Animal Contr

New Directions in the Human-Animal Bond
Alan M. Beck, series editor

Animal Control Management

A New Look at a Public Responsibility

Stephen Aronson

Purdue University Press
West Lafayette, Indiana

Library of Congress Cataloging-in-Publication Data

Aronson, Stephen, 1938-
  Animal control management / by Stephen Aronson.
      p. cm.
  Includes bibliographical references.
  ISBN 978-1-55753-540-5
  1. Urban pests--Control. 2. Wildlife pests--Control. 3. Animal shelters--
Management. 4. Animal welfare--Government policy. 5. Animals--Treatment.
I.
Title.
  SB603.3.A75 2008
  363.7'8--dc22
                        2009008120

For Linda, Peter, and Elizabeth

Contents

Preface

It was at city hall during the last part of my governmental career where I was introduced to the animal control function. I came to city hall in late 1980 to help the city develop a new program budget and to evaluate program performance. After a few weeks, I was asked to add the animal control contract to my other responsibilities. Little did I know that as my career advanced, animal control would follow as my constant companion. My prior experience in auditing, program evaluation, and budgeting proved useful in working through some animal control issues. Yet much what I learned about animal control services was on the job.

At first I believed the animal control issues that confronted me were unique to the city. I shortly came to the realization that other local governments experienced similar concerns and that the program by its very nature was difficult to administer. Surprisingly, I could find no books on how to manage the program. The issues outnumbered the answers, and not every problem had an immediate solution. Many in animal control management learned through experience over the years what worked and what did not; they also consulted with their colleagues in other agencies when they encountered new issues. The published literature in this field concentrated on information about animals and not program administration.

Around 1999, I began contemplating writing a book from the local government management perspective on animal control services. It was my belief then and now there is a need for a book that emphasizes program administration.

This book is based on my own experiences as well as many other sources. For example, I have interviewed animal control directors and managers, various state and local government officials, state wildlife enforcement officers, officials of various animal welfare organizations, veterinarians affiliated with animal control or animal welfare agencies, and private operators providing animal control services.

This book is intended not only for animal control directors and managers, but also for those elected and appointed officials who have oversight and funding responsibilities for animal control programs. Others who are interested in animal control as a public responsibility including animal advocates, students of animal science, public administration, and veterinary medicine may also find this book helpful.

Researching and writing this book made me aware of similarities and differences in programs from one state to another and among communities within the same state. Just as these programs vary in the scope of the services offered, there are also variations in laws and ordinances, organizational structures, and finances. The field of animal control continues to advance, and change is constant. Be aware that information that is current today may change tomorrow.

Data by state, let alone on a national scale, are not well advanced. Developing a body of knowledge that would benefit animal control officials everywhere is making steady progress. It is to the credit of animal control and animal welfare professionals in the United States, Canada, and in other countries that the adoption of best practices in this field has accelerated in recent years. This is due in large part to the leadership provided by national and state animal welfare and animal control organizations, which have led to an increase in the number and quality of training programs offered. The publication of two books in recent years reflects that progress. Both Geoffrey L. Handy's book (2001) and Miller and Zawistowski's book (2004) made positive contributions to the literature on animal control.

My book concentrates on three areas of animal control management including administration, the use of management tools, and delivery of services. This is not a technical book, and the reader need not have a prior background of this program. Rather, this book discusses and explains a range of management responsibilities, issues, and problems animal control directors face. Since animal control serves both people and animals, it is appropriate that the role and impact of stakeholders be addressed.

The contents of each chapter are summarized below.

Chapter 1. An introduction to how the animal control function evolved, major developments since World War II, and a prelude to some dilemmas and challenges that unfold in succeeding chapters.

Chapter 2. Analyzes the kinds of organizations where animal control are located and how these structures differ and their impacts.

Chapter 3. An overview of some of the more important management duties and why they are essential to program administration.

Chapter 4. Explains the use of forms, records, reports, and handouts in administering the program.

Chapter 5. The importance of budgeting and revenues and the need for new revenue streams.

Chapter 6. The details of the contracting process are explained and what local government officials and contractors need to know and steps to take before entering into a contract.

Chapter 7. Focuses on contract content—recommends and explains why certain clauses should be included in shelter and field services contracts.

Chapter 8. Examines management's staffing responsibilities, using case studies and examples to foster understanding.

Chapter 9. Sets forth reasons why interacting with public and private entities are necessary. Examples are provided.

Chapter 10. Assesses the need for communications both within and outside the animal control organization.

Chapter 11. Discusses the use of animal control related Web sites and their value as a management tool.

Chapter 12. Examines the rationale for animal laws and discusses how to enact local animal ordinances.

Chapter 13. Recommends some basic provisions that should be enacted into law and others that are desirable. Several examples of local ordinance provisions are cited.

Chapter 14. Discusses the political environment in which the animal control function exists and how to navigate through difficult and complex problems that are politically charged.

Chapter 15. Recognizes wildlife and exotic animals as an increasing concern of animal control officials and how animal control officials can be prepared when wildlife and exotic animal issues arise.

Chapter 16. Choosing to audit or evaluate an animal services program is a major decision and should not be made hastily. This chapter recommends steps to take before and after making this decision and discusses the impact of the audit or evaluation report.

Acknowledgments

I would like to express my appreciation to the many animal control and animal welfare officials, government officials, and others who gave of their time and shared helpful information and their insights. I could not have written this book without their generous cooperation and invaluable assistance.

Little has been written about the role of private animal control providers. I am therefore appreciative of information about private animal control providers that was made possible by the following contractors: Nancy Graham, Brian Hall, Donald Hannahs, Kerry Payne, and Kathi Pelnar.

This book would not have been possible without the assistance and support of my publisher, Purdue University Press. I would like to express my gratitude for their assistance and especially to the following individuals: Dr. Alan M. Beck, series editor of New Directions in the Human-Animal Bond, who saw the need for the subject of this book and who provided helpful advice and useful ideas; Director of the Press Charles Watkinson was particularly helpful in providing guidance on publishing issues; Bryan Shaffer, who was responsible for the cover design and worked with me to make it attractive to the reader; Rebecca Corbin, who was never too busy to answer my many questions and keep me updated on developments throughout the publishing process; Lastly, Katherine Purple, who served in the critical role of editor. Her conscientious efforts have significantly improved the readability and organization of the text.

Throughout this project there were several people who made important contributions that helped make this book better and whom I wish to acknowledge. Peter Aronson, my son, contributed important and substantive suggestions to Chapter 11. My daughter-in-law Yesica del Moral offered several helpful ideas for the cover design. Dr. Jan Brazzell, Luis Garcia, and Tom Gresham reviewed some earlier drafts and offered helpful feedback and encouragement. Kathy Petlewski helped with library research. Bart Bernstein, author of several books for mental health professionals, enthusiastically served almost from the beginning as my mentor, guiding me through the process from preparing a book proposal to completing the manuscript. I looked forward to our weekly breakfast sessions and his wise counsel. Lastly, I owe much gratitude to my wife, Dr. Linda Brewster Stearns. She was my closest advisor and became a stakeholder in this endeavor.

She served as a truthful and honest critic who told me what I needed to know but did not always want to hear. Her encouragement and loving support helped me to strive to do better. If those reading this book come across shortcomings, they are my responsibility as I failed to heed the good advice of others.

Disclaimer

While performing research for this book it was noted that laws vary by state and within states; there are also differences among local laws and ordinances. The reader should note that the author does not and cannot render legal advice. Only an attorney can provide legal advice. Although the author has strived to use care in preparing this book, the reader should also be aware that the accuracy or completeness of the contents may have been be affected by change without the author's knowledge. If the reader has questions or inquiries on aspects of budgeting and finance discussed in this book, a local government professional in the appropriate jurisdiction should be consulted to determine if the information and strategies in this book are suitable in that particular situation.

Chapter 1

Animal Control Programs: An Overview

This chapter is an overview of the animal control function to help the reader understand the context in which the remaining chapters are presented. The first section in this chapter is a brief historical overview of how animal control evolved in stages from concerns of individuals more than two hundred years ago, to creation of animal welfare organizations, and later to the establishment of state and local animal control entities. The second section is an overview summarizing developments and changes in animal control since World War II. They have also been classified by categories for ease of understanding.

THE HISTORICAL OVERVIEW PERSPECTIVE

The earliest recorded events when individuals publicly spoke out against animal cruelty were a turning point in civilized society. It marked a change in thinking that animals are living beings and deserved to be treated with a humane level of care. Starving, beating, or otherwise inflicting harm upon animals was becoming unacceptable and no longer tolerated by those seeking to protect animals. Perhaps, to a lesser extent, abuse of work animals was perceived by some individuals as self-defeating; if one harmed or destroyed the animals, they were contributing to the demise of their own livelihood. Biblical injunctions over the abuse of animals may have influenced this way of thinking.

The history of animal control agencies in the United States was preceded by efforts of private individuals acting independently of each other who were appalled at the cruelty and abuse that they witnessed and were determined to do something about it. As far back as the 1700s in England, there were people who took notice of cruelty against farm animals and pursued efforts to stop such practices. In 1824, the first Society for the Prevention of Cruelty

1

to Animals (SPCA) was established in England. Concerns for work animals later progressed to include the welfare of companion animals. At the forefront of these early efforts were prominent and wealthy citizens.

Henry Bergh, a philanthropist and diplomat who detested the inhumane treatment of animals in America and particularly cruelty toward working horses, was among the early animal welfare advocates to initiate action to stop the practices. He submitted to the New York State Legislature a charter to create a society to protect animals. The organization, known as the American Society for the Prevention of Cruelty to Animals (ASPCA), was approved by the state legislature on April 10, 1866, and it is reported to be the oldest humane organization in America. Bergh and his allies were also successful in getting the New York State Legislature to pass the nation's first effective animal anti-cruelty law in 1867. That same year the Society began operating the first ambulance for injured horses. The Society also operated the animal control service for New York City from 1894-1995.

Around the same time in San Francisco, James Sloan Hutchinson intervened in the inhumane behavior of two men who were dragging a screaming boar off to market along the street's rough cobblestones. The incident moved Hutchinson and a group of fellow humanitarians to establish the San Francisco SPCA in 1868, which described itself as a "national leader in saving lives and raising the status of companion animals."

In addition to the anti-cruelty efforts of Henry Bergh and James Sloan Hutchinson, Caroline Earle White was a noted pioneer in these early efforts. She founded the Women's Humane Society in Philadelphia in 1869, and the American Anti-Vivisection Society in 1883.

In 1877, delegates from twenty-seven humane societies from ten states met and founded the American Humane Association (AHA) whose mission is "to prevent cruelty, abuse, neglect, and exploitation of children and animals and to assure that their interests and well-being are fully, effectively, and humanely guaranteed by an aware and caring society."[1]

Today, the AHA provides a range of services to local animal welfare organizations including funding, training, and advocacy across the United States.

Other national organizations that played important roles in the development and advancement of animal control programs were founded after World War II. In 1954, what is now known as the Humane Society of the United States (HSUS) was established. The founders were a dissatisfied faction from the American Humane Association who wanted to address animal cruelty and animal protection for all animals. Today the HSUS is the largest animal protection organization in the world and has devoted considerable resources to aiding local animal shelters and animal control organizations. Among the services offered and its accomplishments are: Animal Care Expo, the largest annual educational conference and product and service exhibition for the animal care and control community, first held in 1991; publication of *Animal Sheltering Magazine*; offering a consulting service for animal shelters; and founding Humane Society University, an educational component.

Another national organization of note is the Society of Animal Welfare Administrators (SAWA), formally organized on April 25, 1970. SAWA was created to offer paid executives of humane organizations an opportunity to network with their peers and to exchange and explore ideas and concerns. Part of the "Statement of Purpose" reads, "Over the years SAWA has evolved with its original statement of purpose continually in mind. SAWA's foremost goal is to encourage and promote a professional approach to management of animal care and control agencies."[2]

SAWA holds an annual national conference, offers a certification program for animal welfare executives, and focuses on current animal welfare issues.

In 1978, the National Animal Control Association (NACA) was formed at a meeting in Englewood, Colorado. This was a milestone in the professionalization of the animal control field as its purpose was to offer training to animal control agencies. NACA conducts an annual training conference for animal control personnel and two training academies scheduled in cities across the United States. NACA also offers consulting services to animal control agencies and makes available information and publications about animal control services.

National and State Organizations

By 2007, each of the major national organizations had developed its own priorities and interests, although overlap exists among the organizations because their missions are similar. NACA's priority is the training of personnel who perform animal control services. SAWA's constituency is the leaders and executives of animal welfare and animal control entities. AHA and ASPCA both have outreach functions that serve local animal shelters. HSUS, the largest of the organizations, has gradually focused increasing attention and resources on many animal control issues. Although there are differences among the major national organizations, there is a surprising degree of cooperation because of mutual interests. Representatives of national organizations frequently participate in each other's programs.

Associations of animal control officers can be found in at least forty states. A second animal control organization was formed in California in 2007. The new organization, the California Animal Control Association, is in addition to the California Animal Control Directors Association that was established in 1976. Some state organizations are small and may hold only one meeting or conference per year. Others are more active throughout the year, engaging in lobbying state legislatures to enact new laws and offering training programs. All state associations are committed to training and professional development of their members. This is illustrated in the following mission statement of the Virginia Animal Control Association:

To Advance the Profession of Animal Control by:

- Serving as a resource for the development of quality, standardized training

- Facilitating communication between public and private animal agencies

- Initiating and supporting responsible legislation for the protection of the public and animals

- Providing a united voice for animal care and control professionals throughout Virginia[3]

Throughout the country numerous private animal welfare organizations have sprung up in response to residents' concerns who were upset by what they perceived as cruelty to animals and the abandonment of dogs and cats. Animal groups with special interests work with publicly funded animal control organizations to promote adoptions and offer temporary care of dogs and cats with special needs. Over time, some began see themselves as self-appointed overseers, monitoring the performance of public shelters and animal control agencies.

Selected Milestones

The following events are a few chronological examples of selected milestones in the development of the animal welfare and control functions. Humane societies and local SPCAs have played important roles in promoting the humane care of companion animals, were the first animal welfare organizations in their respective communities, and were instrumental in efforts to fund animal control programs. Some of these animal welfare organizations were later funded by local governments to become animal control service providers in their respective communities.

1863	City of Los Angeles established a public animal pound.
1866	American Society for Prevention of Cruelty to Animals was founded in New York City.
1868	San Francisco SPCA founded.
1868	MSPCA formed in Boston.
1868	Oregon Humane Society founded. It is reported to be the third oldest humane society in the United States and the oldest in the West.
1877	spcaLA (Los Angeles) was founded.
1888	The Kansas Humane Society was founded and "...has provided shelter to homeless animals and promoted animal welfare in the Wichita area."
1895	Los Angeles County by law established pound districts and in 1937, the County established a Pound Department.
1900	The New York State Humane Association was organized.
1911	Animal Refuge League was established in Portland, Maine.
1913	Tulsa SPCA started as an all volunteer group.
1915	The American Humane Association established "Be Kind to Animals Week."
1946	Los Angeles County opened its first publicly funded animal shelter in Downey, California.
1954	Humane Society of the United States was established.
1958	Michigan Association of Animal Control Officers was founded.
1961	Florida State Animal Control Officers Association was organized.
1966	Federal Animal Welfare Act was passed.
1978	The National Animal Control Association was formed.
1979	Louisiana Animal Control Director's Association was organized.
1989	"No kill" animal philosophy began to emerge when a California man wrote an article condemning euthanasia.

MAJOR DEVELOPMENTS SINCE WORLD WAR II

Many major developments in animal care and control occurred after World War II. New shelters were built by municipalities and counties to replace outdated and overcrowded facilities. Shelter medicine emerged as a new veterinary specialty that brought professional medical care to shelter animals. The movement to spay/neuter shelter animals spread across the country, and animals adopted from shelters are increasingly required to be sterilized before being placed in new homes. This has been the key element in response to tackling the problem of pet overpopulation.

Training programs for field and shelter personnel became available at the state and local levels and are now mandated in many states. In addition, in-service training programs for shelter administrators and animal care executives are now offered through animal welfare organizations, community colleges, and universities. These include both certificate and academic degree programs for those employed in the animal care field.

Animal laws, some of which had not been revised in years, have been reviewed and changes enacted to meet new needs and to address new issues. Among the changes enacted into state laws and local ordinances are those imposing more control over dangerous animals, restrictions on giving away or selling animals in selected locations, microchipping requirements, and holding animal owners more accountable for their pets. Behind the changes have been the efforts of individual animal advocates of many persuasions who have joined with animal control officials and other animal welfare organizations when their interests coincide.

The changes came about for two primary reasons. First, protecting public health and the safety of humans and animals required greater governmental intervention, because the issues affected large numbers of people and animals. Second, there was a realization that appropriate care of dogs and cats and assumption of animal care responsibilities by owners could not be left to voluntary compliance. Experience had shown that more regulation was necessary. Only through regulation could authorities convince animal owners that there were consequences for acting irresponsibly and allowing their animals to become nuisances or dangers to the community.

Creation of numerous animal welfare organizations involved cooperative ventures with animal control agencies that benefited shelter animals. Animal welfare organizations such as Petfinders.com and Pets 911 promote adoption of animals, help public and private shelters publicize the availability of their adoptable animals, and have facilitated the return of lost and found animals to their rightful owners. Rescue groups also assist public shelters by accepting animals for foster care (including special needs animals) and finding animals new homes. Not to be forgotten are organizations like Maddie's Fund, established to finance a "no-kill nation." This organization funds special and often innovative animal welfare projects, some of which include participation by animal control agencies.

Summarizing Developments by Categories

There are simply too many positive developments to list here, but summarizing those developments by category will give the reader an idea of how much change has taken place in the past one hundred years. Some changes or developments may fit into more than one category or could be listed in new categories.

Animal Behavior and Control Concerns

- Passage of leash laws to prohibit dogs from wandering at large, causing property damage, and creating safety issues for local residents.

- Nuisance animal provisions to address barking dogs as well as noise and nuisances caused by other animals such as peacocks and other fowl.

- Requirement of rabies inoculations to prevent the spread of disease.

- Passage of dog licensing laws as part of rabies prevention and to collect data on the size of local dog populations.

- Enactment of dangerous dog laws holding owners more accountable for the actions of their animals and restricting the movement of these animals.

- Establishment of dangerous dog registries.

- Regulation of wildlife and exotic animals to protect animals and humans.

Enhancing the Life of Animals in Humane Ways

- Pet adoptions as the preferred method of resolving the problem of impounded stray and abandoned pets.

- Creation of rescue groups to find suitable homes for dogs and cats of a particular breed (or mixed breeds) and animals of other species.

- Establishment and funding of spay/neuter programs to help reduce the number of unwanted pets and to reduce the risk that unwanted animals would be euthanized.

- Establishment of no-kill animal shelters to enhance the chances of more pet adoptions by keeping and caring for animals for longer periods of time until staff can find them new homes.

- Transfer of animals between shelters in different parts of the country to make more animals available for adoption where adoptable animals are in short supply.

- Enactment of anti-tethering laws.

- Establishment of national animal welfare organizations that aid adoption promotion, publicize information about lost and found animals, and help shelters to create their own Web pages.

- Creation of dog parks where animals can romp and exercise.

- Laws prohibiting dog fighting and cockfighting.

Professionalizing the Animal Control Industry

- Creation of national, state, and regional organizations of animal control personnel to address animal control issues and to foster training and professionalization of animal control personnel at all levels.

- Developing consensus among professionals on selected issues (e.g., Asilomar Accords).

- Promoting and implementing ideas, methods, systems, or standards that are effective and/or humane (best practices).

- Development of policy and procedure manuals.

- Creation of animal shelter advisory bodies.

- Contracting for animal care and control services with qualified contractors.

- Creation of training certification programs by law.

- Development of advanced training curriculums and sponsorship of national and regional conferences for animal control personnel.

- State regulation and/or inspection of animal shelters.

- Audit/program reviews of animal control programs.

- Building alliances of animal shelters, rescue groups, and nonprofit animal welfare organizations to promote pet adoptions and to work cooperatively on matters of mutual interest.

- Implantation of microchips in companion animals and the use of microchip scanning devices to help return lost and found animals to their rightful owners.

- Expansion of outreach efforts to educate animal owners and the public about animals.

- Development and implementation of software programs to automate some animal control tasks.

- Grants to animal control programs for special projects.

- Creation and use of Web sites as an outreach effort and for more effectively managing resources.

- Online bulletin boards to publicize lost and found animals.

- Publication and distribution of newsletters and availability of pet care literature to animal owners and the general public.

- Use of television including cable TV programs to promote pet owner responsibility and a better understanding of the needs of pets.

- Development of strategic plans establishing goals and objectives for animal care and control entities.

Creation of Modern Humane Animal Shelters

- Increased use of architects with animal shelter design experience to design new state-of-the-art shelter facilities utilizing new technologies and materials to aid in promoting a healthy environment.

- Construction of shelters with quarantine enclosures.

- Construction of indoor and outdoor runs.

- Construction of veterinary clinics to provide on-site spaying/neutering but also to treat sick and injured animals.

- Inclusion of education centers and gift or pet supply shops in shelters.

- Location of shelters in areas easily accessible to the public.

- Separate housing for dogs, cats, wildlife, and livestock.

- Inclusion of separate rooms for puppies and kittens offered for adoption.

- Visiting rooms for people to visit one-on-one with animals they might wish to adopt.

- Separate euthanasia units utilizing more humane procedures.

SUMMARY

Animal control as a public function had its origins in England in the 1700s when some citizens took notice of the abuse and cruelty to farm animals and began efforts to protect the welfare of animals, which led to the establishment of the first Society for the Prevention of Cruelty to Animals in England in 1824. By 1863, the first public animal pound was established by the city of Los Angeles. In 1866, the American Society for the Prevention of Cruelty to Animals was chartered by the New York State Legislature. Other national and state associations followed.

Many more developments leading to improvements in animal control services occurred after World War II. Training programs for animal control personnel became available, and animal laws, some of which had remained unchanged for many years, were reviewed and new provisions added. When viewed by categories, the changes in animal control programs can be seen as wide ranging and affecting all aspects of the programs.

Notes

1. American Humane Association, "How American Humane Began," www.americanhumane.org/about-us/who-we-are/history/.

2. Society of Animal Welfare Administrators, "About SAWA," Statement of Purpose, www.sawanetwork.org/.

3. Virginia Animal Control Association, "About VACA," http://www.vacaonline.com/pages/about-vaca.php.

Chapter 2

Types of Animal Control Organizational Arrangements

Animal control services are delivered through various organizational arrangements in the public, nonprofit, and private sectors. This chapter describes and analyzes various organizational formats for providing animal control services and how local governments decide how services are going to be delivered. Local issues, resources, priorities, and leadership on animal control issues have an impact on animal control decisions. Animal control is a governmental responsibility, and local officials decide if the program will be operated in-house or outsourced, unless the decision is determined by local law or charter provisions. These same officials also decide which department, agency, or unit is a suitable fit for animal control. Local officials increasingly recognize the need to have a good administrator oversee animal control, leading to decisions that may place animal control in a department with functions that have little in common with animal control but is headed by an experienced department director.

The transfer of animal control functions from one department to another is increasing as local officials become dissatisfied with performance under the current organizational arrangement. According to the *Ukiah Daily Journal*, the animal control department in Mendocino County, California, which had been overseen by the County's Executive Office, was absorbed by the Department of Public Health and transferred to that department's Environmental Health Division. The newspaper reported: "The shift will allow Public Health—which balances regulatory responsibilities with community outreach, a common trait with Animal Care, officials noted—to aid in an increasingly important public education role as the department's streamlining lessens its regulatory tasks."[1]

The big question continues to be where to place animal control services. The public sector finds animal control in many locations in the local

11

government organizational structure, and it seems to be an impediment to standardization as there is an altogether willingness to locate it anywhere in the organizational structure or not at all. Local government administrators who have limited knowledge of the program may find it a difficult fit in some departments other than public safety or health. Is it because animal control is not viewed as a public safety or health function or because some administrators will not accept it in their agencies because this function has little or no relationship to the agencies' other responsibilities?

Viewing animal care and control as either a law enforcement, code compliance, or a health related service comes closest to giving it a stronger and more rational identity because at the heart of the program is the enforcement of local and state laws. Assigning animal care and control to a law enforcement or code compliance agency conveys a message to the animal owning public that animal problems will be treated with an enforcement priority. Animal services programs operated under the umbrella of a health or environmental health department signals they are more compatible with the outreach efforts of health agencies that have a mission to protect public health and the environment supported by its law enforcement authority.

When this function is outsourced to the nonprofit sector (e.g., humane societies and other animal welfare organizations), it would seem at first glance to be a logical choice as their mission is to protect the welfare of animals. A closer look reveals some anxiety among nonprofits performing this service. Even if they are fully or partially compensated for their efforts, it can impact their organizations in unexpected ways as discussed in a later section in this chapter.

How Organizational Structure Impacts the Animal Control Program

Local officials ultimately decide if animal control is a law enforcement responsibility, neighborhood service, health or environmental program, or should be a separate animal welfare function. The tasks performed are similar regardless which organization is assigned this responsibility. The differences are in how the program is administered, amount of resources allocated, and established priorities. The animal control function can be found in public works, parks and recreation, finance departments, and the city clerk's office. When animal control services are outsourced to the nonprofit sector, these services may be provided by humane societies, SPCAs, or other animal welfare entities. There are also private operators including veterinary facilities that provide sheltering and impoundment of animals and/or field services.

Program goals and objectives may be similar, regardless of the type of organizational structure, but each organization has its own operating culture that impacts day-to-day operations and priorities. For example, organizational culture may have some bearing on how a police officer issues a citation for a leash law violation versus a citation issued by a humane officer employed by a humane society. Each approaches the job differently because of training, experience, and organizational policies. Ultimately what matters is whether the program has the resources and committed staff to carrying out its mission. An underfunded program, a shortage of trained personnel to carry out needed duties, lack of needed equipment, and an inadequate shelter facility have all been highlighted in reviews of animal control agencies as impediments to the delivery of services provided, organizational format notwithstanding.

A look at organizations known to have responsibilities for animal control services indicates that animal control programs can usually be found in any of seven types of organizations:

- Public safety (police/sheriff)

- Code compliance

- Public health or Environmental health

- Separate department

- Intergovernmental entity

- Humane society or other nonprofit animal welfare organization

- Private operator

Animal Control as a Public Safety Function

Local governments that assign animal control responsibilities to police or county sheriff's departments have made law enforcement a priority. The public will believe that animal control programs operating under the auspices of police or the sheriff will have more visibility and have greater support. Since public safety agencies are operated on a twenty-four hour schedule, there is always a live person to take the calls, although there may be limited service during nights, weekends, and holidays. Law enforcement personnel in these agencies also provide additional sets of eyes that are alert to animal control problems. Animal control officers operating under police or the sheriff see themselves at least in part as enforcement officers who often share the same radio frequency as peace officers even if they are civilians specializing in animal related matters.

Animal control officers who are civilian employees in a law enforcement agency may report to either a civilian supervisor or to a sworn police officer. Cedar Hill, Texas, has two animal control officers in the police department who report to a civilian communications supervisor. The shelter facility is managed by another city. The entire animal control program (field and shelter services) in Corona, California, is assigned to the police department. Other police and sheriff's departments authorize officers and sheriff's deputies to enforce animal laws, thus augmenting the animal control officer(s). When animal control authority is given to peace officers, violators have a greater chance of being cited due to the fact that there are more police officers on duty than animal control officers.

Peace officers may serve as role models for animal control officers. ACOs assigned to police or the sheriff's departments learn from these peace officers how to interact with the public and how to enforce laws. A police department has the advantage of having established leadership and management and is usually better funded than other local government departments. If animal control has operational problems and is perceived to be ineffective, it may be transferred to police or the sheriff for greater control and supervision with the expectation of improved performance and an emphasis on enforcing animal control laws. A case in point is Van Buren County, Michigan, as reported in the local newspaper:

> In response to continual complaints regarding the lack of response and/ or lack of enforcement within the VBC Animal Control Department, responsibility of Animal Control was recently turned over to the VBC Sheriff Department. With this shift of responsibility, residents will see improved services and a much more user-friendly Animal Control office.

> Sheriff Dale Gribler stated that many changes will be implemented within the Animal Control Department, with the first major change being that all animal control personnel working in the enforcement division, will be licensed police officers, who have attended the police academy and have taken a two-week course on animal control laws. "Van Buren County will be the first in the state to have licensed police officers working in Animal Control enforcement. The officers will be trained and familiar with animal control laws, providing residents with a level of professionalism that was previously lacking said Gribler."[2]

Animal control personnel will find that the culture of a police or sheriff's organization is more structured and procedurally driven. Repeat violators of animal laws may find themselves under closer scrutiny by police or the sheriff if animal control is assigned to either. In smaller cities where police are multitasking, animal control may be a better fit when supported by senior police officials. Although police officers and sheriff's deputies may have animal control responsibilities, higher priorities are still reserved for crime prevention efforts, enforcement of criminal laws, responding to crimes in progress, and other law enforcement emergencies.

When a police department is responsible for animal control it may result in having additional animal control officers without the cost of adding personnel as is the case with the police department in Barre, Vermont. The town animal control officer is a civilian employee of the police department, but town ordinances state that town police officers may also enforce some provisions of town ordinances related to animals.[3] This increases the number of personnel who may enforce animal control ordinances.

Animal Control as a Code Compliance Responsibility

Code compliance is a community outreach program where officers enforce various local codes to keep neighborhoods clean, in good repair, prevent and control blight, and curb neighborhood nuisances. Some code compliance officers are empowered to enforce animal control ordinances. Animal control takes on a law enforcement priority when animal problems are defined as neighborhood nuisances and assigned to code compliance.

Loose running dogs and cats, noisy animals, odor caused by animal waste, and pets that cause damage to the property of others may be viewed as neighborhood nuisances if they interfere with the quality of life of neighborhood residents. If local officials target neighborhood improvements as a priority, they may assign the enforcement of animal control laws to code compliance, since it has authority to issue citations and prosecute cases. Code compliance officers have found that homes with multiple and noisy animal problems have also been cited for trash accumulation, parking of inoperable vehicles, and numerous sanitation violations, all of which contribute to neighborhood deterioration.

The following case study based on an experience in a Western U.S. city demonstrates how animal control and code compliance working together helped solve a neighborhood problem that also included animals:

> Animal control received several complaints about a number of noisy dogs on private property in a semi-rural part of the city. When an animal control officer (ACO) went to the property, he found it fenced and locked and could only observe the dogs from a distance. Even at a distance, he saw that the animals were without food and water, and he noticed trash, litter, and junk cars and trucks on the property. After several

unsuccessful attempts to contact the property owner and the tenant, the officer contacted the city's code compliance division for assistance. Code compliance had cited the property owner in the past for various code violations and knew the history of the problems on this property. A code compliance supervisor obtained a search warrant to enter and search the premises. The supervisor, accompanied by two animal control officers, a veterinarian, and two police officers, went to the property and sought admittance from the tenant. Using the intercom at the front gate, a police officer informed the tenant that they had a search warrant to enter the property and that the gate should be unlocked immediately. The tenant came and unlocked the gate and admitted the official party.

The veterinarian and the ACOs examined the dogs. The dogs looked scruffy and dirty, but they had food and water at the time the veterinarian was present, but the kennels where they were kept were muddy and in disrepair. The veterinarian determined that there were insufficient grounds to impound the animals. However, code compliance officers found numerous violations that they were able to cite and, with the concurrence of animal control, took over the case because of several non-animal related code violations. The code compliance officers, assisted by ACOs, were able to have the animals removed from the premises and placed in new homes, because the owner surrendered the animals to local authorities. The other code violations were corrected after the city attorney became involved in the case and contacted the property owner.

Animal Control as a Health Agency Program

Where there is state oversight of local animal control programs, the responsibility may be assigned to the agriculture department or to the state health department. At the local level some health and environmental health departments are charged with providing animal control services, thus sharing responsibility for disease control efforts for humans and animals. The rationale for health agency involvement is to prevent the spread of rabies, to vaccinate animals, and to educate animal owners on how to care for their pets. Health agencies may offer low cost spay/neuter services and rabies inoculations as part of their community outreach efforts to promote public health objectives.

Local health agencies with animal control responsibilities include: the city of Irving, Texas; the village of Oak Park, Illinois; Henderson County, North Carolina; and Saint Louis County, Missouri. Although health agencies may emphasize the health aspect of animal control, the scope of animal control services provided are comparable to those offered by other entities (e.g., sheltering of impounded animals, field services that respond to calls for assistance for sick, injured, or nuisance animals, sales of dog licenses, and enforcement of animal laws). The city of Irving, Texas, Department of Public Health and Environmental Services notes picking up deceased animals as well as stray and wild animals among its responsibilities. Some health agencies such as the Saint Louis County, Missouri, Department of Public Health emphasize the public health aspects of animal control on their Web site: "One of the most important things that animal control officers can do is to investigate animal bites. Rabies is transmitted by wild and domestic animal bites and is usually fatal. Officers place animals that have bitten people under observation and make sure that the threat of rabies is reduced."[4]

As a public health program, animal control enjoys the advantage of having immediate access to an epidemiologist who can provide assistance with animal disease issues. Animal control programs that are not operated by a health agency will need to go outside the organization for assistance with disease control issues that may delay needed action. When a veterinarian is in charge of an animal control program in a health agency, this trained medical professional is able to address disease prevention and control and can interact more quickly with an epidemiologist on staff, if needed.

Health functions generally have a stable if not a priority funding level, because some duties are mandated by state law. An animal control program under a public health or environmental health agency would seem to be afforded some protection from budgetary reductions. Although health agencies are more sensitive to and aware of animal health problems, they may have no better control over the animals they impound than other agencies and are just as likely to have little or no history of the animals they take into custody. The shelters under their control share potential for the spread of contagious animal diseases as other facilities, even when rigorous preventive measures are implemented.

Animal Control: Stand Alone Agency or Component of Another Department?

When an animal control program is part of another agency it is subject to more internal oversight, but as a separate department, the animal control director would seem to have a freer hand to carry out the organization's mission and perhaps higher status as a department head. City managers and county executives usually allow their department heads considerable autonomy and flexibility in how they implement their programs.

An animal control program as a stand-alone entity does not necessarily benefit from more resources, more management expertise, and input that a larger department with several operating divisions can offer. There is also no assurance that it will be immune from budget cuts and program reductions when other departments are not spared this fate. For these reasons, the head of a stand-alone entity needs to develop good relations with a number of local government officials and demonstrate that the program is meeting objectives and deserves continued support.

As a separate, stand-alone organizational entity, every service provided to the animal control agency from outside the agency will come at a cost, and a charge will be levied (either as a direct charge or as overhead). When animal control is one of several component programs in a department, the cost of services provided directly to animal control within the larger department or from outside the department are either apportioned among departmental units or programs or are included in the department's overhead, which is then apportioned to all cost centers in the department. The following example illustrates these points:

> The animal control program is one of several operating divisions that comprise the city's health department. The department has three support divisions: human resources, finance, and building maintenance, each of which provide specific support services to the operating (or line) divisions and are funded by charges through an internal service fund to those operating divisions that receive direct appropriations from the local governing body. The cost of providing each support service is apportioned among the operating divisions on a formula or percentage basis. In other words, the internal service fund finances the operations of the support units, and the monies for the internal services fund comes out of the budget of each operating division to pay for support services they receive. Charges levied for support services to operating units will fluctuate from year to year due to usage and cost increases.

Should a stand-alone animal services department encounter serious operating problems, it may be at a disadvantage as it lacks the support and resources of being part of a larger department. A department head who has oversight of an animal control program in his or her department has several options. The director can delegate great latitude to the subordinate manager to get the job done, or the department head may maintain an arm's length relationship to the animal control program for various reasons including: lack of understanding about the program, the small size and funding level of the program, or simply the high confidence level that the department director has placed in the program manager. The third option is to maintain closer control over those who manage the animal services program in the department. Department heads with animal control as one of their several responsibilities may not always be knowledgeable about this program and may be skittish about giving greater autonomy to that program manager given that this program is politically charged.

Splitting Animal Control Responsibilities

Animal control responsibilities are sometimes split between two organizations, one public and one private, or between two public entities. Splitting the responsibilities means dividing accountability, and coordinating the efforts of each entity becomes more complex. The split may be due to costs or the fact that no single provider is able to offer both field and shelter services. A local government may employ one or more animal control officers to respond to calls for service and emergencies but might not have its own shelter to house stray and abandoned animals. If this is the case, it will be necessary to contract with another organization for sheltering. Local humane societies, SPCAs, veterinary offices, and other governmental entities may assume some responsibilities. For example, Kilgore, Texas, has one animal control officer but contracts with the Gregg County Humane Society to shelter the animals. Once the Society takes custody of the animals brought to the shelter by the animal control officer, there are three possible outcomes. First, the animal may be returned to its owner if possible; second, the animal may be placed in a new home; or lastly, the animal may be humanely destroyed if it is not claimed by its owner or is not suitable for placement.

There are other examples where animal control services are the primary responsibility of one agency but one or more tasks are assigned to another organization. The Riverside, California, Police Department is assigned the primary responsibility under city ordinance to enforce a law that prohibits fairgoers from bringing their animals to street fairs. Police were experiencing animal control problems at the city's weekly downtown area evening street fair. Some pet owners were bringing large dogs as well as snakes and other animals to the street fair and frightening fairgoers. The police proposed banning animals from the street fair by amending the city's animal control ordinances and authorizing animal control officers to enforce the new law. The county that contracts to provides animal control services to the city, while sympathetic to the problem, was not anxious to assume primary responsibility in this matter. A compromise was agreed upon. The proposed ordinance change authorized both animal control and police to enforce the new law, but it was deemed primarily a police responsibility.

Examples of splitting responsibilities for animal control services are found in smaller cities and towns, although larger jurisdictions also do it when the community does not own its own shelter. The cost of building a shelter for a small dog and cat population may be out of reach for some communities. Other jurisdictions prefer to outsource this responsibility because they do not have the knowledge and experience to operate an in-house program. The problem of not having one's own shelter means that the provider of shelter services may at some point in time choose not to continue to provide this service. Since most communities have a limited number of facilities that can house multiple animals, this leaves the client scrambling to find another facility with space to accommodate more animals at an affordable cost.

There are other variations of divided responsibility where two or more municipalities share animal control duties. One jurisdiction may operate and dispatch calls to animal control officers in the field, and another jurisdiction may operate a shelter to provide temporary housing and care of the animals. Sharing the costs and also taking advantage of the available resources in each jurisdiction may make sense to the parties. Splitting responsibilities can be mutually advantageous when the roles of each party are clear and each party is a willing participant. There will, however, be issues to address.

- Who will own and operate the animal shelter?

- Who will be responsible for shelter repairs and improvements?

- How will shelter costs be allocated?

- Who owns the animals once they are impounded, and are there exceptions?

- What happens to dead, sick, or injured animals picked up by animal control officers?

- Will sick or injured animals be treated by a veterinarian, and who will pay the cost?

- If responsibilities are split, how will each party be held accountable?

The first two questions address of the responsibility of operating and maintaining the shelter and allocating costs to other participating jurisdictions whose animals are impounded at the facility. Will there be a per-animal, per-day charge, or will some formula be used to allocate operating expense? The cost of building or buying a new shelter can be expensive, but it gives local governments more control over the program and most important, an assurance that they have a place to house the animals. If two or more local governments jointly own a shelter then each may derive a benefit from having an equity interest in the facility. If one jurisdiction wishes to withdraw from that arrangement, its share could be considered for purchase by the other entity or entities. A third concern is raised, because if the responsibilities are split, it may not be clear which entity has custody of the animal or at what point in time legal custody is transferred from one entity to another. If an animal owner sues to regain custody of an animal or for the loss of an animal, this question takes on greater significance. A fourth concern focuses on the need for treatment of sick or injured animals and related costs as an element of humane care. This last concern requires a written understanding of the responsibilities of each party and the need to keep good records.

Animal Control as an Intergovernmental Entity

Animal control problems overlap city and county lines, as stray dogs, cats, and wildlife regularly cross jurisdictional lines with impunity. Viewed from a regional perspective, animal control services, in theory, can muster more resources to cover a larger geographical area if several local governments fund the effort.

There are many reasons to form a regional animal control agency. Some believe that a uniform, if not an improved level of service, will result when several local governments join together and pool their resources. Economies of scale are expected when a regional approach is suggested, although it is unclear whether the results have shown this to be true. Those interested in the regional approach need to carefully estimate the costs. Consulting with officials of other regional animal control entities may help to gain a better understand of the issues and finances. Politically, a regional animal control agency removes animal control controversies from city hall or the county government to a regional entity governed by a board comprised of representatives from the participating jurisdictions. The idea appears straightforward (e.g., one entity serving a multi-jurisdictional area) rather than several agencies operating independently, but again, there are issues to consider.

- How will the organization be funded and governed?

- Will the entity provide services directly, or will it contract for service?

- Will there be provisions for member jurisdictions to withdraw and/or for new jurisdictions to become members?

- How will the entity achieve financial stability?

- Will participating jurisdictions have to adopt the same ordinances and fees?

- How will equity in real estate and other property be apportioned?

- Will the participating jurisdictions contribute in-kind services? If so, what services can they provide, and what is the value of those services?

Regional animal control organizations serving multiple jurisdictions are found in several states. California and Wisconsin, respectively, offer examples. The Southeast Area Animal Control Authority (SEAACA) presently provides service to thirteen local governments in a portion of Los Angeles County, California. The Milwaukee Area Domestic Animal Control Commission (MADACC) serves all nineteen municipalities in Milwaukee County, Wisconsin.

Actions taken in October 1975 and January 1976, led to establishment of SEAACA when three cities, Downey, Norwalk, and Pico Rivera, formed a Joint Powers Agreement. SEAACA was formed as an alternative to the increasing costs of animal control services and as an alternative to the unacceptable level of service rendered by public and private animal control agencies. Other cities were admitted to membership in later years.

The Authority is a regional agency operated under the direction of a governing body composed of representatives selected from the member cities. The Director of SEAACA who reports to the Authority's governing body is in charge of its day-to-day operations.

MADACC, a regional animal control agency, serves all nineteen municipalities in Milwaukee County. This entity was formed under the authority of Wisconsin Statute 66.0301 to create an intergovernmental commission. MADACC is governed by a board of directors and an operations committee that consists of seven members who have the responsibility for providing direct oversight of the organization's operations. Actual operation began on December 14, 1998.

> The purpose of MADACC is to provide: shelter, care and disposition of stray dogs and cats, the search and recovery of lost pets, county quarantine services of biter animals for rabies observation, REFERRAL services for wildlife problems, and to promote responsible pet ownership through client education and the licensing of dogs and cats. To accomplish these goals, MADACC utilizes a variety of resources through networking and coordination with metropolitan area humane societies and rescue groups.[5]

Animal control responsibilities in the city of Milwaukee are divided between a city agency and MADACC. Nuisance animal problems are handled by the Department of Neighborhood Services through its Environmental Health and Nuisance Control Section. The Department is responsible for receiving complaints of animal nuisances, animal bites, rabies investigations, issuance of dog and cat licenses, animal fancier permits and kennels, dangerous animals, and pet shops issues. Issues of stray dogs and cats are the responsibility of the MADACC, which is charged with performing field and shelter services, euthanasia, and offering adoption services for stray dogs and cats and animals turned in by their owners.

Other Municipal or County Departments Operating Animal Control Services

Other local government departments and entities are also known to provide animal control services. In 1979, the city of Crestwood, Missouri, established an animal control division in its Department of Parks and Recreation. Similarly, a division in the Department of Recreation and Parks of Yonkers, New York, provides animal control services. Yonkers has a single animal control officer, but the Department's park rangers also perform animal control duties. A more unusual arrangement is the Coweta County, Georgia, Animal Control Department, which is the responsibility of the Warden of the Coweta County Prison. Animal control and mosquito control services are provided to the city of Tyler, Texas, through a contract with the Northeast Texas Public Health District. Animal control services in Creve Coeur, Missouri, are a responsibility of the Health and Welfare Division of the City's Public Works Department. The Community Services Department of the city of Bowie, Maryland, operates the animal control program but is also responsible for public buildings, code compliance, senior citizen services, recreation, and historic properties and museums.

Animal Shelter Advisory Bodies

Any discussion of animal control organizations needs to acknowledge the role of animal shelter advisory bodies. Some publicly operated shelters have created advisory bodies to provide input and ideas and to undertake specific tasks. They can be useful as a sounding board for animal control officials and to reflect community concerns. Politically, they can provide support for the decisions of elected officials on animal related matters. These committees, commissions, or boards are part of the animal control organization and are mainly advisory in nature, but they may exercise a limited oversight function if so designated. Members include lay persons, veterinarians, and those with animal welfare backgrounds. They provide input to those who manage the programs and to elected officials who appoint them. These bodies should not be confused with appeals boards and hearing boards, which are different entities with administrative duties and quasi-legal standing.

Where an animal shelter advisory body exists, it is usually established by action of the local government's elected governing body or by law. City council action established the Animal Shelter Committee of Salinas, California. State law in Texas requires every animal shelter to have an advisory committee. An animal shelter advisory committee in Texas must have at least four members of whom at least one member each is a licensed veterinarian, a public official, an employee of the animal shelter, and a fourth position is reserved for a representative from an animal welfare organization. The committee must meet at least three times a year, and members serve a term of two years, although some Texas cities have larger committees.

Shelter advisory bodies can be found in Arizona, California, Florida, Maryland, Michigan, Nevada, and North Carolina. It is a contract requirement in the agreement that one California city has with its animal control provider, a county agency, that there must be a shelter advisory board.

The purpose of an advisory body needs to be clearly defined so as not to infringe on the day-to-day operations and management of the shelter and related animal services programs. Their meetings may be regularly attended by animal activists who offer their input and recommendations.

These advisory bodies offer a forum for its members, animal activists, and others to bring issues and ideas to that body for discussion and to suggest ways to improve the animal control program. This forum may be the first to hear about emerging animal issues in the community. Those who serve on this body and those who attend its meetings help perpetuate and strengthen accountability where public funds are spent for welfare of animals.

Checklist for Creating an Effective Advisory Body

The value of an advisory body lies in its ability to tap the experience and talents of its members. It is advantageous that its members reflect various skills, experience, and background to bring their viewpoints to the table. Unless the law dictates otherwise, several steps can be taken to ensure the effectiveness of this entity.

- Solicit the names of potential appointees from members of the local government's elected governing body and/or publicly advertise the availability of seats on this panel.

- Persons interested in becoming members of the advisory body should be invited to complete a short questionnaire about their experience and interest in animals and any qualifications they can offer and to identify if they are affiliated with any other animal welfare organization and the nature of that affiliation.

- Consider in consultation with the animal control director how the advisory body can be of help to the director and staff and identify duties to be assigned to the advisory body.

- Limit the term of each officeholder, but have overlapping terms. The initial appointment should be for one year with a limit of two renewals of two years each. This will prevent stagnation and will result in adding new members with new ideas.

- Determine how often the panel should meet.

- Adopt by-laws on how the advisory body shall operate.

- Maintain written minutes of all meetings for at least the minimum period of time the law requires.

Duties of an Animal Shelter Advisory Body

It is up to local elected officials to decide whether there is a need for an animal shelter advisory body except where it is required by law.

The city of Rowlett, Texas, described the duties and composition of its Animal Shelter Advisory Board as follows:

> The Animal Shelter Advisory Board is appointed to advise and assist the city in complying with state statutes regarding operation and maintenance of its animal shelter. The board consists of seven members (who must by State statute include at least one licensed veterinarian, one city staff member, one person whose duties include the daily operation of an animal shelter, and one representative from an animal welfare agency) appointed to two-year staggered terms and two alternate members appointed annually. The board must by State law meet at least three times per year. The city's staff liaison is as designated by the City Manager. The board is strictly advisory in nature to the City Council.[6]

The Pima County, Arizona, Animal Care Center Advisory Committee has as its purpose and tasks the following:

> Serve in an advisory capacity to the Pima County Board of Supervisors and to the Manager of Pima Animal Care Center;
>
> Review and evaluate the operations of the Center in order to make recommendations in writing to the Board of Supervisors for the formulation of guidelines to assure that;
>
> - the Center's operations are conducted in the best interest of the public health and safety
>
> - and The Center keeps pace with the most modern practices and procedures of animal care and welfare
>
> Review complaints from the public concerning policies of the Center and make recommendations for resolving them to the proper authority.[7]

The Pima County Advisory Committee has twelve members, of whom eight represent specific animal related organizations, one a public educator, one a member of the county board of health, one a county resident representing the disabled community, and one representing the city of Tucson. The manager of the Center serves as an ex-officio member. The Committee's makeup assures that the views of various animal welfare organizations are heard. Rowlett's Board is required by state law, whereas Pima's Committee, which has a limited oversight function, is established by ordinance.

NonProfits as Animal Control Providers

Throughout the United States, nonprofit animal welfare organizations provide a valuable community service in caring for stray and homeless animals and helping find them new homes. Some contract with municipalities and counties to provide animal control services. Many deliver an acceptable or a superior level of service, but like their public sector counterparts, they have their share of problems and issues.

Although some humane societies and SPCAs have expressed interest in providing animal control services, others have either shied away from that undertaking or have discontinued providing the service. One local government official expressed the opinion that interest in contracting by some animal welfare organizations is based on adding a new revenue stream to offset the costs of funding their other humane activities and perhaps to attract new donors. Many animal welfare organizations have found providing animal control services is neither lucrative nor immune from criticism by the public, and these same groups have been faced with other dilemmas. They are challenged about what to do with too many unwanted animals, not enough animal adoptions, irresponsible animal owners, and limited public funding.

Information about the internal operations of nonprofits that perform animal control services has been based on what they report to their clients and audits and reviews conducted of their animal control activities. Some humane societies may have separate units that perform animal control duties, but most blend their animal welfare activities and animal control duties together. This makes it difficult to determine the actual cost of animal control services, provide accountability, and measure the effectiveness of services. Many nonprofit entities apportion the costs of providing animal control based on the percentage of time their employees spend on animal control duties versus other activities of the organization. Some organizations charge for the sheltering of each animal on a daily basis.

Case Study

The following case study is based on an audit of animal control services of one nonprofit animal welfare organization and is an extreme example of contracting gone awry:

> The county contracted with the organization for many years to perform animal control services on its behalf. Several municipalities also contracted for services with the same nonprofit. When the contractor asked the county for additional funding, the county agreed to the request on condition that the contractor cooperate with a performance audit requested by the county. The audit was requested because county officials had several unanswered questions about animal control issues. The audit team consisted of individuals with animal control management experience as well as accounting and financial audit credentials. Among the key findings by the auditors were the following:

- The contract terms were so general that neither the contractor nor the county knew what was expected under the contract.

- The allocation of expenses to the animal control side of the contractor's business and the credit of revenues attributed to animal control were questioned. The auditors were unable to separate animal welfare functions from animal control duties. About 80% of the contractor's expenses were charged to animal control, but the auditors could not document that they were justified.

- The contractor did not give priority to responding to animal control complaints about barking dogs or stray dogs. Instead, priority was given to investigating animal abuse and cruelty cases that are the focus of humane societies and SPCAs that do not contract for animal control services.

- The accuracy of data reported by the contractor were questioned by the auditors and some available data requested were not provided.

- Minimal training was given to animal control officers. The provider's policy required animal control officers to receive most of their training on the job from co-workers. Although the budget allocated funds for specific purposes (e.g., training and a capital equipment purchase), those monies were not spent for those purposes and in at least one instance training funds were spent on the contractor's nonprofit side.

- Officers *chose* which field service calls they would answer.

- The contractor had the capability to track response times to complaints but did not do so.

- Many contractor-generated reports including field services reports, calls received and completed, shelter intakes, animal outcomes, telephone calls on hold, and total service delivery were difficult to understand and were not useful for management purposes or for reporting to policymakers.

- New activity numbers were created for each call, even those that were duplicates of the same complaint.

- The contractor was unwilling to provide data on the number of animals from individual jurisdictions it served, so the auditors could not analyze shelter costs or validate the allocation of costs to other governmental clients.

Case Study Commentary

Because the contract was written in such general terms, the auditors were not able to determine what services were required, let alone hold the contractor accountable for performance. The fact that public monies were accepted and used by the provider creates an important additional reason for accountability. If approximately 80% of the nonprofit's expenses were charged to animal control, what functions would the contractor perform if it had no county and municipal contracts? The failure of the contractor to provide data on the number of animals from each individual jurisdiction it served and some other requested data suggests the contractor did not fully cooperate in the audit process. That the auditors were unable to analyze shelter costs and verify the accuracy of the allocated costs to the local jurisdictions raised a red flag on the accuracy of the contractor's cost allocations. The county, too, must share blame as it agreed to a contract, the terms of which failed to protect the county's interests and was poorly monitored by the county.

Role of the Board of Directors

Nonprofit humane societies and SPCAs are governed by boards of directors. The director or manager who is responsible for day-to-day operations is generally appointed by the board and, in turn, the director appoints staff. Although the director is usually the liaison person acting for the nonprofit in its relations with the client jurisdiction, the board of directors is the legal contracting party. The board, which must approve the animal control contract, sets policies, approves the organization's budget, and is expected to provide oversight of programs and services. The board chair or individual board members may or may not interact with local government elected officials on issues from requests for increased funding to contract issues. Too often, local governments that enter into contracts with nonprofit animal welfare organizations to provide animal care and control services pay too little attention to the board's role, let alone recognize that once a nonprofit organization assumes a governmental responsibility, it needs to be more accountable than when it is acting solely in its nonprofit capacity, because it is accepting public funds to carry out a public function. The following case study is an extreme example of how a board of directors failed this responsibility.

Case Study

The city retained a consultant to audit its animal control program due to a number of complaints received by the city council. Animal control services had been contracted to a local nonprofit animal welfare organization for many years. During the course of the audit, the consultant found that the organization's board of directors held no public meetings and was not accessible to city officials or to the public-at-large. The consultant reported that the board's inaccessibility denied local residents (including animal owners) the opportunity to bring animal control matters before the board and provide valuable input to improving service.

More importantly, the consultant pointed out that the board of directors even denied access to city officials who had placed full responsibility for animal care and control into the hands of that board. The city was therefore unable to change policies, procedures, or even obtain correction of service deficiencies, because it could not communicate directly with the board of directors except through the organization's executive director. Consequently, citizens and pet owners alike perceived the city as not being responsive to their needs. The consultant recommended that the city consider alternative solutions for providing animal care and control services (including continuing with the organization but with some changes). The consultant concluded that the board of directors failed to realize and recognize that assuming the responsibility entrusted to them by the city meant that they needed to operate as a semi-public body accessible to the community and be accountable for the use of public funds.

Animal Control Performed by NonProfits: The Differences

When animal control services funded with public monies are performed by animal welfare organizations rather than directly by local governments, there are noticeable differences.

1. The nonprofit's mission is different from animal control. Nonprofit animal welfare organizations are in business solely to protect and advance the interests of animals, whereas animal control programs are both regulatory and protective of animals and people. Animal control has two priorities: (1) protect people from sick or dangerous animals and (2) protect animals. Nonprofit organizations have as their mission the welfare of the animals. This includes finding homes for unwanted pets through adoptions and to prevent animals from being destroyed if possible. Other aspects of their mission include promoting pet population control through spay/ neuter programs, educating the public on how to care for their animals, and conducting investigations on animal cruelty.

These priorities of nonprofit organizations may conflict with their animal control duties that may require animals to be destroyed to enforce local animal control ordinances that can bring the nonprofit animal welfare organization into conflict with irresponsible pet owners and the public.

2. The relationship is governed and limited by contract terms. Contracting with nonprofit animal welfare organizations may provide less accountability to their governmental clients for two reasons. First, the contract with the governmental client is governed as well as limited by the terms of the agreement. Second, humane societies and other animal welfare organizations are governed by their respective boards of directors, which are not public entities nor directly accountable to the public. An attorney can advise whether the board of directors of a nonprofit animal welfare organization funded in part with public monies is acting in a quasi-public role and what responsibilities it may have to a governmental client.

3. Nonprofits that contract to provide these services may resist efforts of the local government client to exercise strict control over their operations and will regard such efforts as unwarranted. The nonprofit animal welfare activities are not the client's concern. Nevertheless, it may pose a dilemma for both parties if revenues and expenditures for animal control services cannot be separated from animal welfare functions since public funds are used to deliver animal control services.

4. The nonprofit does not set policy. Animal welfare organizations do not set public policy but rather carry out public policy in accordance with the terms of the contract, which defines the scope of services to be provided. In other words, any powers they possess are derived from the contract or authority delegated to them in law by the client jurisdiction. This is not to say they do not influence policy or recommend animal control policy.

5. Nonprofits are not required to provide animal control service. Animal welfare organizations that choose to provide animal control service to local governments can also decide to discontinue providing those services in accordance with the terms of their contract as they are private entities and are not mandated to perform these services. Only government may be mandated to provide this service. If the local government does not own or control a facility to temporarily house impounded animals it can be a difficult issue to resolve. It takes time to build a new facility, and locally there are limited facilities that can meet these needs. Hiring government employees as animal control officers can be accomplished in a much shorter time than it takes to move into another shelter facility.

There are many reasons to discontinue providing services. Continued funding at what is perceived to be an inadequate level to meet contract requirements, lack of local political support from elected local officials, a feeling of being overburdened by those duties, and a perceived conflict with their primary humane mission are among reasons most often cited for discontinuing animal control service.

The Local Government Perspective

Municipalities and counties entering into contracts for animal control services with animal welfare organizations such as humane societies and SPCAs are contracting with the board of directors and not with the staff of the organization. The board of directors is ultimately accountable for the success or failure of the animal control program. The contract document should identify the role of the board of directors with respect to delivery and accountability of animal control services to the local government client. The local government client should insist that a representative of the board of directors be included in any contract negotiations and that the board should be accessible to the governmental client if needed. This can prevent problems in the future. Although most contract matters are worked out between the governmental client's management staff and the nonprofit's management staff, access to the board of directors may be needed from time to time.

When local government officials have disagreements with their nonprofit provider, the local government client may have contributed to the problem by limiting their involvement in animal control contracts for several reasons. Local government staff are not charged with day-to-day operating responsibilities, but rather with oversight duties that bring them into contact with the contractor on an as-needed basis. There is an arm's length relationship in the day-to-day operations predicated on the belief that outsourcing means there is a degree of separation between the client and the contractor, because the contractor, whether a nonprofit or a private operator, is not a public entity, and the relationship between the parties is governed by the terms of the contract.

Local governments are paying for a service to be performed by an outside entity, and the bottom line question is whether the client is satisfied with the quality and cost of service. How the contractor is organized internally to perform that service has not mattered in the past to the local government client. This view fails to consider that the contractor's internal organization has everything to do with how services are delivered and how costs are allocated to the client. Further, it discourages transparency and accountability in the performance of a publicly funded service. Finally, local government officials have often been reluctant (and perhaps rightfully so) to insert themselves into the contractor's internal operations unless there is an overriding public interest or legal reason to do so (e.g., allegations of cruelty to animals brought to the shelter through the animal control function, fraud or embezzlement involving government funds, false data reporting, or contract violations).

Animal Control Services Provided by the Private Sector

Smaller jurisdictions may find that outsourcing animal control services to a private for-profit contractor to be a viable option, if a private operator exists. University Park, Texas, is a useful example. The city employs an animal warden but has no animal shelter. Animals that need to be impounded are taken to a local veterinary clinic that is under contract to the city to provide temporary housing for strays and animals placed in custody.

A small community with an animal population of only few hundred dogs or cats will find it beyond its means to construct or acquire a shelter facility and to employ a full-time animal control officer. A private firm or even a single individual under contract may provide a level of service that meets minimum local needs at an agreed upon price. That service is most apt to be limited to impounding sick, injured, or dangerous animals. Spay/neuter services, animal adoptions, and humane education programs are left to nonprofit animal welfare organizations such as humane societies. Like their counterparts in the nonprofit sector, for-profit operators do not set policy but implement public policy set by their clients. They also have the option to discontinue service pursuant to the terms of the contract. Unlike humane societies and other animal welfare organizations that provide both animal welfare and animal control services, the for-profit operator performs only animal control services and does not face the potential conflicts that could arise when the same entity performs both animal welfare and animal control services.

Private operators providing animal control services have been doing business in Alaska, Alabama, California, Massachusetts, Minnesota, and Wisconsin. The owner of a one-person company in Brainerd, Minnesota, contracts to provide animal control field services to fourteen local governments in Crow Wing County, Minnesota. This one-person operation serves a county population of 55,000 people, which in summer swells to nearly one million in that lake region. Sometimes the operator reports working eighteen-hour days in summer, the busiest season. The client jurisdictions reportedly save on worker's compensation and medical insurance and do not pay for overtime, a common animal control expense in larger jurisdictions. The operator supplies his own vehicle and provides his own insurance coverage. When animals need to be impounded, they are brought to local shelters. He is vested with authority to issue citations under state law and pursues cases in court as necessary. As a self-employed contractor, he sets his own work schedule, which also gives him flexibility in exercising his contractual obligations. This owner is a member of that state's animal control association and has participated in a NACA training program.

Northampton, Massachusetts, contracts with a private operator for animal control service for that city. The contractor submitted a bid and was awarded a three-year contract for field and shelter services. She rents her shelter facility and provides twenty-four hour, seven-day-a-week service and has one assistant. The city has contracted with her since 1992, but she has been in animal control work since 1983, when she worked as an assistant to the former contractor. She operates through the police department and reports to a police captain. She is also a special police officer with the Board of Health.

Another sole proprietor contracts to provide field services only to eleven jurisdictions, of which eight are in Minnesota and the remaining three are in nearby Wisconsin. All eleven are within an eighty-mile radius of the proprietor's business location. The largest community served has a population of just over 11,000 people. The contractor bid on each contract, but often there were no other bidders. Contracts are for one year, but one jurisdiction has a five year contract. Animals that need to be impounded are brought to one of two humane society shelters with whom her client jurisdictions contract to house impounded animals. One shelter is in Minnesota, and the other is in Wisconsin. This operator is a certified euthanasia technician and has twenty-five years of experience working with animals in an animal shelter and a veterinary hospital. Response times are reported to be about an hour, and calls are usually answered the same day they are received. Citations are issued as needed by the contractor who is authorized to do so by nine client jurisdictions. Two jurisdictions require their respective police departments issue the citations after receiving the necessary paperwork from the contractor. Her telephone number is published, and her hours of operation are 7:30 a.m. to 7:30 p.m., although she is on call twenty-four hours a day.

Although most private animal control operators serve smaller communities, there are exceptions. Anchorage, Alaska, with an estimated population of 251,000 people, contracts with Animal Licensing and Placement Services (ALPS), a subsidiary of Doyon Universal Services, JV. The company bid on the contract, and the current contract is for four and one half years and was extended for another year. The company provides a wide range of animal control services. The shelter facility is owned by the municipality, and both Anchorage and the contractor share maintenance responsibilities. The firm employs nearly twenty-five full-time personnel, and the day-to-day operations are under the direction of the Center Manager who is a veterinarian with over nineteen years of veterinary practice experience. The organizational structure of the Anchorage Animal Care and Control Center has six key individuals reporting directly to the Center Manager. Four of the six are authorized to serve as the acting Center Manager when that official is absent.

SUMMARY

Where to place animal control in the local government structure can influence both its priorities, how its responsibilities are carried out, and public perception. Operating under police or sheriff, animal control has the immediate backup support of law enforcement officers experienced in enforcing laws. It also sends a message to the public and animal owners that animal laws will be enforced and that animal control officers are part of law enforcement. Public safety functions have a higher priority in the budget process, so animal control may have an advantage when the program is under police or the sheriff's department.

It is not uncommon that property code violations cover animal problems such as odor, feces, and too many animals on the property. Animal control officers operating in a code enforcement organization often work in tandem with code compliance officers to abate the nuisances as a single case and to expedite resolution of the problems. Here, too, animal control is considered an enforcement function.

As a health agency program, animal control activities include rabies prevention, animal bite investigations, spay/neutering, pet adoptions, and educating the public about responsible pet ownership. Disease prevention and control and the welfare of domestic pets often pursued in combination with educational and community outreach are the preferred approach taken by public health and environmental health agencies. Enforcement of animal control laws through issuance of citations and legal action are also pursued if other measures have not been successful. In addition, health services generally have stable and often priority funding because some agency functions are mandated by local and state laws.

Animal control as a stand-alone department or entity may have more flexibility to initiate new and innovative ideas to promote its goals and objectives. The potential disadvantage is that if the department fails to meet its goals and objectives or if it becomes embroiled in controversy, it could be vulnerable to program and/or budget reductions, outsourcing, and management shake-ups.

Nonprofit organizations providing animal control services may not only be a good fit for some communities, but they may be the only option. These organizations have to reconcile their animal welfare mission with their animal control responsibilities. By outsourcing this service, some accountability may be lost. The contractor's role and responsibilities are defined by contract and law.

Private for-profit contractors that provide animal control services generally serve smaller jurisdictions. Anchorage, Alaska, is an exception. The organizational structures vary as do those of public and nonprofit entities. Whereas private contractors may consist of only one or two people providing limited animal control services, others may have several employees. Small towns that hire private contractors may desire only a minimal level of service (e.g., answering emergency calls and impounding animals as needed). Private operators meet a need when there is no governmental animal control program or nonprofits able or willing to meet this need or the private operator offers the lowest price.

Notes

1. Freedland, Seth. "Animal Control Shakeup: Now Under Public Health." *Ukiah Daily Journal*, October 15, 2005.

2. Klinger, Deborah. "Sheriff Takes Over Animal Control." *Paw Paw Courier Leader*, November 8, 2004.

3. Town of Barre (Vermont), Departments, Public Safety, Police Department, Animal Control "Nuisances Control Ordinance," sec. 4-92 (c). www.barretown.org.

4. Saint Louis County, Saint Louis County Health, "Animal Control Services," http://www.stlouisco.com/DOH/environ/animals/animals.html.

5. AboutUs. Animal control organization in Milwaukee Wisconsin, "Description," http://www.aboutus.org/MadaCc.com.

6. City of Rowlett (Texas). City Hall, "Boards and Commissions, Description of Boards and Commissions, (as of July 7, 2009)," Animal Shelter Advisory Board. http://www.ci.rowlett.tx.us/rowlett/.

7. Pima Animal Care Center, "Pima Animal Care Advisory Committee," http://www.pimaanimalcare.org/aboutus/advisory.asp.

Chapter 3

Management and Administration of an Animal Control Program: An Overview

INTRODUCTION

This chapter presents an overview of some aspects of managing an animal control program that have received insufficient attention in recent years. These include the recruitment and hiring process and the many tasks performed by management including those related to personnel, training, budgeting and finances, communications, and the role of the sole practitioner. The subject of managing an animal control program has been much discussed, but that discussion has mostly emphasized the goals and objectives on the animal care side at the expense of the administrative and business/financial responsibilities. In addition, government officials and the public do not have a clear idea of what is needed to effectively manage an animal control program. It is all too easy to ignore that when shelter animals receive humane care, program goals and objectives have been met, and the animal control program is given high marks, it is *because* of good management.

Managing an animal control program is more complex than it appears. It is much more than assigning or performing a myriad of routine tasks. An animal control director needs to be a person of many talents. These include to name a few:

- Demonstrate leadership
- Use available resources effectively
- Supervise staff

- Develop and implement the budget

- Communicate effectively with individuals and groups within government and outside

- Be skilled at planning

- Knowledgeable about new technologies

- Have a broad understanding of animal laws

- Be politically attuned

Program Variations, Changes and Issues

What also makes managing an animal control program both challenging and unique are differences in local priorities and local support. Not surprisingly, local governments have begun to recognize that an animal control program needs professional management. A look at some of the differences in programs and changes that have occurred in this field helps explain the challenges facing program management and some of the outstanding issues to be addressed.

- *Variations in scope of services, available resources, and community size.* Small towns and cities with small animal populations often can afford to employ only a single animal control officer. The officer's primary responsibilities include responding to service calls to impound stray, abandoned, and dangerous animals, rescue sick or injured animals, investigate nuisance animal complaints, and conduct cruelty investigations. Duties may also include maintenance of a shelter or kennels, care and disposition of the impounded animals, issuing citations, and appearing in court as needed. The one-officer program in some communities may be low budget with limited service and few laws to enforce, but in other localities there may be numerous state and local laws to enforce. Some officers have had the benefit of prior experience or training, but others have to learn on the job. Programs in large urban areas may employ a dozen or more personnel in a variety of positions. Staff duties may range from treating sick or injured animals at the shelter to providing adoption counseling, removal of wildlife, and conducting outreach activities. As funding increases, more services are expected and training becomes a higher priority. Today, many urban communities that have experienced rapid population growth have animal control service that has not kept pace with growth in both human and animal populations.

- *Support among local government officials varies considerably.* Some elected local government legislative bodies, city managers, and senior county administrators clearly recognize animal control as needed public safety and public health functions and perhaps as a quality of life issue and are supportive of efforts to improve and professionalize the program. Local government support of the animal control function may also be seen as a quality of life issue with a connection to maintaining attractive and livable neighborhoods. In other communities, local officials continue to view animal control as a nonessential service that can be scaled back or even eliminated when there are revenue shortfalls. Unfortunately, many public officials fail to comprehend what it takes to manage this program and the resources that are needed. In recent years, animal control directors supported by animal advocates and the general public have made great strides in educating and persuading local public officials to budget more funds for animal control and to enact stronger laws to address persistent animal problems.

- *Professional management is on the increase.* Today, those who manage animal control programs often come from the management ranks of humane societies and other animal welfare organizations where they became involved because of their love for animals. There is increasing movement of managers from one agency to another as newer and greater opportunities become available. For many years, animal care and control was not recognized as a profession or as a necessary governmental responsibility. Consequently, there was no management track or career path for individuals who aspired to become animal control directors and managers. Often, people were promoted from within as they gained more experience and knowledge, but salaries were low and recognition of their contributions to animal welfare were lacking. Even today some directors and senior level managers enter this field for altruistic reasons. Their commitment to improving the lives of domestic animals has benefited the animals and their communities.

     There have been other changes as well. Larger animal care organizations are turning to those who have earned college degrees in nonprofit management, business administration, animal science, and related fields such as public administration to lead these agencies. This is a recognition that the administrative and business side of the program is also important. These changes appear to have been influenced by the efforts of animal welfare associations that have taken the lead to increase professionalization in this field. The Humane Society of the United States, the American Humane Association, the National Animal Control Association, and the Society of Animal Welfare Administrators are among national groups that have sparked efforts to professionalize the field. State and regional associations have also contributed to professionalization by presenting topics of current interest and offering training at their conferences, workshops, and seminars. Another factor contributing to greater professionalism is the recognition by manufacturers of new digital technologies that animal control agencies can benefit from new computer-based software programs. In the past ten years, community colleges and universities have created curriculums for training students for management positions in animal welfare organizations.

- *Animal services are increasingly recognized as a needed, regulatory, governmental function.* The increase in the number of community animal issues may have led to a recognition by local governments that these issues are also humane issues, and they have turned to some national animal welfare and animal control organizations for assistance . Residents in communities without animal control services are becoming increasingly vocal in demanding that local officials provide these services in a professional, humane way as the number of calls about animal problems increase. This has resulted in appropriation of funds for animal control in response to community demands for animal services. Many times complaints about animals mask the real problem, which is a dispute between neighbors. This adds to the program's workload and is another dimension of this governmental function.

Defining Animal Control Management

Managing an animal *care* and *control* program means giving management the authority and resources to provide direction, leadership, and oversight of those tasks, activities, and programs that protect animals from harm and abuse by people and protect people from harm by animals. Managers are also decision makers, innovators, and mentors of staff. Animal control management, as opposed to the care and protection of animals, is becoming a specialized body of knowledge developed over the past one hundred years and is still evolving. This body of knowledge encompasses an understanding of a number of subjects that are needed to support the achievement of goals and objectives. These subject areas include new technologies such as the use of computers and software programs, use of microchip scanning devices, budgeting and revenues, law enforcement and legal issues, personnel and training, and a variety of administrative duties.

It is management's responsibility to represent the animal services agency and to be an effective communicator and animal advocate to public officials and the public alike. Management may be charged with carrying out policies established by law or resolution or may develop new policies and procedures consistent with broad goals approved by elected officials. Some directors/managers may have more leeway in setting program goals and objectives and how they will be achieved.

ROLE OF MANAGEMENT

What Do Employers Look For In a Director Or Manager?

This is a good question, but it is easier asked than answered due to variations in local programs and philosophical differences held by local officials. Job descriptions are one place to look for the qualifications sought. For example, a careful reading of the job description used to recruit for the position of Animal Services Director of Alachua County, Florida, to head a division of the Public Works Department reads in part:

> This is a highly responsible administrative work directing and supervising the Animal Services Division.

> An employee assigned to this classification is responsible for directing the enforcement of animal control laws including cruelty investigations in Alachua County, as well as supervising the operation of the Animal Shelter Facility. Work is performed in accordance with County ordinances and other applicable legislation. Work is performed under the direction of a higher level supervisor and is reviewed through reports, conferences, and observations of results achieved.[1]

A reading of the full job description indicates the need to be responsible for planning, organizing, and directing the work of staff, acting as the public face of animal control, responsibility for the preparation of the budget, interacting with other government agencies, and recommending and implementing policies and procedures for compliance with state and local laws, rules, and regulations. Skills needed include the ability to develop objectives for Animal Services and to communicate effectively to establish working relationships with co-workers, other departments, and the general public. The position requires a bachelor's degree in one of four designated fields of study and three years of responsible administrative /managerial experience. The job description emphasizes the enforcement role of the director, and the skills required include "thorough knowledge of the principles and management practices of animal services." The duties are complex, and anyone who has accepted this position must have experience and possess a variety of skills.

Champaign County, Illinois', job description for Animal Control Director listed among the primary duties: responsibility for employee training, budget administration, researching and enforcing state and county animal laws, and creating and modifying ordinances relating to animal control. A four-year college degree is required.[2]

The job description for Animal Control Director of Pinal County, Arizona, notes that this position is not covered under the County's merit system, and the director serves at the pleasure of the appointing authority. The description reads, "The most critical and time-consuming responsibilities include policy implementation, direction of programs /service delivery, and resources management in a major department or major functional area of the organization."[3]

A review of numerous animal control agencies found that comparatively few veterinarians are serving as directors and top managers in this field, but they bring a needed perspective to the position. A veterinarian who is appointed to head an animal control program, because of prior medical training, brings problem solving and diagnostic skills to the position. Someone with a law enforcement background will understand how to enforce the law and interact with violators. A director with a background in nonprofit management and knowledge of animal welfare issues brings fund-raising and organizational experience to the position. Which one is a good fit for the position will be determined by those with hiring authority.

Job descriptions list desired skills, education, and experience, but there are subjective factors that interviewers take into account. Personality, responses to questions, ideas offered, and overall demeanor are critiqued. Managers are also decision makers, innovators, and mentors of staff.

The interviewer is silently appraising whether the applicant can interact positively with people, project leadership traits, and command respect from others. Some opinions formed by the interviewer will be based on knowledge of the applicant's prior experience. How the applicant answers questions during the interview may be an indication of how the applicant would respond in specific situations. During the interview, both the applicant and the interviewer are quietly sizing up each other and wondering if this is a good match and if there is a mutual comfort level between them. Another important but subjective consideration is whether the applicant is politically astute and capable of handling politically charged issues. The interviewer may use a hypothetical problem to assess the applicant's skills.

Individuals both inside and outside government may have input into the recruitment or selection process. Local residents with an interest in animal welfare can be a positive force in influencing the selection of a qualified and experienced professional. However, there are others who may have their own agenda and may try to exert influence in the hiring decision in order to advocate on behalf of someone whom they perceive is supportive of their views.

The Candidate

Those who have applied for the management position need to research the organization and make inquiries whenever possible to find out as much as possible about the position. Newspaper articles, an audit report, and calls to other animal control professionals in that state are starting points. Gather enough information to determine whether to continue to pursue an application for the position and to identify the issues that might arise during the interview. Information conveyed by the interviewers or hiring authority during the interview process may not necessarily be a complete picture of what is happening in the organization.

Applicants for the management position who get to the interview/candidate phase should inquire about funding levels. What is the size of the animal control budget? Has the budget increased or decreased over the past five years and by how much? During the past five years, have program services expanded, and has there been an increase or decrease in the size of staff? Has the community experienced rapid population growth and how much has it grown? What is the animal population of the service area and how many dogs are licensed?

Learning how the employer acted in the past may be an indication to how it might act in the future. The more that is known about the program, the better. An informed applicant is a wiser one.

If there is an opportunity to meet with staff one-on-one during the interview process, additional insights can be gathered about the organization and staff. Asking staff to identify what it considers the organization's strengths and weaknesses may lead to new ideas.

Listening carefully to what is said (or not said) by those who have the hiring and oversight authority can be critical. Whether it is the city manager, county executive, the city or town council, the county governing body, or perhaps the head of a multi-purpose department where animal control is located, the views of each individual can be important because of their respective roles in setting priorities, policies, and making resources available.

The New Manager

A new manager who is also new to the management ranks may bring a fresh approach to the program along with enthusiasm, drive, and new ideas. Initially, the new manager is in a unique position, because he or she will have a short period of time to become familiar with the organization and assess any problems inherited from a predecessor. New managers should carefully observe operations, ask questions, and take notes. That time can be used to informally evaluate the skills and performance of staff and determine what changes, if any, need to be taken to improve operations.

Local government officials, however, may be in a hurry to tackle existing problems and issues publicized in the media or in an audit report. A new manager will be expected to not only show improvements on the animal side of the program, but also the business and administrative sides. Every animal control organization is different, and the new manager may have to move forward cautiously, whereas an experienced manager will be more confident and will know how to proceed. This means that all activities and cost centers need to be reviewed. Attention needs to be given to what is funded in the budget, how it is prepared, cost control measures, personnel, training, and if the organization is in compliance with federal, state, and local requirements.

Expenditures should be reviewed to determine if they were authorized, if funds were spent for the intended purposes, and if there are unusual spending patterns that could be problematic. Personnel matters should be addressed in a timely manner so that vacant positions can be filled as soon as possible or, in the case of an employee problem, addressed before it worsens.

The Interim Director or Manager

An interim director or manager may be placed in charge of the program or organization for various reasons. This is apt to occur when the director has been terminated or has retired. An interim director provides a level of continuity until a permanent replacement is appointed. Interim management may also be brought on board to address deficiencies reported in an audit or program review or to address problems where prompt action is required.

Sometimes an interim director will be asked only to gather information about more complex issues to be addressed later. Not all interim managers or directors will have an animal control background, but most will have some management experience and have to be politically savvy. This person may also need to reach out to animal control critics who have been pressing for change to acknowledge their concerns. The following case study illustrates how an interim animal control director might act.

Case Study

John is a recently retired state labor department director with little knowledge of how an animal control agency operates. He is a prominent local citizen, well respected in the community, and has had many years of experience as the head of a large state agency. This led the city manager to ask him to serve on an interim basis as the city's animal control director following publication of a critical audit report of that department and the sudden retirement of the department's long time director. John and the city manager met with two representatives from the state animal control directors association to seek their help in prioritizing some needed changes. Acting on advice from the association's representatives, John moved quickly on a number of fronts.

He met with a group of local animal owners who had filed complaints about shelter operations, listened to their input, and extended an offer to work with them on mutual concerns. A computer analyst from the city's information technology department was brought in to develop a computerized tracking system that would identify and track every animal entering the shelter. The new system would replace a manual intake report for each animal that contained little useful data. A veterinarian was hired as a short-term consultant to train shelter staff on how to administer euthanasia by injection, replacing the old gas chamber. The holding period for animals impounded at the shelter was extended from three days to five days to allow more time for animal owners to reclaim their pets. Following the extended holding period, adoptable animals would be fed and cared for a minimum of five additional days to in order to find them new homes. Last but not least, John implemented some needed changes in staffing assignments based on the auditor's findings.

The Experienced Manager

Hiring an experienced animal control director/manager enables the new hire to assess the organization more quickly, and based on previous experience, he or she will know what to look for and what questions to ask. Experienced managers know they cannot afford to ignore some issues just because they may be time consuming and difficult to resolve, whether it may be a disciplinary case, long-standing computer problems that takes time and money to correct, or reading through lengthy statistical reports. Some of the least appealing tasks are also the most important from a management perspective. Reviewing detailed reports that provide useful statistical data from one time period to another are necessary in measuring progress and uncovering problems and issues. These detailed reports contain data such as number of impoundments by species, the number of animals returned to owners, number of adoptions by species, and the number of licenses sold by category that managers will need to make important and informed decisions.

The 25 Questions Newly Appointed Animal Control Managers Ought to Ask (but not all at once)

Asking the right questions is a must-do for managers, because the answers may be the key to improving how a task is performed, streamlining an activity, or operating more efficiently or economically. The following questions are suggested as a guide for newly appointed managers/directors.

> 1. What are the primary goals and objectives of the animal control program, does the staff understand them, and how are they going to be achieved? Are any goals/objectives considered unattainable, and why?

2. Are budget expenditures in line with revenue and expenditure projections? Are some line items substantially under budgeted or grossly over budgeted, and why?

3. What do the intake statistics say? How do they compare with the data from prior years, and how do they compare to other animal control shelters of comparable size?

4. What percentage of live animals admitted to the shelter are adopted, destroyed, or returned to owner?

5. Are there issues that should receive a higher priority, and why?

6. When was the last time management met with elected officials as a group?

7. When were local animal ordinances last revised?

8. Are there any ordinances that are not being enforced, and if so, why not?

9. Did prior management promptly return phone calls and inquiries from elected officials and the media?

10. What are senior local government officials and elected members of the local governing body saying about the animal control program, and what action, if any, needs to be taken?

11. What types of local ordinance violations are most frequently reported, how does that correlate with citations issued, and what measures have been taken to address these issues?

12. Is the public complaining about their experiences with animal control officers in the field? If so, what is the nature of those complaints? What is the response from the animal control officers? Would additional training be of help?

13. Are shelter visitors offered assistance from staff without having to ask for help? Is there adequate staff to provide that assistance, and has staff received customer service training?

14. Is staff time being used efficiently?

15. Is staff evaluated on a regular basis? If so, what do the written evaluations say? If there have not been any evaluations, why not?

16. Are training needs being met on a timely basis, and if not, why?

17. What do payroll records indicate about overtime and absences?

18. Are work schedules in harmony with peak visitor periods and heavy workload periods?

19. How often are the kennels cleaned each day? Are shelter and animal care procedures adequate, and are they being followed and charted? Are there issues with disease within the shelter? How do the kennels appear to a first-time visitor? Would you be willing to adopt a pet from this shelter based on what you see or hear?

20. Is there an adequate tracking record prepared for each animal entering the shelter, and is that record updated as needed? Is this process computerized?

21. Are there written operating procedures in effect, and does staff follow procedures in all activities? If not, why? Are some procedures in need of revision and are there some staff duties where procedures are needed but have not been developed (e.g., euthanasia, adoptions, animal impoundment/care, and dispatching calls for assistance)?

22. Are animals kept at least the minimal number of holding days as required by law? If not, why?

23. Are local newspaper readers writing letters to the editor or talking to reporters about unhappy experiences with animal control? Is there a procedure for receiving and processing complaints and a record of actions taken?

24. Are additional resources needed for some activities, and if so, which ones and why?

25. Are there capital needs to be met, at what cost, and how will they impact the program?

The role of the director at times parallels that of coach and mentor. It requires leadership and the ability to develop strategies and make decisions. Managers need to take the initiative in setting the direction for the organization and determining how goals and objectives can be met. The support of elected and senior level local management officials will strengthen the authority of the director to act. The director's effectiveness depends in part on the animal control team sharing not only the director's vision for the organization, but conscientiously carrying out its responsibilities.

Understanding the Organization

A manager needs to have a sense about the culture of the program or organization. There needs to be an understanding of how the organization functions and the role of staff and volunteers if there are any, before consideration is given to change that culture or its mission. Some organizations have a work culture developed over a long period of time that may not be easy to change. New managers cannot expect to change an organization or employees' attitudes overnight. Some veteran employees may be set in their ways and will be reluctant to change how they carry out their duties. People generally fear major change, because it is something new about which they are not familiar. Change must be handled carefully and with a positive approach.

Building Bridges

An animal control director has a strong incentive to network with individuals and groups in government and in the animal welfare community. The support of both is critical where the humane care of animals and the enforcement of animal laws are priorities. Building working relationships begins inside the animal control organization, before building relationships outside the organization.

Staff members should be included in this effort to the extent possible. Those who sell licenses at the front counter, staff who care for the animals in the kennels, the animal control officers in the field who handle complaints and emergency calls, and the veterinary technicians who keep the animals healthy comprise the animal care team and should be enlisted in the effort to build good relationships with the public, rescue groups, community veterinarians, and others. Staff members are the *public* face of animal control, because they have direct contact with the public, the media, rescue groups, and animal owners. The program is judged through the interactions that the public, animal owners, and others have with animal control staff. It is a matter of building *trust* as well as developing communication, cooperation, and competence in the organization.

Outside the animal control organization, it is important to build bridges or relationships with entities and individuals that can be of help to the animal control program. Exhibit 3-1 lists organizations and individuals with whom outreach efforts should be undertaken and relationships developed.

Exhibit 3-1

Bridge Building Internally and Externally

Internal bridge building

Animal control staff

Elected members of the local governing body

City manager or chief county administrator

Local government finance director/treasurer

Police or sheriff

Department head to whom the manager reports

Employee association (union) reps

Animal control advisory bodies

Local government purchasing office

Information technology staff

External bridge building

Local humane societies and other animal welfare and rescue groups

Animal advocates

News media

Local veterinarians and the local veterinary society

Animal control officials in nearby jurisdictions

Chamber of commerce

Service clubs (Kiwanis, Rotary, etc.)

Local public school officials

State wildlife agency, state health department, and state agriculture
department

The public

Developing an animal resource list. A list of potential resources to call seeking answers to questions, assistance in emergencies, temporary boarding facilities for large animals, and a listing of state wildlife personnel to contact for wildlife problems should be kept readily available at all times, and copies of this listing should be given to each staff person. Chapter 15 discusses wildlife in greater detail. See Exhibit 3-2 below. Each resource should be contacted prior to adding them to the listing to make sure the list is as accurate as possible and to clarify services that each resource can offer. Any potential costs should be noted next to each listing, and if applicable, the days and hours of operation and a toll-free telephone number should be noted. Arranging in advance a fixed price for those services where there is a charge levied can save money and reduce uncertainty.

Exhibit 3-2

Essential Resource Support List

- Map of service area with contact names and the telephone numbers for animal control in neighboring jurisdictions

- List of licensed/approved wildlife rehabilitators and their locations and telephone numbers

- List of temporary boarding facilities for large animals, livestock, and some wildlife

- List of professional wildlife trappers

- Contact persons at all nearby law enforcement agencies

- Breed (of dog) rescue groups, cat rescue groups, other rescue groups by species

- Individuals who will foster animals

- Contact numbers and names of individuals at the state wildlife agency

- Contact numbers for animal behavior specialists and obedience trainers

- Persons to contact and their telephone numbers at the nearest zoo

- Telephone numbers of all shelters, rescue groups, and sanctuaries within forty miles

- Telephone numbers for all veterinarians and animal hospitals within thirty miles, noting emergency and after-hours procedures

- Rabies exposure contact list, including after-hours protocols

- Contact person at the state agency that regulates/inspects animal control facilities

- City, town, or county government attorney

- List of dealers who sell/rent traps

- Sources that rent or loan livestock trailers

- List of beekeepers in the area who can offer assistance in emergencies

You can't do everything, but what you do should be done well. There is a physical limit to how many activities and tasks staff can effectively pursue as some activities take more time than anticipated and some are more important than others. Prioritize activities and tasks. Some might be outsourced for reasons of economy and efficiency or put on hold until needed resources become available to perform them in-house. The following case study is useful in understanding limitations.

Case Study

The town of Thompkins, a community of 87,000 people, has two animal control employees, of whom one is part-time. The annual budget is $94,000 and covers the cost of salaries, the operation of a small office, fuel and utilities, and a truck to answer calls. Current staff provides limited five-day-a-week response to calls for service and maintains a three kennel outdoor shelter.

Local animal activists have been pressing the town council to fund a low cost spay/neuter program with a part-time veterinarian to perform the surgeries. The cost of this proposal aside, the chief animal control officer believes that current priorities set by the town council are all staff can handle within the current budget and funded service hours. These priorities include responding to calls for assistance for sick, injured, and dangerous animals within three hours and enforcement of town animal ordinances. He demonstrated through his records that the number of leash law violations has dropped nearly 30% since he began speaking to students at local schools and educating pet owners through his monthly column in the local newspaper. He noted that 85% of calls for service in the field are now answered within ninety minutes or less. He expressed his belief and provided supporting documentation that adding spay/neuter surgeries would require more time of current staff and would negatively impact current services, when a cheaper alternative is available. A local veterinarian agreed to offer a reduced rate for spay/neuters of dogs and cats to low income individuals. The town council deferred action on this proposal until the town manager and the chief animal control officer could pursue discussions with other local veterinarians and report back to the town council.

Strategic Planning: Looking at the Future

Strategic planning is another important tool of management to help shape and guide the animal control program/agency to operate more effectively in *future* years. Up to this point, the discussion in this section has concentrated on the *present*. The focus has been on the recruitment, skills, and experience of managers, the manager's need to understand the organization, and the need to develop relationships with individuals and organizations that will help animal control better perform its responsibilities.

What is strategic planning, and why is it important to an animal control program? Strategic planning is a process that involves making choices and decisions about the role of the agency in future years, what it needs to accomplish in future years, and how it is going to get there. It may mean defining or re-defining the agency mission based on needs for the future and setting new objectives for the future. Mission, vision statements, and strategies are elements of the process.

Municipal and county governments and nonprofit organizations are increasingly utilizing the strategic planning process to more effectively serve their constituents and target groups. Animal control programs may have their own strategic plans or may be a component of the local government plan or that of a nonprofit organization that performs animal control services.

Animal control agencies that have their own strategic plans include: the county of San Diego (California) Department of Animal Services, the Clark County (Washington) Animal Protection and Control Division, and the municipality of Anchorage (Alaska) Animal Care and Control Program. A strategic plan was developed in Baldwin County, Alabama, in which private organizations and local government animal control agencies participated under the auspices of Maddie's Fund to increase animal adoptions and decrease euthanasia.

SPECIFIC ADMINISTRATIVE DUTIES OF THE ANIMAL CONTROL MANAGER

Meeting the community's animal needs requires giving attention to the business and management side of the operation. Managers must understand and take responsibility in matters of funding, laws, staffing, training, facilities management, technology, and communications.

Funding. Annual budget appropriations are the fuel that keeps the programs operating. Management needs to make funding happen by being active advocates of the program through the budget process, periodic meetings with other government officials, and outreach to the community. However, the revenue side cannot be ignored as it feeds the expenditure side. Fees and charges need to cover the costs of those services for which they are levied unless local officials are willing to subsidize lower fees and charges. The animal control director should calculate how much it costs to house and feed an animal for a day by species and if the impound fee covers that cost. A word of caution: fees should not be set so high that the animals are not reclaimed by their owners. Most animal services programs are not self supporting, which is all the more reason to encourage efforts to explore new revenue options. Recommendations for revenue enhancement should be proposed when submitting budget requests. Management should ask that any additional monies realized from new revenues be earmarked for animal control and added to the operating budget.

City managers, chief county administrators, and budget staff first review the budget requests before they go to the elected governing body and will need to concur that the requests are justified and comply with budget guidelines. Next, local elected officials will conduct public hearings on the budget. Animal control management, whether a public agency or a contractor, will be questioned on details in its proposed budget and will need to explain and justify its funding requests. Requests for new equipment, supplies, and staff or salary increases should be carefully prepared and documented. Further discussion of the budget, revenues, and expenditures are found in Chapter 5 .

Laws. Management has three primary roles in enforcing animal laws. The first is to support, assist, and counsel those who enforce the laws. The second is to identify loopholes and shortcomings in local ordinances and state law and to work to implement needed changes. The third is making sure that the program complies with state laws (e.g., provide humane animal care and disposition of animals, hold animals for periods specified in law, and meet training requirements). Chapter 12 examines animal control laws from the perspective of management, and Chapter 13 discusses desirable provisions to enact into law.

Staffing. The importance of staffing the program should not be underestimated. Recruiting, hiring, training, and retaining qualified staff is a big challenge when salaries are low, attrition is high, and the career ladder is limited. Comparing salaries paid by other agencies for similar positions can be useful. Managers need to recommend salary levels that will help retain staff. When recruiting staff, think about the following questions:

- Does the applicant have prior training and/or experience in this field, and how well will it serve this organization?

- What training will this person need, how soon can the training begin, and at what cost?

- Has the applicant's references been checked?

- Why does this person want this job?

- Does this person possess good interpersonal skills?

Training for staff. The need for trained staff is critical because of the need to know how to cope with a variety of animal situations, some of which may be both urgent and unexpected. It is management's responsibility to make sure that every staff person understands his or her respective job and can competently perform the duties assigned.

Animal control officials need to have a well prepared rationale on the need for training and to "sell" it to those local officials who control the purse strings. When funding problems arise, training cannot be allowed to be one of the line items cut in the budget, because it is a critical program tool. Consider for a moment the following reasons why training is needed.

Training benefits all employees.

- Initial training and specialized training saves money in the long run. For example: A city's animal control program has been harshly criticized in the media because some employees had been accused of not treating animals humanely. Some officers were reported to have improperly enforced animal laws, and the animal shelter has experienced episodes of contagious disease that, according to local veterinarians, could have been largely prevented had employees been trained in disease prevention measures. An audit was conducted in response to these charges, and a training plan was recommended for all employees. The cost of new training and audit expense will now cost the city more than if it had budgeted training initially.

- An organization that places a high priority on training also enhances self confidence in its staff and fosters the ability to deliver an acceptable or higher level of service.

- Training is knowledge. Animal care and control comprises a complex body of knowledge about a wide range of subjects and issues, some of which is specialized and is more effectively learned in a classroom setting where history, science, theory, laws, and case studies are used to convey understanding of subjects from qualified instructors.

- The use of new technologies is increasing and rapidly changing. Only through curriculum-driven organized training programs can staff be kept up-to-date on new developments.

- Training is one of the most basic ways to professionalize the organization and improve performance and motivation.

- When accompanied by competitive salaries, trained and motivated employees develop an allegiance to the organization that can lower the attrition rate.

- Trained personnel who follow policies and procedures are less apt to operate outside the scope of their employment and create liability problems. For example, if a plaintiff's attorney can prove that an employee was improperly trained or did not receive training that may have been required by law, the cost of settling a case could exceed the cost of the training. Therefore, all training should be documented.

Training for directors and managers. Training and continuing education for agency directors, managers, and supervisory staff are as important as the training needs for those whom they supervise. Being aware of the need to acquire new skills recognizes that to become a better manager one must always be willing to learn and keep up with advances in this field. If, for example, there is a need to better understand the budget process, enroll in a course in budgeting or read a good text on how to prepare and implement a public sector budget. Talk with those who are knowledgeable about budgeting on what managers need to know about budgeting.

Senior management staff in most animal control entities try to allocate funds to be used to attend at least one conference a year and some meetings of state or regional animal control associations. These are helpful as they have speakers present topics of special and current interest, and it is an opportunity to keep up-to-date on new developments in the field and to network with colleagues.

As professionalism continues to grow in this field, more animal welfare organizations are encouraging their members to enhance their management skills and pursue professional development opportunities. One group that has implemented such a program is the Society of Animal Welfare Administrators (SAWA). This is the first program to target agency directors and executives exclusively. SAWA's program is a certification process for those who work in the animal welfare and animal control fields. It is an effort to professionalize the field and to add legitimacy to the work that they do. Since the program began in 2003, fifty-seven individuals have been certified through an examination process. The purpose of this program is explained in the following description:

> ...to distinguish the knowledge, skills and achievements of high-level managers working in animal welfare and protection; to support best practices within the profession; and to broaden the understanding among those making hiring decisions and the general public of the specialized qualifications required to successfully lead non-profit organizations and government agencies dedicated to animal care.[4]

Commenting on this program, SAWA President Harold Dates said, "it demonstrates to the public that we care about what we do."[5]

Facilities Management. Maintaining an animal facility is labor-intensive. Older shelters require a greater effort to keep clean to prevent the spread of disease, because materials used in construction twenty-five to forty years ago are less effective in controlling the spread of disease than new materials in use today. Older facilities also cost more to maintain. The layout and age of the physical facility can limit how it can be used. Consequently, shelter managers need to focus their attention in two critical areas of facilities: sanitation and disease control and layout and safety.

Sanitation and Disease Control. Given that the history of most public shelter animals is an unknown because they are strays or were abandoned can make disease prevention and control difficult despite taking protective measures. Shelter management should work closely with the shelter veterinarian to keep the shelter clean and sanitary and to implement protocols designed to protect the well-being of impounded animals. A useful reference on shelter sanitation and disease control is Miller and Zawistowski's recent book, *Shelter Medicine for Veterinarians and Staff.*[6]

Layout and Safety. The dream of every animal control director is to have a new state-of-the-art animal shelter. Since this is not always possible, other measures must be taken to make the shelter inviting to the public so that they will want to adopt a pet from this facility. Shelter managers should request safety inspections of their facilities if one has not been conducted in the past two years. The effort can help to detect unsafe conditions affecting animals, staff, and the public and to bring the facility into compliance with federal and state requirements. A number of articles have been written on how to make the shelter more inviting to the public and how to display animals for adoption. Often overlooked in older shelters might be the need for isolation kennels for biter animals and the use of materials for noise abatement and hearing protection. These topics are also discussed at conferences and workshops. A staff review of how space is currently used and how to make better use of available space is time well spent.

Technology. Twenty-first century data needs impact animal control management in new ways. New technologies help promote more efficient, effective, and economical operations. Microchipping of pets, a technology that has been around for several years, continues to gain in popularity as it increases the chances of a lost pet being returned to its owner if the microchipped animal is scanned. Some communities are now requiring all dogs be licensed and microchipped. The cost of implanting a microchip is about $10 to $15 per animal, but it can be considered as a form of insurance in case a pet is lost or stolen and somehow finds its way to an animal control agency. Web sites are increasingly being used by animal control organizations as tools in reaching out to the public at large. They offer much useful information. Many sites allow the visitor to download forms and request assistance, learn about available services, and legal requirements that must be met by pet owners. Chapter 11 discusses and assesses the value of animal control Web sites.

Technological advances have made available, user-friendly, computerized software programs that are able to record and store data, generate many types of reports, and perform tasks that previously were prepared manually, thus saving time and money. See Exhibit 3-3.

Exhibit 3-3

Examples of Features of Animal Control Software Programs

- Tracking incoming animals
- Licensing: issuance of new licenses and renewals
- Logging incoming calls
- Preparing statistical reports
- Matching lost animals with reports of animals found
- Recording animal complaints
- Maintaining animal tracking records
- Recording animal medical history
- Recording citations and impounds
- Recording traps on loan
- Recording calls dispatched
- Tracking animals in quarantine
- Listing of individuals who want to adopt certain breeds
- Recording financial transactions

Electronic Communications (telephone and e-mail)

An area of management responsibility that deserves more attention is incoming communication from the public. Great attention is merited, because this may be the initial contact with the agency, and it can leave a lasting, but negative impression if the caller or visitor has had an unhappy experience. The most common forms of communicating with animal control are incoming telephone calls and e-mails.

Telephone calls. Local government officials receive complaints from individuals who have been unable to reach a live person at animal control by phone, have experienced long delays on the telephone, or constant busy signals. This can lead to delays in responding to calls for service. Too many animal control agencies install telephone systems that are inadequate to handle the volume of calls received or no longer meet the needs of a growing organization. Often the caller becomes confused or irritated by multiple choices on the menu or finds that the menu does not address the caller's need for contacting the shelter.

If management finds that there are problems in receiving incoming calls, several steps can be taken to address the issue. Contacting the local telephone service provider and requesting an evaluation of current level of service is one option. Another is to seek advice from the dispatch supervisor or manager of the police or sheriff's dispatch center, as these organizations are experienced in handling large call volumes, requests for emergency response, and are familiar with equipment and software needed to operate a communications center. Third, contacting a few large animal control agencies to learn how they handle and dispatch calls can be instructive. Local cable television companies can be a good resource because of the high number of incoming calls they receive at their customer call centers.

An assessment of the current telephone system should include gathering and analyzing the following data:

- Number of calls received per day, per month, and annually

- Volume of calls received by category of call

- Number of calls received by hour of the day

- Number of calls received after normal business hours

- Number of canceled calls in queue

- Number of calls received by priority of call

E-mail. A number of animal control Web sites permit or even encourage messages or requests for service (except emergencies) to be sent by e-mail. What is important from a communications standpoint is that e-mails be answered or acknowledged within a reasonable period of time, say the next regular business day. The sender can also verify electronically that the message was sent.

THE SOLE PRACTITIONER

Books about management presume there are several people to be managed, but many animal control programs have only one person who is charged with all animal control responsibilities. How does management apply to one person who might be an employee or contractor who operates with minimal supervision and possesses considerable leeway in carrying out the duties of the position? This section takes a look at the one person animal services program from a management perspective.

Many small communities in the United States provide limited animal services where only one animal control officer is employed. The service provided is mainly about responding to calls for service with an emphasis on field services and *control* duties as opposed to the daily *care* of animals in a shelter environment. When there is only one person employed to handle all aspects of animal control, the position may blur the duties of employee (or contract employee) and manager.

The challenges. This *sole practitioner* must multitask, if for no other reason than there is no one else to do it. The role of the sole practitioner is a constantly shifting one. During the work day, without skipping a beat, this person takes on the duties of animal rescuer, transporting an injured animal to the veterinarian, issuing citations, impounding dangerous animals, referring some calls to other organizations, picking up and disposing of a wild animal in a trap, acting as an animal educator, program administrator, strategic planner, and problem solver combined. Local government officials do not always understand the role and scope of responsibilities of animal control, but that has not deterred them from assigning a multitude of tasks to the community's only animal officer. This is a lot to expect of one person and in some instances may prove to be both difficult and possibly dangerous.

Help may be a phone call away, but it might take time for police or the sheriff to arrive on the scene. But they are not animal experts. Although the solo animal control officer may be assigned to a law enforcement agency, that officer generally works alone. Even though other law enforcement officers are available to assist in an emergency, the single animal control officer must be self-reliant most of the time. This means that the officer needs to try to manage and control each situation he or she might encounter to the extent possible. One animal control officer in a small city described her position and responsibilities as " isolated," because there is no one else to turn to for advice, to exchange ideas, or to commiserate about mutually shared experiences.

When a sole animal control officer needs help from specialists such as a wildlife expert, the officer may have to wait up to several hours before the nearest game warden or wildlife specialist can arrive at the scene because of the travel distance or other pending priorities.

As the solitary animal control officer, the person in this position might ask himself or herself the following questions.

- Do I have sufficient training to cope with situations that I encounter every day? If not, where can I receive this training and at what cost?

- Are there established priorities I should follow, or do I need to set or recommend priorities?

- If someone was working for me, what advice would I give that person about how to handle this situation?

- How should I handle a confrontation with an angry animal owner whose demeanor I deem to be threatening?

- If I don't know the answer, who can I turn to for help?

- What can I do to diffuse a tense situation? What strategies should I use? Who can I turn to for advice?

The opportunities. The following case study illustrates how one animal control officer developed a successful strategy to address local coyote problems.

Case Study

Anne is the sole animal control officer in the town of Harrington Falls. During the past three months, several complaints about coyote sightings were reported to the local police who referred them to Anne. When she answered these calls she found that people were leaving food outside for coyotes to eat. Small pets and children were often left outdoors unattended in areas where coyotes were reported. These animals were getting into trash cans that were not adequately secured and rummaging for food. Pet food was left outdoors for long periods of time when the food and the pets should have been removed and brought indoors.

Anne realized she needed a plan that would publicize the problem, and she also needed to have residents take steps to discourage coyotes from wandering through their neighborhood. She presented her action plan to the town manager to whom she reported. He endorsed her plan and also provided some funding for this effort.

Anne had flyers printed explaining the problem and listing steps residents could take to discourage coyotes from roaming about and feeding in residential neighborhoods. She distributed the flyers at local schools for students to bring home to their parents. Copies were left at veterinary offices, and the local supermarket permitted her to post the flyers in the pet food section. She also wrote a letter to the editor of the of the local newspaper explaining the problem and seeking the public's cooperation. A county-wide cable television channel agreed to air public service announcements about the problem.

During the next ninety days, the number of coyote complaints dropped by nearly 65%.

Anne repeated her efforts the following year during the periods when coyotes were about to be active, and again she had good results. She also wrote some short articles in the local newspaper.

The sole practitioner also needs to set aside time on a regular basis to keep up-to-date on new developments in the field, pursue training opportunities, and reach out to the public. The following suggestions are offered:

- *Networking.* Network with other animal control professionals in the region or state. This can be very helpful in learning how others handle certain types of animal situations without having to reinvent the wheel. Join and attend association meetings and make contact with others at the meeting. They can become friends as well as colleagues and are just a phone call away. Occasionally meet with other animal control officers from other jurisdictions for lunch. Offer to meet halfway if the distances are too far. Join a national association. Their conferences are informative and offer training sessions in a number of subject areas.

- *Training opportunities.* Explore training opportunities. There are many available options throughout the state. Community colleges, universities, animal welfare organizations, and Internet sites are among those offering programs for animal welfare personnel. Consider how the course will help in performing daily tasks. Reading articles in periodicals published by animal welfare organizations is another way to acquire knowledge as they relate the experiences of others or offer new information that others can use. Some national animal welfare organizations offer training programs scheduled in cities across the country that can be particularly beneficial to sole practitioners. Here are a few examples:

    American Humane Association (AHA). AHA offers programs at various locations each year. These include: animal fighting investigation and euthanasia workshops. AHA also publishes a series, known as Operational Guides, that contain information that can be useful to a sole practitioner interested in self-study.

    Humane Society of the United States (HSUS). HSUS offers a wide range of publications including *Animal Sheltering* magazine. Training opportunities are available through its Humane Society University from basic shelter topics to leadership development. Their annual national conference, known as Animal Expo, offers a number of sessions addressing topics for those seeking in-service training opportunities.

    National Animal Control Association (NACA). NACA operates a comprehensive training program for animal control officers and other law enforcement officers who have animal control duties. Their courses cover topics from basic to advanced aspects. NACA also publishes other helpful materials including a training guide for animal control personnel.

- *Write a newspaper article.* Write an occasional article for the local paper about a specific animal problem or offer advice on the care of pets. People care about their pets and want to learn more about caring for them. This is not only good public relations, it is a form of community service and demonstrates leadership. This outreach to the community opens up a new line of communication to pet owners and local residents. It may lead to improving the relationship between animal owners and the local animal control officer. Tip: Arrange for publication for a low-volume call day because you will receive a number of calls pertaining to the article on the day of publication.

A plan is needed to help manage the sole practitioner's many tasks efficiently and effectively. The plan should set goals and objectives that the practitioner wants to accomplish. These goals and objectives become a target to be reached. Some may not be met for one reason or another, but there may be success in meeting others. These successes are not just program achievements, but become personal accomplishments.

Being the only local animal control officer means making decisions that in a larger organization might be made by a supervisor or senior level management or require approval of a supervisor. The officer in the smaller community has a better understanding of the community through more direct interaction with local residents in a variety of situations. The officer's generalist role fluctuates from demonstrating leadership while being an educator and a rescuer to enforcing laws. The sole law enforcement officer is likely to be better acquainted with and interact more frequently with local officials than an animal control officer in a larger animal control agency. This enables the officer more opportunities to communicate with local government officials.

SUMMARY

How an animal control program is managed depends on a number of factors that are community specific. Variations in available resources and size of the community impacts the scope of services provided. The extent or lack of political support impacts funding and how the program is managed. However, there is good news on three fronts. Local elected officials are increasingly recognizing the need for enacting stronger laws, and they have been appropriating more resources to address animal issues and improve the quality of service delivered and efforts to professionalize the field continue to increase.

Employers have many expectations when hiring animal control directors and managers. The interview phase is a critical aspect of recruitment, and although both parties look at it differently, the commonality is the sharing of information that impacts on the hiring decision. The successful candidate must be someone who possesses many skills. The recruitment and selection process may involve others both within and outside government who may try to affect the hiring process and the final selection of a candidate. Those who fill the top management ranks in this field come from other governmental animal control agencies, law enforcement, nonprofit animal welfare organizations, and a smaller number come from the veterinary profession. Although their backgrounds and experiences differ, each brings useful and often different skills to the job.

Candidates for management positions, whether they are managers new to this field, interim managers, or experienced managers making a career move, need to understand the culture, strengths, and weaknesses of the organization. Managers must have a vision for the organization that they are able to communicate to staff and gain their support. Administration of the program requires management to take the lead and get involved in matters of funding, training, facilities management, technology, communications, and enforcement of laws.

Lastly, a chapter on management needs to acknowledge the unique and valued role of the sole practitioner who performs a variety of tasks in this gray area of employee and management responsibilities. The sole practitioner is an important professional in the care and treatment of the community's animals, without whom there would be more human-animal issues.

Notes

1. Alachua County, "Employment," Classification Specifications, Animal Services Director, http://agency.governmentjobs.com/alachua/default.cfm?SearchLetter=A&Action=AgencySpecs&AgencyID=779 or http://www.co.alachua.fl.us.

2. Champaign County, Illinois Local Government Information Center, Position Descriptions, "Animal Control, Director of Animal Control," http://www.co.champaign.il.us.

3. Pinal County, County Jobs, Job Descriptions; "Category: 1000-Department Heads, 1014 Animal Control Director," http://co.pinal.az.us/HR/PDFs/Descriptions/1014.pd.

4. Society of Animal Welfare Administrators, Certification; "Candidate Information Booklet," Certification Mission Statement, http://www.sawanetwork.org/pdf/SAWACandidateInformationBooklet2009. Version. pdf or www.sawanetwork.org/.

5. Telephone conversation with the author on July 14, 2006.

6. Lila Miller and Stephen Zawistowski, ed., *Shelter Medicine for Veterinarians and Staff* (Ames, Iowa: Blackwell Publishing, 2004).

Chapter 4

Forms, Records, Reports, and Handouts

INTRODUCTION

Even in the supposed world of paperless technology we still need hard copies of documents. We live in a world where forms, records, reports, and handouts are essential to the operations of business and government. Without them, communication would be less effective, data collection would be more difficult, and complying with legal requirements would be problematic. Written or electronic documentation is evidence of accomplishments, compliance, and communications as well as problems. There are many reasons why forms, records, and reports are prepared and why handouts are printed and distributed. They are process-driven and help standardize daily practices, which contributes to increased efficiency and effectiveness. Animal control is a governmental function that by law requires the collection of large amounts of data. Every day in each activity of this program, numerous tasks, communications, and transactions take place. In addition the various forms, records and reports provide the basis for both oversight and accountability, a hallmark of governmental operations. Completed forms, records, and reports provide evidence that may have legal significance. Written or electronic formats communicate information, identify the sources, and provide the ability to track events, people, and of course animals. Paperwork is part of normal business practice, without which it would be difficult for the program to function. The human mind cannot store and retrieve the enormous amounts of data that need to be generated and used in this program. Handouts provide a simple readable format for communicating a message that can link to forms, records, and reports.

FORMS

Forms are part of a work process and must have a purpose and save time. They can be pre-printed written or electronic documents that when completed, generate needed data, expedite or request a service, communicate policy, and convey messages or instructions. Completed forms serve as long-term records of past action(s) and any subsequent updates. The following example illustrates the value of one simple form known as a "door hanger:"

> The city received a complaint about an animal problem at a specific address, and an animal control officer (ACO) was dispatched to that address to discuss the matter with the animal owner or occupant. When the officer visited the address, no one was home. The ACO left a form hanging from the exterior doorknob explaining the purpose of the visit. The occupant or animal owner was encouraged to call animal control if there were any questions or need for additional information.

> The door hanger was a notice of possible violation of the animal control ordinance. The officer checked one or more boxes next to categories of problems on the form. There was also a designated space on the form for the officer to write any remarks and to insert the date and time of the visit as well as the officer's name and badge number. One copy was left at the residence, and the second copy was returned to the animal control.

The purpose of this form was to notify the animal owner or occupant at that address about the possibility of a violation of the local animal ordinance. The message on the form reminded the animal owner of his or her pet owner responsibilities. Although no citation was issued nor a violation observed during the ACO's visit, the form would become part of a record at that address and evidence of a visit by the ACO. Using this form, the officer checked the appropriate box, which gave the reason for the visit, saving time and effort by not needing to write in longhand a detailed, explanatory message.

How Forms Are Used

Every form has at least one purpose, although some serve multiple purposes. The format varies from one jurisdiction to another. The exception are forms where the state dictates the content and format. Each jurisdiction has its own set of forms to meet its needs, which may be greater or less than a neighboring community. The following forms are some of the more common examples in use in animal control organizations and may be needed to comply with law. It should be noted that forms often change or are revised.

- *Adoption application form/contract.* This form is an agreement signed by the person adopting the animal from a shelter who has agreed to specific terms and conditions. Increasingly, animal shelters are using the adoption form plus personal interviews to find suitable matches between animals and potential adopters who are interested in long-term commitments.

- *Animal bite report.* These forms are used to gather information about the bite victim and the animal for both medical and law enforcement reasons. The form may contain space for the investigator's remarks and for the animal's caretaker to agree to the terms of confinement.

- *Animal complaint/problem or request for investigation/field service request.* This form is used by a complaining party to report a problem or to file a complaint with an animal control agency. The form will usually note the date that the form was received, and a case number is assigned to each complaint or problem received. Some jurisdictions offer an online form that can be transmitted electronically.

- *Animal noise complaint.* Increasingly, agencies are offering an online form to report noisy animal complaints that can be submitted electronically. The form contains instructions for the sender and indicates how the complaint will be processed.

- *Animal rescue groups.* Rescue groups are playing a greater role in helping public shelters adopt more animals. Increasingly, shelter management needs to have more information about these groups to determine their authenticity and to develop viable working relationships with them. Some animal control agencies ask rescue groups to complete a written questionnaire that is intended to solicit needed information. Other agencies have contractual agreements that spell out the terms and conditions when animals are transferred to rescue groups.

- *Animal trap rentals.* A signed trap rental form obligates the borrower to return the trap in good condition after being used to trap an animal, and the renter promises to pay for a trap that is lost, stolen, or destroyed. The one page agreement may be accompanied by additional pages with trapping instructions and a checklist on how to prevent animals from getting into a home. This form could conceivably be transmitted electronically.

- *Foster care application.* This application form is designed to obtain information about an individual interested in providing temporary care of an animal(s) from the shelter. Information provided on the application is used to match an animal with a compatible party/household. The questions asked on the form and the answers received help determine if the fostered animal will receive humane care in this temporary environment and to determine if there are problems that could negatively affect the foster care of the animal or the animal's caretaker.

- *Complaint/witness statement.* This form is usually a simple, one-page document containing a written statement by a witness in a case being investigated by animal control.

- *Shelter volunteer application.* This document is used to screen potential volunteers at the shelter. The form is completed, signed, and submitted by the applicant. The form may request personal information about the applicant including any arrests or convictions for felonies or misdemeanors. The application may ask the applicant to sign a "hold harmless agreement" to absolve the shelter of any liability in connection with volunteer services.

- *Dog license/registration application.* This is one of animal control's most important documents because it is evidence that an animal has been licensed. The process may be referred to as dog registration as it is known in some states (e.g., Texas). The form must be accompanied by a valid rabies certificate to show compliance with state law and/or local ordinance. The certificate is returned to the animal owner with the license tag or registration document. Some jurisdictions use only one form for both the initial license purchase and the renewal. Others use two types of license applications: one for the initial license and another for the renewal of the license. There may also be a standard format for a license application in some states. Some local governments require a separate license application for a pit bull. Some forms may be printed in English and in Spanish or in other languages

- *Cat licensing.* Local governments may have optional cat licensing, and others that have mandatory licensing may use a separate form for cats.

- *Lost/found animal report form.* An animal owner can submit a written description of his or her lost pet, or someone who has found another person's pet can use the found form to report this information to animal control. The form(s) may be available online and downloaded and submitted electronically, or the person who uses the form can deliver it in person to the animal control office.

- *Permit applications for special animal facilities or establishments.* Some local and state governments require special permits to operate a kennel, pet shop, cattery, animal shelter, zoo, grooming shop, guard dog service, or other type of facility where animals are kept, cared for, bred, or sold. Use of this form helps animal control track these operations as some must be inspected as required by state or local law.

- *Declaration of change/relinquishment of pet ownership.* When the former owner gives up ownership of the pet, the former owner must sign the form. This same form or another form may need to be signed by the new animal owner who takes full legal responsibility of the animal.

What Animal Control Managers Need to Know About Forms

Animal control managers, before developing a new form or evaluating the need to continue using an existing form, need to ask the following questions:

- What is the purpose of using this form, and can it be used for more than one purpose?

- Who will be using the form?

- Where in the organization will the form be used (e.g., by office staff, in the kennels, by officers in the field, or primarily by the public)?

- When will this form be used?

- How will use of this form benefit management?

- How often is this form used during a one year period?

The six questions determine the usefulness or value of completing and processing a form. If the public is using to the form to request a service, is it to make animal control more accessible and user-friendly to the public or to expedite the request? Can the purpose of this form be met in another way or with another form already in use? Can the form be transmitted by e-mail or does it need to be submitted over the counter in person or by mail? Is the form time sensitive (e.g., does receipt of the form need to be time stamped when received by animal control)? Does the form require that other documents accompany it, such as a rabies vaccination certificate when applying for a dog license? Forms that are completed and filed can be accessed by management at any time when specific information is needed. Thus it serves as both a retrieval mechanism and institutional memory.

Forms should be easy to use and to understand. They should contain clear instructions on how to supply needed data, and the purpose of the form should be apparent. Forms that are to be used by the public should have the name of the agency, its address, and telephone number printed on the first page. Application forms provide a factual record of a transaction that will meet requirements in law such as the purchase of an animal license or registration. If any of the forms have legal significance, they should be reviewed by an attorney before being placed in general use. All forms should be reviewed at least once a year for any needed updates and changes.

Finally, forms used are a reflection of management of the organization. User-friendly forms are viewed positively. Those that are difficult to complete or are not clear in their meaning convey a negative impression to the user. Animal control staff members should be asked for their input and ideas. Staff should note any comments from the public about forms submitted to animal control. If the public continually asks how to use a particular form, then it needs to be re-evaluated.

RECORDS MANAGEMENT

Records provide a chronological history of actions (or lack of action) and data to substantiate performance, compliance, and other information of a factual nature or interpretation of events. States define what they deem to be records. The importance of records is demonstrated by this statement from the Retention Schedules of the Missouri Secretary of State, Robin Carnahan:

> Everyday local government offices throughout Missouri produce records that document the right of citizens, the actions of the government that serves them and the history of the community in which they live. It is the responsibility of local government to effectively maintain and manage these records and to ensure the continued preservation of those records of essential evidence that have enduring and permanent value.[1]

How are records defined? Records are defined in state law, and each state has its own definition as shown by the definitions of records found in New Mexico and Missouri laws. Under New Mexico law, public record "means all documents, paper, letter, books, maps, tapes, photographs, recordings and other materials, regardless of the physical form or characteristics, that are used, created, received, maintained or held by or on behalf of any public body and relate to public business, whether or not the records are required by law to be created or maintained."[2] Missouri defines a record "as [any] document, book, paper, photograph, map, sound recording or other material, regardless of the physical form or characteristics, made or received pursuant to law or in connection with the transaction of official business.[3] This definition includes those records created, used and maintained in electronic form."[4]

Since animal control is subject to provisions in state statutes and local ordinances, certain procedures must be followed to comply with the law, and there may be prescribed procedures on keeping records that are deemed evidence or proof of compliance with law. Records also serve to verify that specific transactions took place. Proof of service that a determination and order of a hearing board was delivered to a recipient at a particular address on a particular date is one example. Written or computerized records keep track of various activities and tasks in the program through a filing process that allows both rapid and easy retrieval.

Animal control programs have two types of records: internal shelter records and external field service records. Internal shelter records are maintained to keep track of daily business in the shelter including the administrative office. These include sales of animal licenses or animals registered, adoption data, animals euthanized, animals returned to their owners, calls received at the shelter, financial data, and personnel records.

External field service records are documentation prepared by animal control officers working in the field answering calls for service, conducting field investigations, issuing citations for violation of law, and responding to animal emergencies. They are reports that record what has taken place during a field call. The maintenance of truck logs (mileage, number of calls answered, and the time per call) are included in this category. Other field reports prepared by animal control officers include animal captures, removing dead animals, transporting injured or sick animals to a veterinarian, and interviewing animal bite victims.

Animal control records are kept for several reasons:

- *Legal mandate.* State or local law requires that certain records be kept on file. These include personnel records of those employed in animal control and record of animal licenses sold. For example, the California Food and Agricultural Code Section 30502 states that "Any dog license tag which is issued by any city and county or city constitutes compliance with this division if it is issued pursuant to an ordinance which does all of the following: (a) Substantially complies with this division. (b) Provides for the wearing of the license tag upon the collar of the dog.(c) Provides for the keeping of a record which shall establish the identity of the person that owns or harbors the dog" (Enacted 1933, amended 1993).

- *Tracking purposes.* It may be necessary to file a particular document by subject category or by owner address to record complaints. For example, numerous complaints about a particular dog at a specific address can be a factor in how animal control decides to address the latest complaint because of past history.

- *Documenting actions taken and possible need for follow up action.* Adoptions are an example. A person signs an adoption contract with an animal shelter, pays a spay/neuter deposit, and promises to have the adopted animal sterilized by a future date. An animal control staffer not having heard from the adopting party by the compliance date calls to inquire if the animal has been sterilized and to obtain proof that this procedure was performed. If the animal has been sterilized and proof of such action is rendered, the sterilization record or the proof of such action is then filed at animal control and the matter is closed as the adopting party has met the contractual obligation.

- *Records retention/ permanent preservation of documents.* State law and/or local ordinance may require as part of records retention schedules that certain records be retained for a period of time. Texas law requires that "Daily or weekly activity reports or logs on animal shelter or animal control operations, including field officer reports, kennel log sheets, statistical summaries, logs of response to animal-related incidents etc. RETENTION: 1 year."[5] License records and animal permits must be kept for at least three years.[6]

- *Court cases.* Case files of lawsuits and prosecutions must be kept on file as these documents cover certain time periods, events, and actions that may be referred to if needed, such as appealing a verdict in a case.

- *Storage of animal control operational data.* Records of the number and species of animals impounded, adopted, euthanized, or returned to the owner are among the statistics kept to indicate workload, program costs, and to measure program performance.

- *Budgeting and accounting purposes.* Financial records of cash received, receipts issued, monies spent, and amounts budgeted and encumbered are needed to provide accountability and to determine if the funds were received and spent for authorized purposes. These records need to be available for inspection if a financial audit is conducted.

What Animal Control Directors Need to Know About Records

Keep accurate records and find out what records the law requires be preserved. Failure to keep adequate records may not only be non-compliant with state or local law or contract, but even more important, it may be difficult to carry out assigned responsibilities if records are incomplete or missing. Poor record keeping reported as an audit finding has become a problem for a number of animal control programs. Confidential records (e.g., personnel records) need to be kept under secure conditions.

Records need to be filed in a system that makes the records easily accessible. It is the director's responsibility to see that each record is properly and accurately completed, and if copies need to be transmitted to other agencies or individuals, that it is done in a timely manner. On occasion, the director should pull a sample of records by subject from the file, check them for accuracy, determine if the person creating the record can be identified, and if the record contains needed data. The policies and procedures manual should describe the approved process for creating records and what data the records will contain. Record content can then be measured against the requirements in the manual.

How Records Are Used

Records in animal control programs are used in endless ways. They are used to track the number and types of complaints received and those that require a response. Information about medical conditions and treatment of animals in custody are maintained, and data from the records can be provided as needed. Records provide evidence in support of budget requests and to account for revenues and expenditures. The fact that records must be kept for at least a stated time period benefits management should it need to look at data generated from past activities. Records are also used to verify that procedures were properly followed.

Workload volume and the complexity of that workload can be found by examining records. Personnel files are used to obtain information about employees and for determining training needs. When programs are evaluated, reviewing records helps determine the level of performance and provides accountability.

Computer software programs are able to quickly retrieve vast quantities of data and to convert data into readable hard copy reports used by management and others. Every aspect of managing the care of animals from intake to disposition of the animals can be quantified and converted into reports. The data available includes (but is not limited to) impoundment duration, medical condition, and any treatment that might have been rendered prior to adoption, whether the animal was spayed or neutered, complaints lodged against animals or their owners, and an animal's licensing status. Lists of lost and found animals entered into an automated system can checked for possible matches. Software packages are also used to manage inventories of supplies, track financial transactions, and maintain an up-to-date inventory of licensed animals.

RECORDS RETENTION

Records retention schedules indicate how long records must be kept before they can be discarded. More to the point, however, the retention schedules identify in greater or less detail the actual documents kept by animal control organizations. Exhibit 4-1 lists many types of records kept by animal control agencies, some of which must be retained for specific periods of time as required by law.

Exhibit 4-1

Common Types of Records Maintained

Statistical reports	Veterinarian service bills
Animal case history cards	Animal licenses/registrations
Investigation reports	Animal complaint notifications
Animal census reports	Citations for violation of law
Ownership verification records	Owner claims
Rabies certificates	Release of animal data
Adoption data and contracts	Animals vaccinated
Animal bite reports	Patrol reports
Animals euthanized	Daily or weekly activity reports
Kennel log sheets	Quarantine reports
Warning notices issued	Reports to health officers
Animal medical records	Rabies test request records
Inventory of animals impounded	Pentobarbital records
Kennel cage card for each animal	Animals spayed/neutered
Reports of lost/found animals	Personnel and training records
Financial records	Dangerous dog determinations
Calls for field service	Exemptions from licensing requirements

How long must records be retained? It varies from one to six years or more, depending on the state. Texas requires that applications for animal licenses or permits be kept until they expire or are revoked, plus three years if the permits or licenses were granted. If the permit or license was denied, the record must be kept until the date of denial plus one year from the date of denial. Complaints received from the public or from other agencies regarding animal control issues including the possible violation of animal control regulations must be kept until the matter is resolved or the complaint is dismissed, plus three years. Dog bite reports must be kept three years in Alaska[7] and Texas,[8] two years after bite report in Missouri,[9] and six years in Montana.[10]

Requests for Animal Control Records

Animal control records of a governmental agency can be requested by the public. States have public record laws that govern which records are public and need to be produced on demand and which records are deemed confidential or are exempt from public access. The public is entitled to view and to obtain copies of public records but may be charged for reproducing copies.

Directors of animal control agencies should seek guidance on any request to produce documents requested under a public records law. There may be legally mandated time frames during which records must be given to the party requesting them. It is best to get all public record requests in writing so that there is a clear understanding of what is being sought. A duplicate set (or list) of any documents produced as a result of a public records request should be kept by the animal control agency. The important thing to remember is that anyone who asks for a record under a public records law is entitled to see and have a copy (at a cost) as long as the document is not exempt under law. Some local governments have public record request forms that formalize the process for asking to see and/or obtain copies of government documents.

Some jurisdictions may occasionally offer workshops that explain the workings of the state's public records law. Attend those workshops, if possible. Larger animal control agencies are also more publicly visible than smaller ones and are more likely to receive more requests for public records.

What kind of records are requested? The answer is everything. A person whose unlicensed dog ran away and was eventually found by animal control and later adopted by a third party may be upset and want to know the policy for holding animals at the shelter, how long this particular dog was held, and whether the shelter staff made an effort to find the owner. A local resident unhappy with the animal control program has asked to see specific reports in an attempt to show that the program is inadequately managed. The media, in connection with a story about to be published in the local newspaper or to be broadcast on television, may request documents under the state's public records law.

Examples

- A local newspaper reporter is conducting an inquiry about shelter operations following some anonymous complaints to the city council by some unhappy shelter employees. The reporter initially made the requests to have copies of the euthanasia statistics for the three most recent years. The request was made by telephone, and the animal control director asked that the request be in writing. The written request was submitted by e-mail, and the information asked for was delivered to the reporter by the postal service as well as electronically within two business days.

- City A contracts with City B (the "contractor") to provide shelter for its animals and for field officers to answer calls to assist animals in need and to respond to various animal problems. The contract calls for the contractor to provide, on a monthly basis to City A, the number and type of complaints received about the quality of service performed in City A and how each complaint was resolved. A reporter asked City A for a list of those complaints for the most recent twelve month period including both open and closed cases. The request asked for complaints received from the contractor and those received directly by the city from complaining parties. City A responded by mail and electronically that it did not have those reports. The reporter then queried City A whether the contractor was in violation of a contractual duty to provide the reports. City A replied that it was a legal question and therefore cannot be answered. The attorney of City A informed the city's staff member handling this public information request that if the records do not exist, they need not be created. The reporter then challenged the response by replying that it was not a legal issue, but a rather a contractual obligation, and again insisted that City A answer this question. The city declined to respond further and the reporter dropped the matter.

- A representative of an animal welfare group affiliated with some national animal rights organizations requested the city council pass an ordinance prohibiting the exhibition, use, and performance of live animals in any circus, carnival, or other public display. The matter was referred to city staff for review. When the staff report recommended that the city take no action on this matter, the group's representative requested under the state's public documents statute a copy of the personnel records of the person who authored the staff report. The city denied the request because employee personnel records are exempt under law in that state.

REPORTS

Reports are a major source to internal and external communications. They assume many forms (oral, written, electronic, photographs, and special exhibits). Both management and non-management staff prepare reports. A report may be a statement describing in detail an event or situation (e.g., the impact of people bringing their pets to a public street fair and the related problems). The agenda and actions taken at a meeting of the animal shelter advisory commission may be prepared as minutes for distribution to local officials and made available to the public. The animal services director may be asked to prepare a report describing and assessing the potential impact of a new state law requiring longer holding periods for animals impounded at the shelter. A judicial opinion affecting animal control operations may be the subject of a report by the shelter manager to local government officials.

Among the more common reports that come to mind are those recording the facts and findings of an investigation such as animal cruelty or abuse or an animal bite incident. Management prepares other reports on specific topics both on its own initiative and at the request of others. Reports are transmitted to city managers, county administrators, health officials, and local government elected officials for both informational and decision-making purposes. Reports are used by animal control management to defend its decisions, to refute criticism, explain problems and issues, offer recommendations for change, or to request additional resources. Some reports are for internal use only and may include budget or funding issues, equipment needs, or a confidential personnel matter.

Some reports are based on data gathered by staff, and staff may have initiated or contributed other input included in the report. Regardless of who prepared the report, its content has the potential to impact the program.

What Animal Control Directors Need to Know About Reports

The content of the report and to whom it is sent will impact how it is interpreted and how the reader will respond. Reports on animal control issues submitted to local governing bodies may need to include some background on the subject, as the recipients receive large packets of reports prior to their meetings, and the reader may not remember all of the details previously provided because of the large volume of data that governing body members receive. Another reason for including background data is because elected officials may have only infrequent contact with this subject and are not involved in day-to-day program operations. A report on the same subject to the city manager or the chief county administrator may be shorter and have a somewhat different focus if the subject has been discussed previously with that official who has prior knowledge of the subject.

Whether a report is requested by others or is prepared at the initiative of the director or manager, if it is important enough to write, it is important enough to write it clearly so that the message is unmistakably conveyed. Long, rambling reports are not well tolerated by the recipients and for that reason may be given little weight. The subject of the report needs to be concise and as objectively presented as possible. If the subject matter is worth writing about, it is worth taking the time to have it logically organized. It may take a few drafts before the tone and content are in balance. Accuracy in a report is a must. If providing some background information will help improve understanding, then it should be included. If the report writer needs a response by a certain date, the date should be mentioned in the document, and there needs to be follow-up if there is no response. Sometimes asking a knowledgeable and respected colleague to look it over and offer comments can help, because some issue or fact may have been overlooked. The following scenario illustrates how one animal control director reported and explained a problem and suggested a temporary solution.

Scenario

The director of the county's animal control agency, after reviewing the number of calls for service received from specific unincorporated county areas, concluded that there were problems to be addressed. The geographical areas in question were some distance from the county shelter. After discussing the matter with the supervising animal control officer and with sheriff's deputies serving those areas, she concluded that her agency needed to have faster response time in those areas.

Records indicated that the areas in question had experienced a 35% increase in the number of calls for service. New housing developments were completed, new residents had moved into these housing tracts, and more tracts were being built. Her agency began receiving more calls from the new homeowners requesting assistance with wildlife problems, dogs at large, and reports on dog bite incidents. The new housing tracts were more than an hour's travel time from the shelter but were in close proximity to each other. The response time, particularly for emergencies, was unacceptable. There were no humane societies in or near those areas that could be of help, nor were there any commercial kennels nearby where animals could be impounded temporarily. The sheriff's department operates a small substation within nine miles of all the new housing tracts.

The director met with the sheriff to discuss the problem and asked the sheriff if she could assign an officer to operate out of the substation for a six month period while she worked on a long-term solution to this problem. She proposed transferring an officer full-time on a temporary basis to that area. An animal control officer who lived within thirty minutes from the substation offered to take this short-term assignment and to respond to afterhours calls. The sheriff was currently handling animal emergency calls at night and on Sundays and weekends when there was no animal control officer on duty to serve those areas. The sheriff offered to work with the animal control director and provide backup to the animal control officer, as it impacted the workload of the sheriff's agency, too.

In her report to the county's chief administrator, the director explained the problem, presented workload data, discussed the issues and costs, and presented options, which she prioritized. Temporary kennels were requested to be located at the sheriff's substation. She devised a plan for caring for the impounded animals and for a relief officer to be assigned to the substation when the assigned officer was on vacation, on sick leave, or had to appear to testify in court. The sheriff submitted his own report to the chief county administrator concurring with the animal control director's assessment and recommendations.

HANDOUTS

Why include handouts in a discussion of forms, records, and reports? Handouts are a means of publicity, because they convey messages or instructions and may supplement information on forms to educate through short messages and to note upcoming events. They are neither mandated by law, nor essential to conducting business, but they augment other means of communications and may have some impact on desired results. They also help raise the level of awareness. How to obtain a dog animal license, how to care for a pet, adopt an animal, or rent a trap can be summarized in a flyer or pamphlet. Although handouts are neither a form, record, or report, this category of materials, which includes but is not limited to flyers, pamphlets, posters, brochures, and newsletters, are inexpensive means of communicating with animal owners and the public. Handouts can be used communicate policy and legal requirements and act as a reminder to take some needed action. They should be readily available to anyone who expresses interest in their content. Someone who adopts an animal at the shelter and has signed an adoption contract may also receive a pamphlet containing questions and answers about pets and how to detect animal medical problems.

Handouts provided at the shelter and at other locations around town can help promote and publicize events, opportunities to volunteer, and educate people about an animal topic. They may include materials about wildlife, why the rabies disease is a public health problem, and measures that can be taken to prevent the spread of rabies. Handouts can be used to promote low cost spay/neuter programs and to solicit donations of supplies, consumables, and money to be used to care for shelter animals. Some pamphlets on animal topics are generic and can be purchased at discounted prices. Others are available without charge from pet product manufacturers.

SUMMARY

An animal control program without forms, records, reports, and handouts would be hard-pressed to keep track of its activities, respond to animal needs, and handle requests from the public. All are ingredients in the work process. Written and electronic communications are evidence of accomplishments, compliance, and problems and violations of law. Forms are one part of the process for carrying out responsibilities but also contribute to the standardization and repetitive nature of some tasks. They must have a purpose. Data generated by forms are used to process transactions by staff and the public.

Records management is also about maintaining forms, reports, and other documents such as statements that provide a chronological history of actions (or inaction). Maintaining specific records are required by law and must be kept for minimal periods of time as determined by retention schedules before they can be discarded. Other records are kept for reasons of oversight and to measure performance. Governmental records are public documents, unless the law says otherwise.

Reports are an essential management tool for gathering information, offering recommendations, estimating costs, drawing conclusions, assessing conditions, and prioritizing needs. Reports submitted by animal control directors to higher level management become a basis for decisions that impact the program.

Handouts that appear in various formats are tools for providing instructions for completing forms, publicizing events, and discussing animal topics. They augment other forms of communications and may help in achieving desired results by raising the level of awareness.

Notes

1. Missouri Secretary of State, Archives and Records, Local Records, Retention Schedules, Municipal Government, "Municipal Records Retention Schedule" (accessed May 5, 2006). http://www.sos.mo.gov/archives/localrecs/schedules/municpl.asp.

2. *New Mexico Statutes Annotated*, sec. 14-2-6 (E) 1978 (accessed May 5, 2006).

3. *Missouri Revised Statutes*, sec. 109.210(5) (accessed May 30, 2006).

4. Missouri Secretary of State, "Municipal Records Retention Schedule."

5. Texas State Library and Archives Commission, Records Management. Local Schedule HR, Part 6: "Animal Control and Health Records" sec. 4850-01 (accessed May 4, 2006). http://www.tsl.state.tx.us/slrm/recordspubs/hr.html.

6. Ibid. Sec. 4850-03.

7. State of Alaska, "Local Government General Records Retention Schedule: Schedule Number 300," PS-24, September 2001. http://www.archives.state.ak.us/pdfs/records-management/local_gov_schedule.pdf.

8. Texas, Ibid. Sec. 4850-02.

9. Missouri, Ibid. "Municipal Records Retention Schedule," Record Series Title, 0101, "Animal Bite Records."

10. Montana Local Government Retention and Disposition Schedules, Animal Control, Record Schedules for Local Government Records, Montana, Local Record Forms and Retention Schedules, Municipal, Municipal Records, Record Series, No. 9, MR5, "Montana State Rabies Submission Notification Records." http://www.sos.mt.gov/Records/Local-Forms.asp.

Reference

American Humane Association, *Record Keeping, Operational Guide for Animal Care and Control Agencies*, n.d.

Chapter 5

Budgeting, Revenues, and Fund-Raising

INTRODUCTION

This chapter discusses the role of management in the budget process, program finances, and the need for increased revenues, because money is the catalyst that drives the animal services program. It bears repeating that it is a governmental responsibility, and local officials are increasingly being urged to give more attention to finding additional resources for this program. The cost of an animal services program is at least $4.00 per person per year,[1] and the budget for a basic program can cost a $100,000 or more annually. Animal control programs are personnel intensive and one-time start up costs can be substantial, particularly if a shelter facility is needed.

FUNDING THE ANIMAL CONTROL PROGRAM

The Animal Control Director's Role

Management in larger agencies will delegate the day-to-day task of preparing the budget to others because of the time it takes, the mechanics of assembling the data, and the calculations needed to develop cost estimates. However, budget software programs are making preparation easier, because many calculations can be prepared electronically. The budget is one of management's most important responsibilities, and it is also a management tool that can help shape program direction, because it is the program's spending plan. The animal control director must be knowledgeable about the entire budget process, how the budget document is prepared, and the data needs for the budget document. The proposed budget must be carefully prepared and accurate. Power-Point presentations to local governing bodies showing statistics, photos, and listing accomplishments are increasingly common when departments present and defend their proposed budgets.

Program management needs to anticipate questions from other officials involved in the budget process and be prepared to answer those questions. The budget is not a giveaway process. It is about ranking the importance of proposed expenditures, and animal control is one of many programs competing for limited public resources. The choices will be made by senior administrative and elected officials based on need, priorities, and the political environment. Directors need to listen carefully to what city managers or county executives and budget officials are saying about the local economy and how it will impact revenues to finance the budget. Comments and suggestions made about this program by elected officials, administrators, and others will have a bearing on budget requests.

Larger agencies where animal control is one of many (and often diverse) programs usually have a central budget staff that assembles data and develops the budget with input and assistance from animal control personnel. The head of a small animal control agency may have limited access to assistance and must assume a greater day-to-day role in developing the budget because of limited staff. Animal control directors can be advocates for their program all year, but their best and final opportunity to influence decision makers is when they are making a personal presentation of the proposed budget before the local governing body. Accomplishments need to be highlighted, and requests for more resources should be explained and documented. Local residents who support increased funding for animal services constitute another force on behalf of animals, but their efforts should only supplement those of the animal services agency. There are several aspects of the budget process where the director's knowledge of substantive program issues can be put to good use.

- The director should review and be able to justify requests for substantial increases for existing activities. For example, the impact of inflation on purchases of goods and services, salary increases, equipment replacement, and new state mandates that add to or increase contract costs may need to be cited. One-time funding requests and how they will impact the program are important to the presentation, and the decision on these requests may be based on how they are ranked by priority. When the program has failed to meet some expected goals and objectives, be prepared to discuss why and explain what steps will be taken to obtain the desired results. Sometimes objectives are not met due to unanticipated circumstances or were beyond the control of the program. If so, they should be noted.

- Citing the per capita costs of the animal control program and how it compares to similar programs in other communities can be used to demonstrate that the program may be underfunded.

- All local officials are aware that finding more funding sources is an ongoing challenge, and the animal control director may be asked to discuss revenue generating efforts and to analyze revenue trends over the past three to five years.

- Efforts to contain program costs are always a concern, and the director should explain how costs are monitored and where savings have been realized.

- Local animal advocates and elected officials will be keenly interested in reducing the number of animals put to sleep and increasing the number of adoptions. These concerns will be raised at budget hearings, and if the program is to receive additional resources, it may be predicated upon increasing the number of adoptions and euthanizing fewer animals.

General Fund Appropriations

Local animal control programs (whether government operated or contracted) are usually financed by annual appropriations from the local government's general fund. This fund derives its revenues from a number of sources including but not limited to property and sales taxes, various fees and charges, and revenues from the state. Most programs are not self-supporting because it would mean higher fees that animal owners and others would be reluctant to pay.

Annual program appropriations will usually be incrementally increased (barring any projected revenue shortfall), even if the level of service is unchanged, simply to keep pace with inflation. Some line items will require higher allocations based on the last year's usage and/or increased costs. Wage and salary increases approved in a prior year may result in new salary ranges and added personnel costs. Rising fuel costs for vehicles means it will cost more to drive the same number of miles in the next budget year and will need to be reflected in a larger line item amount for vehicle fuel. Conversely, some line item allocations in next year's proposed budget may decrease because the current year's spending levels were less than projected.

Cost Centers

Costs centers are elements in the local government budget process and can be applied to animal control programs. The first step is defining what is meant by cost center as used in this exercise.

Cost center definition. The term cost center refers to a grouping of related tasks and services, the total cost of which makes up the cost center. It includes salaries and wages, personnel benefits, needed supplies, equipment, and services. Cost centers indicate how much a particular service costs to provide in total, what expenses are charged to this cost center, and when measured against the output can determine whether it is worth the price.

Field services is an example. The total expense of having officers respond to emergency and non-emergency service requests in neighborhoods and other locations, conduct routine patrols, investigate cruelty cases, and enforce animal laws would needed to include salaries and wages, overtime costs and benefits, vehicles to transport officers and animals, fuel for the vehicles, vehicle maintenance, liability insurance, radios, cell phones, supplies needed to write and issue reports, citations, and warnings, and personal equipment carried by each officer or in each vehicle. Officers may even carry and use personal laptop computers in their vehicles.

An in-house veterinary clinic is another cost center and one that generates revenues. Having an in-house veterinarian and assistants to examine and treat sick and injured animals and perform spay/neuter surgeries is both convenient and beneficial, but at what cost? The clinic as a cost center can identify the costs of treating animals in-house compared to treatment by an outside veterinarian. Also to be considered is employee time and cost of transporting animals to a local clinic for the same services and having only a veterinary technician on duty at the shelter.

The general fund budget will contain cost centers at the program and sub-programs levels, and appropriations are approved at those levels. Some elected officials may have a particular interest in specific line items and may wish to discuss them, although city managers and county administrators would prefer they concentrate on the total program. The animal control budget for Bloomington, Indiana, consists of four cost centers: animal shelter operations; animal control/ field operations; volunteer coordination; and humane education/public relations. The budget is an incremental one, and performance is factored into the budget process. Each cost center includes a description of proposed goals for the next fiscal year.[2]

Enterprise Funds

Some animal services programs are funded through an enterprise fund and not the general fund. Enterprise funds are stand-alone funds that are used to account for those activities and services to the public that are financed or supported mainly through charges paid by the users. In other words, it is self-supporting or expected to be nearly self-supporting. Revenues from license fees, penalties, and other fees and charges such as impound and boarding fees and other services charged by animal control to its users are used to pay for day-to-day operations. North Branch, Minnesota is an example. This city contracts for animal control service with a private provider. Revenues from dog licenses support part of the cost of providing services with most of the remainder coming from "impound and animal-collection cost to the animal owner."[3] Dependence on revenues generated by the program requires a concerted effort to renew existing licenses before they expire and to identify new animals that need to be licensed.

Special Funds

Municipalities and counties have had to be creative in developing new and stable funding mechanisms. The animal control parcel tax and the property tax increases are two recent examples.

Animal Control Parcel Tax. Voters in Paradise, California, in 2004, approved Measure N, which levied a $1.00 per month tax on every parcel in the town for the sole purpose of funding the operation and maintenance of animal control services. The reason given for advocating this measure was that due to cutbacks in state funding, the animal shelter that was heavily supported by the general fund would otherwise have to close. Voters were very supportive of the measure, which had little to no opposition.[4] An Animal Shelter Special Fund was established, and all revenues are deposited into this fund from which expenditures are made. Some small appropriations from the general fund will continue to be needed because of operating cost increases. Another lesser reason for general fund assistance is because the county's administrative fee for processing the parcel tax was a little larger than expected. In the first year, the fund broke even, and in the second year, it needed some assistance from the general fund. Overall this funding mechanism may find favor in smaller communities where local residents are sympathetic to animal needs and where local government resources may be even more limited.

Property Tax Increase. Animal control in Washoe County, Nevada, is a county-wide function performed by Washoe County Regional Animal Services. Previously there was only one shelter in the county operated by the city of Reno, and it was old and inadequate. A new county owned and operated shelter serves the entire county.[7]

Services are funded by a property tax increase of up to $0.03 per $100 of assessed value approved by Washoe County voters in November 2002. In 2003, the county agency began serving the city of Sparks, and the city of Reno in July 2005. A Regional Animal Services Fund was created to track revenues and expenditures of proceeds from the voter approved tax. The county also receives revenues from animal licenses, impound, and boarding fees. Adoptions are offered through the Nevada Humane Society, which is located in the same facility as County Animal Services.[5] There are two reported advantages of this funding mechanism. Each municipality gets to use the funds previously spent on animal control for other purposes, and a broader tax base is created by taxing across the county.[6]

Retention of Fees

Programs operated by a local government animal control department or operated as a program within another department could be offered an incentive to allow them to retain at least a portion of the increase in license fees collected. The monies retained in the program (without reducing the appropriation) could be spent for specific activities. This rewards revenue raising efforts and adds more needed resources.

Some jurisdictions that have outsourced this program have negotiated a fixed contract amount to be paid to the provider, but in lieu of higher compensation that would have fully funded the contract, the client jurisdiction has allowed the contractor to keep some or all of the fees, charges, and penalties collected. This can be problematic if the client does not know the size of its dog population, how many dogs are not licensed, or the value of the revenues retained by the contractor.

- Unless the local government knows much revenue is being collected and/or the potential to be collected each year in license, adoption, and other fees and charges, accountability is diminished unless the contractor is required to report the revenues to the client. The client may be relinquishing more revenue than is necessary, if the revenues retained by the provider are deemed greater than the value of the services delivered.

- When a contractor must rely on revenues collected from animal owners for services rendered, there is the possibility of collecting amounts that are incorrect or unauthorized. To preventive this from happening the client should establish approved fees and charges and direct the contractor to post them posted in a conspicuous location in the shelter for all to see. All expenditures and revenues related to the services provided by the contract should be subject to review by the client as authorized in the agreement.

- Periodically, revenues generated by the contract should be evaluated to determine if they are still relevant, should continue to be collected, how much it costs to collect, and how much the revenues offset program appropriations.

Brief Overview of Budget Preparation

Local government operated animal control organizations adhere to a budget preparation process that begins soon after the last budget was approved and implemented. There is a budget calendar that lists chronologically the steps in assembling the budget document, when each task in the process is to be completed, and to whom/where budget materials and data are to be submitted. Budget instructions and forms are distributed to each department to use in the process, and dates are assigned to each department when their respective budget proposals will be reviewed by other local government officials. The budget instructions explain how to calculate personnel costs, estimate energy and utility costs, and list prices of equipment, furniture, and some consumable supplies. The instructions may also explain how centralized charges are allocated to various funds and departments. Periodic budget meetings that all departments are asked to attend are held so that those participating in the budget preparation process will be kept informed on issues as they develop and have an opportunity to ask questions and for budget officials to monitor progress. Animal control managers in government programs should be present at these meetings, if requested.

The discussion and approval of the budget may take some twists and turns, despite efforts to keep to a timetable. Changes, amendments, cutbacks, and increases can happen up until the date the final document is ratified. The final, approved budget document crammed with financial data may be several hundred pages or more and lists by year the actual expenditures in the past year(s), the budgeted amount, any amended amounts, and the proposed appropriations for the next fiscal year. The public budget document may contain only the highlights and summaries, but the approved working copy contains the details.

There may be a supplemental budget process to decide what new funding requests will be approved if there are additional resources available. Departments may be given an opportunity to make a case to support funding for new activities. During the fiscal year after the budget is approved, it may be necessary for a department to return to the governing body to request additional funds due to some unforeseen circumstances.

Contractors and The Budget Process

Animal control contractors are also affected by the budget process. They have to meet budget deadlines set by their local government clients. Although an animal services contract may be multi-year, funds, including monies to pay for contracts, are usually appropriated on an annual basis. It should be noted that some contracts contain a clause that if the funds are not appropriated, the contract is no longer in force. The funding for additional years may already have been determined and is contained in the terms of the agreement. If the contract is up for renewal, the negotiations for renewal and the cost of the contract will need to begin sufficiently in advance of the expiration date.

The contractor will need to submit the requested contract amount in time for it to be reviewed along with funding requests from other departments and other organizations. Any proposed changes in the level of contracted services that affects funding will need to be reviewed and at least tentatively approved before the budget is presented to elected officials for final ratification.

Any issues that will need a larger appropriation to cover cost increases such as increased insurance premiums will need to be resolved early in the budget process before the proposed budget is submitted to elected officials. The line item budget is impacted by past history, current prices, salary changes, state mandates, and available revenues.

The process varies depending on whether it is a public agency or a contractor, although there are similarities. The contractor's proposal will usually be considered as a total dollar amount but is still subject to detailed review if increased amounts are requested. A contractor's budget request and the public agency's request may be both incremental and each may contain line item detail. The contractor, however, has to show a profit or gain some other tangible benefit for its efforts. A governmental entity performing as contractor may derive a tangible benefit by allocating some of its overhead expense to its governmental client(s).

Some proposed costs are based on prior year's expenditures but may need to factor in price increases for supplies and materials or allow for an inflationary increase tied to the Consumer Price Index (CPI).

The client as a public entity is always concerned about how costs are allocated and how to control them. If there are other animal control clients, each client government wants some assurance that it is not paying more than its fair share. The answer lies in how expenses are defined as animal control related and how they are allocated to the client government. There is no single method used to charge client jurisdictions for animal services. Rather, there are combinations of ways that charges are determined and levied.

The contractor's budget proposal ought to include estimated revenues by category and how those revenues will be allocated. Some contracts specify that the contractor may retain some or all of the monies, while other contracts say all revenues belong to the client, and the contractor only collects those revenues as the client's agent. There are agreements that specify that revenues be distributed in other ways. A program audit will review those expenses labeled as animal control-related to determine if they are necessary to providing animal control services and if they have been allocated fairly to the client(s).

Nonprofit entities. Some nonprofits may also charge a flat fee for each animal impounded at the shelter for a minimal number of days or a per call charge for answering calls in the field. Responses to field service calls may be charged on an hourly basis that is intended to cover the cost of the officer and vehicle or it may be a flat fee per call. Calls after regular business hours may incur an additional charge and/or be treated as an overtime personnel cost. This may be acceptable in smaller jurisdictions because of the limited number of animals impounded and the low number of service calls. A contractor may choose to allocate animal control costs on a mutually agreed upon dollar amount or on a percentage or formula basis. For example, if 28% of the animals brought to the shelter by animal control personnel are from the client's service area, then 28% of the cost of operating and maintaining the kennels, which includes feeding and caring for the animals, would be charged to the client through a cost center.

If the contractor is a humane society or other organization engaged in animal welfare activities, it may charge the animal control client for that portion of its staff time and other resources (medications, supplies, etc.) needed to provide animal control services. This might include a share of the society director's oversight time and a portion of the time of clerical and administrative staff and a proportional share of the cost of a veterinarian's services. The contract amount paid by the local government may be a specific dollar amount or it may be on an actual cost basis that is capped at a specific dollar amount, beyond which no further expense is allowed without further approval. If the contractor is simply on call when needed, there may be a pre-approved on-call charge.

Governmental entities. Governmental entities contracting to perform animal control services for other jurisdictions also prepare line item budgets, and costs may be shared with their clients. The client cities or towns are not burdened with the capital costs of building or acquiring a shelter facility or having the responsibility of operating their own programs. The public entity contractor benefits from the additional revenues it receives, which helps to offset its own operating expense.

Another common arrangement is to form a regional animal control agency and apportion costs to each member government by population, perhaps taking into consideration square mileage of the service area, animal population in each jurisdiction if known, the number of animals impounded, or the number of service calls per jurisdiction. Cost allocations of services can be more complex if some member governments desire some services but not others. For example, one city may need to shelter its animals but prefers to sell its own animal licenses and provide field services with its own employees. Some support services like budgeting and accounting, radio dispatch, or minor building repairs may be assumed by one or more of the member entities.

Municipalities that contract with counties or other municipalities for animal services may pay a portion of the overhead charges levied on county or city departments through an internal service fund. In one west coast county, the county animal control agency receives support services from other county departments, which are charged back to the county animal control agency through the accounting system. Animal control, for example, may be charged for a certain number of hours of an attorney's time in the county attorney's office that the attorney spent on animal-related matters.

The billed amount may be based on an estimate or actual time spent on animal matters. Similarly, the county finance department may bill animal control for a portion of the cost of accounting services provided to every county department. In turn, animal control will pass on a smaller part of those internal charges to its municipal clients. Departments that provide support services to animal control are funded through an internal services fund whose monies come from departments like animal control that receive appropriations from the general fund. When the animal control budget is prepared, animal control spreads the costs that were charged back to animal control to the animal control's clients as explained in the following example.

Example

A county provides animal control services by contract to several cities and towns. Each year, the county through animal control, a division of a larger department, presents its proposed line item budget to each contract municipality for its input and review. The proposed budget shows the various internal support costs (charges imposed on animal control from other county departments and by the department where animal control is located) and that animal control must include in its own budget. The line item budget contains cost centers for each municipality that contracts for services and how much of the internal support costs and other line items that impact on animal services have been charged to each municipality.

Among the support services charged are custodial services, mail delivery by the county unit, and a portion of the cost of operating the county's telephone system at the animal shelter. Also, each municipality's cost center is allocated a portion of the cost of clinic operations at the shelter and a portion of the cost of the kennel staff.

In the above example, where several municipalities and the county share services, staff, and other resources, all parties share in the costs. If only one municipality contracts with the county for field services, the vehicles and officers assigned exclusively to that city would be charged entirely to the city. If the client municipality needed to use a portion of other animal control services or supplies to support field services, then those services and supplies needed for field services would be charged to the city in some mutually agreed upon way.

It should not be inferred that when a governmental client contracts with another governmental entity, it will cost less than performing the service in-house, but it could cost less. Charges levied and how costs are apportioned will determine if is more economical to contract than perform these functions in-house.

Private entities. Private contractors need to make a profit, but they also need to be competitive and responsive to stay in business. As noted earlier, one private contractor was allowed to retain all license fees collected and fees and charges paid by animal owners. A contractor may have agreements with several municipalities and different compensation agreements with each.

Unique arrangements in outsourcing local animal control services are not uncommon. A western city, for period of less than two years, contracted with a newly formed private firm for services. The contractor operated the city-owned shelter and was compensated for actual defined expenses up to the dollar limits set by the city. The city compensated the contractor for training costs, overtime, employee benefits, holiday pay, and workers' compensation insurance. When the contract took effect, the contractor was advanced funds by the city to cover payroll and other immediate expenses.

THE BUDGET DOCUMENT

Budget Issues

During the preparation of the budget, numerous issues will arise that have funding and policy implications. The following issues are among those that frequently impact animal control programs.

Cost of service and program problems. The two big issues that surface at budget time are the spiraling costs of providing service and how to address new problems that inevitably require more resources. Animal control management would be well advised to bring these issues to the attention of appropriate local officials in advance of the budget review together with ideas on how to address these issues. This will give all parties more time to consider all of the options.

If services are outsourced and local officials and the contractor cannot agree on the amount to be funded, the contract can be continued on a month-to-month basis until an agreement is reached. It may be necessary to return to the local legislative body for an additional appropriation to fund the contract or to pursue other alternatives.

Making choices. The use of cost centers in preparing a budget establishes a "price" to provide a particular service. It also gives decision makers a *choice*: to fund or not fund this service or to allocate monies that would have been used for this cost center for some other purpose. When the cost center is part of a program performance budget it allows decision makers to compare and contrast costs with the *results* achieved rather than simply reducing some line items in order to stay within revenue projections. A decision on whether to fund or continue to fund a cost center will be more *rational*, because a *value* is placed on the service and some level of priority can be assigned to it. Reducing a line item may have little to do with a particular program or activity and is often an arbitrary decision to reduce costs and can perhaps harm the program in other ways.

Commingled funds. If the program is outsourced and public and private funds are commingled, if allocation of expenses is questioned, or if it is suggested that public funds may not have been spent for intended purposes or revenues were not properly credited to the animal control side, there may be problems. The following case study indicates how one nonprofit provider of animal control services came under fire for just these reasons.

Case Study

A local animal welfare group (hereafter referred to as AWG) contracted with two cities and three towns to provide an animal control program consisting of shelter, field, and licensing services. AWG presented yearly to each client a line item budget that contained approved, estimated, and actual revenues and expenditures for the prior year and those proposed for the next fiscal year. Rapidly increasing costs over the past several years led several clients to question how costs and revenues were allocated. Based on a financial review by one client jurisdiction, the following issues were raised:

- Why were some donations to AWG that resulted from mailing purchased licenses or renewals, the expense of which was charged against the animal control contracts, not credited as animal control revenues?

- Why was some capital equipment expense that one municipal client and other client jurisdictions believed they had earmarked for the purchase of two new animal control vehicles instead used for other unauthorized purposes on the nonprofit side of the operation?

- There appeared to be some overcharges to the contract clients for certain field services that were not related to animal control duties and that only benefited and generated revenues for AWG's animal welfare programs.

AWG appeared to count substantial portions of its animal welfare activities as animal control functions that raised another question of what services AWG would provide if the local government contracts were discontinued.

Personnel overtime costs. Although a program may have established operating hours, there will often be occasions when an animal control officer will be called out in the middle of the night or after regular business hours to assist police or the sheriff at a crime or accident scene where animals need to be cared for and impounded. Overtime expense needs to be budgeted to pay for the on-call officer, but also the types of calls that are subject to an overtime response should be defined in the contract and prioritized. Escalating overtime costs can be problematic and needs to be carefully monitored.

Unanticipated expenses. Sometimes a call for service may result in an unanticipated expense that should be charged to another party as illustrated by the following example.

Example

The police raided a cockfight late one night and arrested the promoters of the event and several owners of birds that fought at the event. The animal control contractor was called to the scene to impound the birds, which needed to be held until the criminal case had gone to trial and the case was deemed closed. The contractor charged the city's animal control contract nearly $50,000 for caring for seventy-five birds for almost a year.

The city contracted with the local humane society and specified that the society must respond to calls for assistance when requested by police. The contract was silent about who was responsible for animals impounded at police request. The city's finance director agreed to pay for the overtime charges from the animal control budget, but he believed costs of the long-term impoundment were a police matter as criminal charges were bought under criminal statutes and not under local animal ordinances. The finance director discussed the matter with the police chief, and it was agreed that the impoundment costs would be paid out of the police budget. When the contract was renewed, this loophole was closed.

Training costs. Costs of training animal control officers, shelter, and office personnel should be a mandatory line item in the budget, but not all jurisdictions budget for training. Funds should be used for courses that offer training to personnel performing shelter, field, and administrative duties. Included in the line item should be food, lodging, and transportation related to the training, if needed. If training is state mandated, management should inquire whether the state funds the training. Conferences and meetings should be budgeted separately unless training is the primary reasons for attending. Each jurisdiction has its own budget policies and procedures and how it defines line items.

Percentage increases and CPI. Providing the same level of service from one year to the next without enhancing the level of service will still cost more due to salary and benefit increases, increased costs of supplies and materials, and inflation. Some contracts stipulate the amount of the increase, expressed in dollars or a percentage change from one year to the next. This locks in costs for future years. Other agreements base increases on changes in the Consumer Price Index (CPI), which is published monthly in the three major metropolitan areas and bi-monthly in other metropolitan areas.

BUDGETING FOR A NEW ANIMAL CONTROL PROGRAM

Local governments exploring the possibility of implementing an in-house animal care and control program as opposed to outsourcing these services will need to consider start-up expense in addition to ongoing operating costs. The cost of a new facility is an expense to be funded in the capital budget and often financed through the sale of bonds and may require several years of planning. The financing, acquisition of land, design, and construction of the shelter are beyond the scope of this chapter.

When estimating the cost of developing a new animal control program, a starting point is identifying services and potential cost centers. It is suggested that they include at minimum: administration, shelter operations, and field services. Each cost center can be further divided into start-up costs and ongoing operating costs, which consist of personnel and non-personnel expense. The following example is intended to acquaint the reader with some of the more common cost factors in preparing estimates for a proposed budget. Local needs or legal requirements may mean that other costs be included. This exercise constitutes a starting point for estimating program costs.

Budget Preparation: An Exercise

The following exercise includes a format for estimating the costs of implementing a new animal care and control program. This exercise is intended only as a guide to preparing the budget. Municipalities and counties may have more or fewer line items in their budgets and may use different terms to define items in the budget. In the following exercise, the salary and benefits of the director is charged entirely to the administrative cost center. Alternatively, the cost for this position could be spread instead among each cost center in proportion to the amount of time the director spent on each cost center. If the director spent 40% of his or her time on administrative matters, then 40% of the personnel costs including benefits would be allocated to administration. The remaining 60% of that person's time would be charged to the other two cost centers. Each cost center would list under "personnel costs" a portion of the director's time with an assigned dollar amount.

Administration as a Cost Center

This cost center includes administrative and clerical personnel, call center, license sales, finance and records management, and purchasing. Additional line items may be needed depending on local needs, requirements, and circumstances.

Start-up Costs (one-time expense)

Office furniture (desks, chairs, etc.)	$_____
Filing cabinets/supply cabinets	$_____
Telephone lines and equipment and installation charges	$_____
Fax machine, fax line, and installation charge	$_____
Computers, computer work station, and related equipment	$_____
Computer software, supplies, and services	$_____
Calculators	$_____
Initial office supplies	$_____
Initial training	$_____
Printed forms	$_____
License tags	$_____
Microwave	$_____
Refrigerator	$_____
OTHER:_____	$_____

On-going Expense

Personnel costs

Director/manager	$_____
Secretary/dispatcher(s)	$_____
Account clerk(s)	$_____
Customer Service Clerk(s)	$_____

     Note: Personnel costs include salaries, budgeted benefits, overtime, retirement, etc. Human resources and budget staff can assist in identifying those elements that need to be included in preparing estimated personnel costs.

Non-personnel costs

Telephone and fax charges per month x 12	$_____
Energy costs per month (gas, electric) x 12	$_____
Other utilities (water, sewer, refuse) x 12	$_____
Equipment rental/leasing (copiers, postage meter)	$_____
General office supplies	$_____
Printing and postage	$_____
Equipment maintenance	$_____
Travel and meeting expense	$_____
Training	$_____
Private car mileage	$_____
In-service training	$_____
Advertising	$_____
Memberships and dues	$_____
Books and publications	$_____
Memberships	$_____
OTHER:_____	$_____

Shelter Operations as a Cost center

This cost center includes but is not limited to the care and feeding of animals housed at the shelter, veterinary medical care as needed, and maintenance of the kennels. Local needs and requirements may mean additional line items.

Start-up Costs (one-time expense)

Uniforms for kennel staff	$_____
Maintenance tools	$_____

Special equipment needed for the kennels:
Examples: hoses, high pressure cleaning
    equipment, freestanding stainless cages
    (various sizes and types) Special animal-

related supplies such as feeding bowls,
water dispensers, cardholders for cages,
ID bands, dry food feeders, animal
grasping devices, portable animal
carriers, special gloves for handling
animals, euthanasia supplies $_____

Initial training for kennel staff $_____

Microchips and microchip scanner $_____

Hand trucks $_____

Wheelbarrow $_____

Storage containers $_____

Washing machine and dryer $_____

Portable kennels and cages $_____

Fire extinguishers $_____

Chains and padlocks $_____

Lockers for staff $_____

OTHER:_____ $_____

On-going Expense

Personnel costs

Supervising shelter attendant $_____

Shelter attendant(s) $_____

Overtime/holiday pay/standby pay $_____

Temporary salaries/wages $_____

OTHER:_____ $_____

Non-personnel costs

Insurance $_____

Telephone line(s) x 12 $_____

Energy costs (gas, electric) x 12 $_____

Other utilities (water, sewer, refuse) x 12 $_____

Special kennel supplies:

Examples: disinfectant, cleaning supplies,
cat litter, ID bands, euthanasia supplies,
air conditioning filters $_____

In-service training $_____

Professional, technical, and other
services (animal disposal, insect
extermination, veterinary services) $_____

Protective gear $\quad$ \$_____

Animal food $\quad$ \$_____

Medical supplies/pharmaceuticals $\quad$ \$_____

Printed forms (cage cards, etc.) $\quad$ \$_____

Travel and meeting expense $\quad$ \$_____

Memberships $\quad$ \$_____

Clothing replacement and personal supplies $\quad$ \$_____

Advertising $\quad$ \$_____

OTHER:_____ $\quad$ \$_____

Field Services as a Cost Center

This cost center includes but is not limited to responding to calls for service including emergencies, animal rescues, cruelty and bite investigations, law enforcement, and assisting in setting traps. Local needs and requirements could mean additional line items.

Start-up Costs

Vehicles (truck and transport box) $\quad$ \$_____

Uniforms for field officers $\quad$ \$_____

Truck radios and pagers $\quad$ \$_____

Cell phones $\quad$ \$_____

Personal equipment for each officer $\quad$ \$_____

Portable cages, various sizes $\quad$ \$_____

Special equipment assigned to each vehicle $\quad$ \$_____

Pre-employment medical exams $\quad$ \$_____

Initial field training $\quad$ \$_____

Animal traps, various sizes $\quad$ \$_____

Office supplies $\quad$ \$_____

OTHER:_____ $\quad$ \$_____

On-going costs

Personnel costs/salaries, wages, and benefits

Lead or supervising animal control officer $\quad$ \$_____

Animal control officer(s) $\quad$ \$_____

Overtime pay $\quad$ \$_____

Temporary salaries/wages $\quad$ \$_____

Memberships $\quad$ \$_____

OTHER:_____ $\quad$ \$_____

Non-personnel costs

Fuel and oil for vehicles $_____

Vehicle maintenance $_____

Animal food and/or bait for traps $_____

In-service training $_____

Vehicle and liability insurance $_____

Protective gear $_____

Printed forms (citations, warning notices) $_____

OTHER:_____ $_____

REVENUE SOURCES

A distinction needs to be made between funding an animal control program versus revenue sources. The former is about providing the operating monies. The latter as used in the context of this chapter is about augmenting the primary funding source (e.g., the general fund). This distinction is important, because licenses and penalties, permit fees, and adoption fees, although they generate revenue that goes into the general fund, are not usually enough to fully fund most animal control programs. It should be noted that some fees were not levied primarily for revenue potential. Adoption fees may cover some or all of the cost of altering an animal that will go to a new home and other related expenses.

One of animal control's most vexing issues is finding ways to increase funding to meet increasing needs for service. In some cases, a replacement for general fund appropriations may be necessary because of economic conditions. Developing new revenue sources and maximizing existing ones are an ongoing management challenge. Among the most common revenue sources to augment the general fund are licensing, fees, charges, and grants.

Licenses. Licenses are generally required for dogs, but some local governments also require licenses for cats, regardless of whether they are indoor or outdoor pets. Potbellied pigs may also be subject to licensing requirements if they are kept as household pets. Licensing can be a substantial revenue producer in large cities with thousands of dogs and cats if the licensing effort is well managed. Animal licensing has generally operated on the honor system. Renewal notices are sent to remind animal owners to renew their licenses, but few resources are devoted to license inspection efforts or to follow-up on renewal notices. There is little incentive for animal owners to renew expiring licenses, unless animal control officers happen upon an animal at large.

Laws vary by states, but usually dogs that are three to six months in age are required to have a license and to be vaccinated against rabies. Many owners are conscientious and renew promptly. Others let the licenses lapse and take their chances that they will not get caught, knowing being caught means they will have to pay late fees in addition to the cost of the license. If the dog wanders at large or causes problems in the neighborhood, there is an increased likelihood that animal control will get involved and will check to see if the animal is currently licensed. Some dogs owners have been known to hide their animals if they learn that their neighborhood is about to be canvassed for unlicensed pets.

There are three primary reasons why animal license sales have been flat. First, most jurisdictions do not have full-time canvassers. Even if there are full-time canvassers, it is difficult to visit every home and every street more than once a year. The cost of a canvassing effort is not always cost effective as it needs to be offset by the sale of licenses and because many people work during the day and are not at home. Second, most communities have no idea of the size of their dog and cat populations and make little effort to find out. It is estimated that at most 25% to 30% of the local dog population is licensed as required by law. The percentage of cats licensed where it is required by law is even lower. Lastly, licensing, whether it is the purchase of a new animal license or a license renewal, has been dependent on voluntary compliance with little follow-up effort.

License sales can be increased in several ways:

- Require the owners of all animals adopted from the shelter to purchase a license before the animal leaves the shelter, even if the animal is below the age when a license is required.

- Make it more convenient to purchase an animal license. Encourage pet shops and veterinarians to sell licenses and compensate them for this service.

- Require all veterinarians to report rabies vaccinations to the local animal control agency. Information reported should include breed of animal and name, address, and telephone number of the owner. This information can be checked against the license database.

- Require pet shops to report to the local animal control agency the sales of dogs and cats and the name, address, and telephone number of the person who purchases the dog or cat, and then follow up with a telephone call or by mail.

- Partner with the local water and electric utility at least once a year to identify addresses where dogs are observed or known to reside, and compare them to the database of licensed animals. Broadcast public service announcements on radio and television about animal licensing requirements.

- Ask local retailers that sell pet food and pet supplies to post small flyers about licensing requirements in a prominent location.

Some local governments require miniature pigs (potbellied pigs) to be licensed or registered. They include Riverside County, California; Boulder City, Nevada; Kenosha, Wisconsin; and Vancouver, Washington. Licensing has more than a monetary value as it forces pet owners to be more responsible by having their animals vaccinated against disease and by having information about the animals and the owners in the animal control database.

Mandatory cat licensing is in effect in some communities, and others are weighing the rationale for doing so. Local governments requiring the licensing of cats include Wauwatosa, Wisconsin; King County, Washington; Madison, Wisconsin; Tulsa, Oklahoma; and Snohomish County, Washington. Snohomish County cat licensing is mandatory in the unincorporated areas of the county and in those municipalities that participate in the Regional Pet Licensing Program. There continues to be opposition to mandatory cat licensing, but some advocates of cat licensing say that licensed cats are less apt to cause problems.

The price of the license needs to cover the cost of processing, otherwise it becomes a subsidy. An analysis of the factors that make up the licensing costs can help determine the fee to be charged. This issue needs to take into account lower license fees for animals that are spayed or neutered.

Some jurisdictions offer a discount to senior citizens who license their pets, although they may limit the number of animals eligible for the senior citizen discounted license fee. If license fees have not changed in several years, it is not keeping pace with increased costs. Management should present to policy makers data to support increasing the license fees, explain the benefits of licensing animals, and propose increasing the locations where licenses are issued. Licensing fees should not be set so high as to deter owners from licensing their pets.

When the majority of dogs are licensed, animal owners are rightly assuming responsibility for their pets, and both they and their animals benefit in a number of ways. The increased revenue from license fees helps offset program operating costs as well. The following are common examples of animal license fees by category:

Dog license: altered animal

Dog license: unaltered animal

Cat license: altered animal

Cat license: unaltered animal

Senior citizen: altered dog/cat

Senior citizen: unaltered dog/cat

Late fee: non-senior citizens

Late fee: senior citizens

Replacement charge for lost license tag

Altered animals (spayed or neutered) are licensed at a lower rate than unaltered animals as required by law. Another approach is to impose a minimum fine of say $100 for any owner found to have an unlicensed animal. This will require advance publicity and perhaps a short grace period during which owners can purchase a license without incurring a penalty. It also puts owners on notice that this is a new requirement that will soon be implemented. This will get the owner's attention because of the cost. It will also lead to an increase in the number of licenses issued, and license revenues will be easier to collect in the future.

Another aspect of licensing is the issuance of kennel permits. In areas where multiple dogs or cats are allowed by zoning ordinance, the owner should be required to obtain a kennel permit and would need to meet certain conditions for the care of the animals. The permit fee needs to factor in the cost of an annual or semi-annual inspection of the premises where the animals are kept.

A well-planned campaign to increase the number of licensed animals ought to factor in cats as well as dogs, as cats are an animal control problem too. The campaign needs to include substantial penalties for failure to comply with law in order to get animal owners to meet their legal obligations. Seattle, Washington, has a Strategic Enforcement Plan, and in 2004, adopted a "zero tolerance policy" as it pertains to leash laws, scoop law, and pet license enforcement.[7]

Fees and Charges. Make a list of all authorized fees and charges, and analyze them to determine if they are still relevant. If they are still relevant, are they still being collected, and does each fee or charge levied cover the cost of the service provided? If not, it may be time to think about an increase. Among the more common fees and charges authorized are the following:

- Animal license/registration fees

- Impound fees (fee to return the animal to the owner)

- Boarding fee

- Quarantine fee

- Animal relinquishment fee (owner initiated)

- Litter relinquishment fee (owner initiated)

- Euthanasia fee (owner requested service)

- Trap rental deposit/fee

- Service call to pick up owner's animal (at owner request)

- Dangerous/vicious dog registration fee

Fees or charges for impounded and/or unlicensed animals returned to their owners are often levied at a lower rate for the first offense. Each additional offense increases the cost to the owner. Redemption fees or charges were established to cover the cost of the service provided and to deter frequent violators. However, it a minor revenue source. Failure to license an animal may incur penalties that are considered as late fees, because they were not renewed on time. A monetary penalty or late fee can range from a few dollars to half the cost of the license or more.

Penalties. Penalties for animals running at large or depositing animal waste (pooper scooper law violations) also vary. Usually penalties must be paid within a designated number of days to the jurisdiction where the offense occurred or at the local animal shelter, and the matter is closed when the penalty is paid.

Adoption Fees. Shelters impose adoption fees to either help offset the costs of the adoption process or to cover the full costs incurred, which increasingly covers a number of services for which a single fee is charged. The fee may include the cost of the spay/neuter surgery for the animal, vaccinations, installation of a microchip, and licensing/registration of the animal as may be required by law. Adoption fee revenue may go into the general fund or may be earmarked to pay for spay/neuter surgeries for low income residents.

Grants. Grants are awarded for specific purposes on a one-time basis. Some do not allow the monies to be used for operating expense but only for defined purposes or to produce certain results. Often a grant application may allow an animal control entity to undertake a project that otherwise stood little chance of funding. Some grants may help fund a new activity that requires the local government to match the grant amount under some formula. If the activity is successful and if grant funds are no longer available, the municipality that received the grant may be willing to commit to continued funding of the activity with local monies. Further information about grants and other assistance available to animal control entities can be found at http://www.lib.msu. edu/harris23/grants/2animal.htm. Resources listed at this Web site include animal welfare organizations and private foundations.

Revenue sharing (vehicle license plates) Twenty-three states have authorized the issuance of what is commonly called "animal friendly license plates." Examples include Delaware, Illinois, Georgia, Mississippi, New Mexico, Oklahoma, Ohio, and Texas. The purpose of these specialty plates is to generate revenues to help fund pet population control programs. Only some of the twenty-three states have actually begun issuing the plates. Those that have not yet issued the plates are still awaiting a minimum number of committed buyers before they will manufacture the plates. The features of the program vary from state to state. In some states, local governments or animal control agencies are eligible for these revenue sharing funds to be used for sterilizing dogs and cats. In other states, revenues generated from the sale of these plates are shared with only one designated organization.

Some states that have not authorized the issuance of these plates have opted instead to allow taxpayers to donate monies by designating an amount on the state income tax return that will go to address the problem of pet overpopulation through spay/neutering of companion animals. Examples include Colorado, Maine, Oklahoma, and Illinois. Both Oklahoma and Illinois also issue the animal friendly license plate. Further information can be found at www.palc.org.

Special sales tax on pet food. It seems that a very small tax on pet food (1/4% to ½%) to be used exclusively to support animal care and control services would be a logical approach to help close the gap between rising expenditures and shrinking revenues. The underlying concept is that those who have dogs and cats should pay to support these services. A broader revenue base would be created that would extend to all owners of dogs and cats. The tax burden would be spread among more people, and each would find that the amount of taxes paid per purchase would amount to only a few pennies. Those who do not have pets will not be affected by the tax, nor are they the ones who create the need for animal services. The number of animals each year that require a response from animal services is increasing due to pet owners with a disposable animal mentality. Since there are not enough new homes to place unwanted pets, more animals are being euthanized.

Opposition to a tax on pet food has been ongoing from the pet food industry. North Carolina, in 2004, considered an increase in its pet food inspection fees, but a bill in the state legislature died a quick death. Multnomah County, Oregon, considered a sales tax on pet food, but it was defeated when the pet food interests marshaled its formidable resources against it. In 1997, a 1% tax on the retail sale of pet food was urged by the state animal control association in Kentucky but also failed to pass. An opportunity to improve the welfare of animals, reduce the pet over-population problem, and protect the public has consistently been defeated.

Donations. Increasingly, governmental animal control entities are soliciting funds from the public and encouraging the donation of not only money but pet food and any supplies and consumables that can be used to make animals at the shelter more comfortable. Some entities have even established special revenue funds to accept monetary donations, which are then earmarked for specific program purposes. The following story is based on the author's personal experience.

Many years ago, the author received a call from a local resident who often called animal control about neighborhood animal problems. She wanted to donate her old car to the animal control program in appreciation for their work in caring for animals. However, the car had to be removed from her property that day. A call to the police garage produced a tow truck that was quickly dispatched to her home, and the car was removed. The car was later sold at auction, and the proceeds transferred to the animal control program.

The donation was not without a minor complication. The city had not established a fund for animal control donations as they were quite rare at the time. The city council had to formally accept the automobile as a gift before it could be sold at auction. A word to the wise: establish a fast track procedure and create a fund to accept monetary and non-monetary donations.

Other revenue sources. In addition to those revenues discussed above, animal control programs are raising additional revenues through dog walks, silent auctions, pet contests, and through the effort of organized volunteer groups. They have copied the efforts of humane societies and animal rescue groups. According to *Business Week*,[8] pet owners spend $41 billion annually on their pets. This figure indicates there are untapped opportunities to appeal to pet owners for needed funds. Why not sell ads in the shelter newsletter? Shelters that offer obedience classes, a veterinarian led workshop on basic pet care or pet nutrition, or a workshop on cage birds can draw more people to the shelter, can charge modest fees for these services, and may draw more donors. Some shelters operate pet supply stores, the profits from which go into a special fund to be used for designated purposes.

FUND-RAISING IN A GOVERNMENTAL ENVIRONMENT

Raising funds for a publicly supported animal care and control program as a *necessity* is a new concept for governmental officials and one which the public who are the taxpayers have only just begun to grasp (and slowly, at that). Citizens pay property and sales taxes to support the delivery of governmental services, and asking them to directly donate out of their own pockets to this program for services that many may believe are mandated by law is apt to generate a negative response. Local government funds that provide animal care services through a public shelter or an animal care and control contractor does not usually mean that a premium level of services will or can be delivered, despite such expectations from animal owners and the public. It takes a carefully crafted effort to educate the public that government, which provides services that the private sector cannot or will not provide, is not able to deliver all of the services animals need for creature comfort and health reasons. Spay/neuter services to help reduce pet overpopulation, some specialized veterinary services, and implanting microchips are a few examples of animal needs where public funds may not be available or mandated by law. The fund-raising appeal must clarify and emphasize that monies raised from this source will be used to augment services required by law and will not be used for enforcing laws, prosecuting violators, paying staff, or for overhead expense. If people who care about animal welfare, want animals to have these services, they must realize it comes at a price. This is where fund-raising become necessary, particularly in today's economy. Most animal shelters provide only temporary housing and care of impounded animals and do not have the resources beyond basic custodial care.

Today's recessional economy has highlighted revenue shortfalls at the local government level that have affected animal care and control programs. People must realize that with high unemployment, mortgage foreclosures, and overextended credit, animal shelters must also be hurting. This means that impounded animals may be receiving only a very minimum level of service as more displaced animals are taken into custody, as more homes go into foreclosure, and as more families have to relinquish their pets. It is important to note at this juncture that funding an animal care and control program and fund-raising for the program are separate and distinct efforts that are clarified in the following section.

Funding Versus Fund-raising

Funding. The monies to operate an animal care and control program, as noted elsewhere in this book, are a public responsibility usually financed through the local government's general fund from fees, charges, and tax revenues. Sometimes monies are distributed down to local governments by the state for delivery of services mandated by state law. Local government funds are used first for those services required by law (e.g., enforcement of animal laws through employment of officers to enforce those laws, investigation of animal cruelty and abuse, administration of a licensing program, and operation of a shelter to care for impounded and quarantined animals). The remainder of the appropriation or any additional funding may be used in accordance with local priorities and needs.

Fund-raising. Fund-raising is the process used by governmental animal care programs to raise money from public and private sources for services over and above the minimal level services required by law. Examples of how monies raised by fund-raising efforts are used are discussed later in this chapter. It is important to note that fund-raising efforts need to emphasize three points. Number one is how the animals will *directly* benefit from the infusion of these monies. Number two, there must be an appeal to those who love animals and are advocates for their cause. Through their help, animal care and control programs can help realize the goal of reducing pet overpopulation and finding good homes for these abandoned animals that cannot be achieved with limited governmental funds alone. The third point to note is that fund-raising revenues will be used for animal care and needs that government does not provide.

Nonprofits such as humane societies, SPCAs, and other animal welfare organizations are almost entirely dependent on donations and fund-raising efforts with which they finance their programs. In times of economic downturn, these groups are also vulnerable to revenue shortfalls. A key difference is that nonprofits understand and have mastered the process of raising money. They know which efforts work and which ones do not, so they may schedule some of the same events from one year to the next because of their past successes. They know how to target their donor base and will reach out to potential donors. Some nonprofits hire professional fund-raisers to manage their campaigns.

Many local governments still lack fund-raising experience and have been slow to seriously commit to raising monies from outside sources despite increasing needs, more animals passing through their doors, and recent economic trends that show little hope of receiving more governmental financial support.

Grants as a Fund-raising Source

Grants from public and private sources can be used as way to fund special needs of animal services programs, but there are limitations. Grants are temporary funding sources and may constitute a one-time receipt of funds for a specific project or purpose. There is also the competition factor. Applicants are competing against programs in other jurisdictions for a portion of the available monies, and some proposals will rank higher in priority than others. Notwithstanding, grant applications should be pursued and should be considered in addition to other fund-raising efforts.

Strategies for Fund-raising for a Publicly Supported Animal Control Program

Officials of any publicly supported animal care and control program who are contemplating a serious fund-raising campaign to raise a substantial sum of money need to keep four factors in mind.

1. *How will these funds be spent and how will they help the organization achieve its goals and objectives?* There will be no shortage of ideas on how to spend these funds. Rather, the concern should be on establishing priorities on how the animals will benefit from these expenditures consistent with goals and objectives.

2. *How can we reach our fund-raising objectives ?* Fund-raising takes time and planning. There is a need for those with fund-raising experience who can identify issues and help develop a successful fund-raising plan.

3. *Funds raised must be committed for the direct care or benefit of the animals and should not pay for mandated services.* This reassures donors and participants that their monies will be spent for animal needs that could not otherwise be met because of limitations on governmental appropriations.

4. *The use of these funds should reflect local needs.* In other words, the purpose(s) for which the money is spent should reflect some need(s) that is a locally determined priority. It will be easier to raise funds when there is a consensus on the need.

The following are some key steps to consider in formulating a strategy. Each step should build upon the one before it, but the order of each step taken could vary due to local factors.

Financial and legal advice. At the outset, discuss fund-raising with your jurisdiction's finance director and attorney to find out the requirements to be met and options to consider. For example, creating a separate fund for donations and/or creating a 501 (c) (3) charity separate from the governmental entity that delivers animal care services could be considered. Are there any legal issues to be considered? Do you understand how a 501 (c) (3) entity functions? What are the limitations and requirements imposed on this type of organization?

Focus group(s). Larger animal control agencies, particularly in urban areas, may wish to consider the use of a focus group to generate views about the current program and the animals' needs.

A focus group is a process whereas six to ten people at the same session provide information about a particular service or product. The participants are encouraged to offer their opinions, and the group can be used to assess some proposed new ideas (e.g., fund-raising ideas). The focus group should be led by a qualified facilitator who will develop and guide the participants as they respond to series of carefully prepared questions.

A focus group may be helpful in gaining a better understanding of the public's views of this program. This can be particularly helpful if in the past the program/agency had experienced unfavorable publicity and there is a need to improve its image.

A focus group may help answer the following questions:

1. What do dog and cat owners and other animal advocates really think about the animal control agency? Are their views favorable, negative, or mixed?

2. What is the visual impression of the physical shelter facility? Are there facility changes that could easily be made to give it a more inviting appearance?

3. What kinds of fund-raising efforts are most apt to succeed in this community?

4. Who are the potential target groups to contact for donations or to participate in events that will help raise funds?

Fund-raising advisory panel. The creation of a panel of individuals with fund-raising experience and who are also knowledgeable about animals and the community can help generate ideas for raising money to help shelter animals and/or address the issue of pet overpopulation. Some members may include local fund-raising professionals willing to donate a few hours a week or a month to help the animal services program. Others may be lay people who have had experience as volunteers helping to raise funds for other community organizations or who have played key roles in organizing and managing special events. The panel could be either be a task force of short duration for a special project or event or part of a long-term effort to attract volunteers who possess needed special skills and are sympathetic to your needs and those of the animals. Others on the panel may be knowledgeable and influential community leaders who can help tap other community resources. Lastly, this group can help reduce the time it takes to learn about fund-raising based on their knowledge and experience.

One local jurisdiction in need of renovations to its animal shelter mobilized volunteers who had marketing backgrounds to drum up support to pass a bond referendum to finance a new shelter. This effort deserves mention, because it was a successful political campaign that called attention to the needs of the animals that could not be financed through the annual budgetary appropriation process, and it mobilized the community to get behind this effort with their votes. Garnering public support is essential whether it is to seek individual donations or to secure a vote in favor of a bond referendum that community will fund through a long-term financing plan.

Raising money takes time, hard work, and commitment, and the fund-raising process itself covers a span of time. It is not an effort conceived on day one and on day two the donations come rolling in. The next section discusses some ideas on how to build local support to achieve your goals to help the animals.

Promoting Local Support

Raising funds through donations, sponsorship, and hosting special events depends on residents of the community knowing about your existence, understanding your mission, and why they need to support your work whether with money and/or non-monetary contributions.

The following example helps illustrate this point. A visit to the Howard County Animal Care and Adoption Center Web site, www.petfinder.com/shelters/MD106.html, in Columbia Maryland, asks the following request of visitors:

> You can now help the animals as well as the environment by donating newspapers and aluminum cans to be recycled, as well as your used cell phones. These donations will be used to raise needed funds for emergency veterinary services and other shelter necessities. Give some thought as you "PAWS" for the cause. Your donation could help save a life.

Local veterinarians. One of the more obvious sources of support can be local veterinarians since they are experienced animal care professionals who understand animal needs and play an important role in animal care in the community. Even if your shelter already has a good working relationship with the local veterinary community, now is the time to reach out to this segment of the community to ask for their help with your special needs and promoting events. Veterinary support for your program is essential and should not be taken for granted.

The local press. The local newspaper is another important source of support and local information about what is happening at animal care and control. An article in the paper and perhaps an editorial supporting your mission can help encourage revenues to your organization for projects and events.

Local civic and community groups. Lions, Kiwanis, and Rotary are among the many local civic groups where an animal control director may have an opportunity to speak to their audiences to help foster a better understanding of the role of the local animal control agency. Neighborhood associations, local schools, and houses of worship also present opportunities to reach out to the citizenry to discuss the role of the animal control agency and the needs of the animals. Consider for a moment preparing and presenting a short video that visually highlights animal needs in the community. Volunteers with videotaping experience can be a source of help in this effort.

Some denominations including Roman Catholic and Episcopal churches hold "Blessing of the Animals" services on or about October 4 in remembrance of St. Francis of Assisi's love of all creatures. Some Jewish synagogues and Lutheran churches have been known to offer pet blessings, too. Following the service, some houses of worship have held other animal-related events at which local animal welfare organizations have benefited from donations of food and proceeds from these after-services events. For example, Emmanuel Episcopal Church in Orlando, Florida, at its "Blessing of the Pets" service on October 4, 2008, collected pet food and toys that were donated to shelters in Orange and Seminole Counties.

Outdoor and radio advertising and public service announcements. Do not forget people who drive or ride to work each day on public transportation. They can be reached through billboards on heavily traveled main streets and highways and on advertisements posted in and on buses and other forms of public transportation. Another potential audience is those who drive to and from work and listen to the radio. They also listen to the public service announcements.

Appeals for donations: some examples of animal needs. A visit to some animal control agency Web sites indicate that they ask for monetary donations, specific items that are needed, and volunteer labor for special projects. Examples of how monetary donations will be used include purchase of pet beds (Fayette County Animal Control, North Carolina), purchase of medicine, equipment, and supplies (Friends of Animal Care, Inc. for Broward County,

Florida Animal Care and Regulation Division), and helping to fund the Ani-mobile, a mobile surgical and adoption van (Friends of the Chicago Animal Care and Control for Chicago's animal care and control program). Examples of donations of specific items needed at the shelter include dog and cat food, newspapers, leashes, and collars (Savannah Chatham Metropolitan Animal Control, Georgia). A microchip scanner, color printer, and stainless steel dishes are among the many items found in the wish list of the Great Falls, Montana Animal Shelter, which also seeks the volunteer services of certified electrician and a locksmith for special projects. The Albuquerque, New Mexico Animal Welfare Department has asked citizens in that city if they are willing to con-struct dog houses for the agency to give away to those who have requested them to shelter their dogs.

What Some Jurisdictions Have Done to Fund-Raise

Dog walks. People who love their dogs may be enthusiastic about participating in a dog walk with their pets. Awards might be given for special categories of entries. A suggested donation for each animal participating in this event could be directed for specific animal care efforts (e.g., spay/neutering, groom-ing, specialized medical care).

Dinner dance. This particular type of fund-raiser enables the donor to enjoy a social night out and an enjoyable meal, knowing that monies raised will be used to help animals. Another incentive for participants would be if a portion of the donation is tax deductible.

Pet photos. Arrange to have a professional photographer or a highly skilled amateur take pictures of pets or both owner and pet for a moderate fee, some or all of which will be donated to the animal care and control program. Car-ing animal owners spend considerable sums of money on creature comforts for their pets, and a quality portrait of the animal mounted in a frame in the owner's home can be a treasured keepsake.

Raffles and silent auctions. Donations from local businesses and individu-als, whether products or services, are a popular way to raise funds for the ben-efit of animals. Costs are minimal (perhaps some advertising expense), and the donors and/or sponsors receive credit and recognition for their contributions. This fund-raising mechanism might be included as part of another event.

Proceeds from purchases to be donated to animal care and control entities. Three examples come to mind. Kroger food stores offer a "Kroger Neighbor to Neighbor Donation Program." The program "will allow churches, schools (k-12), or any 501 (c) (3) charitable organizations the opportunity to earn a portion of $1 million that will be donated annually." Further information can be obtained by contacting Kroger Neighbor to Neighbor, 19245 Memorial Drive, Shenandoah, Texas 77385 or at Kroger's Web site, www.krogerneighbortoneighbor.com.

Scrip is another way to raise money. Scrip is a prepaid gift card or gift certificate that can be used like cash. Organizations buy scrip at a discount and resell it at the list price. The difference between the discount price and the list price can become the donation to the 501 (c) (3) organization. A buyer of scrip gets the full value. Everyone has to eat, including animals. Why not encourage the purchase of scrip to be used at local food stores and other establishments to purchase pet food and pet supplies. The cost to the pet owner is only the cost of the pet food, which would be purchased in any event. Using scrip, other animals will benefit, and there is no cost to the buyer of scrip. Additional information about the use and benefit of scrip can be found at the following Web sites: www.glscrip.com or www.scrip.com. According to www.scrip.com, "every nonprofit organization regardless of its size, nature, or mission can benefit from scrip fundraising." Animal control entities that wish to participate in this program must have a nonprofit status.

A third example is to arrange to have selected local merchants or service providers donate a portion of their profits on selected days to the local animal care and control program. Potential participants might include pet shops, animal grooming services, and other retailers.

State fund-raising efforts. As noted in the "revenue sharing" section above, some states have allowed taxpayers filing state tax returns to donate money for spay/neuter surgeries to address the problem of pet overpopulation. The Colorado state tax return is one example. Donations help fund grants to various animal care entities including animal control agencies. The Colorado donation is tax deductible. Information about the Colorado program can be found at www.SaveColoradoPets.org.

SUMMARY

The budget is the spending plan, and the money is the fuel that feeds the delivery of animal control services. The preparation of the budget needs to be a major concern of every animal control director as the budget sets program priorities. The director's role is to prepare and defend the proposed budget and to request the resources needed to meet program objectives.

Most animal control programs are funded by local government general funds, although some are financed by other means. Enterprise funds and various special funds have been used to varying degrees to finance animal control services. Some contractors are allowed to keep animal control-related revenues they collect, but there are issues about this means of compensation.

Contractors budget animal control services in a number of ways, some are in combination with others. A fee may be levied per animal for each animal brought to the shelter. Others charge an hourly rate for field services. If the contractor takes in animals from several jurisdictions or from the public and the client's service area, the cost to the client may be based on a percentage of animals from the client's service area as a proportion of the total number of animals housed at the shelter. Contractors may choose to spread their overhead among the clients served. When several jurisdictions share animal control services and a common facility, costs may be shared among the participating governments on the basis of some formula. One major ongoing issue is determining how costs are to be allocated and what constitutes an animal control-related cost.

When budgeting for a new animal control program, early identification of cost centers is a necessary step in the budget process. The development of a proposed line item budget along the lines of the budget preparation exercise presented in this chapter can help estimate start-up and ongoing operating costs.

Development of new revenue sources and maximizing the potential of existing ones can be challenging. Some revenue sources such as animal licenses and penalties have been underutilized, while other actual or potential revenue sources such as revenue sharing and a special sales tax on pet food have not caught on or have been opposed by business interests.

Raising additional funds for an animal care and control program from private and public sources to augment governmental support has become a new necessity and a concept that the public has only just begun to grasp. Governmental funding alone will no longer meet all of the needs of animals as more animals are abandoned or owners have had to relinquish their pets to shelters as the economy takes its toll on the people whom the animals depend on for care.

The distinction between funding and fund-raising needs to be made clear. Governmental revenues support basic and mandated services, but fund-raising from private sources, events, and in some instances, from public entities can provide for those special needs when governmental funds are not available or are insufficient.

A serious fund-raising effort on behalf of an animal care and control program requires a plan of action, commitment, and volunteers who can use their prior experience to help the animals. Some key steps need to be considered in formulating a strategy to raise funds.

Promoting local support for the program is critical, because until the community knows of your existence and understands your mission, they cannot be expected to support your work. Finally, fund-raising efforts must have as part of its core message that the monies raised will be spent on the direct care or benefit of the animals and will not be used to support mandated services or overhead.

Notes

1. Geoffrey L. Handy, *Animal Control Management: A Guide for Local Government* (Washington, D.C.: International City/County Management Association, 2001) 3.

2. City of Bloomington, Indiana, City Departments, Controller, City Budgets, 2006 City Budget, "Animal Care and Control Budget," www.bloomington.in.gov (accessed September 2005).

3. City of North Branch, Minnesota, City Departments, Police Department, "Animal Control," www.ci.north-branch.mn.us/city/depts.html#Police.

4. Town of Paradise, California, *Voter's Pamphlet: Measures, Analyses and Arguments*, Measure N, 2004.

5. Washoe County, Nevada, Budget Home Page, Library of Budgets, FY07 Budget Book, Special Revenue Funds, "Regional Animal Services," http://www.co.washoe.nv.us (accessed February 9, 2007) and telephone interview with Jean Ely, Animal Control Director, Washoe County Regional Animal Services, February 9, 2007.

6. Telephone Interview, Jean Ely, Ibid.

7. City of Seattle, Washington, Seattle Animal Shelter, *Strategic Enforcement Plan*, Effective March 1, 1998, Updated August 2007. http://www.seattleanimalshelter.org/strategy.html#4. No longer available online.

8. Diane Brady and Christopher Palmeri, "The Pet Economy," *BusinessWeek*, August 6, 2007, 44.

Chapter 6

Contracting for Animal Services

INTRODUCTION

Local governments that fund animal control services must decide whether to provide services in-house or outsource them. This is a major decision affected by many factors including cost and scope of services desired. Local governments may be faced with the fact that some animal control functions are mandated by state law, and they must provide them somehow, although some municipalities and counties have failed to do so. This chapter explores the option of contracting for services from several perspectives:

- Common issues to consider when contracting for services
- Critical steps in the contracting process
- Contracting options
- Perspectives of client and contract provider
- Contract termination and impact

Local government as the client determines the scope of services to be provided. The scope of services depends on available funding and competing priorities for other governmental functions. Because contracting is at the discretion of local government officials, funding, terms, conditions, and scope and level of service vary considerably from one jurisdiction to another.

Reasons for Outsourcing the Service

Local governments outsource this responsibility in whole or in part for many reasons. The community may be so small that it cannot afford to hire staff and maintain a shelter facility, or it has no animal control experience or expertise in this field. Financial resources may be limited, or the community does not own a shelter. There is a widely held belief that contracting is cheaper because contractors have lower overhead costs. There may be little support in the local governing body to undertake the needed services in-house because of start-up costs and perhaps fear that once begun, animal control may continue to grow both in cost and in scope as the animal population increases.

Some municipalities contribute a specific dollar amount for this purpose to a local humane society or SPCA to help those organizations offset some of their costs for providing these services in the absence of a government operated program. At best, this is a temporary solution for all concerned. Humane societies and SPCAs are finding after a few years that these contributions are inadequate to cover the actual costs of service and want to renegotiate the arrangements. Other nonprofits choose to limit their involvement in animal control to sheltering animals brought to their facilities.

Issues of accountability and whether a public or private entity can do a better job aside, the local municipality's financial condition, local priorities, and politics will be important factors in deciding whether to outsource this responsibility. The size of the local dog and cat population also influences the decision making process for two reasons. First, a community that impounds just a few hundred animals a year may be unable and unwilling to add more personnel to the public payroll because of government's overhead and the permanency that is expected when adding new staff. Larger communities with substantial pet populations that impound several thousand or more animals may similarly conclude they do not have the wherewithal to build and operate a facility large enough to meet the needs of a growing community. Contracting is therefore seen to have several advantages. A nonprofit provider's staff members are not public employees and are compensated less than public employees. The contractor already has a facility, less overhead, and there can be an arm's length relationship that many clients desire. A local government interested in outsourcing this service will need to look hard to find a private or nonprofit operator that has the operating capacity and is willing to perform these tasks. In some cases, contractors have been less than enthusiastic in accepting animal control responsibilities, but agree to do so because they realize it is their mission to help animals in need.

A looming question is: Are there available and willing entities in the private or nonprofit sectors willing to perform this service? The number of humane societies, SPCAs, other animal welfare organizations, or private contractors in any county or region of a state that are able and *willing* to contract with local governments to perform these services is limited. Some simply do not want governmental involvement, but others welcome the opportunity because they believe they can do a better job. Local veterinary clinics have been known to contract to impound animals in some communities. After a search, it often comes down to acknowledging that there is only one available provider, making competitive bidding moot. A request for proposal (RFP), often the preferred option, is discussed in a later section of this chapter. Since response time can be critical (and is also a performance measure) when answering calls for service in the community or transporting animals to a shelter or for emergency medical treatment, shelter and field staff need to be in close proximity to the service area.

Some local governments operate their own shelters but contract with another organization for field services. In the past, local governments gave inadequate attention to the contract until costs started to escalate or questions about the service arose. The focus is all too often on cost containment. Inevitably, both the client and the provider have to revisit these issues as needs and circumstances change and costs continue to increase.

Not all animal control professionals believe that animal control services should be outsourced to the private sector. The most frequent motivator for government to contract out for this service has been to save money.

UNDERSTANDING ANIMAL CONTROL CONTRACTING

Animal Control is Unique

The unexpected is often the norm when performing animal control services, whether in-house or by contract. For example, a contract to house impounded dogs and cats takes on an unusual twist and unexpectedly reduces kennel space when the sheriff raids an illegal cockfight and twenty-five gamecocks have to be impounded until the trial of their arrested owners takes place (perhaps six months in the future). These animals need to be held as they are considered evidence at trial. Impounding dozens of mistreated, sick, or injured dogs and cats seized from a hoarder can quickly fill and strain the capacity of a small shelter. A field service contract that normally covers calls about dogs and cats suddenly has animal control officers and local police responding late at night to a neighborhood invasion by a band of feral pigs. The pigs have dug up lawns, ripped out underground sprinkler systems, and when confronted by animal control and police officers, charged at both. Animal control is unique in the following ways:

- Unexpected and sometimes dangerous animal situations can occur at any time.

- Service calls and sheltering may require temporary housing of wildlife, livestock, and other species that require special accommodations.

- Animal emergencies know no set hours. When human and/or animal lives are in danger, a response may be needed whether it occurs day or night. After-hours calls are unpredictable and can add to contract costs.

- Animal control personnel need training that covers unusual and dangerous situations as well as knowledge about many species of animals, because animal control is often the first responder in an emergency.

- Lastly, animal control personnel have two very different sets of clients: animals and people.

Contracting Basics

The following points should be considered when pursuing the contracting option.

1. A local government that owns a shelter facility should not be in a hurry to give it away or sell it to a contractor or to any other party without giving thought to where impounded animals will be housed in the future should the contracted service terminate.

2. Local animal ordinances should be reviewed and updated before signing an agreement with a contractor. Otherwise, the contractor may not have adequate authority to enforce local laws.

3. Contractors that have a capital investment in the contract will want to recoup that investment over the term of the contract. That is partly why the parties sign multi-year agreements and for the client to lock-in costs for future years. Should the contract be terminated early, capital investment and reimbursement may be at issue.

4. Budget adequately. An underfunded contract can soon lead to disagreements and termination. More importantly, a supplemental appropriation may be necessary to continue needed services in the short term.

5. Appropriate funds for training, and specify how these funds are to be used. Training is the key to improving the quality of service. It is not a fringe benefit, nor is it a perk. It is a business requirement and needs to be documented that designated training was provided.

6. Both parties need to negotiate in good faith if the contractual relationship is to survive and a needed level of trust maintained.

7. Both parties need to meet periodically to discuss any issues that arise and to review reports submitted to the client. This keeps lines of communication open and helps ensure a satisfactory working relationship.

Getting a Contract That Meets Local Needs

A contract is more than an agreement between parties and more than a "meeting of the minds." It is the *legal* basis for which one party promises to deliver certain goods or services to the other party in exchange for an agreed upon sum of money or other compensation. Beyond promises, payments, and legal standing, the contract, if carefully written, can serve as a form of measuring stick in which the recipient (the local government client) can determine whether it received all that it paid for and if the quality of the services delivered is acceptable.

For example, a local government anxious to reduce the problem of dogs running at large on city streets and other public places may want to specify in the contract that complaints about animals running at large merit a higher priority response. The contractor might be required by the terms of the contract to provide documentation to support its progress in this area and how the problem is being reduced in scope. This might include maintaining data indicating when the call for service was received, when it was dispatched and answered by an officer in the field, and the outcome of the call.

A written contract needs to describe the intent of both parties. The larger the contract amount, the greater the need for accountability and specificity in describing the obligations of all parties to the agreement. Attorneys play important roles in interpreting what the parties want and the agreed upon terms. An attorney can advise which clauses should be included and any requirements in state or local law that may impact them. The fact that new and unanticipated circumstances may develop in the future is reason to draft some provisions more carefully than others.

Contract Examples to Meet Local Needs

Example 1. A town with horse owners and horse corrals can expect equine problems. If the town contracts for animal control services, and if horses at large are an animal control responsibility, then the contract (and local animal ordinances) need to contain provisions for horse impoundment, related equine tasks, and applicable fees and charges.

Example 2. A city with high population density that contracts for animal services should consider contract provisions and ordinances that apply to nuisance animals (including noisy ones) and appropriate disposal of animal waste (pooper scooper laws).

CRITICAL STEPS BEFORE SIGNING A CONTRACT

Before contracting for service, a local government needs to identify the type and extent of animal problems in the community, how to address them, the types of services requested, and what services are to be prioritized. Addressing these issues will require analyzing data extracted from animal control records for specific periods of time. Local governments will need to have and make available data on the size of its dog and cat population and service request statistics for the most recent three to five year period. Data should be shared with potential contractors as they develop cost proposals.

Issues to Consider Before Contracting

Before contracting for service, review the following questions and attempt to answer each. Some or all of these questions can be addressed through Options A or B that follows.

1. Have cost estimates and a proposed budget been prepared if animal services is also being considered as an in-house function?

2. Does the local government client have the subject and management expertise and financial wherewithal to provide animal control services within the local government organization?

3. Have local government officials who will be involved in the decision arrived at a consensus on how to proceed?

4. Are there one or more local entities that could assume animal control responsibilities? Which ones might be interested? Local entities could include a nonprofit organization, another governmental organization, or a private contractor like a veterinary clinic.

5. Do potential provider organizations have the experience and personnel to do the job?

6. Are local animal ordinances adequate and legally enforceable? Will a contractor be authorized to enforce them?

7. Are there pet limits per household? If not, how will the absence of animal limits impact the service provider's workload and cost of service?

8. If sheltering is needed, who will provide the shelter facility? What is the condition and size of that facility? If the facility is owned by the local government client, who will be responsible for maintaining it?

9. What problems in the current operation, if any, need to be addressed and at what cost?

Option A: Preparing a Staff Report

The local governing body of the jurisdiction, the mayor, city manager, county executive, or others who may be vested with authority, may assign staff to research the above concerns and prepare a written report addressing them. The report needs to provide detailed estimates on the costs of proposed services as well as alternatives. The local government's budget and purchasing officials can help in preparing cost data. Others to contact for information include other animal control agencies, the state animal control association, and local veterinarians. Hiring an animal control consultant is another alternative. The report should include a history of animal control in the jurisdiction to familiarize the reader with past problems and issues and current and future needs.

Animal census. A staff report or committee report should estimate the number of dogs and cats in the community. The American Veterinary Medical Association has formulas to estimate the number of pets in a community. A dog and cat census is another approach and one that offers greater accuracy. A newly created city that is going to provide animal control for the first time needs an animal census. The size of the animal population is a predictor of the number of dogs and perhaps cats that should be licensed and also helps to estimate the number of animal control officers that may be needed to meet the anticipated workload.

A one-time canvass by utility meter readers of every address in the city is a worthwhile expense as it can help estimate the total number of dogs as well as the number that need to be licensed and vaccinated for rabies. Meter readers for the local electric or water utility visit each property on a regular schedule and would be appropriate for this task. The utility has a computerized listing of all residential and commercial properties and generally note in their data base if there are animals known to be on that property as a means of alerting meter readers for their personal safety. Prior to undertaking any canvass an attorney can determine if there are any privacy or legal issues to resolve.

Option B: Ad Hoc Task Force or Committee

An alternative to the staff report is to appoint an ad hoc task force of individuals with interest and experience in animal welfare issues to prepare a set of recommendations. The task force might include a veterinarian, a police official, a few governing body members, and some local residents. This option encourages community consensus and support and can be a valuable resource to the elected decision makers. A task force or committee offers the decision makers some political cover through community input.

RFQ and RFP

Identifying organizations qualified to provide the needed services should begin as soon as possible. Staff needs to prepare a request for qualifications (RFQ) to identify organizations that may have the experience, expertise, and interest to provide those services. A sample cover letter and RFQ are found as Appendices 6-1a and 6-1b. The RFQ can be mailed to designated organizations, made available for down-loading on the city's Web site, or advertised in selected animal welfare publications and in the local press.

Organizations that respond and appear qualified can subsequently be sent requests for proposals (RFP) prepared by the local government. The RFP should contain sufficient detail so that the respondent can adequately reply to the terms of the proposal. The proposal should contain information about the city, its population, square miles, description of the service area, the current status of its animal control program, and the service(s) being requested. If the RFP is being solicited by a county, will the service area include the entire county or only the unincorporated areas?

Decision makers need to be specific in describing the services they want to be provided in an animal control program. These services should be prioritized in the RFP, and a separate cost estimate should be requested for each activity, if needed. The following are examples of requested activities:

- Sheltering lost, stray, impounded, or injured animals, the quarantining of dangerous animals, and the number of days animals are to be impounded or quarantined

- Field services to respond to complaints about animals and requests for service, such as aiding an injured animal, responding to dog bites and attacks, and enforcement of state laws and local ordinances

- Licensing or registration of pets

- Animal adoption programs

- Scheduled rabies clinics

- Spay/neuter services

- Basic veterinary care at the shelter

- Euthanasia, pick up, and disposal of dead animals

- Community outreach efforts to educate the public and pet owners

The more information local government has about a potential animal control contractor, the better it is able to make informed decisions. Borrowing the term "due diligence" from the business and financial world, local government officials should do their homework (e.g., gather as much relevant information as possible that relates to the contract work of a potential vendor). Some of the concerns and information can be requested through the RFP. The client jurisdiction's attorney and finance director should be included as participants in the RFP process. The following concerns are intended as illustrations of matters to pursue through the RFP process:

1. Does this contractor serve other public clients, and if so, who are they, and how long have they been clients? Ask for the names of these clients and their telephone numbers and then call them.

2. Ask these clients if they are satisfied with the level of service received.

3. Inquire whether the client's contract costs increased during the contract period, what was the percentage increase, the actual dollar amount of the increase(s), and the reasons for the increase(s).

4. Have there been any recent major changes in the management of the contractor's organization, and if so, why and how might it affect a new contract?

5. Do any of the contractor's clients have unresolved issues with the contractor?

6. How does the contractor provided accountability to its governmental clients?

7. What is the animal control/business experience of the principals in the contractor's organization?

The responding organization then submits a proposal pursuant to the requirements/terms of the RFP. The RFP should have a closing date and time for responses. A sample RFP for the impoundment and boarding of animals is presented in Appendix 6-2.

Splitting Responsibilities without Deleting Accountability

Splitting the responsibility for animal control services requires coordination and the means to hold each provider accountable for its performance. The contract needs to specify the tasks to be performed by each party.

Example. A city may own and operate the animal shelter and perform activities associated with that facility such as the care and feeding of impounded animals, treatment of sick or injured animals, sale of dog (and/or cat) licenses, and animal adoptions. Field services may be contracted out to another governmental entity such as a county agency or to a nonprofit or for-profit firm. This will require clear delineation of tasks by each provider. Even cities that own their own shelter may choose not to operate it directly and may contract with another entity, public or private. Some local governments may not have a shelter but employ animal control officers (field officers) to answer calls for service and to perform tasks normally associated with the field operation of this program. These contractual arrangements vary greatly from one jurisdiction to another. When responsibilities are split between two or more entities, the question is how to hold each accountable for its own actions and how they will coordinate with each other. Consider the following scenario.

Scenario. Town A contracts with the county to provide field services within town limits. Shelter services are provided by the local humane society to both the town and the county, because neither one has a shelter facility. A county animal control officer on patrol comes across a cocker spaniel running at large on a county road, picks up the dog, and places it in his vehicle's animal holding compartment. The animal had no collar or license tag and is brought to the humane society where it is impounded. Paperwork is transmitted from the animal control officer to a shelter employee who signs off on having received this animal. One copy of the paperwork is kept by the society, and the other copy is retained by the county. Presumably, a society employee scanned the animal for a microchip as required by the contract, but no microchip was located. A clerk at the shelter prepared a tracking form for this animal and entered the data into the computer. The clerk went on vacation the next day, but the society's computer crashed, and yesterday's data entries were lost. The society claims the animal was held the minimum three days required by law and then was adopted by an out-of-county individual. The dog's owners, who lived in Town A, were away on vacation and returned to find their dog missing. The dog's caretaker, who had been searching for the animal for three days, did not locate it at the shelter. The owners charged that the town, the society, and the county failed to hold the animal for the minimum three day period, and the owners produced evidence that the animal was licensed and had an implanted microchip. The animal's owners threatened to sue all three entities. What are the issues, and what would you do if you were the animal control director?

Accountability issues can be addressed through informal meetings of the parties from which consensus is reached and then implemented by written provisions in the contract. Another option is to seek advice on specific questions from the state association or other jurisdictions that contract for services. An attorney can also be a useful resource when accountability questions involve potential liability.

CONTRACTING OPTIONS

When it comes to contracting for animal control services, there are several possibilities to consider. Saying that there are "choices" could be misleading, as every option is not available in every locality. The following sections examine some of the major options currently in use.

Contracting with a City or County Animal Control Agency

There are municipal and county animal control programs that are able to provide services to other jurisdictions. These entities also understand how public sector decisions are made and the constraints under which they are made. The lines of communication and accountability between a city and a county, between two cities, or between a town and a village can be readily established. Understanding the fiscal constraints and the political environment of each entity can foster an effort to develop a more regional approach and may take advantage of economies of scale. Adopting one set of animal ordinances and fees for all participating entities can simplify enforcement and administration. There are currently no data that conclusively show contracting with another governmental agency for services will cost less than contracting with a nonprofit or private provider, but governmental overhead can be higher than the private sector. After working through cost estimates, however, there may be an economic advantage in a regional approach with several jurisdictions participating. When there is a level of mutual trust and good relations between the governmental entities, it can be a mutually beneficial arrangement and one where accountability and cooperation work hand in hand. There are other matters to consider, including political relationships and frequent personal interaction on other projects, services, and issues of mutual concern. Counties and the municipalities often contract with one another and/or share the cost of selected services. Contracting for animal control services with an entity where there has been a past history of a relationship and perhaps a greater comfort level may carry more weight in some cases, even if the cost of services is a bit higher than those of another provider. On the other hand, if past contracting experience with a county or municipality has been problematic, there may be an unwillingness on the part of one or both parties to enter into any new agreement for services.

The Shelter Ownership Issue

A local jurisdiction contemplating contracting with another unit of government to provide animal sheltering services may want to explore the value of investing in an ownership interest if a new facility is to be built. A financial analysis is needed to estimate construction, land acquisition, equipment costs, and future maintenance expense of the facility as well as how those costs will be allocated among the parties. An ownership interest in the shelter facility is a form of insurance to assure animal occupancy rights and create ownership equity in the facility. It encourages a long-term sheltering commitment that can be financed over a period of years. Communities that share joint ownership interest in a shelter facility also have more say in its operations.

If two or more jurisdictions house their animals in a facility to be built, owned, and operated by a third party for its animals, but houses animals from other jurisdictions, to what extent will the client jurisdictions be subsidizing the construction and acquisition costs if they do not have any equity in the facility? Would it be more economical for two or more local governments to build their own smaller shelter? Consider the following two case studies.

Case 1. Center City and Northville, the two largest cities in the county, and five smaller cities contract for animal control services with the local SPCA. Each of the seven cities recently received a letter from the SPCA's executive director informing them that the SPCA will discontinue providing animal control shelter and/or field services for all jurisdictions, effective fourteen months from the date of the letter. The letter further explained that the SPCA's board of directors had concluded that the animal control contracts were no longer compatible with the SPCA's primary mission of providing animal welfare and pet adoption services. About 35 percent of the SPCA's revenue came from the governmental animal control contracts. The city managers in the seven cities were surprised by the SPCA's announcement.

The impact varied by community, as some cities owned their own shelter buildings but contracted with the SPCA for field services, whereas other cities had their own field officers but brought the impounded animals to the SPCA-owned shelter facility. Each community scrambled to identify options and future costs. A few communities asked the county government to help with the matter. The county, after some internal deliberations, expressed an interest in building a new county-wide shelter to serve all cities and the unincorporated county areas. However, the county declined to consider joint ownership or an equity interest in the facility by these cities. The county's preliminary cost estimates to house the cities' animals were nearly double the amount paid by the cities to the SPCA. Each jurisdiction had just over a year to develop a solution. What would you do?

Case 2. Two local governments, one a city and the other a county, each faced the need to find a shelter facility after being served notice by the local humane society that it was going to discontinue sheltering city and county animals and would no longer provide field services to the city. County employees performed field services in the unincorporated county areas but utilized the society's shelter to house the county's animals.

City and county working together located a former manufacturing plant that was for sale and had adequate space to house both city and county animals. The county financed and purchased the land and building on behalf of both entities. The county agreed to perform all animal control services for the city (including sheltering the animals). The city, in turn, agreed to pay for a one-half ownership of the shelter building. The costs of purchasing the property, renovations to the building, and annual maintenance were assumed by both parties and amortized over a twenty year period. At that time the city would receive a one-half ownership equity in the animal shelter portion of the building. Both parties were thus assured of having a place to house their animals for years to come. The terms and conditions for the purchase and renovations to the shelter facility were stipulated in a written agreement signed by both parties.

Joint Powers Authority (JPA), Special District, or Joint Ownership

The cost of a city or town operating a comprehensive animal control program can be a financial strain, because most animal services programs have not been self-supporting. There is often a need for overtime and for keeping animals for extended periods of time in cases of quarantine and when animals are part of a lawsuit or evidence in a criminal case. Several local governments, including both municipalities and counties, may conclude that it is mutually advantageous to take a regional approach to providing animal control services and share the cost of operating a shelter and providing field services to each participating jurisdiction. The key advantages are cost sharing, a large degree of certainty and long-term participation because of the legal commitment, some economies of scale, uniform operating policies, procedures, and laws, and one set of employees to serve all participating entities. If additional field officers are needed to address a problem in one community on a short-term or one-time basis, personnel can be assigned temporarily for that purpose.

A JPA can be utilized when two or more public agencies (e.g., counties and cities) establish a joint effort to work on a common problem, fund a project, or act as a representative body for a specific activity. The advantages and disadvantages of creating a JPA should be carefully evaluated.[1]

There are several ways this arrangement can work, but two are outlined here. First, each public jurisdiction participating in the arrangement contributes its share to the operating costs according to some agreed upon formula. A governing board with representation from all participating jurisdictions selects a director with day-to-day oversight responsibilities who also hires staff. The director reports to the board. The board approves the budget, which is funded by appropriations from the participating local governments.

Another option is to have the board contract with another organization such as a public jurisdiction, a nonprofit animal welfare group, or a for-profit contractor to operate the program. There are variations of this model in use. The following examples illustrate two regional approaches to delivery of animal control services.

Example 1. SEAACA (Southeast Area Animal Control Authority) a joint powers authority created in 1975, provides services to 13 Southern California cities near Los Angeles. SEAACA is an independent public entity but is funded by the participating jurisdictions. SEAACA was formed by the cities of Downey, Norwalk and Pico Rivera and other members of the joint powers authority were added later.

Example 2. Tri-Cities Animal Shelter in Cedar Hill, Texas, near Dallas, provides animal shelter services to three small cities: Cedar Hill, DeSoto, and Duncanville. Each city contributed one-third the cost of acquiring the site and constructing and equipping the shelter. Each city owns an undivided one-third interest in the project site and the facilities. Maintenance and operating costs of the facility are allocated on a pro rata monthly basis according to each party's use of the facilities not paid with revenues from the operation of the facilities. A three member management committee (with one representative from each city) is responsible for the ownership and operation of the shelter. The shelter's director and staff are all employees of the city of Cedar Hill. Each respective city operates its own field services. Animal control officers in Cedar Hill and

Duncanville work for their respective police departments. Duncanville also operates the animal control dispatch center for all three cities and the center's staff members are employees of that city.

Contracting with a Humane Society, SPCA, or Other Nonprofit Animal Welfare Group

Local humane societies and SPCAs often contract to provide animal care and control services. Some humane societies and SPCAs perform animal control duties at least in part to help underwrite the cost of their basic mission (e.g., to promote the adoption of stray and unwanted pets and other humane activities including spay/neuter services and a community outreach program with an educational component). As long as the society's or SPCA's mission does not conflict with the philosophy and goals of the governmental animal control program, it may be a mutually beneficial arrangement for both parties. Initially at least, these nonprofit organizations see themselves as being able to provide a more humane and higher level of care to animals. A government shelter is seen by some as the final destination for unwanted animals that are deemed to have little chance of being adopted and beginning a new life in a new home.

Why would a nonprofit animal welfare organization want to contract to provide animal control services in the first place? Nancy Lawson in a 1998 article in *Animal Sheltering* magazine offered this explanation:

> Humane organizations often sign contracts so they can work more closely with government to make positive changes for animals, increase their presence in the community, and, most importantly, directly help greater numbers of animals by enforcing laws against abuse and neglect.

Lawson raises eight issues for humane organizations that take on animal control contracts:

1. Is your concern for animals enough to make it work?

2. Will a government contract bring more money into your shelter?

3. Are you ready to enforce laws?

4. How will contracting affect your relationship with supporters and other citizens?

5. How will a contract affect your autonomy?

6. How can you show your importance as a public service?

7. Are you ready to play hardball?

8. How far are you willing to go to get what you need?[2]

Lawson's questions are a reality check for those nonprofits that think they would like to provide animal control services. A nonprofit entity may be able to provide animal control services at lower cost, but cost alone should not be the deciding factor if the service is no better. A comparison of personnel costs between a government program and one operated by a nonprofit will show that government's costs of doing business can be higher due to the wage scale, overhead, unions, and laws and regulations that apply to the public sector.

Depending on the relationship between the provider and the client, occasional program changes requested may be problematic if the provider adheres strictly to the contract terms and insists on negotiating any requested change, no matter how small.

Contracting with a Private (for-profit) Contractor

There are a smaller number of private animal control contractors compared to nonprofit animal welfare organizations in the United States that perform local animal control services. None are known to operate animal control programs on a nationwide basis. Outsourcing animal control services to a private, for-profit operator first depends on whether there is an operator interested in performing these services. Some private operators are individuals who left public sector animal control and set up their own business to bid a contract in a specific jurisdiction. Any jurisdiction considering contracting with a private firm would be well advised to find out as much as possible about the background of the principals and whether they have the experience to provide the needed services. Due to the fact that an animal control program can require considerable capital investment for the purchase of vehicles, equipment, supplies and staff training, the financial ability and business experience of a private operator can be critical when large numbers of animals are considered and there is a need to hire several employees.

It is doubtful that animal control contractors will enter this field on a national scale any time soon for several reasons:

1. A contract would have to be of multi-year duration if the contractor was to amortize its capital investment. Since local governments budget primarily on an annual basis, municipalities and counties may be reluctant for both financial as well as legal reasons to enter into a long-term relationship with a private contractor unless cost containment measures were in place, future contract costs were locked into the agreement, or there were other incentives.

2. Small jurisdictions would need to combine their resources and contract as a combined entity to make it profitable for a large-scale private contractor. Political differences could make this difficult to achieve.

3. Animal control is a labor-intensive operation both in the shelter and field operations. If a private contractor has to add staff to meet needs but was limited to increases linked to the CPI (consumer price index), it would negatively impact profits.

4. Local governments, when faced with budgetary constraints and competing requests for resources, are focused on the need to cut costs, and contracting is the option they most often look to as a solution. At first glance, it would seem like an opportunity for a private contractor to provide services. If a municipality or county continues to experience revenue shortfalls over a multi-year period, a private contractor may see little likelihood to grow the business in that jurisdiction.

5. Lastly, a large-scale contractor would need to develop a business model that will take into account differences from state to state and from one locality to another.

Other Perspectives on Contracting

Private sector animal control contractors (both nonprofit and for-profit) provide their services for a variety of reasons. Some are *asked* by local government officials to provide the service when the local government is unable or unwilling to assume or continue to exercise that responsibility or desires to change providers. Dissatisfaction with the level of service or the cost of service provided by a public sector agency may encourage public officials to look to the private sector to operate the animal control program and to correct existing problems.

Humane societies and SPCAs have been known to approach local government officials to ask for the opportunity to operate the animal control program. These groups believe that they have the experience and expertise to provide a higher level of service than the public sector at lower cost. If their animal welfare mission is compatible with performing animal control responsibilities, they are better positioned to save and help animals by promoting pet adoptions, educating the public about pet owner responsibility, and offering low cost spay/neuter services.

Other private sector groups may view animal control responsibilities as a new revenue opportunity. Nonprofits that view animal control as a revenue opportunity see public monies as a way to offset some of the costs of operating their other animal welfare activities or to develop or expand their base of donors for their fund-raising efforts. Once they assume animal control tasks, their donors may view them in a different light (e.g., as providers of a government service that kills animals and not necessarily as an animal welfare or animal rescue advocate). The rationales for providing animal control services notwithstanding, these groups provide a needed community service. Compensation received often does not cover the full cost of providing the service and may amount to a subsidy to the client jurisdiction.

The client's views (the local government client) about contracting and the reasons for doing so are well known. Contractors have their reasons as well. Nonprofit groups such as local humane societies, SPCAs, and other animal welfare organizations have taken on animal control responsibilities for several reasons. Some animal control duties are similar to their animal welfare mission (animal rescue, adoptions, fostering, and spay/neuter services) and offer an opportunity to help more animals and to educate the public about pet ownership. There are also differences. Enforcing animal laws, helping to prosecute violators, and coping with large numbers of impounded animals that cannot be turned away may require new strategies that they must be prepared to accept along with greater public scrutiny.

Some nonprofits view animal control revenues as a way to partially offset some of their fixed operating costs. They may become animal control providers as a result of circumstances in the community. A critical audit report of the publicly operated shelter or non-governmental provider has sometimes brought local animal welfare advocates together to develop and submit a proposal to take over the local animal control program. This is apt to occur when local officials have lost confidence that the current provider is able to correct the problems.

Private, for-profit operators providing pest control services may see animal control as an unmet local need and an opportunity to grow the business. Some are already providing animal-related services. Others are currently working with animal control agencies and local governments to respond to wildlife problems or act as back up when the animal control provider needs assistance in an emergency or provide service when animal control personnel are off-duty or unavailable. This may have helped them build a good reputation locally and acquire new clients.

Some private operators with prior animal control experience started the business with the intent of serving a specific jurisdiction in need of the service and believed they would be the lowest bidder or the only bidder. Contractors also have expectations from their client governments:

- That the governmental client will provide the contractor upon request with available data and information that will allow the contractor to prepare cost proposals as accurately as possible.

- That the governmental client will negotiate in good faith.

- That the governmental client should not expect the contractor to subside the client's need for services.

- That local authorities will support them by giving them powers to carry out their responsibilities and will listen to their recommendations to improve service.

The Downside for the Contractor. What is the downside of private sector contracting from the contractor's perspective? The public may view the animal control provider primarily as an enforcement agent of local government and not be aware of its humane activities. This can hurt the provider's fund-raising efforts for its animal welfare activities. Although the enforcement of animal control laws, euthanizing of some animals, and animal impoundments may be necessary, it should not be assumed that it has everyone's support. Rather, these functions may generate complaints and negative publicity even if the contractor's actions are justified. When combined with difficult contract negotiations, negative publicity, and having to continually ask for additional funding, it is not surprising that some contractors may become discouraged and serve notice of their intent to discontinue service.

The Business/Administrative Side. Some nonprofits providing these governmental services have become too dependent on government funds as the primary revenue source of their operating budgets. This raises the question of why they are in business. Is it primarily to provide animal control services or to operate as a humane society? The problem arises when the nonprofit does not maintain separate cost centers and combines its humane and animal control services. This makes it more difficult for the client local government seeking accountability and transparency to determine how the governmental funds were spent and the actual cost of providing the governmental services. It may even come as a surprise to nonprofits and for-profits that periodic, detailed reports are required and that documentation is required to substantiate the contractor's performance. Government funding is accompanied by the requirement of accountability and audits. Public monies are not dispensed without strings attached.

Negotiating the Contract

Local nonprofit organizations that contract to perform animal control services have an uphill battle at budget time when requesting increased resources from the client government. The contractor needs to be well prepared going into contract negotiations. Documentation to support funding requests and provide evidence of accomplishments should be brought to budget hearings and meetings. Since local governments are contracting with the nonprofit's board of directors, the contractor's staff person (executive director or manager) should be accompanied to the budget hearing and to some selected meetings by a member of the board of directors to remind local government officials that it is contracting with the board and that the board is an active participant in this process.

During contract negotiations and at budget time, the contractor may need to contemplate whether it is prepared to discontinue contracting for services if the requested resources are denied or are simply not available. The local government client is also aware that any contractor can walk away from the contract after giving proper notice, so there is a mutual incentive for the parties to bargain in good faith and have a cooperative relationship. A contractor should consider the following questions before proceeding further:

- If we are not funded at the level requested, will we need to reduce the level of service provided, and if so, will some activities have to be curtailed, and which ones?

- What will be the impact on the client if the service level is reduced?

- Can we cover our fixed costs if we no longer are a contract service provider?

- How will our organization fare if the contract is terminated, or what do we stand to lose if we no longer provide animal control services?

- How budget-dependent is our organization on the animal control contract (e.g., what percentage of our budget comes from the animal control contract)?

- Will we have to terminate staff if there is no contract?

- Do we have a plan to survive as an animal welfare organization without an animal control contract?

What Happens When a Contractor Wants to Call It Quits?

This is an increasingly frequent occurrence. Animal welfare groups are finding numerous reasons to discontinue providing animal control services under contract to local governments. These groups are saying that their primary mission of operating various animal welfare activities (including pet owner education, adoptions, and animal rescues) are in conflict with animal control services they provide. Some groups report that it costs them more than they are paid to provide the service. The president of the Morgan County Humane Society in Indiana explained why her organization declined to renew its contract with Morgan County:

> [Marsha] Ebert said the expense of having someone do animal control is climbing. She said the increased cost of gas, vehicle maintenance, employee salaries, insurance, and other factors have made it impossible for the society to continue with animal control. The expense of caring for animals involved in legal actions also created a financial bind for the shelter.[3]

Subsequently, the county increased its funding to the Society, and a van was donated to the Society by the sheriff. In 2007, the Society continued to be the animal control provider for Morgan County.

The real cost of providing service to the client may be beyond the client's willingness or ability to pay. The inability to hire and retain good employees is another reason. When client demands, criticism from the public, or the client's failure to understand the contractor's perspective arise, animal welfare groups may decide it just is not worth the trouble. Service delivery problems, unpleasant experiences with animal owners, and adverse publicity are other contributing factors.

A minimum one year cancellation clause in the contract is a reasonable request to allow the client time to find an alternative. This is especially important for shelter services. Too often the client does not think long-term. Requiring adequate notice to terminate is important. Most local government clients, when entering into a contract, have not given any thought to alternative service delivery in the event the contractual arrangement does not prove satisfactory. It takes longer to implement new service than most clients realize. What can be done to meet service needs on a short term basis?

Interim Solutions. If the contractor is providing field services, these tasks could be assumed temporarily on an emergency basis by local police or the sheriff, but services would be limited. Another municipality or other local government agency that operates an animal control department may be willing to respond to emergency calls for a short period, which allows some time to recruit, hire, and train local animal control personnel or find another contractor. Service in the interim may have to be limited to dangerous animals at large, bite cases, and rescue of animals in distress. Lower priority calls such as leash law violations and noisy animal complaints may have to wait. The existing contractor may be willing to continue service on a month-to-month basis for a few months to allow the client to develop other arrangements.

Providing shelter for animals on an interim basis will require a search for facilities that have space and are willing to take animals for a short period of time. The possibilities include a commercial boarding kennel, a veterinary clinic, or another local government shelter facility. Communities with large dog and cat populations may have to house impounded animals at more than one location due to lack of space at any one facility.

A third scenario is constructing temporary animal cages or runs with a roof and protection from harsh winds and rain and locating them on government property. Some manufacturers of animal enclosures offer outdoor, freestanding chain-link pens and animal runs. Some models offer protection from the sun's rays, and others have roofs. Some vendors may be also be able to assist with installation. Manufacturers of chain link fencing and portable buildings can be helpful in crafting temporary animal housing solutions. These include fabric-covered and metal or fiberglass portable animal shelters designed for all types of weather. They can be erected in a relatively short time. Trailer manufacturers and dealers may be another resource for the temporary housing of small pets.

SUMMARY

Although animal control is a public responsibility, governmental decision makers may opt to outsource these services rather than perform them in-house. Costs, need for a shelter, lack of expertise, and a reluctance to grow the bureaucracy are among factors in considering outsourcing as the preferred choice. Some local officials want an arm's length relationship to animal control, and contracting meets that need.

Careful planning and consideration of a multitude of issues is essential before entering into any contractual arrangement in order to meet local needs and priorities. A staff or committee report that examines issues, requirements, and costs is needed early in the contracting process. The RFQ and RFP process is the most useful for finding potential providers and how they would propose to deliver the services. If responsibilities are to split between two or more providers, how to hold each accountable must be addressed. Attorneys and other specialists can be valuable contributors in this undertaking.

Thought must also be given to what might happen in the future, should the contractor wished to discontinue service. Too often it becomes a matter of scrambling to find another provider. It is not only a matter of requiring adequate notice to terminate the contract, but identifying interim solutions until another longer term provider is found. Any liability must also be determined.

Last, each of the contracting options, governmental, nonprofit, or for-profit, may meet the client's needs. The availability of local providers willing and able to perform requested services may be limited ,and the choice may boil down to a single provider. Local governments that are considering a regional approach to delivery of services should carefully investigate whether it is in their interest to share in the ownership of a shelter and have some assurance of having animal housing available over the long-term.

Notes

1. Trish Cypher and Colin Grinnell, *Governments Working Together: A Citizen's Guide to Joint Powers Agreements*, (Sacramento, CA: California State Legislature, Senate Local Government Committee), August 2007.

2. Nancy Lawson, "Is Government Right For Your Organization?," *Animal Sheltering*, November-December, 1998, A program of the Humane Society of the United States. http://www.animalsheltering.org/resource_library/magazine_article.

3. Keith Rhoades, "Humane Society opts not to renew animal control contract," *Mooresville-Decatur Times*, August 24, 2005, www.md-times.com, (accessed October 30, 2007 by permission).

Chapter 7

Contract Provisions

This chapter discusses how particular clauses in shelter and field services contracts affect the parties, the delivery of services, and explains the reasons for inserting the specific provisions. Contracts vary in their terms and conditions, because each client's needs are different, the contractor's ability and capacity vary, and the level of public funding is always an issue. When the parties are satisfied that their mutual expectations are reasonable, it can be a win-win situation for the client and provider. The author's explanation of clauses, issues raised, and preferences expressed should not be construed as legal advice. Only an attorney can provide legal advice.

SHELTER SERVICES CLAUSES

Program Philosophy

The first few pages of the contract document enumerate the "program philosophy" or the purpose of the program and what it strives to accomplish. This is an abbreviated version of legislative intent commonly found in federal and state laws. It may be a short statement explaining the need for the program and a summary of the program's activities. The philosophy, in addition to setting forth the purpose and basis of the contract, may explain the benefits conferred and summarize goals and objectives, level of service, and in the example below, the purpose of sheltering animals.

Example. The following statement of program philosophy is from the shelter services contract that one city has with a county animal control agency:

D. *Program Philosophy.* The animal care and control philosophy which forms the basis of this contract includes the following:

(1) Adequate care and treatment of animals while in custody at the Shelter to assure that each animal remains healthy.

(2) Development and implementation of a process for local residents to report lost and found animals, and for the County to identify the animals in the Shelter and inform the inquiring public.

(3) Reuniting lost animals taken to the Shelter with such animal's owner.

(4) Adoption of healthy animals and that all animals adopted from the Shelter are spayed or neutered or that adequate provisions are made for such spaying and neutering if County transfers any animals to another nonprofit corporation or humane society for the sole purpose of providing adoption services.

(5) Development and implementation of a program to provide for the participation of volunteers in the care of the animals and the maintenance of the Shelter and the provision of various programs relating to animals.[1]

This statement emphasizes a humane level of care will be provided to the animals. The "program philosophy" reflects recommendations developed by a task force that identified specific services it deemed necessary to provide. An on-site veterinary clinic to treat sick and injured animals and to provide mandatory spay/neutering of adopted animals was implemented, because the task force deemed it essential to providing humane shelter care.

A contract in the early 1990s between Moreno Valley, California, and a private contractor stated the purpose of the contract, which read in part as follows:

Whereas, the City desires to contract to provide a broad range of animal control activities for the purpose of safeguarding the health and safety of its domestic and wild animals, for promoting the humane treatment of animals and for enforcing City ordinances relating to animal control.[2]

Shelter Services Defined

The term "shelter services" can have a broad or narrow meaning. It commonly means those services, activities, or tasks that are generally provided at or in the shelter facility. These include but are not limited to housing, feeding, treatment of sick/injured animals, quarantine of contagious or dangerous animals, euthanizing animals, locating owners of impounded animals, and the adoption of suitable unclaimed animals. Other responsibilities carried out at the shelter include the sale of animal licenses, supervision of volunteers, and various administrative duties, including keeping records that track all animals entering the shelter and preparation of reports for the client.

SCOPE OF SERVICES

This is the heart of the agreement, because it describes those services that the provider has agreed to perform. The scope of services for sheltering the animals normally includes definitions and some or all of the following duties:

- *Definitions.* Terminology used in the contract that has a special meaning or interpretation needs to be expressed in a clause(s) at the beginning of the document. Examples of defined terms include holidays when the shelter is closed, contractor, parties, and dangerous animals.

- *Enforcement of laws.* The provider will enforce all relevant provisions of the client jurisdiction's local laws or ordinances pertaining to animals as well as those animals housed or maintained at the shelter or other facility where animals such as livestock may be kept.

- *Quarantine.* The provider will keep in isolation as the law prescribes all animals suspected to be rabid or dangerous to the public at large. The procedure for testing animals suspected of being rabid should be described or referenced in the agreement.

- *Impounded animals.* Animals are held at the shelter for a period of time required by law before they can be adopted. "Animals" customarily refers to dogs and cats but often includes other species. Some contracts exclude certain wildlife from being impounded. It needs to be decided before the contract is drafted who owns the animal once it is impounded as it may have legal implications. Quarantined animals may be returned to their owners according to provisions in law. Animals that are being boarded at the facility are excluded from this definition.

- *Vicious animals.* It can be helpful to have a clause in the contract that any dog or other animal declared to be vicious and either impounded or in quarantine at the shelter shall be deemed unsuitable for adoption and will not be released except as required by law.

- *Equipment and supplies.* The ability of the contractor to perform its responsibilities is dependent on having the necessary equipment and supplies to provide the agreed upon services. Some contracts specify that the contractor will provide specific equipment and supplies including but not limited to vehicles, computers, fax machines, telephones, animal handling equipment for staff, animal medications, forms, copy paper, and cleaning materials. If the client will provide some or all equipment or supplies, it needs to be expressed in the agreement.

- *Sheltering of animals.* Commonly, this means caring for the animals, including providing food and water, safe housing, and basic medical care. Provisions in the contract should specify the level of care for animals in custody and the level of treatment of sick or injured animals. Will all animals entering the shelter receive a basic medical evaluation? When and what level of veterinary care will be available to impounded animals? Will behavioral assessments be conducted? Will all animals offered for adoption be required to be spayed/neutered before being placed in new homes? If horses and other large animals are to be sheltered, does the contract spell out the terms and conditions for custody of those animals as they will require more space and have other needs?

- *Redemption, treatment, sale, and adoption of animals.* The agreement should require a written procedure to be developed and implemented along with staff training to foster a greater effort to return animals to their owners, and if possible, to accelerate adoption efforts. As part of this objective, staff should publicize lost and found animals on the shelter Web site and at least weekly in the local media. A copy of the written procedure should be given to the client together with periodic reports on animals reported lost/found, animals returned to their owners, and animals adopted. Once the owner is located and before the animal is returned to its owner, it should be required that the animal be properly licensed, have proof of rabies vaccination where applicable, and that the owner pay any applicable fees, charges, or penalties before regaining custody of the animal.

- *Spay/neuter deposits.* Where it is shelter policy or a local government requirement to collect spay/neuter deposits for adopted animals or animals returned to their owners, an appropriate clause ought to be included in the contract document.

- *Computer chip detection capacity.* Increasingly, animal services providers are using handheld scanners to determine if impounded animals have been microchipped, making it easier to return animals to their rightful owners. Adding this clause is not simply keeping up with new technology, but increases the chances of an animal being returned to its owner.

- *Species of animals.* Many local governments think of animal control as only dogs and cats, but people keep a variety of species as pets. The public presumes and expects that a call to animal control is the answer to any animal problem, regardless of scope of the problem or the species of animal. This is unrealistic. Species of animals that are a responsibility of animal control need to be defined in the agreement. One city-operated shelter in the Pacific Northwest stated in its sheltering contract that it "reserves the right to refuse acceptance of any animal, where, in the opinion of shelter staff, it does not have facilities, capacity or expertise appropriate or available to accommodate the needs of such animals."[3] Some types of insect problems are best handled by experienced pest control operators, but they could become an animal control responsibility and an unwanted diversion from its mission to care for four legged domestic animals if the exclusions clause is not clear.

Most humane societies, SPCAs, and private sector providers have the experience to handle domestic animal situations and on occasion may offer help with other animal problems such as runaway horses and cattle, foraging coyotes, and small reptiles such as snakes and turtles. One contract between a county and a private provider contained the following clause about which animals will be accepted:

> The shelter shall accept unwanted small domestic animals (i.e., dogs and cats) from County residents, including strays and owner released animals for humane euthanasia. The Contractor shall also accept pigs, goats, sheep, cattle, horses, ferrets, llamas, rabbits, hamsters, guinea pigs, snakes and domestic birds and other animals as circumstances require.[4]

A contract between two municipalities in California excluded some species of wildlife including marine animals. The contract read in part that services apply to "...stray dogs, stray cats, and other domestic small animals, including rabbits, chickens, turkey, geese, and ducks and excluding confined wildlife...such as opossums, raccoons, skunks, or squirrels."[5]

Uninjured or healthy living wildlife were excluded, as are ocean animals. Shelters are increasingly turning to licensed wildlife rehabilitators for assistance with injured wildlife because of requirements in law. When mountain lions, bears, and other dangerous wildlife are sighted in a community, state game wardens and/or other wildlife experts are the ones to call.

- *Livestock.* A schedule of fees covering the impoundment of large animals should be established, and the schedule should be attached to the contract or referenced in that agreement.

- *Licensing/Permits.* If the contractor sells animal licenses, it falls under the scope of services and should be included in the contract. Most licenses sold are for dogs, but some communities require cats, potbellied pigs, ferrets, and other animals be licensed. If other species are required to be licensed, the agreement should so specify. Some communities may require that a permit be issued to keep other animal species. It is also common for licenses to be sold at municipal and county offices and at veterinary offices. The issuance of licenses requires proof that the animal has a valid rabies certificate. The contract should make it clear who is to receive the licensing revenue. Is the revenue to be transmitted to the local government client or shared with the contractor as an incentive to sell licenses or as partial payment for services provided? Regardless, the contractor should be held accountable for all licenses sold at the shelter.

All licenses sold should be entered into the same database. One city paid its provider a fee for each license sold, but deducted any checks or other remittances in payment of licenses that were subsequently dishonored. It should be determined in advance, but not necessarily written into the contract, how and when license refunds and any adjustments are made to animal owners. Reports of licenses sold should be reported periodically to the client by category of licenses sold (neutered, unneutered, senior citizen rate, and multi-year, etc.). This is important in determining compliance with the law.

- *Euthanasia.* Animals that are not suitable for adoption because of temperament, medical, or other reasons may have to be euthanized. If so, the method should be approved by the American Veterinary Medical Association or one that complies with state law. Some jurisdictions require that euthanasia be performed by certified technicians and that the euthanasia procedure be performed in an area out of sight of visitors and isolated from the kennel area.

Euthanasia records may need to be kept for a period of time to comply with state or local records retention schedules. Data kept for each euthanized animal should include breed, sex, color, weight, other distinguishing characteristics, date, time, and location where the animal was found, methods of euthanasia, reason for this method, and the name of the person administering euthanasia.

If the animal control facility is a no-kill shelter, that declaration should be expressed in the contract. If the shelter is a no-kill facility, the parties to the agreement may need to consider the disposition of animals and how long they will remain at the shelter. If it is necessary to euthanize an animal in a no-kill facility, criteria needs to be established that allows this procedure to take place and where the animal should be euthanized. A no-kill facility may wish to include a provision to allow the transfer of animals to a rescue group or other shelter to enhance their chances for adoption.

- *Carcass disposal.* This issue has been problematic for some animal shelters because of how dead animals are temporarily stored and the method of final disposal. Temporary storage of animal carcasses should be kept refrigerated and the storage area maintained in sanitary condition. Dead animals should be disposed of by the shelter in accordance with state law or local ordinances. Should animal carcasses be buried in a local landfill pursuant to environmental regulation, removed by a rendering company, or incinerated? The choice would depend on local circumstances and the law.

- *Pound seizure.* The practice of selling animals from municipal animal shelters to be used in research and experiments is known as "pound seizure." Thirteen states ban this practice. One local official recalled receiving several telephone calls from a firm that did scientific research using shelter animals. The firm's representative offered compensation for taking the animals off their hands quickly and quietly. The offer was turned down . While it would cost more to dispose of the dead animals by other legitimate means, the publicity that could be generated by selling them would be rightfully perceived as inhumane treatment of the animals. The Animal Control Authority of Kennewick, Pasco, and Richland (in the state of Washington) states clearly in its animal control contract that "Under no circumstances shall animals not adopted be sold for purposes of medical research or other activities without the consent of ACA."[6] It is strongly recommended that dead or live animals be neither sold, traded, or donated for experimentation, scientific testing, research, or any commercial purpose.

- *Adoption process.* Animals should only be offered for adoption if they are in good health and in the contractor's judgment have a suitable temperament to be someone's pet. If animals are offered for adoption, the following questions need to be considered when preparing the contract:

- Will mandatory spay/neuter be required before the animal leaves the shelter?

- Is it required by law?

- Will the adopter be required to sign an adoption agreement?

- Will the contractor offer adoption counseling?

- Who will receive the adoption fees?

- Will any part of the adoption fee be refunded if the animal is returned to the shelter?

It is critical that the contract specify that any adult animal (dogs or cats in particular) be spayed or neutered at the time of adoption or within a reasonable period thereafter. It should be a contractual requirement that the contractor follow through on the adoption transaction to see that all requirements have been met. There should be a provision in the contract that it is at the contractor's discretion whether a specific animal can be adopted. Adoption of sick animals may require more monitoring and care by the adopter than is reasonably possible or if in the contractor's opinion the animal is too sick to be released from the shelter and requires longer care in a shelter environment. It is sound policy not to allow knowingly sick animals to be adopted as the animal's condition can rapidly change. If there is any question about the animal's health condition, a veterinarian's advice should be sought.

Experience has shown that when animals are knowingly adopted when sick, the adopters may take the animal first to a private veterinarian for treatment rather than return the animal to the shelter, and in some cases the animal may die despite good veterinary care. Adopters often fail to follow the shelter's policy or the terms of the adoption contract, and subsequently, the animal's condition deteriorates even more quickly. Adopters may unreasonably expect the shelter to not only refund their adoption fees, but pay their veterinary bills as well. An adoption agreement should state the terms and conditions for the return of the animal and the shelter's policy on returned animals. Adopting a sick animal becomes problematic and an unpleasant experience for all concerned.

- *Vaccination clinics.* Scheduling periodic, low-cost rabies clinics where licenses are also sold is a popular and beneficial service with pet owners. It also encourages responsible pet ownership and promotes a healthy animal population. This is a desirable clause to add, if the contractor will provide this service and arrange to have a veterinarian inoculate the animals.

- *Holding periods for animals.* The minimum number of days that stray animals must be impounded at the shelter before being offered for adoption or disposal is usually found in state law. Some contracts adopt the state requirement as the local requirement, but others establish longer holding periods for strays and owner identifiable animals.

- *Payment of fees and charges.* A clause authorizing or requiring the contractor to collect payments for impoundments, boarding, adoption, or other fees and charges (including animal licenses and late license renewal penalties as set by the client) is commonly found in animal control agreements. The schedule of fees and charges should at least be referenced in the contract. Prior to drafting the agreement it should be determined whether revenues collected on behalf of the client jurisdiction should be remitted to the client, retained by the contractor, or credited toward the payment owed to the contractor. The contract clauses about revenues received should specify when and how these monies will be deposited to an account or otherwise transmitted to the client jurisdiction. One small Southwestern city requires that impound and other fees must first be paid at city hall. and then a written authorization would be issued to allow the contractor, a local veterinary clinic, to release the animal to its owner.

- *Maintenance of the shelter.* If the contractor is using a client-owned shelter, the contract should clarify who is responsible for the daily maintenance and any major repairs to that facility. A facility shared by several jurisdictions in a contractual arrangement where there is also a shared ownership interest requires that maintenance responsibility and infrastructure repairs be addressed in the agreement.

- *Shelter hours.* Business hours when the shelter is open to the public can be expressed in the number of hours per week, by days of the week, and the specific open hours each day. Since some months are busier than others, and if it is not known what times of the day the public is most apt to visit the facility, there needs to be some flexibility in setting the hours of operation. It may be advantageous to stipulate in the contract that the days and hours of operation may be subject to change as mutually agreed upon by the parties. This eliminates the need to continually amend the contract, which would require action by the client's legislative body. Naming those holidays in the agreement when the shelter is closed is common in animal control contracts and does not present problems. The contractor should be responsible for publicizing those holidays when the shelter is closed and services are not available. A head count of visitors to the shelter taken at different seasons of the year can help determine when the shelter should be open to the public. Monthly statistical reports can also be used for this purpose. The hours when the shelter is open should be to accommodate the public, and staff work hours should be scheduled accordingly.

- *Service after normal business hours and holidays.* Animal control emergencies (as defined in the contract) can occur at any time of the day or night. Trained, on-call personnel need to be available to open the shelter to receive animals, or there needs to be a way for animal control officers to have access to the shelter so that they can impound or quarantine animals as necessary. Examples include situations where the safety of animals or the public are endangered or where an animal needs to be impounded as a result of someone being arrested by law enforcement officers. Even though the facility is not open to the public at certain times and dates, care and feeding of shelter animals must be provided every day.

- *Missing animals.* Animals mysteriously disappear from shelters from time to time. Any animal missing from the shelter should be reported to the local law enforcement agency as soon as possible. It should be a violation of local law or ordinance for anyone to break into a shelter and/or remove an animal without authorization. A copy of the law enforcement agency's report of the incident should be obtained and filed. Unaccounted for animals, in part, may be the basis for an outside audit or even a criminal investigation, so shelter officials need to keep accurate records to account for all animals in their care. This includes animals impounded at other locations and animals being treated by veterinarians at outside facilities.

- *Complaint log.* A record of all complaints (e.g., dissatisfaction with service) received orally or in writing from the public or through the client about services provided at the shelter or the quality of such services (as opposed to requests for service) shall be maintained by the contractor. These complaints may be about staff and/or volunteers. A standardized form can be used to report and receive these complaints. Periodically, the client should be provided in writing the number of complaints the contractor has received, including those transmitted through the client, and how each complaint was resolved.

- *Client access to the shelter and records.* Contracts commonly contain a provision that the client's authorized representative shall have access to the entire shelter and to animal control records during normal business hours and at other times upon reasonable notice. This helps ensure accountability and gives the client the right to review records should issues arise. The contract should specify those records to be maintained by the contractor and made available to the client upon request.

- *Volunteers.* An effective volunteer program is good for the animals, can be satisfying to the volunteer, and provides a needed assist to shelter staff. If volunteers are used, the contract should contain provisions relating to the terms and conditions on the use of volunteers. The issue of liability for volunteers also needs to be considered. For example, is the volunteer protected if bitten by an animal at the shelter? What liability is incurred if the volunteer makes a representation on behalf of the shelter but is acting outside the scope of the volunteer's duties? The contractor should report to the client at least twice a year the number of volunteers participating in the program, their duties, and how they have contributed to the program. A contract between a city and a county where the county performed animal control services for the city contained the following provisions: Personnel employed at the Shelter in the performance of shelter related activities shall be designated as County employees and any and all volunteers engaged in shelter activities shall be under the auspices of County. Use of volunteers at the Shelter shall be determined by County on behalf of City. County shall establish and implement policies and procedures for volunteers consistent with the provisions of this contract.[7]

- *Materials and information.* A provision requiring the contractor to provide complimentary educational material to the public helps promote pet owner responsibility and information about humane care of pets and advice about wildlife. Animal care information brochures, including the benefits and need for spay/neutering and humane animal care, should be visually on display and available to anyone visiting the shelter facility. Some materials are readily available free or at low cost from national animal welfare organizations and from some pet product manufacturers. Some pamphlets can also be purchased from other sources in large wholesale quantities at low cost. Other information for dissemination to the public can be prepared in-house and placed on display. Careful thought should be given to the types of printed information available to the public, perhaps in languages spoken locally, in addition to English.

- *Training.* The client has a right to expect that the contractor's staff is adequately trained to carry out its responsibilities. The agreement should require that the client be provided documentation as proof that staff is properly trained and that the training meets state and local requirements. It is useful to include a clause in the contract that requires that the contractor provide evidence that kennel staff has been trained in the care and feeding of the animals, how to provide first aid to animals in distress, and how to clean and sanitize kennels and cages. Clauses requiring training of field personnel should also be added. Some states have requirements for training field officers. Similar requirements should be implemented for staff that sell licenses, process incoming animals, handle adoptions, prepare and maintain records, and receive and dispatch calls for service. Since some states mandate training for shelter technicians before they are allowed to perform euthanasia, a clause in the contract requiring that training meets state requirements may be needed.

- *Contract duration and termination.* This is a particularly important clause as it can affect renewal or cancellation of the contract and costs in future years. Contracts normally require a minimum notice to cancel or renew to be expressed in days, months, or years. If the contract terms permit, the agreement can be kept in force on a month-to-month basis as a stopgap measure to prevent interruption of service while the parties work to resolve their differences.

One county wrote into its agreement with a city that the agreement was a one-year contract that is automatically renewed for additional one-year terms up to a maximum of "x" years unless cancelled by either party with one year's written notice. The one-year cancellation clause allows the client city time to find alternate arrangements. The term "adequate notice" to cancel needs to be defined by the parties. A sixty-day cancellation clause in a contract with a small town that impounded only a few hundred animals a year may be adequate. A city where the local dog and cat population may exceed 50,000 animals and where up to 15,000 animals pass through the shelter in a single year may need a year or more to find new shelter space. The larger the contract, the greater the need for longer cancellation notice because of the number of animals involved. Contract terms can vary from one year to several years to prevent disruption of service and to lock in costs for a future time period.

Some contracts may be terminated for cause only if the problem cannot be cured within a specified period of time. Other agreements state that the contract can be terminated by either party without stating a reason, provided that proper notice (as defined in the contract) is given.

Terminating a contract for cause is not without problems. One city found to its detriment that its contract with a local animal welfare organization continued year after year, because the contract read that the agreement could be cancelled only for cause and only if the contractor failed to cure the breach within the time frame allowed by the agreement. Every time there was a problem that impacted the contractor's performance, the contractor was notified of the breach of contract, and the problem was cured within the time allowed. However, there were always new problems arising, and the relationship between the parties continued to be unsatisfactory. Finally, when it came time to renew the contract, the city attorney, at the urging of city staff, amended the agreement to say that the contract could be canceled by either party with adequate notice and no reason be given. Seven months after the last contract renewal, the city gave notice to cancel the agreement.

A word of caution to contractors is in order at this juncture. Contractors should be careful not to place total reliance on contracting with any one client jurisdiction, particularly if the contractor is a non-profit animal welfare organization whose budget is built around the client's need for services. A client's financial and political position can change suddenly and can negatively impact the provider. Some contracts contain a clause that says if the client fails to appropriate funds for the contract by a certain date, the contract terminates.

If the contractor has a capital investment in shelter and field operations that is expected to be amortized over the term of the agreement, severing the contract early may raise issues about recouping that investment. What happens to property purchased by the contractor with the client's funds if the contract terminates? One Georgia county required that the property be returned to the county:

> Equipment and supplies purchased by the Contractor with contract funds shall be the sole property of Fulton County and be marked and inventoried as such, with a copy of the inventory forwarded to Fulton County. All finished and unfinished documents and materials prepared by the Contractor in accordance with contract services shall become property of Fulton County.[8]

CLIENT OBLIGATIONS

Local government clients have been known to provide supplies, equipment, and services to support their providers in performing their contractual responsibilities. These in-kind contributions may include forms, animal license tags, radios, vehicles, some types of training, legal assistance in prosecuting violations of animal law, and publicizing information about animal control requirements. Client commitments may reduce the amount needed to fund the contract but may also offer expertise and services that the contractor cannot easily provide.

COMPENSATION

There are also differences in how monetary compensation is determined from one locality to another. Contractors have been compensated in a number of ways. The following methods of determining compensation are illustrative of the differences found in local animal control agreements.

- *Charge per animal.* A charge is levied on every animal brought to the shelter from the client's service area. The charge for dogs may be higher than for cats, and livestock charges may be higher than both. Calculating sheltering costs based on a fee levied on each animal is more common in shelters serving very small communities where there is a low volume of animals entering the shelter through the animal control program. One shelter levies a flat per-month charge to its client government in addition to charging for each animal admitted to the shelter. This flat monthly charge is levied even if no animals are admitted to the shelter in any month.

  Some shelters collect and retain impound and boarding fees and other authorized charges when owners come in to redeem their pets. If the shelter is allowed to retain these fees and charges, it should be required to account for these revenues to the client because of their economic value. An understanding of how much owners have paid to redeem their animals and how many owners were willing to pay these fees and charges is an indication of how much their pets mean to them and the extent of pet owner responsibility. Some owners will abandon an animal at the shelter rather than pay the charges incurred.

- *Compensation based on an expense budget.* A line item budget is prepared listing all personnel and non-personnel costs and may include a separate line item for overhead associated with providing animal control shelter services. The amount paid by the client is based on the approved budget, with some negotiating taking place between the parties. If the provider serves several governmental jurisdictions, the costs are apportioned to each based on some formula. The formula may take into account the population of each community or the number of animals impounded from each in any given time period. There may or may not be separate cost centers for each activity or subprogram. Each client jurisdiction served ought to be a separate cost center. A cap may be established that limits spending to the amount appropriated by the client's governing body. This could be problematic if the number of animals processed through the shelter in a year is substantially higher than projected.

- *Annual per capita assessment.* Funding the shelter operation among several local governments may be based on the same per capita charge levied on all participating entities based on the most recent United States census count for each jurisdiction. For example, a per capita charge of $1.60 per resident in a local population of 152,082 people would result in an annual charge of $243,331.20. This method is in use by four New England cities. A city in the state of Washington paid its contract provider a per capita fee based on the population estimates provided by a government agency. In addition, the provider was allowed to retain all impound and board fees, late penalty fees, and all licensing fees collected from the client's service area. License fees collected at the client's city hall were also turned over to the provider less a 10% administrative fee that the client retained.

- *Population plus assessed valuation.* A California city that contracted with a county for shelter and field services agreed to pay a percentage share of the net program cost of the animal control program, which was determined by the county that contracted with a local humane society. The city's percentage share was based on a formula of one-half of the relative population of the city to that of the county plus one-half of the city's assessed valuation plus the cost of the county administering the licensing program less any revenues received by the county or the humane society.

One county preparing to contract with several municipalities proposed allocating costs to each based on the number of calls received from each municipality. Compensation for services is sometimes found in an attachment to an agreement. Other contracts make no mention of compensation, so presumably, funding was authorized and that information is recorded elsewhere. The common thread running through most contracts that have a fixed dollar amount for the contract term is that the contract amount is paid in monthly installments. The contractor may submit a monthly invoice to the client, or the client routinely submits a payment monthly as stipulated in the agreement.

OTHER SHELTER CLAUSES

- *Performance incentives.* Performance incentives have been used to reward a provider who exceeds expectations or to encourage meeting specific objectives. For example, a contract provider that increases the number of animals adopted above the target set for the year by the client could be compensated a fixed dollar amount. Paying a fee for every license sold should encourage a greater effort to sell animal licenses. One city agreed in its contract to share 15% of the total revenues raised by the provider in excess of the revenues targeted for each fiscal year by the city. Some jurisdictions that allow their providers to keep all revenues received including license fees are including those revenues as part of the compensation package rather than as performance incentives.

- *Records retention.* This is a common contract clause. State laws require that selected animal control records must be kept for a period of one year or more in accordance with the state's record retention schedule. Required records and the amount of time they must be kept vary by state. Some local governments have their own retention requirements for keeping records before they can be destroyed. For example, among records to be retained by Montana local governments are euthanasia (four years), animal licenses and permits (three years), quarantines (one year after quarantine is lifted), and incident reports about potentially dangerous animals for the life of the animal or fifteen years. Utah requires that animal bite reports be kept for five years, New York requires that anti-rabies protection certificates be kept five years, and Rhode Island requires that animal complaint files be kept for three years.

- *Contacting animal control by telephone.* It should be required that the contractor have a published telephone number for both regular business hours and after-hours emergencies.

That number should be publicized by the jurisdiction that contracts for service with its provider. Local law enforcement agencies should also have an unlisted number to reach animal control quickly and vice versa. One county animal control agency that is also a contract provider uses a private answering service to receive calls when the shelter is closed. If the call is deemed to be an emergency, the answering service operator can contact the on-call officer by pager.

THE CONTRACT DOCUMENT

Generally, one contract document will suffice when contracting for both shelter and field services. Some written agreements can be twenty pages or more, but one- or two-page written agreements have been found in some small communities. Multiple contracts are not uncommon, particularly if there is more than one service provider. The client government should draft the contract for several reasons. There are numerous standard legal provisions that must be written into the agreement, and attorneys for local government clients know these requirements. Also, the local government client needs to understand local animal issues and establish service priorities in the contract. The process of preparing the agreement involves discussion of the client's needs now and in the future and clarifying issues and priorities to be addressed. The contractor, in turn, will have an opportunity to review and comment on the proposed agreement and to recommend changes and negotiate details from the provider's perspective.

The city of Riverside, California, contracted for field and shelter services with Riverside County and had four separate lengthy contract documents, and each was technically a year-to-year contract. Three separate but related contracts for sheltering, field services, and dog licensing were entered into by the parties.

A fourth document known as a "Sublease Agreement" defined the city's occupancy terms in the shelter facility, the city's share of the costs of renovation, an annual rental charge, and the city's acquisition of one-half ownership in the shelter. The four written agreements were prepared in the belief that if there were separate agreements for each major service, should one of the documents be subjected to legal challenge, the others would still remain in force. Two of the written agreements, one for field services and the other for shelter services, each contained the following provision: "It is the intent of the parties hereto that the three contracts shall be considered as an integrated contract, and that if the contracts have overlapping procedures, each such procedure shall be considered as supplementing and not superseding the other."[9]

FIELD SERVICES CLAUSES

Program Rationale

The underlying reasons for providing field services in the community (in addition to being required by law) is to protect public safety and public health. The following rationale for providing field services is contained in a clause in a contract between a city and county in California:

> City is desirous of contracting with County to provide a broad range of animal control field services for the purpose of safeguarding the health and safety of the population of the City of...and the health and safety of its domestic animals, and for the purpose of promoting the humane treatment of animals and the stimulation of public support for enforcement of city ordinances relating to animal control.[10]

What is Field Services?

Animal control officers in their vehicles answering calls are the visible public face of animal services in the community. These individuals in the forefront of enforcement and rescue efforts are the foot soldiers of animal control work. How they perform their responsibilities impacts on the quality of service and how the public perceives them.

"Field services" generally refers to those tasks or duties performed by animal control or humane officers who respond to calls for service, answer complaints about animals, and rescue animals in distress. These officers need to have the authority to investigate cruelty cases, enforce laws, and be trained to handle a wide range of animal issues and problems. Investigating a barking dog complaint, taking sick or injured animals into custody, or rescuing an abused animal are all in a day's work for these officers. The agreement needs to identify in writing those tasks and responsibilities assigned to the field services component. Some field officers also are involved in outreach efforts such as speaking to community groups about the role of the agency and how to care for pets.

Scope of Services

The following section identifies those tasks most often defined as field services activities, many of which are commonly addressed in a written agreement.

- *Authority to enforce animal laws.* This is a necessary clause when contracting for field services, because officers need to have legal authority to enforce animal laws and to cite violators, nearly all of whom they come in contact while on field duty. Those who abuse and neglect animals and those who are irresponsible animal owners need to be held accountable for their actions that affect the community at large. The authority to enforce laws enables officers to issue warnings, write citations, and impound and quarantine animals. Some states may specify how this enforcement authority shall be delegated.

  Another issue that arises when contracting for both shelter and field services is the need for uniform local animal ordinances. When several local governments contract for services with another governmental entity or private provider, the provider entity may ask all contracting parties to adopt basically the same set of animal ordinances, because it is easier to enforce one set of local laws rather than several different sets. If the client jurisdictions agree to make these changes, it should be referenced in the contract.

- *Taking custody of stray and abandoned animals.* Duties include picking up stray animals and transporting them to the shelter where they can receive humane care while an effort is made to locate their owners. Care and treatment of sick/injured stray or abandoned animals is at the core of a humane animal care and control program. Whether or not to provide emergency veterinary treatment in the field may need to be discussed when contracting for field services.

- *Impoundment/return of owned animals at large.* When animal control service providers encounter animals running at large they will usually impound them. This includes licensed animals and those whose owners can be identified. If policy permits, the animal may be directly returned to its owner in the field. This is good public relations, but there is a caveat. Should an officer be given the discretion to return a licensed animal found running at large to its owner in the field, rather than transport it to the shelter, it may be wiser not to include this option in the contract as the policy could change at any time. Additionally, it could lead to a misinterpretation that the animal *must* be returned to its owner in the field when there may be a valid reason to take the animal into custody .

- *Specialized animal services.* Animal control providers as first responders encounter many domestic animal and wildlife problems. They may be trained and experienced to handle some types of animal problems in addition to dogs and cats, but others may require the services of specialists. The problem of urban coyotes that have seized small pets or have approached and threatened small children has sometimes been subcontracted to wildlife specialists to resolve. Contract provisions should state which species of animals are covered/excluded under the scope of service. The client may reserve the right to approve any subcontract on a case-by-case basis to address problems of species not covered under the contract. It should be noted that subcontractors may be subject to requirements in state law regarding trapping or disposal of some animal species.

  Feral pigs and reptiles are often an animal control responsibility, but in other localities, residents having problems caused by some pest animals are referred to experienced pest control operators for needed services. State game wardens are called when particularly dangerous wildlife are present. Licensed trappers or private wildlife experts are sometimes hired to remove selected species that are causing problems. State wildlife officials should be consulted about local wildlife problems where state laws govern removal and eradication. Permits may be required to trap and/or kill some wildlife species.

- *Investigation of animal bites.* This is a standard animal control responsibility and one that impacts public safety and public health if the animal is found to have rabies. The contract should require that animal bites be investigated and should spell out how the contractor will respond. State law or local ordinance may dictate the type of response that is needed and the information to be obtained. Although animal bites may be reported by telephone, officers ought to respond in person to all bite incidents by dogs or any suspected rabid or wild animal. Victims and witnesses need to be interviewed, and in the case of a minor, a parent or guardian needs to be contacted. An effort must be made to locate and quarantine the suspect animal and to determine if the victim has received medical attention.

- *Quarantine of biter and other dangerous animals.* Quarantine of an animal that has bitten someone is required by law in order to observe these animals for a period of time to determine if they show signs of rabies. The procedure for quarantining animals usually found in state and/or local law should be referenced in the contract.

Depending on state laws and/or local requirements, animals will be transported to the shelter to be placed in quarantine isolation for a period of time as designated in law to be observed for signs of rabies or other contagious diseases. An aggressive animal at large that has threatened the safety of people or other animals may be quarantined on the owner's property under terms and conditions set by animal control as authorized by law or quarantined at the shelter.

- *Nuisance animal complaints.* Officers may conduct a field investigation of a nuisance animal complaint or contact the animal owner by telephone or by mail. Nuisance animals are those that may have caused property damage, frightened people, or noisy animals such as barking dogs and crowing fowl like peacocks and roosters. The contract can reference the local ordinance section that applies to nuisance animals.

- *Dead animal pickup.* Some communities make dead animal removal a responsibility of the road department or other agency. If dead animal pickup is assigned to animal control, it needs to be listed in the contract's scope of services. Some animal control providers pick up dead animals at veterinary offices at no charge in exchange for some limited free veterinary service. These are often informal arrangements that do not find their way into the service contracts unless there is reason to do so. Dead animals found on the street or at curbside are not generally a public health problem or a service priority, but they do generate calls for removal, particularly if they are dogs or cats. More calls for dead animal removal occur during hot weather and should be given some consideration in urban areas as a matter of good public relations and for aesthetic reasons.

- *Trapping animals.* Many shelters rent or loan animal traps to residents who want to remove nuisance animals including wildlife. Some jurisdictions will, upon request, send an officer to deliver and/or remove an animal from a trap. If so, this is a field services responsibility and falls under the scope of service.

- *Verification of animal license status.* An officer responding to a call for service in the field should always check the license status of the animal in question. This would apply to any animal that must be licensed by law or must have a permit. Even if the animal is returned to its owner by an officer in the field, the owner should be cited if the animal is unlicensed or has an expired license. Having these requirements in the agreement can help reduce the number of unlicensed animals that have not been vaccinated against contagious diseases and can promote pet owner responsibility.

- *Priority of field services.* The volume, types of calls received, and available resources make it necessary to set priorities when responding to calls for service. This requires defining an "emergency" where response time is critical as opposed to other calls where human and/or animals lives are not in immediate danger. Prioritizing calls for service can be included as a clause(s) in the contract or as an attachment to that agreement that list the order in which calls are to be answered.

- *Dispatch of calls for service.* Telephone calls to animal control is where field service responses begin. The National Animal Control Association found in those animal control programs that they evaluated that "this is the most deficient area of any Animal Control Program."[11] Calls need to be received, prioritized, and transmitted so that the most urgent ones get the fastest response. Consider the following dispatching problem.

Problem

City A contracted for shelter and field services with a local nonprofit animal welfare organization. The city received complaints about the length of time it took to respond to calls for service, and it was alleged that some calls were never answered. This led the city to conduct a review of the field service operation, including the receipt and dispatch of calls for service. The review found that the dispatch center was not permanently staffed, and when the phone rang in the dispatch office, the closest available person at the front counter would run back to dispatch to take the call. Calls were recorded manually, and requests were not relayed to officers in the field until the next morning. Established procedures were not followed in relaying emergency calls to officers in the field.

Consider how the following factors impact the receipt and dispatch of calls for service when drafting provisions on receiving and dispatching calls:

Type and capacity of communication equipment

Number of phone lines

Number of calls for service per day

Busiest call periods

Number of dispatch personnel per shift

Number of priority calls received nights, weekends, and holidays

Waiting time of calls in queue

Number of priority calls for service during business hours

Number of field officers on duty per weekday shift

Number of field personnel on duty/on-call nights, weekends, and holidays

Desired response times versus actual response times

Hours of service

Number of field officers needed

Number of calls for service carried over to the next day

Average number of calls answered per officer per day versus desired number of calls to be answered per day

- *Field service charges.* Some contractors are paid a fixed amount for a defined time period, say monthly, while others may charge an hourly rate. If the contractor is providing both field and shelter services, each ought to be a separate cost center. A proposed budget should be prepared for each cost center. The budgeted amount assumes a defined level of service (e.g., a fixed number of officers, full and/or part-time, and the number of hours and days of the week when service is offered).

  Some organizations charge separately for actual overtime (after regular business hours and holidays and only for priority calls in those periods), while others estimate some overtime costs based on past experience and include a fixed amount or cap in the budget. A client may pay a fixed amount to have an officer on-call, but if the officer answers the call in person, the client may be charged for a minimum number of hours of service, even if the call took less than the minimum time charged.

  Additional use of overtime above the budgeted amount should require the client's approval. If much of the overtime use is attributed to calls from police, the client should be informed, and it may be necessary evaluate the need for these calls and to establish criteria for police calls after regular business hours. Officers in one city's police department routinely called animal control, usually late at night, to remove dead animals from city streets, which increased overtime costs. When the police chief was informed, this practice stopped.

- *Field service logs.* It is in the client's interest to require that the contractor maintain field service logs in each vehicle and to retain those logs for a certain period of time, usually a few years. The logs identify the vehicle and its driver(s), the nature of the call, and the date and time when the call for service was received, when the call was dispatched, and when the driver arrived on the scene. Other information provided in the log should include the disposition of the call, the names, addresses, and telephone numbers of the relevant parties, and number of miles traveled. Maintaining these records makes it easier to audit the service. These records become pertinent if a case is prosecuted or if a lawsuit is filed.

- *Preparation and submission of reports.* This is a common requirement in animal service contracts. Reports submitted to the client based on data generated from officers in the field and from shelter statistics indicate workload and how well the program is meeting its objectives. The client should review the data in each category and compare the data for the same reporting period for the prior year.

- *Training of personnel.* Some jurisdictions take it for granted that field officers are properly trained, or they are given assurances that experienced officers are answering calls for service. When an audit is conducted, training shortcomings are often found. It is always better to err on the side of caution and require in the agreement that field officers must be trained and that the training meets state requirements. The client is entitled to ask for documentation to verify that staff has met state training requirements. If the client appropriates funds to be earmarked for training, the contractor should be required to document that training was completed or explain why training funds were not spent. A contractor that offers only on-the-job training where new employees learn from experienced ones should be carefully monitored by the client.

TYPES OF ANIMAL SERVICE CONTRACTS AND CLAUSES

The following agreements are a few of the many examples of local animal service agreements:

- The cities of Lacey, Olympia, and Tumwater as well as Thurston County, all in the state of Washington, executed an intergovernmental agreement for joint animal service operations that provides field and shelter services to the four governmental entities. The agreement contains clauses covering scope and funding of services, repayment of the shelter debt, and establishment of a policy-making body. One city was designated with administrative and financial duties. An agreement entered into between two New Jersey townships, Wantage and Frankford, provided animal control coverage by Wantage to Frankford when the latter's animal control officer was not available.

- Pierce County, Washington, contracted with a local attorney to conduct hearings on potentially dangerous and dangerous dogs. The agreement enumerated the responsibilities of both parties, the county and the contractor. The county also contracted with a local veterinary clinic to provide emergency care of animals in urgent care situations. The veterinary agreement listed allowed charges for services and potential for discounting the exam charge.

- Three North Texas cities, Cedar Hill, Desoto, and Duncanville, executed an agreement to acquire, own, and operate a joint animal shelter. The agreement included but was not limited to clauses covering funding of the facility, how it would be managed, liability, relationship of the parties, and the term of the agreement.

STANDARD CONTRACT CLAUSES

Attorneys drafting the contract will add a number of clauses that have legal significance. Some are intended to protect one or both parties to the agreement. Other clauses are inserted to comply with law. Examples of these clauses include indemnification, non-discrimination, venue, independent contractor status, and insurance. Because liability is always a potential issue, the client may wish to reinforce its comfort level by writing into the agreement that the service provider's insurer must be authorized to do business in the state where the animal control services are provided. In addition, the client may require the contractor to name the client as an additional insured on the contractor's insurance policy and to notify the client if the insurance is canceled for any reason. A risk manager or an attorney should be consulted in this matter. All insurance documents must be reviewed.

SUMMARY

A contract is the sum of its clauses, and the clauses spell out the terms and conditions. Every clause should be clear in its purpose in the agreement. The scope of service is the core of the contract, as it spells out what the contractor has agreed to perform. Client obligations identify those commitments made by the local government to the provider and may extend beyond monetary compensation. That commitment may include both direct and indirect support to the provider that enables a level of service at a more affordable price or a form of support that one party is in a better position to deliver.

When questions arise about the provider's obligations or if there is a need for clarification, the contract provisions can address those issues after discussion and perhaps negotiation. Some issues are best expressed in general terms where frequent change may be necessary. Some contract clauses are protective of one or both parties, while others help clarify the services requested and define the level of service to be provided. If there are any provisions or words in the contract that cause stress to one or more of the parties or generates conflict, then these issues will require further and separate discussion to arrive at some mutual understanding that satisfies both parties.

Notes

1. City of Riverside, California, *Contract for Animal Shelter Services Between the City of Riverside and the County of Riverside*, (Riverside, CA: City Clerk's Office), 1995.

2. City of Moreno Valley, California *Contract for Animal Services with Moreno Valley Animal Friends*, FY 91/92-FY 92/93, (Moreno Valley, CA: City Manager's Office), 1991.

3. City of Everett, Washington, *Agreement Regarding Animal Shelter Use Between the Cities of Everett and Marysville*, (Everett, WA: City Clerk's Office), 2005. Agreement for services from January 1, 2005 to December 31, 2006.

4. Whatcom County, Washington, *Animal Services Agreement Between Whatcom County and Rustand, Inc. d/b/a Preferred Animal Care*, (Bellingham, WA: Whatcom County Executive) 2003.

5. City of Milpitas, California, *Animal Services Agreement Between the City of San Jose and the City of Milpitas*, (Milpitas, CA: Office of the City Clerk), 2003.

6. Kennewick, Washington, *Personal Services Agreement by and between Animal Control Authority of Cities of Kennewick, Pasco & Richland and Tri-City Animal Control*, "Disposal of Unclaimed Animals," 14. Contract entered into on January 1, 2004 and terminating on December 31, 2006. (Seattle, WA: Municipal Research and Services Center of Washington), www.mrsc.org/Contracts/R5animalcon.pdf (accessed August 20, 2007).

7. City of Riverside, *Contract for Animal Shelter Services*, sec. 4(K), 11. Ibid.

8. Fulton County, Georgia, *Fulton County Animal Control Contract* [with Southern Hope Humane Society] (Atlanta, GA: Fulton County Clerk to the Commission) 2003.

9. City of Riverside, sec. C, 2. Ibid.

10. City of Riverside, sec. A, 1. Ibid.

11. National Animal Control Association, by permission.

Chapter 8

Staffing: Needs, Duties, and Issues

The success of any program is largely dependent on the operators. Animal care and control programs are no different. Some of the key resources needed in this program include funding and political support, laws that meet the needs of the program, a shelter to house the animals, and a capable staff that willingly supports the mission of the agency. This last resource, the human resource or staffing, is the subject of this chapter that examines some factors and issues that affect personnel and the program itself.

THE ABCs OF STAFFING

The following fundamental elements are needed to staff an animal care and control program, because they impact the effectiveness of the program.

The job description. This is the starting point in hiring new personnel or promoting existing staff. The job description is a detailed and customized explanation of the duties and responsibilities of the position, required minimum qualifications (education and/or prior experience), and specific knowledge, skills, and abilities needed perform this work. When a vacancy occurs it is not uncommon and also a good idea to review and update the job description to reflect needed changes. Creation of a new position lacks past history and experience, so writing the job description may require more general language to allow for flexibility in job duties. Obtaining a job description from another animal care organization can be helpful in preparing a new or revised job description. There is often a separate job announcement that lists the compensation for the position and the final date when an employment application for the position will be accepted.

Many animal welfare organizations' publications list available positions and abbreviated job descriptions in animal care and control agencies. Available positions are publicized to their respective memberships, some of which are statewide and others that are national. Examples include the Animal Welfare League of Alexandria (Virginia), California Animal Control Directors Association, the New Jersey Certified Animal Control Officers Association, the Society of Animal Welfare Administrators, the National Animal Control Association, and American Humane Association.

The most common positions in an animal control program are animal control officers (called animal wardens in some states or humane officers if employed by a nonprofit), kennel technicians or kennel attendants, animal control director or animal control/shelter manager, and clerical or administrative positions that go by various names. Animal control entities may also employ adoption counselors, veterinary technicians, veterinarians, animal behavior specialists, data entry clerks, animal license canvassers, and various supervisory personnel depending on size and mission of the agency and the animal and human populations served.

A review of job descriptions in local governments across the country in two of the most common job categories, animal control director or equivalent position and animal control officer, reflect similarities but may include other duties that reflect local and regional differences and needs.

Animal control director. The authority of the director varies depending on whether the director is the agency or department head or manages the program in a department headed by someone else such as the chief of police or the director of health. The first part of the job description will usually indicate to whom the director or the head of the program will report. The director's position is expected to provide leadership, supervision, program planning, administration of the budget, and overall management of the program or agency. Other duties include working with other animal welfare organizations and other animal care professionals, interpreting laws, arranging or providing training for staff, evaluating staff performance, and acting as the spokesperson on animal control matters. Some directors serve at the pleasure of the appointing authority, but others may have civil service protection. Some directors are exempt from the provisions of the Fair Labor Standards Act (FLSA).

Animal control officer (ACO). This is a generalist position with a wide range of duties and responsibilities that are similar in most organizations that perform animal control services. Many of the duties are performed outdoors and away from the shelter but may include tasks at the shelter. ACOs handle animal-related complaints, rescue injured animals, remove dead animals, and may respond to calls involving wildlife. This position calls for administration and enforcement of animal laws and conducting various types of investigations throughout the service area. The ACO in some agencies has responsibility for the care and feeding of the animals at the shelter and maintenance of that facility. Where required, the ACO may inspect pet shops, kennels, animal shows, and exhibits. Some ACO positions are contractual. For example, the job description for animal control officer in Moab, Utah, is a contractual position where the contractor must supply his or her own vehicle and liability insurance. The job description is included in a "job packet" that also contains an employment application. A person in this position must be able to communicate well with people, often in stressful situations, so the applicant must enjoy interacting with people.

The hiring process. Too often, especially in government-operated programs, the recruitment and hiring process can be all-consuming and may appear to overshadow the applicants themselves. Everyone who is interested in applying for a position is entitled to an equal opportunity to compete for the job without fear of discrimination. There are laws intended to prevent discrimination in hiring practices and to give all applicants an equal opportunity to compete for available positions based on how their qualifications meet the requirements of the position.

When advertising and publicizing positions that are unique to animal control (e.g., adoption counselor, veterinary technician, kennel technician, and animal control officer) the positions may be posted in specialized publications to reach those interested in animal welfare and animal control work in addition to generic advertising sources such as local newspapers. This will help increase the size of the applicant pool unless there is an up-to-date list with a sufficient number of interested persons. Posting available jobs on the agency's Web site has become increasingly popular and an effective way to recruit for vacancies in this new age of instant communications. Administrative and clerical support positions may also draw many applicants through local advertizing and posting on the agency's Web site.

Animal control has two distinct client groups: people and animals. Animal control staff needs to have both people skills and compassion for animals. Job skills can be acquired, but personality traits are already well established by the time of employment. Personality is a critical factor in hiring, particularly when the employee has to interact with the public. A probationary period will test how new hires interact with staff, the public, and animals and provide an opportunity for new staff members to demonstrate their proficiency in job-related skills.

Staffing levels. The lack of standardization in this field and the fact that each community's animal control needs vary has made it difficult to arrive at an agreed upon number of employees to staff the program. Determining actual staffing needs with any degree of accuracy is an estimate at best, even with the availability of staffing formulas, but the level of funding ultimately determines staff size. The decision on how many people to employ is influenced by priority given to this program, because despite the best efforts of those in this field, there is no single model that successfully fits all localities.

The variables that can affect staffing needs differ when comparing shelter duties to field operations, just as the activities in each of these two program categories differ from each other.

Selected Shelter Variables

- Number of animals in custody at the shelter daily, monthly, and annually and the average daily animal population in the shelter requiring care.

- Hours of operation (hours when the facility must be staffed).

- Size, layout, and age of the shelter facility.

- Scope of kennel duties.

- Administrative workload including but not limited to issuance of licenses, number of phone calls received, adoptions processed, etc.

Selected Field Service Variables

- Hours of service.

- Number of calls for service.

- Peak call volume periods.

- Number of square miles served.

- Average time spent per call.

- Desired response time.

- Priority of calls.

- Court time.

Orientation. The orientation process is important, because it establishes the future relationship between employer and employee. A well-planned and executed introduction to the organization through an orientation can help develop a new employee into a valued one. It is the beginning of a new relationship and introduces the new staff person to the history and mission of the organization and provides basic information that the employee will need to know. How the orientation process is conducted can have a lasting influence on the new employee and his or her opinion of the organization. The orientation can influence the new person's work performance and relationships with others in the workplace. At minimum, the orientation process should be carefully planned in advance and input solicited from staff. There should be a checklist of tasks to be performed so that a new employee will be correctly processed. The following checklist contains suggestions to include in the orientation process:

- Distribution of an orientation manual or packet with information that a new employee needs to know.

- Brief overview of the history and mission of this agency or the animal control program.

- Completion of various employment forms and documents by the employee including but not limited to payroll information, personnel benefits, and persons the employee would like to have contacted in an emergency.

- Introduction to other employees and their respective duties.

- Medical examination, if required.

- Brief introduction to other animal welfare organizations and other entities and how they interact with animal control.

- Information about upcoming training that the new employee will receive.

Staff duties. When a position is vacated for whatever reason, an opportunity is presented to examine the vacancy and to determine if it is necessary to fill that position, expand the duties to include other tasks, reclassify the position, create a new position with new duties, or leave the position unfilled for a period of time. The following case study offers an example involving staffing, supervision, and span of control.

Case Study

Linda is the director of the local humane society that contracts with three nearby towns to provide animal control services, both field and sheltering. There are five field officers employed by the society who answer calls for service and perform other field-related duties. Since the contracts were first awarded to the society, Linda has had all five field officers report directly to her. She had previously served as the county's supervising animal control officer where other officers also reported directly to her. When she became director, her former position with the county was reclassified from a supervisory position to animal control officer for budgetary reasons. In her current position, she sometimes accompanies other officers on field calls when her presence is needed. Two weeks ago, one of the five field officers submitted his resignation to accept a position in another state where he has family.

During the past eighteen months, Linda has spent increasingly more time developing plans for a new in-house spay/neuter facility, revamping the society's adoption program, and implementing a new software program for tracking animals. She now feels that she can no longer allocate enough time to directly supervise the field officers. She has proposed to her board of directors and to the three town managers that the soon-to-be-vacant field officer position be filled and that a new position of supervisory field officer be established that would perform field related duties and also provide in-the-field oversight of the other five officers. She presented documentation to show the increased workload of the field officers and how her own duties had increased, making it more difficult to directly supervise field staff. Her board of directors and the three town managers supported her proposal, and all three town governing bodies agreed to share the increased costs of the new position. The new supervising officer would report directly to Linda instead of five officers under the current arrangement.

Another idea popular with management is to implement cross-training to meet staffing needs. Agencies with a small staff can benefit by having staff members cross-trained in the duties of other personnel to enable them to perform those duties when the other person is not available or needs help. Individuals who are cross-trained should be considered eligible for promotion when vacancies occur, provided they meet other requirements. Cross-training broadens the knowledge of staff and helps them work more effectively as a team.

On-the-job training. Over the years many animal control organizations have relied heavily on in-house training for financial reasons. On-the-job training (OJT) where a new employee works alongside an experienced or veteran staff member to learn the various tasks of the job is acceptable under certain conditions. There needs to be a training plan, the trainer needs to be carefully selected, and the new employee should be tested for job skills. OJT is workable if the experienced employee has good work habits, performs the various tasks correctly, and the new employee is taught the proper way to perform his or her assignments. If the employee who is instructing the new hire has poor work habits and a new employee is exposed to them, then the new employee is not being properly trained, and the teaching employee is performing unsatisfactorily, thus harming the program.

Formal training programs. Formal training programs sponsored by national, state, and regional animal control and animal welfare organizations offer training on best and safe practices in this field where safety and compliance with law are paramount concerns. They offer credibility, and in some instances, they may be the only way to meet state requirements. Formal training programs provide written materials that the enrollees can use to supplement classroom instruction and their personal interaction with the instructor. Formal training opportunities on a wide range of animal control topics are available for both shelter and field employees and are offered in many locations across the country.

Experienced and veteran employees need training to increase and improve their job skills, to meet new training needs, and to be updated on new developments in this field. New laws, new techniques, new services, and new issues facing animal control agencies highlight the need for training for both new and veteran staff. The following section offers some examples of the types of training available.

Selected Training Opportunities

Several national animal welfare organizations offer training programs for animal control personnel at all levels. Offerings include educational conferences and workshops on special topics and issues as well as an array of written instructional materials, some of which can be purchased for self-study. Many state associations also offer at least one or more training sessions per year, often in conjunction with their annual conferences.

National Animal Control Association (NACA). NACA offers training programs for personnel performing animal control duties (e.g., animal control officers, police officers, and sheriff's deputies engaged in animal control work). NACA offers three levels of training academies that present a wide range of topics relevant to performing animal control duties. The topics include animal behavior, rabies, euthanasia, shelter operations, laws and legal proceedings, court testimony, stress management, blood sports, and four workshops that offer training and certification in four subject areas.

Humane Society of the United States (HSUS). HSUS offers a number of training opportunities for those in the animal welfare field including those employed in animal control services. HSUS' Animal Care Expo is an annual educational conference that draws in excess of one thousand participants representing all levels and interests in the animal welfare field. HSUS also offers on-site workshops, online courses, certificates, and academic programs through its Humane Society University. HSUS presents a biennial conference on disaster planning and the response process. Other HSUS training programs are offered at various locations in the United States.

American Humane Association (AHA). AHA offers two training programs of particular interest to animal care and control agencies: a Shelter Operations School (SOS) and the Shelter Operations School for Managers. In addition, the AHA's annual conference is educationally focused with a number of workshops that explore topics of interest to those in the animal care and control field.

Society of Animal Welfare Administrators (SAWA). SAWA offers a professional certification and continuing education program for executives of animal welfare and animal care and control agencies. There is a suggested reading list of books, manuals, and other materials to prepare for the written exam that has a work experience requirement:

> The Professional Certification Program is designed to distinguish the knowledge, skills and achievements of upper-level managers working in animal welfare and animal care and control; to support the best practices of the profession; and to broaden understanding about the specialized qualifications required for excellence in leadership in this unique field of work.[1]

Code of ethics. Some animal care and control organizations have adopted a code of ethics to guide their employees in their daily duties. Examples include New Bedford and Seekonk, both in Massachusetts. NACA has a code of ethics for its officers and board of directors.

Compensation and retention. Those employed in these organizations need to be reasonably compensated for their work, or there will be an on-going problem of retaining competent staff. A career ladder will help retain ambitious and talented staff, but for small agencies this may be difficult. Employee recognition, personnel benefits, and opportunities for training and networking can help address this concern. When employees believe they are valued in performing a needed public service, it encourages professionalism in the ranks of staff in the organization. Management needs to promote an environment where employees believe in the organization's mission and want to carry out their duties in a professional and competent manner. Yet, retention remains an issue for organizations that perform animal control services, where the work can be stressful and sometimes dangerous and where salaries in some agencies are still below those of other local government functions.

If the starting and top salaries are below those of comparable organizations in the same region, attrition will be a problem. This may require raising not only the entry level salaries to fill vacancies, but the salary ranges of current staff may also need to be adjusted. Government-operated animal control agencies should ask their human resources office to periodically conduct a salary review and to survey other public entities to find out more about salary ranges of animal control personnel including supervisory staff.

Humane societies and other nonprofits that contract to perform animal control responsibilities are aware that their employees are sometimes paid less than their counterparts in the public sector. This offers them a competitive advantage in bidding for animal control contracts. Once their employees have been trained and have gained experience, they may apply for openings in public sector animal control agencies where salaries are higher and benefits are greater. Code compliance agencies in local government where the work is similar to enforcing the local animal ordinances have higher salary ranges than animal control and attract applicants with animal control experience from the public and nonprofit sectors who are seeking increased compensation.

The opposite problem of paying salaries that are too low is paying a new employee at the top of the salary range. Hiring an applicant at the top of the salary range effectively eliminates further raises unless the range changes or there is a cost of living increase given to all employees. A good rule of thumb is not to hire someone above the middle of the salary range. This allows for merit increases for at least the next few years, even if the salary range is not adjusted upward.

Another aspect of the compensation and retention issue that is important to employees is the benefits package. The rapidly rising costs of health care and concerns about retirement needs have sparked great concern among those who work in this and other fields. Employees look increasingly to their employers for a benefits package to meet their personal needs, because it is too expensive for many to buy individual health coverage policies on the open market. Some employers pay the full cost of health insurance coverage for the employee only. Employees who desire broader coverage and/or coverage for dependents may have to pay part of the cost. Employee benefits vary by organization and can be a factor in retaining or failing to retain experienced staff.

Supervision. The role of management is, in simple terms, one of guiding and directing the organization/program and staff with some degree of control being exercised. Supervision is a management task, and supervisors are part of the management team. Supervisors exercise responsibilities on a daily basis to assure that the staff they oversee understands and carries out its duties effectively and efficiently. More specifically, the duties of supervising animal control staff includes:

- Providing guidance and direction in the shelter and in the field.

- Offering advice and assistance as needed.

- Making sure that staff complies with legal requirements.

- Making sure that staff understands and is able to carry out its duties and responsibilities.

- Assuring that staff properly represents the organization to the public.

- Reinforcing the mission of the organization.

- Promoting and reinforcing safe work practices.

- Fostering staff accountability.

- Resolving problems.

The following example illustrates how one supervisor not only supports her staff, but creates an atmosphere where her staff looks forward to coming to work.

Example

Doris is the office supervisor in the animal care and control agency. She oversees four employees with various administrative and clerical duties. She initially trained each person on her staff, but now she sends new employees and veteran staff members to formal classes sponsored by animal welfare organizations. The staff works together as a team, and each person is cross-trained to handle some other tasks in addition to their primary duties. The office is the hub of organization. It is the location where the public first enters the shelter and meets someone on staff, where telephone calls are received, and where calls for assistance are transmitted to officers in the field. Whether it is entering data into the computer on animals admitted to the shelter, issuing a dog or kennel license, posting a list of animals available for adoption, or ordering supplies, staff members handle these tasks smoothly and efficiently. Doris's calm demeanor, friendly and upbeat personality, and support for her staff makes the shelter office a place where one enjoys coming to work each day. She is never too busy to lend a hand for mundane tasks or to take questions from staff or the public.

The next example, based on one city's procedural requirements, illustrates elements of supervision including providing guidance, accountability, legal compliance, and promoting employee safety when euthanizing animals by injection. Because euthanasia drugs can be fatal to humans, the process requires safety precautions be followed to avoid injury to both staff and the animal, and because the animals must be treated humanely.

Example

When an animal is euthanized by injection the procedure must be carried out in a private area away from public view. There needs to be two employees performing this procedure. One must hold and calm the animal while the other person administers the injection. One staff person must stay with the animal until the heartbeat can no longer be detected using a stethoscope. Animals needing euthanasia should be handled in safe and humane manner so as to prevent injury to the people performing the procedure and to the animal itself. Administration of the injection requires the correct dosage based on animal weight and the proper body location where the injection is administered. The employee administering the euthanasia must record certain information on the kennel card including the amount of drug used. The federal government, through the Drug Enforcement Agency, regulates the use of euthanasia drugs, so there must be detailed documentation in the euthanasia logbook and the shelter's computer system. The shelter is also subject to federal audits.[2]

This city requires that the date and time of the euthanasia be documented and the supervisor's initials written on the kennel card indicating that the supervisor has reviewed the kennel card data for accuracy.

Another issue that has recently received increased attention in the media is the question of oversight of the single animal control officer in the community. News reports have highlighted some problems in several communities attributed to animal control officers who work alone and who appear to receive little oversight or direction in their daily work. Senior local government officials ought to revisit how they provide oversight if they have encountered personnel problems where only one animal control officer is employed in a community.

Staff input into the decision-making process. Some decisions will be made only by management or other bodies, but other decisions can benefit from staff input. There will be occasions when management may seek input from staff on how to resolve a problem, how to implement a new idea, or to consider policy and procedural changes. When staff members participate in arriving at a decision, acceptance will be higher, in part because staff input is welcomed and valued, fostering greater understanding of the matter and how it affects employees. Keeping staff informed about matters that affect them helps to minimize personnel problems, because it will be more difficult for rumors to take root if management maintains good lines of communication with staff.

Staff morale. The easy part is recognizing that every successful animal control organization needs to take steps to keep staff morale high. Staff morale can plummet for any number of reasons, can occur unexpectedly, and in some cases may be beyond management's control. For example, a shelter employee with a grievance against management may bad-mouth management to fellow employees and may convince others that they, too, have been wronged, thus spreading dissatisfaction to other staff members. Similarly, when an expected pay raise for all shelter and field staff has unexpectedly been placed on hold by other local government officials because of a sudden financial crisis, it causes distress among staff. In the first example, management may have been caught by surprise when several employees complained to their supervisor about a particular issue being discussed negatively by another employee. Employees should be encouraged to bring work-related personal concerns to their respective supervisors sooner rather than later. In the latter example, the problem at the moment was beyond animal control management's ability to change, but management should have briefed the staff on the matter and should have informed staff that it would follow up.

Staff morale is affected not only by circumstances and events. It is also about employees believing that they are needed and are valued members of the organization who are appreciated for their work. It is much more than simply keeping employees happy. Good communication between management and staff is important, helping to maintain good morale. Open and honest communication, whether on a one-to-one basis or at staff meetings, can help resolve issues, generate useful ideas, and build trust between management and staff.

Confidentiality. There will be occasional situations when management has information that must be kept confidential. Some personnel matters need to be kept confidential as demonstrated in the following example.

Example

John is the lead animal control officer who supervises five other officers. He has been respected and well-liked by those he supervises and by others in the organization. During the past two months, the other officers noticed changes in how John treated them. He has exhibited flashes of anger and has criticized other officers over minor issues. He appeared to be under stress and became argumentative with animal owners with whom he comes in contact. His subordinates dreaded coming to work each day and are becoming frightened of him.

The animal control director spoke to him privately to discuss his work performance. John shared some limited information with the director that he was having family problems. The director suggested that John seek confidential help through the Employee Assistance Program. The problems continued, and John asked for a leave of absence, which was granted. The director appointed another animal control officer to be the interim lead officer and gave him only the briefest information about John because of the privacy issue.

Recognition of staff. Everyone needs and wants to be recognized for their work. The personal acknowledgment of a job well done to someone who has performed exceedingly well or to the entire animal services staff for their efforts under often difficult conditions are all too easy to forget. Employee recognition shows respect for staff, promotes employee retention, helps maintain good morale, fosters organizational stability, and enhances team spirit. Employees should be recognized for special achievements, whether it is the successful conclusion of a difficult cruelty investigation, rescuing an animal in distress under dangerous conditions, or developing or refining an improved work process. One city recognized its animal control staff in a short ceremony where a proclamation was presented to the animal control director at the shelter.

The chairperson of the city council's public safety committee, which has jurisdiction over animal-related matters, initiated a proclamation signed by the mayor recognizing the good work by animal control staff. The committee chair presented the proclamation at a special meeting convened at the shelter. Light refreshments were served, and the chairperson expressed her personal appreciation and that of her colleagues for the work of this agency. Staff was surprised and pleased by this gesture.

Use of volunteers. Caring and enthusiastic volunteers who help animals and staff in a shelter are making a positive contribution to the community. The services provided by volunteers augment the work of paid staff who often are unable to provide that extra love and attention that dogs and cats desperately need. Volunteers see firsthand the needs and the effort that goes into caring for the animals, and they can be a bridge between shelter staff and the community. The experience of volunteers at a shelter is informally communicated back to the community and can have a positive (or negative) affect on the program.

To be effective, a volunteer program needs to be carefully planned and implemented. Potential issues such as liability, rules for volunteers, hours of service, and coordination with staff need to be addressed at the outset. Volunteer programs are neither created or become a success overnight, as it takes time and effort. If a volunteer program is being considered, the following guidelines may be worth noting.

- Volunteers are individuals who are willing to perform needed services of value to the staff and to the animals. Volunteers should never be assigned duties that staff members refuse to do or find distasteful.

- Potential volunteers need to be interviewed to determine if their interests and skills can be matched to those of the organization.

- Use of volunteers should be understood and supported by all staff persons. Volunteers should never be assigned tasks that could be viewed as a threat to staff.

- The volunteer effort needs to be coordinated by someone who understands the mission of the organization and can assist and monitor the services provided by volunteers so that they play a constructive role in making the shelter a safe and caring place for animals.

- There needs to be an orientation program for all volunteers.

- A volunteer handbook and/or policies and procedures for volunteers are basic to assuring that this effort will be successful and to give it the structure it needs.

- Volunteers need to be recognized and appreciated.

PERSONNEL ISSUES

The very nature of an animal care and control program with its stressful work environment and potential for human conflict create conditions that can trigger personnel problems and issues. If these issues and problems are not addressed in a timely manner, they can quickly spread throughout the organization. Even if some staff members have no interest in or connection to an issue, it can be distracting to them nonetheless. This section explores and examines some of the more common issues that are apt to arise.

The law enforcement role. Although animal control officers enforce local animal ordinances and some animal-related state laws, most are not peace officers, and their law enforcement authority is limited. Occasionally, an officer may attempt to intimidate the animal owner or others with his or her powers and may act outside the scope of employment. Appropriate training and supervision can help reduce these risks. It is imperative that these officers be well-versed in how to enforce the laws and understand when they should call for assistance from a peace officer.

Interacting with the public. People are at the very heart of this program. Individuals who come to animal control for help may have lost their pets to whom they are deeply attached and may be quite distraught. That is reason enough for staff and volunteers to listen to the public, show empathy, exhibit courtesy, and display professionalism.

The author recalls hearing a former senior government official speaking before a group of elected officials and management staff on the subject of customer service. The official reminded the gathering that people can always be taught new skills, but by the time someone enters the workplace, his or her personality is already well formed and will not change. Therefore, when considering hiring a new employee for a position where customer service is important, hire someone who likes and enjoys working with people. If that person needs training in a particular job skill, it can be provided. Also, when interviewing volunteers interested in helping at the shelter, consider whether their personalities are conducive to working with the public.

Inadequate staff and resources. There is a cost to the citizens and a negative impact on the program when there is insufficient staff and resources. Morale problems aside, a shortage of staff in the kennels means less care for the animals, less maintenance, and perhaps fewer hours when the public can visit the facility. When there are not enough field officers to handle the workload, those who call requesting field service will wait longer, enforcement of animal laws will be more limited, and there is a greater chance that animal owners will be less inclined to comply with legal requirements knowing that there is less enforcement effort. Similarly, too few staff to monitor licensing and pursue license renewals can lead to a drop off in the number of licensed pets, which means that fewer animals will be vaccinated and more animals will be at risk of contacting some contagious and serious disease.

When the need for more staff and resources is explained and presented in a non-confrontational manner, key decision makers may be willing to revisit these needs because of a legal mandate and impact on the community. There are steps that animal control management can take to highlight and document the need for more staff. Prepare a list of services and responsibilities that are mandated by state statute or local ordinance, the workload volume, staffing needs, and the costs to provide a minimal acceptable level of service. Documentation such as a legal opinion or data compiled from the program can bolster the chances of receiving additional resources. Be prepared to prioritize mandated services in the event that new resources are limited and choices will need to be made.

The problem employee. Personnel issues and problem employees in particular can be disruptive to an organization, distract from the organization's mission, and may become a threat or danger to staff. If ignored, the problem employee can become more than a long-term headache and can undermine both staff and management. Management needs to address the matter before the problem is exacerbated. Human resources professionals should be contacted for advice, if needed. Actions taken by management with regard to the employee should be fully and carefully documented and in accordance with personnel policies and the law, if applicable. Acts by the employee that violate rules and regulations of the organization should be documented. The following case study illustrates one type of problem employee issue.

Case Study

Bill is the supervisor overseeing kennel operations at the city animal shelter where he has been employed for several years. Recently he tendered his letter of resignation to accept a higher paying position at a shelter in another city. After having begun work at his new job, Bill began appearing at his former place of employment several days a week where he was observed talking to his former colleagues and entering and exiting restricted work areas. He was informed by the director that although he was welcome at the shelter, he was not allowed into restricted areas. His new position was in a city forty-four miles away, so it seemed odd that he should be visiting his old work location so frequently. On four separate occasions he was told by other supervisors to stay out of the locker room and the employee break room.

Management soon learned that he was spreading rumors to his former colleagues that he had been forced from his job by management. During the same time period he was visiting his former employer, he had sent what management deemed to be poison pen letters to the city council denouncing and levying false allegations against the director.

Bill had an imposing appearance as he is over six feet tall, weighs about 220 pounds, and is known to have an explosive temper. Three employees complained to the director that they were afraid of Bill and considered him to be a threat. The director notified the human resources director and the city manager of the situation. New security locks were installed for the safety of personnel. When Bill appeared at the shelter on a day when it was closed and then late one night when only two employees were on duty and argued with one of the employees, police were called to escort him from the facility. A restraining order was obtained to prevent him from being on the premises at any time. Police kept the shelter under surveillance for a period of time even though he stopped visiting the shelter.

Other problem employee issues reported in the media include misappropriation of funds, cruelty to animals, unauthorized removal of animals from the shelter, and falsifying reports. Each instance presents problems that unfairly reflect on other employees and on the program and must be addressed as soon as possible.

Misrepresenting opportunities to an employee. Another impediment to retaining employees is when employees have been led to believe that they can be promoted and can expect merit increases, but neither materializes, and the employee is terminated. . The following case study highlights this problem.

Case Study

ABC is a contract provider of animal control services to the county. The terms of the contract call for four state approved animal control officers (ACOs) to be employed to serve the unincorporated county areas. There was only one ACO who was state-approved to perform all duties of the position. Other employees who worked in the kennels as animal care attendants were often sent out on calls that required an animal control officer, but none of the three had completed the state required training for ACOs However, they were given ACO uniforms and ACO badges of authority. If any of the kennel employees went out on field calls and needed to issue a citation, the citation used was pre-signed by the state-approved ACO. Each of the three employees who worked for the contractor had gained enough work experience to qualify for appointment as an ACO, provided they completed the state mandated training curriculum within seven months of appointment to that position. As ACOs, they would be in a higher job classification and salary range and eligible for merit increases.

When hired, each of the kennel workers was led to believe there were ample opportunities for promotion to ACO and supervisory positions and to expect merit increases if their work was satisfactory. The performance evaluations were always negative, however, and there were never any merit increases.

When the kennel employees complained about the lack of merit increases and failure to be promoted, they were given a variety of excuses, and when they complained about working conditions, they were told to "keep quiet and do your job" by the supervisor.

Over a thirty month period, not one employee was promoted to ACO, nor were there were any merit increases given. Kennel staff never gained longevity, because kennel employees were always terminated before a merit increase was due or the promised promotion was given. Yet kennel staff was functioning as both animal care attendants and performing some duties of animal control officers that were outside of their job classification. A few terminated employees filed charges against their former employer with the state labor board, and one former employee wrote a letter to the county governing board alleging that the county was not getting what the contract required. An audit was conducted by the county, and it was found that ABC had not been complying with some personnel requirements of the contract. The county notified the contractor to comply with the contract terms or face the possibility the contract would be cancelled.

Stress. Working in an animal shelter is a stressful job for the staff and for the animals whose care is in the hands of those who work for the organization.

The new and often noisy environment can be threatening to the animals and makes them more susceptible to disease because it lowers their resistance to infection. Psychologists, mental health counselors, academics, shelter managers, and animal control directors all recognize that stress in this field can have a profound effect on an individual's job performance and attitude toward the job that crosses over to the individual's personal life.

Terms used to describe the effects on employees include "burnout," "work related stress," and "compassion fatigue." Each has a specific definition, but they are used to refer to related issues affecting staff. Staff is affected by its continued exposure to abused animals entering the shelter, abandoned animals that are impounded, and by having to euthanize animals.

Shelter managers and animal control directors have turned to consultants to help staff cope with their stress on the job. Compassion fatigue can affect employees in various units of an animal control organization, not just those who care for the animals and maintain the kennels, but those who administer euthanasia, are involved in deciding which animals are to be put to sleep, and animal control officers who experience stress in the field every day.

Discipline and termination. Discipline and/or termination of an employee can be a difficult, unpleasant, if not an emotionally distressing task for any manager or director. Before embarking on a disciplinary process or the act of terminating an employee, it is necessary to follow established policies and procedures. As a rule of thumb, human resources personnel should be contacted prior to instituting disciplinary action or termination. Termination and/or disciplinary actions should be documented. Failure of management to follow personnel policies or other requirements in law can create numerous problems for the employer.

DEVELOPMENT OF A DESK MANUAL

A useful management tool to help a new local government official get up to speed quickly on the functions of his or her department is to ask members of the department's management team to prepare a detailed description of their respective duties and responsibilities to be assembled as a work document called a "desk manual." This multi-page document, prepared by each person at the management level, walks the reader through each major area of responsibility as if the reader is training for the position. The desk manual has several advantages, but three are significant:

> 1. In the manager's absence (due to vacation, sick leave, emergency absence, resignation, or retirement), someone else can temporarily assume the duties of the position with a much shorter learning curve.

2. It enables the person who oversees this position (e.g., department director, city manager, police chief, etc.) to quickly assess which responsibilities of the position must be filled without interruption.

3. It provides a basis for updating the job description, salary range, and/or job title.

A city department director in one Western city asked each member of his management team to prepare a desk manual. The city contracted for animal control services with another jurisdiction, and one member of the city's management team also served as the city's animal control administrator. The administrator submitted a document with the following information:

- A list of the major responsibilities of the position and tasks in each area of responsibility (contract administration and oversight, animal licensing, complaints and inquiries, animal control emergencies, the budget and other financial matters, the animal control hearing board, shelter advisory committee, legal and enforcement issues, and non-contract animal matters).

- Key provisions in the contract, how the contract is administered, and compliance options.

- An explanation of how the city's animal control matters are coordinated with the contractor.

- Common and atypical animal related problems and how to handle them.

- People to call (who are employed by the contractor) on various animal contract-related matters and personnel to contact in other city agencies and outside organizations who help support the animal control function.

The desk manual was written in a tutorial fashion that allows the reader to understand the job functions, the division of responsibilities between the city and the contractor, and how certain functions were carried out to meet contractual requirements, legal mandates, and/or city policies and directives.

SUMMARY

The job description is the starting point in the hiring process as it defines the duties of the position, so it is worth the time to review the job description every time there is a vacancy to see if it needs to be changed. Advertising in specialized or trade publications and on the agency's Web site will attract interest from those seeking work in this field and can lead to more applicants than if advertising was limited to more generic sources such as newspapers.

The success of an animal control program in helping animals and people coexist in harmony depends in large part on how the program is staffed and if the members of the animal control team have the skills to do the job and to work as a team. Management and supervisory personnel need skills to oversee others and must be well-versed in program content and the responsibilities of this program. Management must act ethically and not mislead staff as it could lead to complaints filed against the animal control entity and its management. Recruiting, hiring, and training staff, proper orientation, and enough staff to do the work affects how the work is performed. Communicating with staff is critical, not just for expediting the flow of information, but for maintaining morale, its impact on work performed, and on employee retention. Personnel issues can have a negative impact on an animal control program and need to be addressed as soon as possible, lest they become both a distraction and a disruption.

Notes

1. Society of Animal Welfare Administrators, *2008 Report*, 7, http://www.sawanetwork.org/pdf/SAWA_AnnualReport_2008.pdf.

2. *City of Plano, Texas, Department of Environmental Health, Animal Services Manual*, Section 7.6, Euthanasia, Revised June, 2005.

Chapter 9

Interacting with Public and Private Entities and the Citizenry: Introduction and Overview

Anyone who believes that animal care and control is only about the welfare of animals has not stood in the director's shoes and experienced the pressures and stresses of that job. Managing this program is as much about working with people as animals. A prime example is partnering with animal rescue organizations to find new homes and/or foster care for shelter animals, which is discussed later in this chapter. The welfare of the animals is the paramount concern for all who are working in the field of animal welfare. Providing the care that animals need is only part of the bigger picture. People with a variety of views about pets, wildlife, and exotic animals really make a difference. Some contribute to making our communities better places for people and animals to coexist. Others shirk their responsibilities as pet owners, and there are those who are apathetic to animal needs. Lastly, there are some who present other challenges to animal control directors and managers. The challengers include those who support animal welfare efforts but believe only they know the one best way to ensure the welfare of the animals. There are others who are critical of the work of animal care and control entities and relish their role as self-appointed watchdogs. Some critics rightfully take credit for their efforts to improve agency operations, which has resulted in improved care of animals in custody and has led to more adoptions and new homes for unwanted animals. Consequently, fewer animals need to be put to death. There are other critics whose motives are opened to question.

This chapter is about people and organizations that influence, assist, and support the mission of animal services agencies and those who differ with animal control management on enforcing laws, setting animal policies, and providing care needed for animals in custody. Differences in opinion notwithstanding, animal control officials need to communicate with, cooperate to the extent possible, and garner support of those who have a perceived interest in the welfare of the animals in the community. Understanding the perspectives of the many players in animal welfare and animal care and control is the starting point for developing new relationships and enhancing existing ones with individuals, groups, and organizations. Whether publicly acknowledged or not, they are all stakeholders, and their support or at least their neutrality can greatly impact how successful the agency is carrying out its mission. Support whether it is political, financial, or volunteering at the shelter all count.

Reaching Out to Others: The Reasons and the Need

There are at least two approaches and many reasons why animal control programs need to reach out to the public. One approach is to enhance the public's knowledge of companion animals and wildlife in ways that will lead to greater protection of animals and will also protect humans from being harmed by animals. A second approach is a management effort that reaches out to organizations and individuals that interact with animal care and control in a variety of ways that affect how the agency carries out its mission and the degree of success with which that mission is pursued.

There are four major reasons why animal control management needs to build or enhance existing relationships with organizations both within and outside of government and with private individuals who have a passion for animal welfare and are active on behalf of the humane treatment of animals.

1. Animal control needs to create two-way communication between program staff and the public to promote understanding of animals needs and animal control's role. One path is to convey specific information to the public about the program and about animals. The return path is to listen to and to seek input from the public, animal owners, and others.

2. As a public entity funded with tax dollars, animal control needs to provide transparency and accountability in its operations. Increasingly, agencies are using the Internet as one of several avenues to provide information about their animal control programs.

3. Partnering with other organizations (e.g., rescue and fostering groups) is essential if an animal control program is to succeed in reaching its goals and objectives, because other entities need to understand the role and the value this program provides before they can accept the need for its existence. Animal control cannot operate in a vacuum. It must reach out

more to those it serves and work with those who want to offer their help to make the community a better place for people and animals to coexist.

4. Lastly, building relationships and support in the local community offers the best option for strengthening the program and assuring that it receives the resources it needs.

The Players and Stakeholders and Their Interests

People are increasingly becoming sensitized and repulsed by abuses inflicted on animals. Many caring pet owners are obsessed about their pets as evidenced by billions of dollars spent by pet owners on their dogs, cats, and other pets, but there are still significant numbers of animal owners who abuse and/or neglect their animals. This politically-charged program has several targets that the program would like to reach and these target groups sometimes overlap. One of the most obvious are animal owners and potential animal owners who may adopt an animal from a shelter. A targeted grouping is more properly described as interested parties that share a similarity (e.g., their interest in the well-being and protection of animals, but they have different perspectives on animal welfare). Both groups include players and stakeholders.

Animal owners and the public. The general public and pet owners may have an ongoing or an occasional interest in animal control programs when there is an issue that strikes a chord with them or when they need to request a service from an animal control agency. For example, a local resident may file a complaint with animal control about a neighbor's noisy dog, or an animal owner will have occasional contact with animal control (e.g., to license or register his or her pet). If someone has lost a pet, that pet has caused problems, or the owner has violated or is suspected of violating an animal law, the animal owner will most likely be contacted by a representative from the animal control agency.

The type of animal control transaction and the experience of the animal owner will color that person's opinion of the agency. If the owner was helped by animal control personnel in finding a lost pet, the owner will be happy, and the experience with the agency will be remembered with gratitude. On the other hand, if the owner was given a citation for violating an animal law provision and feels he or she or is innocent of the charge or was not treated "fairly" by an animal control officer, that experience will be remembered negatively. The approach program staff should take is to act professionally and treat everyone fairly. Visitors to the shelter should expect staff members to greet them and offer assistance. This can make a difference in whether they choose to adopt an animal from that shelter and if the shelter is observed to be clean and inviting.

Elected officials. Members of city, town, village, and county legislative bodies, because of their legal and funding powers, shape the scope and size of the program and will determine if there will be an animal control program. Their concerns are that funds be spent wisely for approved purposes, that results can be shown for the monies spent, that the animals are properly cared for, and that the number of animals euthanized be kept to a minimum. Senior administrative management and political officials are the ones to whom animal control directors will ultimately be held accountable, and they may not all be happy, as the *majority* of the elected body has to be satisfied with program results and management's performance. Program managers who are attuned to the concerns of elected officials meet with them periodically, take their calls promptly, and provide them with progress reports are demonstrating that they are responsive to being held accountable. When information from constituents to their elected representatives is passed on to the animal services management, it goes without saying that it requires prompt follow up with both the elected representative and the constituent. If the comments or complaints form a pattern, it may be clue that there is a problem that needs attention.

The elected representatives may know little about the animal control function when first elected, or they may bring their animal owner views to the table. Once in office they will realize that animal issues can be ongoing, sensitive, and often difficult, because those interested in animal issues are vocal and assertive and often have divergent views. It will not be long before they hear from constituents who will give them input about their experiences with animal control. There will usually be at least one or more members of the elected governing body who are dog or cat owners and who may take a greater interest in this function and may even serve as the lead person(s) on animal issues. Animal control management may look to this individual(s) for guidance on some animal issues, particularly if this person has the respect of the other members of the governing body, or this person is knowledgeable about how others on the governing body view animal issues.

If there is a shelter advisory panel where a representative is appointed from the local governing body, that person may become the de facto liaison to the elected governing body. If the local governing body has standing committees and animal control is under the jurisdiction of one of those standing committees, that committee may be the first place that an animal control official will go to in the process of keeping the governing body informed on any animal control matter.

Each local government has its own procedures to be followed when matters are submitted to the governing body. Senior local government officials such as the city manager or the chief administrative officer of the county may need to review and/or approve matters before they are transmitted to the governing body.

Elected and appointed officials like anyone else do not like to be criticized publicly or blindsided on issues that could have been considered in other, less confrontational ways or handled administratively. The following example illustrates this problem.

Example

The town council directed the town manager to instruct all departments to cut their respective budget requests for the next fiscal year by 10% due to a revenue shortfall in the current fiscal year, a similar projection for the next year and with anticipated increases in costs for worker's compensation and the retirement system contributions by the town. Other department directors took steps to find ways to cut their budgets by 10%. The animal control director, when asked by a reporter for the local newspaper to comment on the next year's budget problems, blamed the town council for underfunding his department that he claimed resulted in personnel retention problems, fewer animal adoptions, and more animals having to be euthanized.

Subsequently, an article on the budget was published in the newspaper that painted the elected governing body in a negative light and highlighted the animal control director's comments. This angered members of the elected governing body, one of whom wrote a letter to the editor of the paper defending the council's treatment of the animal control program over the past three years. The writer reported that the animal services budget had risen by 23% over and above increases to cover the costs of inflation and salary increases. The director's comments were regarded by some town hall insiders as the latest in series of outbursts from someone who was not a team player who had intentionally set out to embarrass elected officials.

The director is appointed by the town manager and serves at the discretion of that official. The director was quietly informed several months later that the town manager had lost confidence in his ability to run his department and was asked to retire or have his position downgraded. The director retired soon thereafter.

Senior local government management officials. Appointed senior level local government officials to whom the animal control director is accountable and to whom he or she reports may have their own concerns about how the program is managed or how certain issues need to be resolved. Local government executives look at the big picture and try to work their way through a number of issues in a politically-charged environment. Are there enough revenues to meet spending needs, and if not, what are the options? What are the local governing body's spending priorities, and how can they mesh with top management's assessment of budgetary needs? How should limited resources be allocated among competing governmental functions? Can some budget requests be delayed, and how will a delay affect the program?

The local government executive who is appointed by and responsible to the local elected governing body must weigh the options available and then offer recommendations based on need, amount of funding available, and whether there is political support for the recommendations.

Department director. The animal control director has to retain the confidence of the senior level local government executive about how he or she manages the animal control program. At the same time, the director needs to be a strong advocate for the program but must set priorities when seeking more resources. The director and top management play by a set of unwritten management rules more akin to an informal understanding that means being a team player and knowing when to concede on an issue. Experienced animal control administrators know that tomorrow will bring other opportunities to plead animal control needs or to provide a rationale for a proposed action.

Animal control directors/managers may report to others upward through a chain of command that involves further interaction with another level of management that directly oversees the animal control program. An example would be an animal control program within a larger organization such as health, police, or sheriff's department. Where this occurs, the department director manages several functions of which some may be related. As a division manager, the head of animal control will have varying degrees of autonomy in how the program is operated. There can also be a closer day-to-day relationship between the animal control manager and the department director because of how the organization is structured. When animal control is a separate department, the department director's relationship with the city manager or the chief county administrative officer may involve more personal interaction with the chief executive.

Shelter advisory panels. These committees, boards, or commissions are panels whose members advise animal control management and elected local government officials on animal-related matters. In some states, these panels are required by law. They can be natural allies of program management as they usually have a strong interest in animal welfare. Their role is to provide advice to management and gather input from the public. The panel enables animal control directors to obtain needed feedback on new ideas and proposals. Some advisory bodies have clearly defined responsibilities that are intended to assist both management and elected officials. They are also used to support program decisions and to reflect the views of the communities they serve. Sometimes the views of the members of the advisory body regarding a particular issue may be in opposition to the view expressed by the animal control director.

Other units of government. Animal program officials also interact with federal and state agencies and nearby local agencies on a wide range of animal issues, whether about law enforcement matters or referring matters to these other entities because of jurisdictional authority. In some states, agriculture or health departments may have oversight responsibilities for local animal control programs. State and federal wildlife agencies also may interact with local program officials. These other entities play support roles when their assistance is needed and may join forces to address regional or statewide issues. Establishing relationships with officials in these other entities is a function of management and makes good sense. By asking to be put on their respective mail or e-mail lists, local animal control officials will receive news updates on animal-related issues.

The veterinary community. Local veterinarians are often the first animal professionals to see animals adopted from a shelter in a clinical setting. These professionals may have agreed to offer a free examination to animals adopted from the local shelter. This is a mutually beneficial arrangement for both the veterinarian and the shelter. The veterinarian may acquire a new client as result of this visit, and the shelter has some assurance that the animal will be evaluated by a qualified medical professional at no cost to the animal control program. Since veterinarians are apt to be the first to identify an animal's medical problems, it is important that the shelter manager be promptly informed of such findings, particularly if there is any evidence of contagious disease, since measures must be taken to control the spread of the disease among the shelter animal population. Having a veterinarian serve on the shelter advisory board provides another communications link with local veterinarians who may have treated animals adopted from the shelter. This is important given that most shelter animals have little known history. Veterinarians need to feel assured that shelter officials are taking their input seriously and will take appropriate action, otherwise the relationship with the veterinary community will suffer. If there is a full-time or part-time veterinarian at the shelter, the shelter vet should be encouraged to become a member of the local veterinary society, if for no other reason than to build relationships with other veterinarians.

Volunteers. An effective volunteer program is one that has been carefully developed, supported by shelter staff, and meets the needs of the organization. Management needs to understand what motivates volunteers and to match volunteers' skills with the needs of animal control services. Volunteers are to be considered part of the organization and to assist but not replace staff.

A successful volunteer program at the shelter would benefit from the following elements:

- Having a qualified person who is knowledgeable about the organization should be placed in charge of them.

- An action plan describing the role and duties of volunteers, why they are needed, and ways to acknowledge their help.

- A recruitment and screening process for volunteers.

Volunteering at an animal shelter is not for everyone, nor should every animal control agency have volunteers unless the elements of a volunteer program are in place and the agency is prepared to support the effort of volunteers. If an animal control organization has major internal operating problems, the problems should be resolved before implementing a volunteer program, if the problems could impact services provided by volunteers. Animal control entities, regardless of size, can benefit from having volunteers

The media. It cannot be overemphasized that the media (radio, television, newspapers, and the Internet) through its dissemination of the news, influences what people see, hear, and think about animal control agencies. The media's role fluctuates between reporting positive and negative news. It may report program accomplishments, recognize the heroic efforts of animal control personnel, criticize some aspect of the program, or relate horror stories of animal abuse. The media considers any program in the public domain funded with public monies as fair game when it comes to reporting the news. The media is both a player and a stakeholder. As a player, it contributes to publicizing the availability of adoptable animals as a public service and may co-sponsor some animal-related events. As a stakeholder, it reports the news and monitors governmental activities. Animal control directors recognize the many roles of the media. Members of the media are both allies and critics, as they are free to act and report what they believe the public will need or want to know.

Animal welfare organizations, activists, and advocates. This broadly grouped category consists of those who care deeply about the welfare of animals. In its broadest sense they may include professional dog and cat breeders, humane societies, SPCAs, animal trainers, animal behavioralists, entities that promote spay/neuter services, wildlife rehabilitators, individuals who proudly identify themselves as animal activists, or animal advocates on behalf of dogs and cats.

They may include those who are primarily interested in other animals such as horses, rabbits, gerbils, or cage birds that are sometimes available for adoption at animal shelters. They are stakeholders inasmuch as they have an interest in saving animals impounded in shelters. Their relationships with publicly funded animal control programs varies with the issues. Some groups and individuals work cooperatively with local animal control officials and support the program mission. Others get involved only with issues that they care about or when they have differences of opinion with animal control officials. Others view themselves as monitors of shelter activities, and when they observe or suspect problems in the program they are apt to publicly air their concerns. It is fair to say that their relationships with animal control entities has its ups and downs. There is a healthy skepticism among these groups and individuals that a publicly operated shelter can ever do enough to help animals in need given past experience and funding limits. Some may find it difficult to understand and accept that publicly supported animal control programs have limitations based on available resources, political and legal constraints, and physical capacity. To their credit, some groups and individuals have helped raise awareness of the needs of animal shelters, assisted or led fund-raising efforts, and have become involved as shelter volunteers. These efforts have made a positive difference in the lives of shelter animals.

Other individuals acting alone or in small, informal groups present a challenge for animal control directors who prefer to work with them as allies and not as adversaries. These individuals or small groups may be knowledgeable about some animal issues, but they want their views to dominate, and a few go so far as to interfere with program operations. Animal control management that ignore these groups does so at its peril. Keeping local government officials informed about animal issues, giving them factual information on a regular basis, and taking timely, appropriate action can help contain problems and ward off unwarranted criticism from these individuals and small informal groups. The following example illustrates how a problem almost spiraled out of control when an animal control critic and a shelter employee exacerbated a situation.

Example

The kennel supervisor went to the manager of animal control services and reported that a purebred dog had disappeared from the shelter, the third in the past five months. All had mysteriously vanished from the kennels, and there was no evidence of a break-in at the shelter. The first two missing animals were not reported to the police, because they were believed to be merely recording errors. The animal services manager informed the city manager of the latest disappearance. The city manager recommended that this time the police look into the matter on a confidential basis, and the city manager called the police chief about this matter.

Coincidently, two shelter tech positions were open and needed to be filled. Several applicants were interviewed, and one was hired. Unbeknownst to the shelter staff, the new shelter tech was an undercover police officer. The police also installed hidden security cameras in several locations in the shelter building. Within six weeks, police were able to identify two suspects in the case.

Suddenly, out of the blue, a local animal shelter critic was informed by a kennel staff person who, speaking for himself, without any facts, and without authorization, alleged that someone on the staff had stolen the three dogs, had sold them to unsuspecting individuals, and had pocketed the money. The local critic called a reporter at the local newspaper who called the shelter manager and inquired about the missing dogs just as the police were making other discoveries in the investigation. The shelter manager who had been pledged to secrecy on the investigation called the city manager who called the police chief about the latest development. The police chief called the editor of the local paper and asked that the newspaper not publish anything about the missing dogs as there was an ongoing police investigation and that the investigation could be jeopardized by any publicity. The editor agreed to hold any story until the police investigation was completed and the suspects arrested. Meanwhile, the shelter critic wrote a letter to the editor of the local paper alleging that city officials were covering up the theft of the dogs and that the animal services manager had failed to act on the matter. The letter was not published. The police accelerated the investigation, and two suspects were charged with the thefts just as the mayor received a letter from the animal critic accusing city officials of a cover-up and demanding that the city take prompt action.

Animal rescue and foster care groups. These outside groups are both partners and stakeholders. They play a critical role in supporting the work of animal shelters by augmenting services that shelters are hard pressed to provide (e.g., long-term animal care, foster care, and specialty breed care and adoptions). They also accept healthy animals from crowded shelters or from shelters that have difficulty promoting adoptions. Through these groups, animals that are not quite ready for adoption, have special medical needs, or are so young that they need to be specially fed and cared for are temporarily placed in home environments under the care of committed and capable volunteers. Animal foster care by volunteers helps socialize the animals as well as evaluate them to determine if they are candidates for future adoption. When the animals are ready to be offered for adoption, these groups will hold adoption events and/or advertise animals they have available. The following section discusses some issues and concerns relating to animal rescue groups that impact animal control agencies.

PARTNERING WITH RESCUE ORGANIZATIONS

One of the animal control director's most vexing challenges is to save as many incoming shelter animals as possible. The effort to save these animals and find them new homes can be helped by partnering with animal rescue groups. Animal rescuers, most often thought of as people who help save homeless dogs and cats and work to find them new homes, perform a valuable service to the animals and to the communities they serve. The overwhelming majority of these volunteer groups, which are based out of people's homes, are not only legitimate entities, but many of them engage in valued partnerships with animal care and control agencies in helping to find adopters for shelter animals. It is imperative that animal control directors who encourage relationships with these groups create a level playing field for all participating groups so that each and all are treated fairly. In addition, as a community-based agency charged with animal welfare and law enforcement responsibilities, animal control needs to be aware of individuals and groups fraudulently operating as animal rescuers and to prevent and curtail these operations.

Partnering with these groups can produce a valued relationship that can help meet an agency's twin goals of finding new, long-term homes for these animals and reducing the number that are euthanized. Developing a productive partnership must be carefully planned and implemented. Animal control directors who enter into partnerships with rescue groups may wish to consider informing their local governing bodies of their successes working with these groups. This section provides some background on rescue organizations, how to identify reputable rescue organizations, learn warning signs, and steps that agencies need to take with regard to rescue groups to protect both animals and the agency.

Role of Rescue Groups.

Rescue groups or organizations have as their purpose to provide temporary care of domesticated pets until homes can be found for these animals. In its broadest sense, any group, organization, or individual that takes temporary custody of abandoned, abused, sick, or injured animals for the purpose of finding them new homes may be considered to be an animal rescuer. According to this definition, a nonprofit animal welfare organization and a publicly supported governmental or nonprofit animal shelter could be included in this category. The emphasis here is on the relationship between nonprofit groups of volunteers without their own facilities that receive animals from governmental shelters or from entities that contract to provide animal control services.

The following definition of a rescue group is offered for the purpose of discussion in this section:

> A rescue group or entity is nonprofit and has as its primary purpose to find adopters for those animals temporarily in its custody. Most rescue groups are made up of volunteers who provide foster care for the animals in their homes until the animal can be placed in a permanent home. A reputable rescue group exhibits certain characteristics in their efforts to find good, permanent homes for animals and assures that new animal owners will act responsibly and will provide appropriate care.

Types of Rescue Groups

Most rescue groups that receive animals from shelters accept either dogs or cats, but not both, and these groups are either a "breed rescue" or a general dog or cat rescue. The former will accept only a certain species of only one breed such as a Labrador Retriever, Greyhound, or Chihuahua. The latter group, acting as a general dog rescue or as general cat rescue, will accept any breed of a species (dog or cat) and mixed breeds if they believe the animal is adoptable. Some dog rescuers may limit their rescue efforts to finding homes for large dogs. Other species-specific rescue groups that will accept animals from a shelter include those that focus on rabbits, ferrets, guinea pigs, horses, and potbellied pigs to name a few.

Differences Between Rescue Groups and Local Government Shelters

Local government shelters are usually funded each year through the local government's general fund and are assured of a steady revenue stream. The revenues received may fluctuate from year to year for various reasons, but the funding stream could be at risk if revenue projections are not met. Rescue groups are not guaranteed a steady income stream. These groups need to raise operating funds through donations and events that will generate revenue, because the fees they charge to adopt an animal often are not enough to fully support their work. The rescue volunteers who staff the organization donate their time, use of their homes, and frequently pay the animals' expenses out of their own pockets. Animals who are in foster care live temporarily in the homes of volunteers, since most rescue groups do not have their own sheltering facility. Many such groups are nonprofit 501 (c) (3) organizations and must meet certain legal requirements to obtain this designation.

Why Animal Shelters Partner with Rescue Groups

Working with reputable rescue organizations makes it possible for animal shelters to euthanize fewer animals and to place more animals for adoption. Some public shelters place a high priority on increasing adoptions in-house, but with limited resources, even the best managed agencies recognize that rescue organizations are better positioned to help place more animals in good homes. Although there are hurdles and challenges, the opportunities offered and the successful placement of animals makes the partnership worthwhile. Since public shelters and animal control contractors often have little or no information about the animals they receive, despite their best efforts not every animal will be guaranteed new home. Rescue groups may accept or reject any animal offered to them. Animals that these groups accept for placement need to be observed and assessed to determine what kind of home would be best for each animal. The animals benefit in several ways. Rescue groups monitor the health and temperament of the animals they accept, implant microchips in the animals, and monitor the placement of animals in new homes to assure that the adopter adheres to the terms and conditions of the adoption. The animals transferred from the shelter to a rescue entity have their expenses paid by the rescue group including needed veterinary care. Generally, rescue groups provide a level of care that the animals need to become more suitable for adoption. This may include needed socialization, specialized medical care, and obedience training, if warranted. Animals experience living in a caretaker's home for a short period until the animal is ready to be offered for adoption. Public shelters and animal control contractors often do not have the staff, let alone resources, to care for special needs animals, whereas rescue organizations may meet those needs.

What Shelter Management Must Do to Have an Effective Partnership with Rescue Groups

As indicated earlier in this section, management must make every effort to euthanize as few animals as possible for both humane and political reasons and to actively find new homes for those that are adoptable. The effort to find new homes by partnering with rescue groups requires that management takes those steps necessary to ensure that its rescue partners are reputable and are genuinely concerned about the animals' well-being. Caution and common sense should be followed in pursuing any partnership with animal rescuers. The following steps can help reduce potential problems and foster a mutually satisfactory relationship.

Implement policies, procedures, and laws. At minimum, shelters need to have policies and procedures in place and require a rescue group to sign a written agreement to comply with certain terms and conditions established by the shelter (see: Appendix 9-1 for Floyd County, Georgia's, animal rescue group policy). The policies should require an inspection of facilities where animals are to be housed and check the applicant's references. One provision to include in the rescue group policy is to clearly state that the animal control director or his or her representative retains the right to refuse to release an animal to a rescue group. This provision can be applied to unforeseen circumstances or if the animal control director believes that it is not in the animal's best interest to be placed in foster care or offered for adoption. Animal control directors, in consultation with an attorney, may determine that local ordinances do not cover rescue groups or may be inadequate and may need to be revised. A key reason for implementing written policies and procedures for rescue organizations is to have a level playing field in which all groups are required to play by the same set of rules. A rescue organization that complains to the local governing body that it does not receive all the animals it requests or does not receive all animals of a specific breed should be viewed warily as it may indicate that this group wants to play by its rules, not yours.

Policies that apply to rescue organizations should establish placement priorities. For example, the placement priorities of the Loudon County, Virginia, Animal Care and Control Center (Appendix 9-1) are:

1. Reuniting animals with their owners

2. Adopting animals to new homes

3. Placing animals with breed rescues or other reputable organizations

The department policy further states:

Therefore, the placement of any animal with a rescue organization will not be automatic. The Department will alter its placement priority when, in its professional opinion, an animal has special needs that can be better addressed through placement with a rescue organization rather than through adoption. In certain instances, the department may pursue both priorities simultaneously, making an animal available for adoption while at the same time pursuing rescue placement.[1]

The policies and procedures should require rescue entities that wish to receive animals from animal control to submit an application form with sufficient information to determine their suitability.

Issues to Consider

When developing policies, procedures, and laws, some thought needs to be given to those issues apt to arise in a partnering effort. Here are few examples:

- *Who should have preference in adopting shelter animals?* An argument in favor of preferences given to local residents or the general public is based on the fact that the shelter is funded with public funds, and therefore, individuals should be given priority. Another reason is that it is easier for the public to adopt from the animal control agency whose requirements are less stringent than those of rescue organizations. However, rescue organizations that assume the costs of caring for animals transferred to their care and help to make the animals more adoptable provide a valuable service as they also screen potential adopters to place the animals in long-term homes. Rescue organizations also *specialize* in adoptions, whereas animal control agencies have many other duties, limited resources, and often have more animals that they can successfully adopt.

- *How many animals should rescue organizations be allowed to receive?* Some agencies may limit the number of animals transferred to any one rescue organization in a one-year period in order to treat all groups fairly and to give the public an opportunity to select animals from among many offered for adoption . Rescue entities may accept or reject animals offered to them by the agency, but they will usually accept the ones they expect have the best chance of being adopted. If too many animals are received by rescue groups, it not only gives them an advantage over the public in selecting animals, but could lead to complaints from individual, would-be adopters that the citizens are being treated unfairly at a publicly-funded shelter. It could also cause a backlash from animal welfare advocates and perhaps the local governing body if it receives complaints about preference given to rescuers. Another concern of allowing rescue groups to request and take all the animals they want leaves open to question whether it is in the best interest of the animals, as it offers no guarantee that all the animals the groups receive from animal control will find new homes. The question can also be raised about how many animals a specific organization can reasonably care for at one time. Behind this question is also the thought that the agency does not want to turn over animals to rescuers that are later found to be hoarders or animal abusers. The bottom line is to encourage quality adoptions that will last as opposed to large quantities of animals being sent to rescue organizations, of whom some will be returned to animal control for varying reasons.

• *Should all animals be offered to rescue groups?* Animals that are quarantined, being held at the request of law enforcement agency, or known to be aggressive or to bite should not be made available for transfer or adoption. If an animal is microchipped and the owner can be identified or if there is good reason to believe an animal's owner can be located, the animal should not be released to any individual or group. It is best to err on the side of caution until it can be determined that the owner cannot be found.

Check licensing status. If the state where the shelter is located requires rescue groups to be licensed, shelter officials should check licensing status and inquire of the licensing authority if any complaints have been filed against the rescue group in question, the nature of those complaints, and how they were resolved. Some states that require rescue groups to be licensed have only minimum requirements, so further inquiry is advised. Among those states requiring licensing or registration are Colorado, Georgia, Kansas, New Hampshire, and Virginia. The Virginia law, SB 260 enacted in 2002, requires rescue organizations to keep records, provide oversight of foster homes where they place animals, and send selected annual reports to the state veterinarian. Further information about the Virginia law can be found by typing " SB 260, 2002" in the search box of the "Regulatory Services" link of the Virginia Department of Agriculture and Consumer Affairs Web site (www.vdacs.virginia.gov). Information about animal rescuer requirements in Colorado can be found in the PACFA Newsletter for January 2009 (www.colorado.gov/ag/animals).

Consult with attorney and local law enforcement agency. The shelter's attorney should be asked to assist in drafting and/or reviewing both the application form and the agreement to transfer custody of the animals to an animal rescue organization. Regardless of whether the state requires animal rescuers to be licensed, the shelter director may wish to inquire of the shelter's attorney and the local law enforcement agency if it is possible to check into whether any individuals affiliated with an animal rescue group that has filed an application has ever been convicted of animal abuse or unlawful activities involving animals.

The attorney should be consulted about any legal issues that could arise in the proposed policies and procedures. Questions involving liability, who shall have adoption preference, and whether animals should be transferred only to local rescue groups or made available any group regardless of their location ought to be discussed.

Developing an effective application form. An application form should be required of any rescue entity that wishes to receive animals transferred from a public shelter for placement in a new home. The application form can yield much useful information and can help assess whether the applicant is a suitable adoption partner. Before preparing the application form, make a list of questions deemed important in evaluating the applicant. Asking the right questions on the application form is critical. For example, consider relevancy of the following questions for your agency:

1. Has your organization or any of its officers, members, volunteers, or staff ever been convicted of a crime against animals or a crime pertaining to the welfare of animals?

2. Does your organization and/or its principals, officers, or staff operate a for-profit business under this or another name that sells animals as pets or for research or sells animals for profit via the Internet, newspaper advertisements, periodicals, or by other means?

3. Does your organization sell animals to the general public, and if so, what requirements if any must the new animal owner meet?

4. How many animals has your organization cared for each month for the past twelve months, how many were adopted, and how many were returned?

5. Does your organization have a 501 (c) (3) designation, or its it registered as a nonprofit in this state? If yes, please provide documentation.

6. Does your organization have written policies and procedures on the placement of animals in new homes and/or in foster care? If yes, please provide a copy of both.

7. Ask for at least three references.

8. Ask for contact information for the applicant's veterinarian.

Rank questions in priority order and include the highest priority ones on the application form. The other questions can be asked during a meeting with the applicant or on a supplemental form at a later date. Two examples of animal rescue applications are Floyd County, Georgia, Animal Control and Loudoun County, Virginia, Department of Animal Care and Control. These applications are found as Appendices 9-1 and 9-2, respectively. The Loudoun County policy is also included in Appendix 9-2. Both applications contain questions to be answered and require some documentation to be provided by the applicant.

Make inquiries about the rescue organization. Check references provided on the application form. Shelter officials should also inquire of local veterinarians, other shelters in the area, and national and regional animal welfare organizations to determine if a rescue group applicant is reputable and competent. State health and/or agriculture agencies charged with oversight of animal control agencies and animal welfare are another valuable source of information about rescue organizations and fraudulent rescuers. Should animals be transferred to the custody of a group with a questionable background, the local animal shelter may not only incur potential liability problems, particularly if harm came to the animal(s), but the resulting negative publicity could also damage animal control's reputation and impair its ability to function.

Key Characteristics of a Reputable Animal Rescue Organization

The following are some examples of characteristics exhibited by reputable animal rescue groups:

- Have established policies and procedures to protect the animals.

- All animals are spayed/neutered before the adopter takes custody.

- Animals receive necessary medical care including inoculations, microchips, and are in healthy condition for adoption.

- Animals are kept in foster care under the care and supervision of committed volunteers who monitor and screen the animals to determine what type of home would be a good fit.

- Offer advice and assistance to new adopters.

- All adopters must sign a contract promising to adhere to terms and conditions, and the adopters are screened and receive a home visit.

- The rescue organization will take back any animal if the placement is unsuccessful.

- The rescue organization works in a cooperative way with the shelter from where animals were transferred to its custody.

- The rescue group is a 501 (c) (3) public charity or a nonprofit organization.

- Incoming animals are screened for temperament and health.

- Animals received by the rescue entity will interact with other animals before being offered for adoption.

- The rescue entity does not offer animals for breeding.

- An application form and an adoption agreement (contract) will be required of all adopters.

- The adoption agreement will require that if the animal must be relinquished, it must be returned to the rescue group.

Practices of Those Who Are Not Legitimate Animal Rescuers

Those impersonating animal rescuers will try to deceive and profit from unsuspecting but caring people who are looking to adopt a dog or cat. Bogus rescuers will try to avoid answering questions. Knowing some of the major characteristics of reputable animal rescuers and warning signs to be aware of can help prevent and reduce the number of incidents where animals and people are victimized.

Publicly supported animal control agencies and reputable animal control contractors have a number of tools at their disposal, as noted elsewhere in this section, to determine whether a potential rescue organization can become a productive animal adoption partner. Dishonest individuals or groups that pose as reputable animal rescuers have been around for some time, and an economic recession often brings out the worst behavior of those who are operating a scam. The following are a few examples of how dishonest individuals may operate as animal rescuers. It is important for anyone who cares about the welfare of animals to ask questions and expect reasonable answers from anyone who wants an animal and/or someone who is releasing an animal. Individuals should be warned not to adopt an animal from any organization sight unseen.

The Web site approach. An individual posing as an animal rescuer advertises that if you give your dog to that organization, you can be assured that they will find a good home. Sometimes these unscrupulous individuals may take the name of a legitimate rescue group. They may make promises, and after acquiring the dog at no cost to them, sell the dog to an animal broker who may resell the animal for research or to someone who will use the dog for bait in dogfights.

A dishonest breeder anxious to sell dogs may use a Web site to portray that he or she is an animal rescuer and wants to place the dog in a good home (for a fee, of course). The unsuspecting prospective pet owner has no idea that he or she may be dealing with a puppy mill. Any organization or individual who wants to partner with an animal control agency needs to go through an application process designed to have key questions answered in order to weed out any fraudulent individual or group. Reputable rescuers who work with animal control agencies have protocols they must follow and are careful to protection their reputations.

Free to good home approach. Individuals who have litters of puppies or kittens that they do not want may place classified ads in local newspapers offering the animals free to good homes. Some people who answer the ads may be misrepresenting themselves as a family looking for a new pet and will have a carefully contrived plan and a story that seems believable. The recipient of the animal may then sell the animal to an animal broker for a profit, who in turn may sell it to a dogfighter, to someone who abuses animals, or to a pet shop.

Backyard dog thieves. Posing as representatives of reputable animal rescue organizations, unscrupulous individuals may snatch pets (often valuable breeds) from the owner's yard or even animals at large on the street. Should they be confronted, they may produce paperwork that indicates they have legal grounds to seize the animal, and these bogus rescuers may be wearing official-looking uniforms and driving marked vehicles identifying them as an animal rescue organization.

Why and How Does This Affect Animal Control?

An animal control agency has a major concern for several reasons. First, through the application process and careful screening, the agency can determine whether an individual or organization is a reputable and potential adoption and/or fostering partner. As an agency charged with enforcing animal laws and investigating animal cruelty and abuse, animal control receives complaints that need to be investigated. The role of animal control includes educating the public about animal care, pet owner responsibilities, and providing information to the public. The agency may publicize information about reputable rescuers with whom it partners and issue warnings about persons and organizations fraudulently representing themselves as animal rescuers in an effort to prevent further harm to animals, legitimate rescue groups, and to prevent unsuspecting people from being victimized by these con artists. The Web sites of some animal care and control agencies contain helpful information about animal rescuers.

Some Warning Signs That Animal Control Agencies Should Heed

The following signs should give animal control officials cause for concern, and further inquiry may be warranted before signing any agreement to transfer animals to the applicant. It may find, after further inquiry, that in some cases there were reasonable explanations that should be taken into account.

- The rescue group does not possess 501 (c) (3) status as a nonprofit animal rescue or adoption organization. It should be noted that there are reputable individuals who truly care about the welfare of animals, and who engage in rescue work, but do not possess nonprofit status.

- Other shelters have experienced problems with the applicant group, and those problems have not been resolved.

- The rescue group fails to spay /neuter adoptable animals as required in its agreement with an animal control agency.

- Principals of the rescue entity have been convicted of animal cruelty or have submitted false information on the application.

- The rescue group sells animals to anyone who wishes to purchase them without screening the potential adopter.

- Scam artists ask for money in advance for shipping the animal or to pay a veterinary bill before the animal is received by the adopter who may not have laid eyes on the animal. In fact, the animal may not exist except in the mind of the perpetrator.

- The rescue group transfers all or many dogs out of state. Some shelters that have too many animals in custody may transfer some to shelters in other states that have too few animals to offer for adoption and where the transferred animal stand a better chance of being placed in a new home. As noted earlier, further inquiry is recommended. It should not be assumed that any organization that transfers animals out of state is not a legitimate rescue. Rather, caution should be used when interacting with these entities to be sure that they have met all requirements.

- The rescue group does not inspect the home of the prospective adopter.

- The rescue group requests money up-front.

- The organization has the same or very similar name as another rescue group that is deemed to be reputable.

Sources of Information About Rescue Groups and How They Operate

The following sources may be helpful in evaluating rescuer applicants:

- Wisconsin Dog Rescue: www.widogrescue.com

- Alliance of Wisconsin Animal Rehoming Efforts (AWARE, Inc.): www.aware-wi.com

- Small-Dog Breeds.com: www.small-dogbreeds.com

- Pennsylvania Attorney General: http:///www.attorneygeneral.gov/press, press release from September 17, 2008

COOPERATIVE VENTURES

The players and stakeholders can also be considered as partners in projects with animal services agencies. Examples abound. New veterinarians in the community can be invited to write a guest column in the shelter newsletter about some current animal topic. The readers would benefit from this additional information, and the veterinarian would get free publicity and may acquire some new clients. Similarly, if a veterinarian agreed to give a free physical exam to any dog or cat adopted from for shelter, the vet may acquire some new clients this way. Shelters should also consider asking vets to sell animal licenses and compensate them for this effort.

Sometimes, as a public service, retail shopping malls will permit animal welfare organizations including municipal and county shelters to display dogs and cats available for adoption. This is another opportunity to place animals in new homes. There are also Web-based organizations that will partner with animal shelters to promote animal adoptions and to publicize lost and found pets in an effort to return these animals their owners. People who see animals publicized on the Internet will travel some distances to visit a shelter with the intent of adopting a pet whose picture was viewed on the Web. There are also arrangements between shelters to transfer animals from one shelter to another. It seems that in some parts of the country there are shelters with too many animals that need new homes while shelters in other areas have more requests to adopt animals than there are animals available.

There are other types of cooperative ventures that can benefit public shelters. Some pet product manufacturers will give free pet food to shelters when the products near their expiration dates or if the bags of food have been damaged and cannot be sold but can still be safely consumed. Some shelters have collaborated with nearby veterinary colleges to offer veterinary students internships in shelter medicine. Another opportunity for internships and special projects awaits students enrolled in a bachelor's (BPA) or a master's (MPA) program in schools of public administration who are interested in local government functions. Animal control directors and managers have many administrative and financial projects that can be assigned to students.

Public shelters are adopting techniques used by their nonprofit colleagues who operate animal adoption organizations by scheduling special events to raise the awareness of the plight of abandoned and abused animals and to raise money to help them, which will augment the limited public funds that have been appropriated. Suffice it to say that scheduling special events and fund-raisers to help these animals is a great way to connect with people who care about the animals and to promote the good work of animal care and control programs.

SUMMARY

Animal control is the one governmental function that attracts the interest of a number of players and stakeholders, because people are increasingly concerned about how animals are treated, particularly domestic pets. The highly-charged political climate surrounding the treatment of domestic pets has been the impetus for animal control officials to increase their efforts to reach out to various interest groups and individuals with messages of how to properly care for the animals and to address the ongoing problem of pet overpopulation. Animal control needs feedback as much as the community wants to give its input. As a publicly funded function, its operations need to be transparent, and officials need to be held accountable for their actions. Building relationships with those interested in animal welfare is a positive step toward alleviating the suffering of abandoned, abused, and unwanted pets. There are many program constraints, legal, physical, and financial, which animal welfare activists and others now recognize has limited the effectiveness of animal services programs and agencies.

Partnering with reputable animal rescue groups can help animal control agencies meet the goals of finding long term homes for dogs and cats—and that means fewer animals will need to be euthanized. The costs to animal control to transfer animals to these groups is minimal, if the rescue entities assume the expense of caring for the animal including spay/neuter, microchipping, specialized medical care, and other costs needed to make the animal more suitable for adoption. Animal control must create a level playing field for all participating rescue groups and exercise oversight to make sure that policies and procedures are being followed.

Animal control directors must also pursue other steps to protect the animals and avoid liability and other problems that can damage the agency's reputation. Consultation with an attorney on potential liability issues, development of a comprehensive application form to be required of all rescuers, plus inquiries and a background check are minimum requirements. The characteristics of reputable rescuers, warning signs to watch for, and understanding how fraudulent rescuers operate can go a long way to help the agency, animals, and the public avoid being victimized.

Cooperative ventures with other community-based groups and entities such as veterinarians, shopping malls, and others including pet product manufacturers, veterinary colleges, and students of public administration can reap benefits for shelter animals as well as help animal control officials.

Notes

1. Loudoun County, Virginia, Public Safety, Department of Animal Care and Control, Policy Directive, *Rescue Group Policy*, Effective September 19, 2007. www.loudoun.gov.

Chapter 10

Communications and Relations with the Media and the Public

INTRODUCTION

The effectiveness with which animal control communicates within and outside of the organization and the messages it sends to the public helps determine in large part whether it is successful in carrying out its mission. Those who convey messages and those who receive messages may interpret them differently. Communications assumes many forms from face-to-face discussion to news stories in the print media, radio, television, and the Internet. Other forms of communication include correspondence, formal notices, press releases, and the list goes on. This chapter examines the role of communications both within the program and outside the organization. As evidenced by reports in the media, animal control programs have experienced a wide range of operational problems, some of which could have been alleviated by better managing their communications.

The Communications Role and Needs of Animal Control

Internal communications. Within the animal control program, communications are much more than transmitting information. They are also about listening and learning. The message itself, how the message is delivered, and even the passion or emphasis with which it is delivered are all noteworthy. Instructions and requests to staff are forms of communication used to provide direction in the program. Other examples of communications at work include:

- Explaining the goals and objectives of the organization to staff in ways that will help promote understanding and gather support for these efforts.

- Demonstrating through both oral communication and physical example how to administer first aid to animals.

- Explaining to staff and the public the pet license application process.

- Explaining to staff how to prepare a bite incident report that is clearly written and contains all pertinent information.

External Communications. When staff interacts with animal owners in person, by phone, or by e-mail, what staff say and how it is said can leave a lasting impression on the animal owner who then may form an opinion about the program and staff. Courtesy and compassion, whether expressed in person or over the telephone, ought to leave the visitor or caller with a positive feeling about the staff and a feeling that shelter animals are in good hands. Some visitors to the shelter, after seeing the animals and talking with staff, will develop a greater sympathy for those who provide animal care services and become more sensitized to the problems of unwanted and abused animals. Other visitors to the shelter are there because of problems related to their animals (e.g., a dangerous dog hearing or to return a sick animal adopted from the shelter) and may leave the shelter unhappy regardless of the outcome. If a citizen leaves the shelter upset after interaction with staff or is otherwise critical as a result of this short visit, it becomes a problem that management cannot ignore. There will be times when it will be necessary to tell an animal owner something he or she does not want to hear. It might be that a late fee must be paid for license renewal or that the owner has to pay a penalty for violating the leash law. This may not be easy for some animal owners to accept no matter how diplomatically it is presented by staff.

External communications is about reaching out to more people through the media. Animal control will often seek the media's help to spread the word about achievements, upcoming special events, or to send special but urgent messages. At times the media will focus on reporting program shortcomings and animal control officials may feel they are being treated unfairly.

Open meetings. Communications need to go in two directions. Feedback from the party to whom you are speaking or to whom your message is directed can be valuable. Keep an open mind. Examples include responses to a proposed ordinance change to limit the number of animals per household, a proposal to control dangerous dogs, findings of an audit report, or proposed changes in services provided. The meeting should start with an announcement of the purpose of the meeting (e.g., to hear comments from the public and that no decisions will be made at this meeting). This should be followed by announcing the meeting rules. Each person should be given a time limit to express remarks. Three minutes per person is reasonable. Those presiding at the meeting should refrain from expressing their personal comments, and their remarks should be limited to asking questions to clarify the comments of others.

Role of the Media: What It Reports and Why

The short answer is that the media (primarily radio, television, newspapers, and the Internet) reports the news as it defines the term. The answer is really more complex, but first, what is the meant by the "news"? News, in part, is about a recent happening or event, intelligence, or information. Radio and television present an abbreviated news story that is carried live or on tape for a few minutes after which it moves on to the next story. Other news reports are given more time and space depending on the issue. Radio news often includes interviews with people who are pertinent to the story, allowing the listener to hear responses directly from the person being interviewed. Television has the advantage of being able to present audio and video of people being interviewed, but the coverage is less in-depth because of the short time available. Newspaper and Internet coverage using the written word provide longer coverage with more details. Articles that appear in newspapers about animal control issues may have been prepared over a period of several weeks before the first installment appears in print. The Internet also offers audio and video presentations of some news stories in addition to stories in print.

Radio, television, and the Internet can update their stories as often as necessary over a twenty-four hour period, unlike newspapers that are limited to one or two daily print editions. This, too, is changing as technology advances. Newspapers are now updating their earlier print news stories on their Web sites. The audiences reached by each media segment are different, but there is some overlap. Readers keep up with news events in many ways. Some regularly read newspapers in the morning or during a work break during the day. Others watch television at night at home to get their news. Those who have a personal computer at work or at home may use the computer several times a day to access the news.

What does the media report? The news media reports what it believes is newsworthy in the market it serves. Stated another way, the news covered is what the target audience wants to see/hear or what the media provider believes its listeners, viewers, or readers want.

- *Problems.* Reports of animal abuse including arrests of persons charged with abusing animals, dangerous dog attacks, and injuries resulting from such attacks always get the attention of the local media. Letters to the editor of the local newspaper about a perceived problem at the animal shelter or a call to a reporter from an unhappy local resident about a recent unpleasant experience with animal control may pique the interest of the newspaper, radio, or television channel. The media often learns about animal control issues from both within their respective organizations and from outside sources such as a grand jury, a consultant's report, or through a request for data pursuant to the provisions of the public records act in that state.

- *Human interest stories.* Articles about animals as loyal companions and stories about shelter animals for whom new homes are being sought are popular among media audiences. Efforts to find new homes for unwanted animals strike a chord with the public, and this is an opportunity for shelter staff to promote adoptions by displaying photos of available animals. Discussing the animals' personalities and type of home where they would be a good fit adds to the story and may create an emotional response and trigger a desire to have a pet.

- *Profiles of animal control officials and employees.* The local newspaper wanting to know more about the newly hired animal control director will send a reporter to interview the director. The reporter will probably be interested in the director's views on local animal issues and any changes being contemplated in the program. The newspaper may position the story to introduce the official to the community, particularly if the hiring of a new animal control official was based on recommendations in an audit report or study or as the replacement for a retiring shelter director. Officials interviewed should be careful not to overstate their credentials and experience.

- *Editorials and columnists.* Newspaper and radio editorials offer their opinions on an issue, and they are used to stimulate discussion among readers and listeners. Editorials can also be a rallying cry for action by the community or to pressure local officials to make a specific decision. Some local elected local government officials have used media coverage as their justification to act in a situation about which they may not have been aware. Similarly, newspaper columnists may explore certain aspects of animal control issues that also may stimulate letters to the editor. The writer may present arguments for or against an issue and may interview interested parties to learn their views. Those views may be used to persuade public officials to take a stand or to change their positions.

- *Competition among the media for coverage of an issue.* A public hearing or meeting on a proposed animal control ordinance is sure to draw a large crowd, and the media will be there to report the opinions expressed and questions raised by those in the audience. The local newspaper will assign a reporter to cover the event and a television station will send a reporter and a mobile broadcasting van to the site to interview some of those in attendance and to summarize the proceedings. Journalists in attendance will interview residents, local officials, and animal control staff. Local officials and animal control staff need to give some thought in advance about questions that might be asked and how they should answer them. Being circumspect in responding to some questions may give greater latitude to act in the future, should that be necessary.

- *Local coverage.* No matter how much competition there is for space in the local newspaper, animal control issues are assured some coverage, because they are politically charged, and because many readers are pet owners with opinions on the issue. If there are operational problems at the shelter, personnel issues, questions raised about the number of animals euthanized, questions raised about the number of dog bite incidents, or the number of complaints about dogs running at large in violation of local leash law requirements, be assured the press will find out at some point, and it will be reported to the public. Any publicly expressed suggestions by local government officials to explore ideas on how to stop pit bull attacks will get the attention of the local press, which will then seek the reactions of pit bull owners and other pet owners on the issue.

- *Investigative journalism.* This needs to be viewed differently as it is a more in-depth review of a governmental function (whether the function is performed by a public agency, a nonprofit, or a private, for-profit entity) over a longer time span and is intended to hold public officials to greater public scrutiny. A reporter or team of journalists may prepare and air an investigative report in a series of articles over a period of several weeks. The assignment may be undertaken at the direction of an editor based on knowledge of certain events or decisions made in the public sector or as a suggestion offered by a staff writer covering animal control. Investigative journalism stories about animal control programs can have a strong impact on community opinion. These stories in the media may have a negative focus due to problems uncovered and how the problems were handled by animal control officials. Investigative reports tend to keep the issues alive over a period of time until local officials take corrective action. Sometimes investigative reports include a follow-up in the future to report any changes or actions taken to date.

    The animal control director should react cautiously but may be able to use the reports to make needed changes in the program by working behind the scenes with other public officials to develop an action plan and timetable to correct deficiencies. If the media reports have factual errors, the animal control director should make a concerted effort to provide correct information. Be aware, animal control critics may use these reports to promote their own agendas.

Animal Control's Dissemination of Information

There are many ways to provide the public with information. Educational materials for pet owners can be found in booklets and other handouts available on display at the shelter and other locations for the public to take. Publicizing upcoming events with printed flyers or posters is another option. Materials for public consumption may also be kept in animal control vehicles for field officers to give to people they meet in the course of their daily work. Other means of providing information include press releases, media interviews, public service announcements, a column written for the local newspaper, speaking to community groups, and even paid advertising.

- *Posters, flyers, brochures, and handouts.* Information found in these sources can be displayed in a public area of the animal shelter, available free of charge to visitors. This information need not be time sensitive. Examples include materials on how to care for dogs and cats, the value of having a pet microchipped, and summaries of local animal laws.

- *Press releases.* This form of time-sensitive communication allows management to issue statements, explanation of issues, announcements of new services to be offered, and the appointment of a new director, manager, or new employee who brings qualifications and experience to a specialized position. The director may issue a press release to announce receipt of a grant, the start of a new activity or special project, or other positive news. Press releases may be publicized by the media if time and space are available, or the media may develop a story based on the press release. The value of the press release from management's perspective is that agency controls the content of the information to be distributed, how it is worded, when it is to be released, and whom the media can call for further details.

- *Newsletters.* Humane societies, government animal shelters, SPCAs, and other animal welfare groups publish newsletters for their members and others to promote their activities and services. Among topics discussed in newsletters published by or for animal control organizations are upcoming events, explaining animal laws, educational articles about wildlife, shelter wish lists, profiles on volunteers and staff, stories about animals that need new homes, successful adoption stories, need for donations, and tips on pet care. Among animal control organizations that publish newsletters are: Animal Care and Control of New York City; Oakland, California, Animal Services; Charlotte County, Florida, Animal Control; Milford, Connecticut, Animal Shelter; Charlotte Mecklenburg, North Carolina, Animal Control Bureau; the Animal Services Division of Fairfax County, Virginia; and Mansfield, Massachusetts, Animal Shelter.

  Newsletters take time to write and edit, and there are the costs of printing and mailing. It first should be determined why a newsletter is needed, who will read it, how often it should be published, and what are the costs and benefits. Having volunteers with writing experience prepare the newsletter can reap many benefits.

- *Communicating through community outreach.* Writing a monthly or occasional newspaper column can help in reaching more people in the local community to explain the role of animal control and to promote responsible pet ownership. A newspaper column that answers questions from animal owners or discusses selected animal topics helps build a closer connection between the animal control organization and the community.

   Speaking to local groups can be advantageous to both the audience and the agency, because it can spark a dialogue during the question and answer session. The face-to-face interaction where the audience gets to see, hear, and ask questions of the speaker provides both parties with information and feedback. Examples include problems of loose running dogs in a neighborhood, noisy animals, an animal abuse case, or some policy issue that is seen as problematic by some pet owners. The personal presence of the speaker lets the audience know that animal control is not a faceless entity, but consists of real people who care enough to reach out to the public.

- *Public Service Announcements (PSAs).* These short and to-the-point messages published in local newspapers and broadcast on radio and television augment other forms of communications. Examples of these messages are: "Be a responsible pet owner, have your dog spayed or neutered" and "Protect your pet: have it microchipped." These announcements are published or aired at no charge at the discretion of the media since they are considered filler material. Although these messages have more limited value because of how and when they are displayed, they serve as a reminder of animal control's presence and animal problems in the community.

- *Paid advertizing.* Never underestimate the value of advertising for sending a message or announcing an event. It may be the only sure way the message will reach the intended audience. It should be used only if the benefit is expected to exceed the cost. An advertisement that lists the schedule for upcoming low cost rabies clinics (where animal licenses can also be purchased) or the availability of low cost spay/neutering of dogs and cats can generate increased interest and participation of pet owners. Some newspapers may offer an advertising discount to shelters that make these services available.

Who at Animal Control Should Be Responsible for Communicating the News?

Disseminating news and information about animal control services to the public and the media should be given careful consideration by management. It is important that whatever information is conveyed be accurate, timely, and clear. If complete information is not available or cannot be presented for whatever reason, its best to be truthful and say "I have no further information at this time." If additional information will be available at a later date or time, it might be better to say that further information will be provided as it becomes available. If the spokesperson cannot answer a question, it is better to say "I don't know, but I will try and find out, and I will get back to you [at a later time]."

The size and type of organization may determine whether there is an assigned spokesperson for the organization. Public agencies with a high political profile often employ public information officers to interact with the public and the media. These individuals need to develop relationships with community organizations and the media to gain their trust as a reliable and accurate source of agency information. The spokesperson for the agency must have credibility and be able to communicate well with others in all types of settings and situations.

Large animal control organizations may have a single person act as spokesperson to assure coordination within the agency and to speak with one voice. The spokesperson should have direct access to senior management and may also serve as an advisor on media relations. There may be issues where the animal control director will need to speak rather than the agency's spokesperson. If there are complex policy issues, matters that have a history over time in which the director has more detailed knowledge, or because discussion of a particular issue by the animal control director or manager will carry more weight with the public and/or the media, then the director should assume the role of spokesperson.

The director or manager of a smaller animal control organization is often the spokesperson for that organization, because that person usually has knowledge of the issues and is directly involved in day-to-day operations.

Responding to Media Inquiries for Information

There may be times when the media will want to interview an employee who is very familiar with a particular event, incident, or issue. There should be a policy for staff to follow in responding to media inquiries. When developing that policy or creating guidelines, the following suggestions are offered:

1. The person interviewed should provide management with a summary of questions, the responses given, to whom the response was given, and the date of the response.

2. Inquiries about controversial matters should first be directed to management for its input. In any event, only factual information should be given. An employee's personal perspective should be withheld unless approved by management.

Routine information. Requests for dates for the next scheduled rabies clinic or minutes of the shelter advisory committee (which is public information under state law) can be provided by appropriate staff persons. If the requests are for data on specific activities such as the number of animals impounded, adopted, or euthanized during a particular time period, the requests should be referred to the appropriate person. That might be the spokesperson or a management official. The reason is to make sure that what is requested will receive a correct and accurate response.

Investigative inquiries/requests under the state's public records act. Information from public agencies including animal control entities may be requested by the media under state law that declares certain information and records be made available to the public upon request. The law may specify a time frame in replying to these requests These state statutes go by various names. Most are known as open or public records acts, freedom of information acts, open meeting laws, sunshine laws, or freedom of access laws.

One example is the California Public Records Act (CPRA). CPRA contains specific information exemptions. One exemption is based on the individual's right to privacy, and another exemption is based on government's need to function in a "reasonably efficient manner." Other exemptions include maintaining the confidentiality of investigative records and records relating to litigation. Under the CPRA, private, nonprofit corporations and entities are exempt from the public disclosure. The public may believe that all government documents are open for inspection, but the law may say otherwise. The following CPRA provisions illustrate how the law operates:

- An agency has ten days to decide if copies of the requested information will provided.

- Access to the records is always free, and fees for inspection or processing are not allowed.

- Costs are limited to a per page charge for reproducing a document. That charge is set by the legislature and not by local ordinance. The reproduction charge is typically ten to twenty-five cents per page.

- An agency must justify why it wishes to withhold any records by demonstrating that the record is exempt from the requirements of the law.

- CPRA covers only records that exist. An agency cannot be compelled to create a record.

- Public employee records are exempt under the law.

It goes without saying that these requests should be carefully processed. The following examples demonstrate how the latter two exemptions could be applied:

Example 1. The town contracts with the county to provide animal control services to town residents. The contract requires that the county submit quarterly statistical reports to the town containing data on the number of dogs, cats, and other animals entering the shelter through impoundment or owner turn-in and the number of animals by category that were returned to their owners, were adopted, or were euthanized. The town did not receive the fourth quarter report for the last fiscal year from the county and requested that the county send it to the town. The county replied that the report was not prepared, because the person assigned this responsibility resigned, and the paper records were accidently destroyed.

The local press requested the fourth quarter report under the state's open records act and asked that the report be prepared and provided to them. The town manager denied the request based on an opinion from the town attorney that the law applied only to existing records, and this record did not exist.

Example 2. Representatives of an animal welfare group requested that the county legislature adopt an amendment to the county's animal ordinance to ban circuses that use animals to perform in their shows on the grounds that circuses abuse their animals. The matter was referred to the county's animal control director for input.

The director recommended that no action be taken on this request as the state was already regulating circus animals, and the state's animal control directors association had the matter under study. The representative of the animal welfare group accused the animal control director of neglecting animal welfare and trying to forestall action. The animal welfare group submitted a request to the county executive officer to produce the animal control director's personnel file and any and all documents in that file that may contain disciplinary action against the director. The request was denied as employee personnel records in this state are exempt under the state's public records act.

The media occasionally will publish a story or a series of articles or reports on a particular governmental issue or problem occurring in public agencies including animal control organizations. The media may request data from the agency in preparing the story or report. Notwithstanding, public agencies and nonprofits or private entities that perform animal control services can expect to be scrutinized by the media when public funds are being spent to deliver these services.

There are procedures that public agencies must follow in responding to those requests. Local governments may have policies in place that meet requirements of state law and will apply to animal control if that function is operated directly by government (e.g., city, town, county, special district, or authority).

The rules for nonprofits and for-profit entities that operate animal control programs on behalf of a local government are another matter. However, the media has not been hesitant to hold these latter entities accountable when public funds are involved. The willingness of nonprofits and for-profits to provide data on their animal control operations may be governed by the terms of their contracts or their own policies. Some local governments that are clients of a nonprofit or for-profit organization have had problems obtaining requested data from their contractors even when the contracts contain clauses that require the contractor to make records available to the client.

Bad News and Crises

Animal control directors are not strangers when it comes to crises facing their organizations or to incidents that lead to unfavorable reports about the program and staff. Whether it is about someone's pet that was euthanized by mistake, an animal control officer acting beyond the scope of his or her authority, a report of unsanitary conditions at the shelter, or allegations of theft or embezzlement, each allegation or incident needs to be handled with care. While some incidents are unforeseen, others may have been foreseen, but there was a failure to act. At this juncture, the questions are:

- What should be done, and how should the agency react?

- Are all the facts assembled, or is there a need for further inquiry?

- What will be the media's interest in this matter, and what questions can be expected from the media?

There is a natural tendency to try and minimize the damage and put the best spin on the incident as possible, but it is important to both understand and take control of the situation and develop an exit strategy. It is management's responsibility not only to manage the program but problems and crises as well. The public and aggrieved parties may be more forgiving if agency management makes a genuine effort to remedy the situation and to take steps to prevent its recurrence.

Steps to take internally. Management should first assess the situation to determine if all of the facts are known, and if not, what needs to be done to gather needed information. Will further internal inquiry be needed? Were policies and procedures followed? Are there other individuals (or witnesses) to be contacted? If all of the facts are not known at this time, it is best not to draw conclusions until all the facts are known and evaluated. Management, in order to prevent different versions of the same incident from being presented by staff, should speak with one voice. Only factual information should be given to the news media if there are inquiries. It is often better to say in response to the media that "I do not know" or "I am not aware of the matter you are referring to" if you do not know and then promise to look into the matter. It may be prudent on sensitive matters (e.g., personnel, political, or liability issues) to bring them to the attention of higher officials before discussing them publicly. The following case study illustrates how one animal control director responded to one such issue.

Case Study: Part 1

Mrs. Smith's mixed breed dog escaped from her yard and was found wandering at large by an animal control officer who transported the animal to the shelter. The animal control officer reported that the animal had no license tag nor any identification on its collar. The dog was held according to shelter records for the three day minimum required by law and offered for adoption after that period when the owner could not be located. During the holding period, staff reported that the dog was scanned for a microchip, but none was found. The dog was placed on the posted list of animals impounded at the shelter and was also placed on the list of impounded animals published on the shelter's Web site. Mrs. Smith was out of town when the dog escaped, and a neighbor who was caring for the dog failed to notice that it was missing. Mrs. Smith claims the dog had an ID tag on its collar. Mrs. Smith wants her dog back and has demanded that animal control repossess it from the new owner. When her request was refused, she threatened to sue the shelter for wrongful release of her pet. Due to the possibility of litigation, the director instructed the animal control officer and other staff not to talk to the press or anyone about this matter and to refer all inquiries to the city's risk manager who was reviewing the circumstances with the city attorney.

Steps to take publicly. If management decides to speak publicly on a matter, the reasons for doing so should be very clear: to correct any misinformation that has been circulating, to present any additional pertinent information, to clarify any previous statements or facts, to demonstrate that the agency practices accountability, or to announce steps that the agency is taking to respond to the matter. Where an issue may result in legal action initiated by another party, it is always wise to follow the advice of an attorney before speaking on the subject. The author's rule of thumb is never volunteer negative information to the media, but do not lie or mislead the media. The following case study reveals some of the complexities of a case involving someone's pet.

Case Study: Part 2

When Mrs. Smith, the owner of a dog that was impounded by animal control, learned her animal had been adopted by someone, she requested animal control officials have the dog returned to her, but her request was denied. Mrs. Smith then contacted the local newspaper. The animal control director, in response to a question from a newspaper reporter, replied that shelter policies had been properly followed, and when the owner could not be located, the dog was offered for adoption. According to the director, the animal had been brought to the shelter by an animal control officer on a certain date and held for the minimal holding period required by law. The director refused to speculate on some hypothetical questions raised by the newspaper's reporter or to respond to other questions from the reporter during a telephone call.

The objectives in managing problems and crises is not to make them worse and to resolve them as quickly as possible at minimal expense and/or suffering. The public comments of an animal control official if not chosen carefully or the lack of a strategy or a flawed strategy in responding to a crisis situation may create further problems that may be even more difficult to resolve. Managers who exacerbate situations will learn that there is a personal cost to them and to the organization.

Publicizing Achievements and Other Information

Publicizing the good work or achievements of animal control organizations means being proactive and "tooting your own horn," so to speak. No one can do it better than animal control officials and staff. They have the information at their fingertips, experience working with animals, and a vested interest in promoting and protecting their program.

Highlighting achievements. Shelters that rescue homeless and unwanted animals until they can be placed for adoption, in foster care, or transferred to another animal welfare group provide a needed public function and deserve recognition. As animal advocates, these organizations need to publicize their good work. Increases in the number of animals adopted, placed in foster care, animals licensed, or vaccinated at clinics should be highlighted. Some shelters have been recognized for their accomplishments and innovative efforts to help animals, which can help increase community support. Increasing and maintaining that support is dependent on demonstrating to the public that the agency cares about animals and is getting good results.

Communicating through press releases, speaking to community groups, or being interviewed by the media should all be encouraged to convey good news. Overall, local newspapers have been sympathetic to animal control programs. They have printed photos and stories about shelter animals needing new homes that have contributed to increasing adoptions of those animals.

It is easier to remember and cite the problems and difficulties that face animal control directors and staff on a daily basis, but what about acknowledging the good works of animal control personnel, efforts by conscientious local and state officials, and effective animal control agencies? The following examples demonstrate the good works in this field on behalf of animals

Examples

- Larry Wright, of Jay, Maine, was honored as the part-time "Animal Control Officer of the Year" by the Maine Animal Control Association.[1]

- Les Rowe, animal control services officer for Manteca, California, was named "City Employee of the Year."[2]

- Anthony Dorrzapf, an animal control officer in Fairfax County, Virginia, was awarded the "2005 Domestic Animal Rescue Award" for saving a dog that fell thirty feet and was stranded on a cliff.[3]

- Governor Bill Richardson, of New Mexico, received the "Humanitarian Award from Animal Protection of New Mexico" for his support of animals.[4]

- Upper Freehold Township, New Jersey, was honored for its shared services agreement with other towns to provide animal control services.[5]

- Ingham County (Michigan) Board of Commissioners received "The Hope Award" for promoting humane values and for its support of improvements and programs at animal control.[6]

- Knox County, Tennessee, animal control was awarded the "2006 NACA Outstanding Agency Award."[7]

Some animal control agencies report their accomplishments annually or by fiscal year. The following excerpts are from reports by the Los Angeles County Department of Animal Care and Control.[8]

- Updated Department's Policy and Procedure Manual that had not been revised in about ten years (FY 2003-2004).

- Added a training officer to improve staff development and training (FY 2002-2003).

- Completed the department's first strategic plan (FY 2001-2002).

- Received a special "Productivity and Quality Award" from Los Angeles County Quality and Productivity Commission for a multi-departmental disaster response training program in association with other agencies (FY 2001-2002).

- Trained employees of the Department of Public Social Services and Children on how to recognize animal abuse (FY 2001-2002).

Sending special messages. Publicly funded and operated animal control shelters have had to become more assertive in recent years in publicizing messages they want the public to hear. Increases in animal cruelty cases and the number of unwanted animals that end up in already crowded animal shelters are issues that need to be brought to the public's attention. Animal control officials are also becoming more proactive to demonstrate that their programs are getting results and deserve more funding. Ideas have been borrowed from their colleagues in the nonprofit and private sectors.

Another aspect of communications is reaching out to animal owners and the public to promote special events such as dog walks, pet shows, an open house at the shelter, obedience classes, and rabies clinics. Reaching out to the community for support, whether it is to donate items on the shelter's wish list to make the animals more comfortable, recruiting volunteers to help at the shelter, to solicit donations, to speak out publically for more governmental funding, or just to endorse its activities are all needed. Messages need to be carefully scripted and delivered in a timely manner.

Problems with the Media

Maintaining good relations with the local media, particularly the local newspaper, is a must for every animal control director. Newspapers support animal control's efforts by sponsoring animal-related events as a community service and publishing announcements of upcoming animal events in their calendar section without charge. Notwithstanding, there are occasions when the parties part company amid problems that arise over a particular story or a series of articles about the animal control program. Problems arise for any number of reasons. If the newspaper published information about the program that came from data supplied by animal control, and the data were incorrect, the newspaper is not to blame. If animal control subsequently notified the newspaper of the problem and provided corrected data, the newspaper should publish the corrected data and explain the circumstances. Data given to the press should be checked for accuracy, and a management official should sign off on any data released.

Another problem of increasing frequency is a letter to the editor by someone who has had an unhappy experience with animal control. This may be followed by additional and similar correspondence and calls to a reporter from local animal critics with a litany of complaints about shelter operations and staff performance. Program management should investigate each negative letter to the editor and determine if it has merit. Where appropriate, the letter writer should be contacted, the letter acknowledged, and an effort made to address the writer's concerns. Several letters of similar content may indicate a problem that management was not aware of and needs to pursue. If the allegations by critics are false, they should be rebutted. If their complaints have some basis in fact, management should acknowledge that it will look into the matter as soon as possible and then do so. The following case study illustrates a problem between a mayor and a reporter for a local newspaper.

Case Study

The town's animal control program in recent months had been the subject of three critical letters to the editor of the local weekly newspaper. This was followed by a letter to the mayor from an anonymous employee at the town's animal shelter complaining about the care of the animals and staff morale. The mayor discussed the matter with the animal control manager and was satisfied that the animals were given adequate care, that an effort was made to contact each letter writer, and that all matters raised in the letter had been resolved. The animal control manager noted that the anonymous letter writer was probably an employee who had filed a grievance against the shelter, and that grievance was being processed. The human resources director confirmed to the mayor that only one employee had been critical of shelter operations, and other staff did not share that employee's views. The mayor decided that no further action was warranted on his part.

Less than a month after the last letter was published in the paper, a new reporter for the newspaper called the mayor and asked for all complaints lodged against the shelter in the past year. During the telephone conversation, the mayor asked the reporter to submit his requests in writing and said he would reply as quickly as possible. The reporter objected, said he was not required to do so, and inferred that the mayor was stalling. The mayor held firm and explained that by having it in writing, he would know exactly what was being requested, and the town could then provide a more accurate response. The mayor also invited the reporter to meet with him and the animal control manager to discuss the program. The reporter declined the invitation.

The reporter grudgingly agreed to submit his request in writing The written request cited the state's open records act and called for producing all complaints, oral or written, and the disposition of each complaint for the past twelve months. A few days later, the reporter asked for notes, phone logs, and memoranda pertaining to those complaints. This was followed by another written request for detailed budget information.

The mayor and the animal control manager met with the town attorney to discuss the requests. Based on the advice of the attorney, most documents were delivered to the reporter, and only a few were withheld. After the materials were delivered, the reporter wrote a critical article and inferred that the town had something to hide when some records were withheld. The mayor complained to the editor that the reporter had deliberately misquoted him during one of their telephone conversations and asked for a meeting with the editor of the paper.

SUMMARY

Communication is a necessary element of all animal control programs and is both internal and external to the organization. The success or failure to communicate effectively can be demonstrated by the support or criticism that the program receives from the public. The media plays a key role as a communicator in helping to transmit the message and promote understanding of the role and function of animal control to the public. News is more than reporting a story; it is also about shaping public opinion. Editorials and columnists are catalysts that challenge readers, listeners, and viewers of the news. Although the media is usually supportive of the role of animal control programs, it acts as the conscience of the public and notes when it perceives that animal control has acted improperly.

As a program or as an agency, animal control will always be in the public spotlight, because the public and not just animal owners have strong feelings about animals and domestic pets. This places a burden on animal control, unlike some other governmental functions, to work harder to be a positive force for animals and people.

Communications take many forms, and each form has its advantages and disadvantages, but all are intended to send a message and to reach selected audiences. The message must be clear and concise. Animal control entities need to coordinate the flow of information and speak with one voice, particularly on major issues.

State laws that authorize public access to governmental records enable the media to obtain information that might not be otherwise available. This access is not without some limitations and restrictions. Transparency and accountability are protected by this access and can serve to retain the citizenry's support and confidence in a publicly funded program. One of the most difficult times for animal control agencies is how to manage a crisis and to provide information that will not exacerbate an already sensitive situation. On the positive side, the humane work performed by animal control staff needs to be publicized, and the media continues to be a willing and supportive partner.

Notes

1. Donna M. Perry, "Wright wins award for animal control," *Sunjournal.com*, Jay, Maine, April 17, 2007 (accessed May 7, 2007). www.sunjournal.com.

2. *Manteca Bulletin*, Manteca, California, "When doing more is Les," December 18, 2005, www.mantecabulletin.com.

3. Metropolitan Washington Council of Governments, COG Honors Local Citizens for Service to Animals, "Fairfax County Officer Recognized for Daring Rescue," news release, March 3, 2006 (accessed May 7, 2007). http://www.cog.org.

4. Richardson for President, "Governor Richardson to Receive Humanitarian Award from Animal Protection Group," [Animal Protection of New Mexico] news release, October 6, 2007.

5. Jane Meggitt, "Township gets kudos for sharing services," *Examiner*, Upper Freehold, New Jersey, December 4, 2004 (accessed January 20, 2007). http://examiner.gmnews.com.

6. Ingham County, Michigan, Ingham County Animal Control Shelter, The Humanitarian Awards for 2006, "The Hope Award" (accessed May 7, 2007). http://www.ingham.org.

7. Knox County, Tennessee, "Knox County Animal Control Wins 2006 National Animal Control Association Award," news release, posted June 1, 2006 (accessed May 7, 2007). www.knoxcounty.org.

8. Los Angeles County Department of Animal Care and Control, "Reports of Accomplishments for FYS 2001-2002; 2002-2003; 2003-2004 and 2004-2005," sent to author at his request, April 26, 2005.

Chapter 11

Web Sites: Your Agency's Online Presence

INTRODUCTION

Today it is taken for granted that most organizations have a Web site that explains their functions, communicates messages, and is used to conduct business. Animal control entities, too, need to recognize that people want to connect with them via the Web and to communicate by e-mail. The underlying purpose of an animal control Web site should be to show that animal control staff are professionals in a field that is increasingly becoming more professionalized. The Web site should demonstrate that the agency is not only knowledgeable about animal issues, but also that the welfare of animals is a priority concern. It is also the role of the agency to educate the public about the care and treatment of companion animals and to provide information about local wildlife.

The use of animal control Web sites and Web pages as management tools, sources of information, and as a venue for transacting business are the focus of this chapter.

Have a Game Plan

Simply having a Web site isn't enough; it must be well thought through in terms of content and design. The Web site represents the agency's identity, purpose, and image. Carefully conceived Web sites benefit both the user and the organization. On the other hand, poorly designed Web sites that are difficult to find and/or navigate reflect poorly on the organization and frustrate visitors. Terms used in this chapter should be familiar to most Internet users.

Actual construction and maintenance of Web sites is beyond the scope of this book, but some selected design aspects are discussed in this chapter as they relate to the value and utility of animal control Web sites and Web pages. Generally speaking, though, it is important to start with the idea that a Web site is not a technical asset; because it falls into the category of communications and public relations. Therefore, do not make the common mistake of putting a technical specialist or IT head in charge of the Web site. Rather, approach it in the same way you would a brochure, newsletter, television interview, or redesign of your reception area—think of the message and image your agency wants to convey. Then, later, seek out the appropriate skilled people to make that happen. If you do leave your Web site in the hands of someone whose primary job is server maintenance or systems design, do not be surprised if what you get does little to convey your agency's message. If your budget is limited, try giving an opportunity to a student or group of students at a nearby college.

Perhaps Today's Most Important Medium

Government and business alike communicate and conduct transactions over the Internet and communicate online more than ever before with their respective constituents and customers. Similarly, millions of people using personal computers (PCs) seek information from animal control Web sites and Web pages. In addition to providing information, some of these sites enable the user to request services, download forms, and on some sites, they can process selected transactions (e.g., purchase animal licenses). The more functions you make available online, the less staff time you will have to dedicate to these activities. A small investment in automating certain functions on the Web can pay off in terms of labor savings.

Some governmental animal control agencies have their own Web sites along with humane societies, SPCAs, and other animal welfare organizations, some of whom provide animal control services. Some Web sites market their services and information through outreach to animal owners, potential pet adopters, and others who care about animal welfare. Petfinder.com, a well-known Web site that serves animal shelters, pet owners, and those who want to adopt pets, reports that in its ten years of existence, 10,000 adoptions have been credited to Petfinder and that seven million people visit its Web site every month. Petfinder also carries classified ads for lost and found pets.

Local governments have been good about embracing the Web, and one or more Web pages may be devoted to animal control services, though the quality and the thought put into making the sites interactive varies. First-time visitors and those not familiar with governmental Web sites find little uniformity in the design and content of these sites. Planners should put some thought into making the Web site as easy to understand and user-friendly as popular mainstream sites. Doing so may require the involvement of a more talented Web designer. If contracting, always ask your designer for samples before entering into an agreement. Wherever possible, do not limit yourself to a local vendor; the Web now makes it possible to purchase services from designers anywhere in the world.

Differences in how animal control services are organizationally structured, scope of responsibilities, and how the community ranks animal control services in terms of funding and political priority are also reflected on numerous governmental Web sites. Lack of uniformity in the services provided and differences in Web site design are reflected in the examples, case studies, and scenarios described in this chapter. Often visitors cannot be sure of finding the desired information or the depth of information offered. Given the fact that the Web is often the first place a person will look for your services, this is a real problem. Your agency does not have to offer a lot of services online, but what information and services it does provide should be clearly organized and easy to find.

Basic Information on a Web site

At minimum, an animal control Web site or Web page should contain specific information for anyone wishing to contact this agency or the local animal control officer. Basic information includes the following:

- The name of the organization (or the name of the local animal control officer if there is only one person who is assigned this function), telephone number with area code, an e-mail address, a fax number with area code if there is one, the hours of operation, and a telephone number to call in an emergency if different from the listed telephone number. The hours of operation and the address of and directions to the local shelter where the animals are housed are also needed, as well as a link to the Web site where available animals are shown and an e-mail address. If the shelter has a different telephone number, it ought to be publicized.

- The services provided by animal control should be clearly stated. Some local animal control programs offer limited service, while others have broader responsibilities.

- Unless it is clarified, the public could erroneously presume that animal control is responsible for many more animal-related problems.

- Legal requirements to be met by pet owners should be posted on the Web site or Web page. Some pet owners may not be aware of local requirements or may be new to the community. At minimum, a short summary of these requirements should be listed on the site. These may include but are not limited to licensing, rabies vaccinations, animal limits, and a prohibition on animals running at large.

The Web site as a Means of Communication

Animal control management has learned the same lesson as politicians (e.g., use as many means of communication to reach the public as possible). The Internet offers publicity twenty-four hours a day every day of the year and at minimal cost to communicate the role and *need* for an animal care and control entity, but also to convey educational information about the care of pets. Increasingly, those who use computers are finding information on a wide range of animal topics on both local and distant Web sites, because the Web within a few seconds to a few minutes makes all information locally available.

Some Web sites and Web pages may be compared to advertisements in the business pages of the local telephone directory ("brochureware"). Brochureware is a Web site that does no more than a paper brochure would do. It is not very interactive. Others contain a whole host of information or services available online interactively. Still others contain little more than the telephone number and the name of the local animal control officer.

Some local governments have allocated one or a few Web pages for the animal control function on the local jurisdiction's Web site. Due to server constraints and often because the animal control program is limited in scope, the information provided is limited. Other factors affecting the Web site content include the extent of involvement by animal control officials and staff, input from local government officials, cost of designing and constructing the site, and the experience of those who design the Web pages. Some have given considerable thought to the content and have sought input from many sources. Other management officials have designed the Web site to have a specific focus. Spalding County, Georgia, Animal Shelter is an example. The shelter's Web address is: www.spaldingcountyanimalshelter.com . The shelter's home page states it has a three part mission: protecting the health and safety of residents by "controlling the population of unwanted animals," working to ensure the humane treatment of all animals, and to promote animal adoptions. It is the third goal, which is given greater emphasis on this Web site, and which also is designed to convey a positive image as a place where animal adoptions are regarded as a joyful function and not just a responsibility.

The Web site as a Management Tool and Money Saver

Managing an animal control program requires having a vision for the organization and finding ways to turn that vision into a reality. That vision may be about operating a shelter that does not kill animals and is able to adopt every animal that enters the facility. While this is a noble vision, euthanizing fewer animals and adopting out more animals requires great effort. The shelter's Web page(s) can be used to promote these objectives by reaching out to pet owners to educate them on the care of their pets so they do not add to the population of homeless and stray animals that become an added responsibility of already overburdened animal shelters. These same pages can be used to market adoptable pets by displaying photos of the animals in combination with appealing descriptions of each animal. The Web pages increase the shelter's presence not only in the community, but worldwide.

Would you rather build a Web site for a reasonable, one-time fee or employ someone *full-time* to answer routine questions and address all of the topics frequently found on these sites? This electronic medium with minimal human interface can be accessed at any time of the day or night, rain or shine. These sites are in some respects comparable to the self-service check out machines at some discount stores and food markets. What are the advantages of having a Web site for an animal control agency from a management perspective?

- *Cost-effective.* It is cost-effective, because once it is operational, little staff time is required to maintain the site if it is simply to provide information that does not require continual updating such as name and address of the organization, directions to the shelter, hours of operation, how to contact the organization by phone, and to list frequently asked questions with the answers to those questions. It is like having an extra staff person but without the cost.

- *A medium for communicating, promoting and marketing services/activities.* It is a useful tool to educate the site visitor about pet owner responsibilities and related events and services. For example, information about licensing or registration of pets and rabies requirements together with a summary of relevant animal laws can help make the pet owner aware of his or her obligations in the care and keeping of that pet. Using the site to advertise the availability of specific pets for adoption has already caught fire among people seeking to adopt animals. Some even do long distance adoptions based on seeing the picture and description of an adoptable animal on a Web site.

- *Setting management priorities.* From a management perspective, Web pages can be used to define and explain animal issues directly to the public. It may take the form of an open letter to the community from the animal control director about a particular animal problem or to explain a change in shelter policy, an increase in fees, to announce a moratorium on license fee penalties, or even to boast about some program accomplishments. Management maintains the discretion on how the Web pages are used and what will be displayed.

- *Transacting business electronically.* Forms and documents to be used for transacting business previously available only on request by telephone, fax, or in person can now be made available online and either downloaded as soft copy or filled in and submitted online. Forms available on some existing sites include animal license/registration applications, citizen complaint forms, lost/found animal reports, and applications to become a volunteer.

Make sure you have someone to read all those online forms or answer e-mail in a timely manner. If you want people to use your Web site, then responding to the users is as important as answering the phone. Do not let your site get out of date—as soon as your hours, phone numbers, programs, or other information change, be sure to update your Web site. You can do this by having your designer make a user-friendly Web site that you can easily update yourself from your Web browser, or you might ask a volunteer to handle nothing but the Web site. Of course, you can always pay someone each time it needs an update.

If there is criticism of animal control Web sites, it is because they are impersonal, so try and keep it as friendly and interactive as possible. Web sites are not intended to be used in case of an animal emergency as the sites are not continuously monitored.

Lastly, management needs to be aware of how many visitors (or page views) the Web site receives, how many actual people visited the site, how they found the site, and what they view most. This is valuable feedback needed to improve animal control operations.

TYPES OF AND USES OF WEB SITES

A review of animal control Web sites reveal a wide range of information that is presented in an array of formats, some of which are more comprehensive and/or informative than others, and the ability to navigate sites varies widely. Most are easy to use, but others are challenging. Some sites contain limited information, others are comprehensive in scope, and there are many that fall in between. It is commendable that so many animal control entities have Web sites or Web pages as they are greatly needed. This chapter classifies animal control Web sites into three broad categories to distinguish their respective characteristics and to identify the types of information one is apt to find in each category.

The Type 1, Basic Web Page, or Web site: "Brochureware"

Some towns and cities may be limited by their available resources and staff expertise in what they are able to construct on their Web sites. Others choose to limit the information provided. Animal control may be limited to a Web page or two or just a blurb on the police or sheriff's Web pages. Some larger communities make hardly any mention of animal services on their Web site, and it may be difficult for a novice computer user to locate a telephone number for that service without going to the telephone directory or calling city hall. The following case study illustrates a problem in trying to locate the appropriate animal control agency for one city.

Case Study: A Frustrating Experience

It is Sunday afternoon, and Mr. Jones, the owner of a lost pet, is trying to reach the local animal control agency to report the loss of his dog who had been missing for three hours.

He did a Google search for "(City, State) animal control." The name of the animal control agency and Web site should have immediately appeared. It did not. Mr. Jones pressed "Search," and what appeared next was the city clerk's home page. That page indicated that dog licenses could be purchased at the city clerk's office. The city's home page contained a listing of city departments but did not list animal control. Next, the pet owner searched the county's Web site. Scrolling down through a list of departments, Mr. Jones eventually came to the health department, and by clicking on the links of several divisions in that department, he finally produced a telephone number for animal control, but nothing else on that topic. When calling that number, Mr. Jones was asked to leave a message or to call again on Monday morning.

Any decent Web site should at least contain minimal contact information that allows the user to contact the service provider. These sites require little if any maintenance unless the telephone number, location, or hours of operation change. It is more or less a billboard for all to view.

Type 2 or the Mid-Range Web site

Web sites or Web pages that contain more than basic information, but less than the full menu of animal services found on some of the nation's largest cities' Web sites have been dubbed by the author as "mid-range" Web sites or Web pages. These sites are more descriptive than a billboard, because they provide messages of educational value to pet owners and the public and emphasize responsible pet ownership by offering selected and often low cost services that benefit animals and their owners. They also list animals available for adoption to those interested in acquiring a new pet, whether it is a dog, cat, or some other animal species.

The mid-range site reflects an effort to make the public more aware of its services, to encourage responsible behavior of pet owners, and to encourage pet owners to provide humane care to their pets. The information is intended to educate the reader and also to invite the reader to make use of the services offered. There may even be a few links to other Web sites or to additional Web pages that contain other helpful or follow-up information. This type of site may be monitored part-time by a staff person or volunteer and may require some periodic maintenance

Manchester, New Hampshire, with a population exceeding 100,000, is one example of a Type 2 Web site. Animal control information is divided between two Web sites. The field services component of the program is in the police department and can be reached by going first to the city's Web address: http://www.manchesternh.gov. The shelter operation component has its own Web site found at: www.manchesteranimalshelter.org.

The police department's home page indicates that animal control is one of the seven divisions of this department. Clicking on the animal control link on the police department's home page directs the user to the animal control Web page. This Web page indicates there are two animal control officers in this city, and there is seven day a week coverage of animal services. Hours vary by season, and the user is asked to call the animal control division for hours of operation. There are two links on that page. One directs the visitor to a Web page that displays a brochure listing local animal laws, and states that stray animals are impounded at the Manchester Animal Shelter at 490 Dunbarton Road. The second link, www.manchesteranimalshelter.org, directs the visitor to the animal shelter that is operated under contract by the Friends of the Manchester Animal Shelter (FMAS).

Clicking on the shelter link yields more information about shelter programs as well as six other links that connect to adoptions, shelter events, volunteering, donations, the FMAS Newsletter, and how to support FMAS. Clicking on the adoptions link produces further information about how to contact the shelter by phone, e-mail, and the postal service, shelter operating hours, a listing of pets available, and detailed directions to this facility.

Type 3, The Comprehensive Animal Services Web site: Your Virtual Agency

Some animal control organizations have designed their Web sites to be online alternatives to their offices, authoritative sources of information, and marketing tools to educate and draw people in. It is worthy to note that a Web site that contains many links is apt to reduce the need to make telephone calls to the agency because the Web site addresses those topics. Comprehensive sites can thus accomplish several ends:

- Provide basic information including hours of operation, location, telephone number(s), and services provided.

- Offer links to other Web pages and other Web sites.

- Educate the public and pet owners alike by providing information on the care and treatment of animals and responsibilities of pet ownership.

- Promote adoption of animals needing new homes.

- Provide the ability to send a message to shelter staff online twenty-four hours a day.

- Offer selected services online. For example, filing a request for service or submitting an animal complaint, downloading license forms, or submitting an animal adoption interest form.

- Count the number of visitors to the site. (Do this behind the scenes. Nobody else really cares how many visitors you have had.)

- FAQ (frequently asked questions and answers).

- Pictures and bios for each available animal.

- A "webcam" with live views of available animals.

Not surprisingly, many large animal control organizations also have multi-page Web sites with additional links that provide information about a number of animal topics of interest to the pet owner and Web site visitor. Examples include Palm Beach County, Florida; Los Angeles County, California; and Collier County, Florida.

Palm Beach County animal control is one of six divisions in the county's Public Safety Department. The animal services page has more than eleven links that enables the user to easily click onto other locations that offer additional information about animals. Some of the links are repetitive, but overall, the links provide adequate descriptions that enable the user to correctly estimate the type of information presented in each link. The links offer the user the ability to view and print forms online (e.g., dog adoption release form). The link to "Ordinances" displays a list of all county animal ordinances and a descriptive title for each ordinance. "About Us" will take the user to a Web page that has a listing of fourteen services and programs offered to county residents.

Collier County Domestic Animal Services, located on Florida's west coast, is a comprehensive Web site with an array of user-friendly features for interested visitors. The site makes it clear that outreach to the areas it serves is a high priority. Among the features included are information about lost and found animals, volunteering, frequently asked questions, what is new, and upcoming events. There is an explanation of the department's responsibilities and information, and it is also available in Spanish. The Web address is www. colliergov.net/pets.

Ideally, using the Google search box and typing in the jurisdiction's name followed by "animal control" and clicking on "go" would result in the user being directed to the animal control Web site or Web page. Similarly, typing in the Web address for a particular animal control organization above the menu bar in Google would yield the same results.

Animal Control Web sites Serving America's Fifteen Largest Cities

Residents of America's fifteen largest cities based on population are provided with animal control services either directly by the municipality, by a contract provider, or by another unit of government that has this responsibility. The author reviewed animal Web sites that serve America's fifteen most populated cities to determine if was easy to locate the Web site, the ease of navigating each site, and to identify the types of information (beyond the basics) found on each site. Four cities (New York City, Philadelphia, Phoenix, and San Diego) contracted for animal control services with other entities that are both public and nonprofit. A fifth city, Columbus, Ohio, is served by the Franklin County Department of Animal Care and Control, because animal services is a county function.

Locating the Web site. It appeared to make hardly any difference in locating the animal control agency whether it was government operated or served by a nonprofit entity. San Diego states on the city's home page that animal control is performed by the county of San Diego. A link to the county's Web site is displayed on the city's home page.

Maricopa County, Arizona, serves Phoenix under contract. By Googling "Phoenix animal control," the Web user is directed to the "Environmental Concerns Directory" for Phoenix. A click onto this page shows at the bottom of the list of environmental concerns "Wildlife and Animal Control." Clicking on the latter directs the visitor to the Maricopa County animal control agency.

A similar Google search for the "city of Columbus, Ohio, animal control" notes on the page describing the city's Web site the existence of the Franklin County animal shelter. A search for the "city of Philadelphia animal control" would have caused a page to pop up that had more than five links to PACCA (Philadelphia Animal Care and Control Association), one of which said it is the city's contracted animal shelter. PACCA held the city's animal control services contract until the end of 2008

Navigating the Web sites. Once the user has accessed the Web site of the organization that provides animal control services, it is easy to use the various links to find desired information. The description of the links to specific topics were accurate up to a point. In other words, there was information about the desired topic, but the completeness and depth of discussion of the topic varied from one agency to another.

For example, information about adoptions on some Web sites included the cost of acquiring a new pet (including licensing), spay/neuter requirements, details about the adoption process, and even some information about microchipping. New York City's Web site, www.nycacc.org, offers greater information about pet adoptions. A few cities only posted pictures of adoptable pets but did not include other adoption information.

A search of all fifteen Web sites to find out what to do if a pet has been lost turned up similar disparities. Some only posted photos of lost pets. Others provided links to other Web sites or encouraged the pet owner to visit the shelter to search for the lost pet. Others, such as San Antonio at www.sanantonio.gov/animalcare, list several steps the owner can take to find a lost animal.

Exhibit 11-1 lists the types of information found on these Web sites. Although some Web sites contain either more information or information that differs from other Web sites, all of the Web sites can be broadly described as either Type 2 or Type 3. The focus and the information provided on these sites would appear to reflect priorities, policies, demographics, and geographical location.

Interestingly, San Antonio's strategic plan has as an objective to "update its Web site on a regular basis with information on services, news and programs." The plan also called for establishing a Web site domain name and to continue to expand ListServ.[1]

Commentary. A review of the features of these fifteen Web sites show variations in the information presented. Some features are marketing efforts such as the sale of gift certificates and animal-related merchandise. Other features (e.g., dog training programs, pet food recipes, and a calendar of animal-related events) are intended to attract the attention of caring pet owners and hopefully to bond with them and to win them over as advocates for the shelter and perhaps as potential donors of money or needed shelter supplies.

Listing those services offered by the agency such as dead animal pickup, what to do when a pet is lost, or someone else's pet is found reinforces in the visitor's mind that the agency is a community resource and much more than just enforcing animal laws. Offering information in Spanish and other languages is another example of trying to broaden outreach efforts to the local community.

Don't Forget: It's Advertising

One important thing to remember is that a Web site is advertising, a mechanism for publicity and conveying information. Do not make the mistake of putting your Web site design in the hands of a computer tech—would you entrust the making of a television commercial to a television repair technician?

Therefore, animal shelter directors and managers may find it beneficial to consult from time to time with marketing or public relations consultants on the best ways to make their Web sites most effective in reaching out to people, educating them about pet owner responsibilities, and marketing services and programs. The author observed that some animal control Web sites either have links to other Web sites for other animal-related services or list the telephone numbers to call to purchase animal licenses, report noisy animal problems, or to contact someone about an animal bite investigation and animal abuse. Although these responsibilities are divided among other agencies, it is not only user-friendly to refer the visitor to these other entities, but it promotes interagency cooperation.

Domain Name: Your Online Brand

The easier your URL, or Web address, is to remember and spell, the better. Lots of slashes, dashes, and dots are not going to help people find you. Especially if you want to get the public to remember it, keep it short and catchy (i.e., petregister.wa.com, smallvilleanimalcontrol.net, or WeLoveRodents.org, and since domain names are so inexpensive, you can register new ones just for special occasions like AdoptAStrayCamelWeek.com or SpayThatTurtle.org).

OTHER WEB SITE ISSUES

Lack of Familiarity With Governmental Organization.

There can be a number of difficulties in accessing animal control Web pages on the local government's Web site. Many community residents do not have a working knowledge of the local government's organizational chart, so unless a call is placed to city hall or the county offices, locating animal control on the Internet can be a challenge. Some communities note on a department's Web pages that animal control is a departmental responsibility, but a search for the phrase "animal control" fails to link it to a specific department. In some states, the term "animal warden" or "dog warden" may be a more common term in use rather than "animal control." Examples include Ohio, Illinois, Indiana, Michigan, New York, and West Virginia.

The animal control program may be in a larger department, but determining which department can be puzzling. Unless the user knows the exact department, it can be hard to locate without clicking on the link for each department. As noted in Chapter 2, animal control programs can be found in any one of ten or more locations, some of which are outside the local government organization such as a regional agency or a private provider. Since animal control programs fall under departments such as parks, public works, fire, highways, finance, health, and police or other law enforcement organizations, the name of the agency is not necessarily a clue to locating this function.

There are a number of municipal Web sites where animal control is hard to locate, because it is a unit of a division in a department, and the municipal Web site does not list animal control as a service, nor does it list the services provided by each department.

The Web site Should Contain Current Information

Be sure that the address, telephone number, hours of operation, holidays when closed, and contact information (including after hours for emergencies) is always current and correct.

Language

If there is a sizable Spanish-speaking population, there should be a button on the homepage ("Version en espanol") that allows the user to see a Spanish-language version of the Web site. Basically, the entire site is duplicated in Spanish, page for page, with the same content and navigation. If other languages are commonly spoken in the community served, consideration should be given to how people who speak primarily another language can use the Web site.

Get Linked

Try to get as many related agencies as possible to link to your Web site from theirs. Not only will this help visitors to their Web site find yours, but it will also help boost your ranking on Google. You can suggest the link text yourself.

Addressing Split Responsibilities on the Web site

A review of some animal control Web sites indicate that animal services are split among two or more entities . It is not always clear what services are performed by each entity. Some communities do not separately list animal control on its list of municipal services. Other municipalities do not list animal control services if the service is not directly performed by the municipality, yet it is public funds that are paying a private or another governmental entity to assume this responsibility. This can be confusing to the public. Any community where animal control functions are divided should clearly state which organization provides which services and how to contact the respective providers. Again, ask as many related agencies as possible to link your Web site from theirs.

There are numerous instances where a municipality retains for itself the authority to issue dog licenses but contracts field and/or shelter services to another provider. The following scenarios illustrate a few problems associated with failing to provide clear information and offer suggestions to help avoid confusion.

Scenario 1. City A contracts with a local animal welfare organization to provide field and shelter services on behalf of the city. The city's Web site does not mention who performs animal control services, only that dog licenses can be purchased at city hall. The city's Web page should indicate to the viewer that animal control is performed by another provider. The name, address, and telephone number of that provider should be shown on the city's Web site. It would be even more beneficial if there was a direct link from the city's Web site to the provider's Web site, making it easier for the user to transfer to the appropriate agency. The provider should similarly state on its Web site that anyone who has lost an animal should come to the shelter to look for it, and anyone who has found an animal should call the shelter to report this information. The provider should also acknowledge, if it does not do so, that it only contracts with the city to house lost, stray, or impounded animals.

Scenario 2. City B, in addition to being the sole source for the issuance of dog licenses, employs animal control officers to answer calls for service and also dispatches those calls from a small office at city hall. A contract provider shelters all impounded animals brought to the provider's facility. However, neither the provider or the city indicate the role of each in providing specialized animal control tasks. Only the telephone number of the city clerk is given for those who wish to purchase a dog license. Links on both the city and the contract provider's Web sites are needed to connect the user to either the shelter to locate a lost dog or file a missing animal report or to reach the city's dispatch office to request an officer to make a field call because of an animal problem. In addition to modifying the contents of the respective Web sites, the listing under the city government in the local telephone directory should also be checked to correspond with changes made on the Web pages.

Other Resources

Some animal control organizations are quite small and do not have either the expertise or the funds to create a Web site, but they, too, can have a Web site. For example, Petfinder.com, a nonprofit organization, will help animal control agencies create a customized Web site at no cost to the agency. The site is linked to Petfinder and customized to meet the needs of the particular animal control organization. These sites promote pet adoptions, which is Petfinder's mission. Petfinder requires that shelters that join its organization must provide the following information on the shelter's Web site:

- Who they are

- Where they are located

- How people can contact them

Pawtucket, Rhode Island's Web site, http://www.petfinder.com/shelters/RI13.html, is augmented by a link to Petfinder with whom it partners to publicize a list of its animals that are available for adoption. The Pawtucket Shelter's Petfinder link is www.pawtucketanimalshelterpetfinder.com, which consists of three Web pages devoted to animals available for adoption and the adoption process as well as directions to the shelter.

Another resource is PETS 911. This organization's Web site is www.pets911.com. It also operates a toll-free phone and a bilingual hotline (1-888-PETS-911) to help people on a number of animal-related matters. This organization states as its mission:

> PETS 911 believes that if you consolidate all adoption, fostering, lost and found, volunteer, shelter/clinic and health and training information out there and give the public a single and easy place to find this information, education will substantially increase and euthanasia will decrease. This is our mission.

This organization's Web site has links to a number of animal-related topics and services. It reports that it partners with over nine thousand local shelters and rescues across the country to provide information to the public. The visitor to this Web site can specify by zip code to be directed to nearby local public shelters, animal welfare organizations, animal fostering opportunities, post information about lost or found pets, volunteering at the shelter, and low cost spay/neuter services. If the visitor is seeking information in other parts of the country, all that is necessary is to enter the zip code for the desired locality.

Exhibit 11-1

Features of Animal Control Web sites Serving the Fifteen Largest U.S. Cities

Basic Features

Name of the organization, address (including directions to shelter), telephone number, hours of operation, and services provided.

Additional Features

Adoptions	Advisory board
Advertising links	Animal breeds/species
Animal bites/animal abuse	Animal issues (pit bulls, hoarding)
Animals lost/found	Animal limits
Behavior training	Biography of director/manager
Calendar of events	Career opportunities
Contacts in other agencies about animal matters	Corporate partners
	Dead animal pickup
Director's blog	Disaster preparedness
Dog training	Dog walkers
Donations	Downloadable forms
Education	Employment opportunities/internships
Euthanasia statement/ policy	Feedback form/survey
	Feral cats
Finding a veterinarian/ animal hospital	Fostering animals
	Frequently asked questions
Gift certificates/ merchandise for sale	Health issues
	Laws/ordinances
Licensing	Mission/vision statement
Microchips	Noisy animals
Newsletters/news	First aid/emergencies
Pet food recipes	Post-adoption veterinary care
Photos	Rabies information
Press releases	Rescue groups/partners
Spanish language information	Special reports
	Spay/neuter programs
Strategic plans	Statistics
Traveling with animals	Transactions online
Wildlife	Volunteers

SUMMARY

Animal control Web sites have multiple purposes, and there are often significant differences from one site to another. They provide a means of communication to Web site visitors, are a public relations tool, educate the viewer on animal topics and issues, and offer some services online. Perhaps best of all, it is available twenty-four hours a day. Today, the Internet is perhaps the most important medium of communications and transaction of business. Local governments have embraced the Web, and increasingly, more animal control programs and agencies have a presence online. However, differences in how animal control services are structured organizationally and variations in the services offered are similarly reflected by Web site differences. Every animal control Web site or Web page needs to contain basic information so that the visitor to the site is able to contact the agency or the local animal control officer.

The Web site is a management tool for carrying out its mission and it can help save money. It requires management to think creatively and to prioritize how the Web site will be used. It is also a means to publicize the program and to advertise its services. There are different types of Web sites. Some are very basic, but others are more comprehensive. Larger agencies are likely to provide more information and are easier to navigate. The nation's fifteen largest cities have varying online presence. Some Web sites for the fifteen largest cities are easy to navigate, but others are more difficult, and it depends on how the site was designed.

A few Web site issues are worth keeping in mind. Many Web site visitors are not familiar with how local government is structured, let alone familiar with all of the services it provides. If the Web site is poorly designed, it becomes problematic. If there are sizable numbers of people who primarily speak a language other than English in the community served and the Web site does not offer a language option other than English, then the site is not realizing its potential to reach a larger audience. A third issue relates to splitting animal control responsibilities. If animal control services are divided among two or more entities, it would help if each entity linked its Web site to the other providers' Web sites.

Notes

1. City of San Antonio, Animal Care Services, Animal Care Services Advisory Board, Five-year Strategic Plan, "Animal Care Strategic Plan," August 2006. www.sanantonio.gov/animalcare/.

References

1. Jared M. Spool, Tara Scanlon, Will Schroeder, Carolyn Snyder, Terri DeAngelo, *Usability: A Designer's Guide*, (San Diego, CA: Academic Press, 1999).

Chapter 12

Animal Control and the Law

The legal basis for many services and responsibilities provided by animal control programs and agencies is found in state statutes. Animal control has different meanings, scope, and activities that depend in part on the state where the services are provided, what state statutes say, and local animal issues. Changes in state animal-related statutes like other state laws are influenced by input from animal control officials, animal welfare organizations, and others. Over the years, states have added new laws or amended older ones in response to new needs. New laws have emphasized a more humane approach to animal regulation, but at the same time, these laws have imposed more requirements on animal owners, holding them more accountable for their actions and those of their animals. Some changes in state laws impose mandates on local governments. Some mandates are state funded to offset the new local government expenses, but others are not.

A major source of information on animal laws by state is the Animal Legal & Historical Center of the Michigan State University College of Law. The Web site is http://www.animallaw.info. All states have animal laws of which some apply only to dogs, cats, and other domesticated pets. Fortunately, animal laws in most states are assembled, published, and consolidated by the state or by private entities. In California, for example, state laws pertaining to all species of animals are published in a small single volume by the State Humane Association of California. Every animal control agency and every animal control officer needs to have a copy of all local ordinances and relevant state statutes in the jurisdiction served by the agency and some familiarity with federal statutes like the Animal Welfare Act.

State Laws

States may enact laws as authorized by their respective constitutions. State animal laws or statutes impose minimal levels of compliance upon animal owners and obligations on subordinate forms of government (e.g., cities, towns, and counties). Statutes also authorize or enable local governments, which derive their powers from the state, to undertake certain responsibilities or activities. These include establishing animal license requirements, operation of an animal shelter, and prohibiting dogs from running at large. Municipal and county codes are enforced locally and are adopted by cities, towns, villages, and counties. Local attorneys will interpret whether the local government can enact certain types of ordinances, and this applies to animal control matters.

Animal laws have public policy objectives reflecting the views of the communities that enacted the laws and should have the support of various animal welfare organizations. These laws include provisions either requiring or encouraging certain responsibilities by animal owners and/or local governments. The two-tier dog license structure in some states is an example. Dogs that are spayed or neutered pay a lower license fee than unaltered animals. The message is clear to every dog owner: it costs you less to license a neutered animal, and you are acting in the animal's best interests. This encourages owners to have their animals sterilized, which helps address the problem of pet overpopulation, as altered animals are believed to diminish many of the negative behaviors which animal laws seek to address (i.e., aggressiveness and roaming). Another example is a state requirement that any dog or cat adopted from an animal shelter must be spayed or neutered, which is increasingly becoming public policy through law in many states.

Other state laws establish controls over local governments to ensure that both animals and people are protected, to discourage offensive animal behaviors and harmful acts against animals from occurring, or to delegate specific enforcement powers to local animal control officers. Laws are enacted for many reasons, and any one statute may have several objectives.

Laws contain penalties for violations, but in many cases the penalties have been ineffective. Violations are often misdemeanors and may carry fines as low as $10 to $50. This makes it all too easy for violators to pay a small fine but not change their behavior. This has led to rapid changes taking place at the local government level, as municipalities and counties faced with increased animal problems have made their ordinances more restrictive, have increased monetary penalties, and have imposed additional non-monetary penalties on animal owners such as strict confinement requirements for animals deemed to be dangerous, prohibitions on keeping certain species of animals, or in some cases, removal of animals from the community.

State statutes can be classified into broad categories that help to understand the meaning and purpose of those laws. A review of the following four broad categories helps place the laws in perspective.

State Mandates. This category of laws imposes obligations on individuals and local governments. For example, some states require that dogs and perhaps cats must be licensed by the age of three, four, five, or six months, but it is not uniform. Other states merely allow local governments at their option to license dogs and/or cats (e.g., Kentucky, South Dakota, and Texas). If they choose to exercise the option, state requirements must be followed when issuing licenses, and the issuance of licenses is linked to providing proof of rabies vaccinations, a requirement in all states. Other state mandates include how animals will be euthanized, the type of rabies vaccine to be administered, how dogs are determined to be dangerous, and how dangerous dogs are regulated. Some state statutes even designate which municipal office will issue dog licenses.

Proposed state mandates may generate controversy, and despite amendments to arrive at a compromise, may still have to be withdrawn. A case in point is Assembly Bill 1634 (AB1634) known as the California Healthy Pets Act that was withdrawn by its sponsor in early July 2007. This proposed law would require all dogs or cats over the age of four months to be spayed or neutered. Opposition came from some members of a state senate panel and from animal interest groups, although the bill had the support of animal control officials.

Enabling Legislation. These statutes empower local governments to pass ordinances addressing many types of animal issues including but not limited to dogs and cats running at large, operation of an animal shelter, ability to contract for animal control services, and setting fees for animal licenses. There is an erroneous assumption by some members of the public that municipalities and counties are required to have an animal shelter to house stray dogs and cats. There is more apt to be state enabling legislation that allows local governments to establish shelters should they choose to do so. In South Dakota, a statute gives county commissioners power under state law to establish a pound or pounds and appoint pound masters in areas outside of municipalities.[1]

A Connecticut animal statute addressing animal shelters contains provisions, both mandating action as well as enabling legislation, that gives local governments options on how to meet the mandate.[2]

Connecticut law mandates that cities and towns must provide and maintain an animal shelter for dogs, and the state agricultural commissioner may adopt regulations on how such shelters will be constructed and maintained. State law also allows cities and towns to meet these requirements in several ways: through a regional dog pound, through impoundment by a licensed veterinarian or licensed veterinary hospital, at a licensed commercial kennel, or a dog pound maintained by another city or town or some facility approved by the state agricultural commissioner.[3]

State Law as a Policy. When state legislatures enact animal laws they are setting public policy for the benefit of people and animals. Spaying/neutering of dogs and cats adopted from animal shelters, holding owners accountable for damages caused by their dogs, and requiring owners to confine dogs in heat are among examples of laws with policy implications. In enacting these provisions, legislatures are not only making sterilization a legal requirement, but also are taking steps to reduce the pet overpopulation problem (e.g., Missouri, New Mexico, Texas, and Montana). Holding owners accountable for their animals' behavior is another effort to place the responsibility where it belongs and to assist victims who otherwise might have an uphill battle in seeking a remedy.[4]

Conferring Enforcement Powers and "Prevent and Protect" Provisions in Law. Other statutes empower local law enforcement officers, whether they are animal control officers, code compliance officers, humane officers, or police officers, to enforce provisions of animal law. Some states have enacted provisions that say any interference with an animal control officer in the performance of official duties is a misdemeanor or worse. Provisions have also been enacted that prohibit leaving a dog or cat in an unattended vehicle, endangering the health or safety of the animal (Maryland). Animals left in closed cars on hot days have died from the effects of high heat in the vehicle.

What Happens If There Are No Laws or Laws Are Not Enforced?

Although state and local governments have enacted animal laws and ordinances that support their animal control programs, there continue to be jurisdictions without animal control programs and few if any local animal ordinances. Some jurisdictions for financial reasons choose to ignore state mandates that require local governments to enforce provisions applicable to dog and cats. Other local governments have chosen not to regulate until some major incident occurs and public opinion forces local officials to act. The phrase "animal control" infers there is authority to act, although the degree of authority varies from one jurisdiction to another. If local laws or ordinances do not exist, animal control personnel cannot exercise their responsibilities. Before examining how animal laws form an integral part of animal control programs, consider the following scenario where animal owner requirements are few and enforcement efforts lacking.

Example

State statute in State D allows but does not require local governments to enact local laws requiring that all dogs over the age of four months be licensed. The law requires that there must be a higher license fee for dogs that are not spayed or neutered. Another state law independent of licensing requires that all dogs must be vaccinated against rabies. State law is silent on whether local governments must have an animal control program or maintain an animal shelter. It is also silent about dog owner responsibilities.

Mr. B owns seven dogs, which he keeps outdoors on his quarter acre property. The town where he resides has a dog licensing requirement, but it is not enforced. Nor does the town have a leash law. Less than one hundred dogs are licensed each year out of an estimated dog population of 3,500. Mr. B does not have licenses for any of his animals. The town does not provide any animal care and control services. It is unknown if any of Mr. B's dogs have been vaccinated against rabies or if they receive regular veterinary care.

His dogs are frequently at large, and one day two of his dogs got loose, bolted from his yard, and attacked a four-year-old child who suffered internal injuries, required several stitches, and had to be hospitalized. A police officer happened upon the scene and rescued the child from further harm, but not before the officer had to shoot one of the dogs because it charged at him. Neighbors reported to town officials that on several occasions, one or more of Mr. B's dogs were at large and menaced other pets being walked by their owners. Town officials took no action. Each time complaints were filed they were either ignored by town officials or the mayor said the town had no authority to act. Complaints were also filed with the town about the odor of animal waste emanating from Mr. B's property.

Following the child biting incident, the police chief asked the town council to enact animal ordinances, hire an animal control officer who would report to the police chief, and empower police officers to also enforce animal ordinances if they witness violations.

Commentary. This example is troubling for many reasons. There is a public safety issue inasmuch as one or more of Mr. B's dogs have been shown to be dangerous. Since rabies vaccinations are state mandated, and it is unknown whether Mr. B's dogs were vaccinated against rabies, there is an increased risk to public health. Clearly the town needs to rethink the regulation of domestic pets.

Rationale for Enacting Laws and Ordinances

Problems caused by some domestic animals led in large part to passage of laws to protect people as well as animals. It was also caused by the failure of pet owners to take responsibility for the actions of their pets. Voluntary efforts to ensure appropriate animal behavior and to protect both the public at large as well as other animals have had limited success. Some animal control organizations prefer to continue to emphasize educating animal owners on their responsibilities over the law enforcement approach to get animal owners to comply. Overall, dangerous dog incidents and animals at large have been the motivation for proposing and enacting new and more restrictive ordinances.

Passage of animal laws has had many purposes and also conveys a message. First, the enactment of local and state animal control laws created a "legal toolbox" that can be used to resolve animal problems when other efforts failed. Second, these laws and ordinances very directly convey the message that animal owners will be held accountable for their animals' actions if laws are violated. The laws also serve as a reminder that keeping dogs and cats is a privilege that can be revoked.

The Failure of Voluntary Compliance

Many animal owners obviously prefer voluntary compliance, because it imposes no legal obligation to act responsibly. If voluntary compliance worked so well, why are so many animals impounded each year as strays? Why are thousands of pet owners cited each year for leash law violations?

There are many reasons. First, some animal owners do not value their pets and view them as disposable commodities if the animals do not live up to the owners expectations or the animals cause problems. The increase in animal abuse and dangerous dog incidents are examples. Second, educational efforts, while they are to be commended, are only a form of voluntary persuasion, and the results have been difficult to measure. Third, animal control has fewer deterrents and that contributes to reduced success of voluntary compliance. There are too few animal control officers to monitor animal behavior, and some local governments have only one animal control officer. Due to the small number of animal control officers in each community, they are simply spread too thin. Much of an officer's time is spent responding to calls for service on an established priority basis. Finally, as noted earlier, penalties for violations, until recently, have often been weak and ineffective.

This is changing as local officials have determined that nuisance animals and dangerous dog incidents require firm action to meet public demands for remedies. De Soto, Texas, is a recent example. The De Soto City Council enacted a new ordinance to take effect on October 1, 2007, that defines and bans dangerous dogs from that city and increases the penalties for dogs at large if there are repeat incidents. A fourth dog at large violation will cost the owner $2,000.

Voluntary compliance works best when there is a strong law enforcement deterrent and significant monetary penalties. For example, when motorists approach a traffic signal that has turned red, they stop. A police officer cannot be at every intersection to monitor traffic, but sober motorists know enough to realize that they run the risk of having an accident or worse if they drive through a red light. The injury/accident/death factor is a strong deterrent in addition to any penalties that may be levied by the motorist's insurance carrier, receiving a citation by a police officer, or loss of a driver's license.

Efforts to educate the public about how to care for their pets need to be pursued simultaneously with law enforcement efforts. This requires staffing and funding for both educational outreach and enforcement together with enactment of laws that firmly address issues at hand. Animal educational efforts have often fallen to animal welfare organizations, whereas enforcement has been an animal control responsibility, but this is changing also as animal control agencies increasingly are trying new ways to educate animal owners.

Here are a few examples in recent years where local officials turned to the law to remedy community animal problems:

- Sherwood, Oregon, approved an ordinance to fine anyone $250 who failed to clean up after an animal under the person's control defecates in a public place.[5]

- Minnesota approved a law effective January 1, 2005, imposing restrictions on wild animals after a seven-year-old girl was attacked by a four hundred pound Siberian tiger.[6] Owners of bears, lions, tigers, chimpanzees, and gorillas would be required to register with the local animal control authority.[7]

The Law as a Preventive Measure

Consider laws as tools to be used if needed. Enacting laws before they are needed, based in part on past history and future needs, is simply a preventive measure and good management. The absence of applicable laws to address a particular type of egregious behavior or problem means that considerable time and effort will be spent looking for other options that might help resolve the issue.

Drafting of most amendments and new ordinances usually occurs as a result of a horrific incident or a series of incidents that have generated complaints from the public, thus putting pressure on local officials to act. It is also the time when public support is at its highest. This is not to say there is a consensus on what needs to be in the ordinance. Rather, it is a call for action. When rushed to pass new legislation, there is but a short window of opportunity to examine the issues and develop an adoptable ordinance. Hastily prepared legislation may not address the problems and may instead generate significant opposition from the public that could doom its passage.

If there is no immediate crisis, and where politically possible, it is better to pursue a comprehensive revision of the animal control ordinance one time than to do it piecemeal. A complete revision or a new set of ordinances where none previously existed allows numerous issues to be examined at one time and will result in a more effective body of laws. All of this requires a strategy.

Strategy for Enacting an Ordinance or Amendment

Passage of an ordinance to meet a specific local need(s) is an exercise in legal draftsmanship and navigating through the political and public relations process. It is political because the topic is usually controversial, and those who support or oppose the proposed provisions will speak out and contact their elected representatives to convey their views to protect what they see as their personal interest. For example, professional dog breeders will step forward to oppose animal limits and mandatory sterilization of dogs and cats. The public relations process comes into play when trying to sell the local elected governing body and the community on the need for the ordinance.

There needs to be strategy that will carry the ordinance ideas forward into a firm written document, the outcome of which will be a new local law or ordinance. The following issues should be considered when crafting a strategy.

- Who will draft the ordinance provisions? Will it be only an attorney, or will others be involved?

- Will community input be sought before the proposal is submitted to the elected governing body for its review and comments?

- Who, what, where, when, and why? Who is the target group that the ordinance desires to reach? What is the purpose of the ordinance? Where does the ordinance fit in the scheme of animal control activities? When will the ordinance take effect? Why is it needed?

Since proposed local laws/ordinances are submitted to the local governing body for its review, there should be an opportunity for the public as well as governmental officials to review and offer comments prior to introduction of the ordinance. The biggest single mistake local government officials make when it comes to drafting and presenting a proposed animal control ordinance or amendment is to fail to take time to explain its purpose, anticipate the public's reaction, and to consider questions that may be raised. More commonly, the proposed ordinance or amendment is placed on the agenda of an upcoming city council or county governing body meeting as the case may be, and elected officials wait to see how it plays out. Potential and actual problems need to be identified and worked out in advance of the public meeting so the proposal can be presented with strong and broad support to ensure its passage.

The proposed ordinance or amendment needs to be explained, both orally and in writing. A handout that summarizes the contents of the proposal and addresses anticipated questions and offers answers will help defuse opposition and promote passage. Copies of the proposed ordinance or amendment and the written handout needs to be available at or in advance of the public meeting.

Elected officials could argue that they do not take these extra steps for other proposals that come before their respective body, nor are they obligated to do so here. True, but animal control issues are unique and more sensitive and controversial. If it is deemed that there is an urgent need for the proposal, then the time spent to draft it will be for naught if it is hastily presented and opponents are allowed to derail it without having the facts. Local officials must be prepared to explain and justify new legislation, backed up by factual data. The public's mind needs to be put at ease that the proposal is not an attack on pet owners, but about protecting the public and/or their companion animals.

Another useful but different strategy for enacting a local animal ordinance was developed by Mike Burgwin, a former animal control director. His approach encompasses determining the need for and creating a demand for an ordinance and the use of a committee to write the appropriate provision(s) into the municipal or county code.[8]

Explaining the Proposed Ordinance to the Public

Before presenting the proposed ordinance or amendment, those responsible for carrying the ball on this matter need to consider potential questions that could be raised and how to respond to those questions. The following illustrations offer some examples.

If the proposed ordinance limits the number of animals per residence, regulates animal breeders, or makes it a violation to allow dogs to run at large, the following questions and answers are offered as a guide in preparing a response.

Question: Does the proposed ordinance limit the number of pets I can have, and do I have to get rid of some of my animals if I am over the limit allowed by law?

Answer: No one will be required to give away or otherwise dispose of their animals if they possessed the animals prior to the date the law takes effect. The law limits each household to three dogs and cats in any combination. Individuals who have more animals than allowed by law when the law becomes effective can keep their pets as long as the pets and the owner live at the same address. If the animal dies, if the animal moves to another location, if the pet owner moves away, when the property is sold, or when new occupants move in, then and only then will the limit take effect. This is called a grandfather clause.

Question: I have raised Bedlington terriers as show dogs from my home for more than twenty years and breed them periodically. I have been active in numerous professional dog fancier groups, and in all of the time I have lived in this city I have never had a complaint lodged against me by my neighbors or by animal control. Why are you doing this to me? I am a law-abiding citizen.

Answer: Thank you for raising this question. First of all, you are neither the problem nor the target. You can continue to raise your breed-specific dogs as long as you are in compliance with local zoning regulations, you keep your premises clean, and you take care of your animals. You will need to fill out an application to obtain a breeder's kennel permit and pay the annual fee of $100. If any of the dogs are over the age of four months, they must be licensed as required by state law. When you apply for the permit you agree to its terms and conditions. The committee that developed the proposed ordinance included some professional breeders like yourself who are sensitive to your concerns. While we have had problems with owners of multiple animals, those who are responsible animal owners have nothing to fear, and we appreciate your understanding and cooperation.

Question: Why are you requiring dogs to be on a leash? Loose running dogs are a minor nuisance at best. My dog never gets loose. Why are you after those of us who are responsible pet owners? This law is unnecessary and unfair.

Answer: During 2005, animal control responded to 145 complaints about loose running animals that were causing property damage or attacking other dogs. There were eleven bite reports filed and investigated and six reported incidents of dog packs frightening children in school yards when schools were in session. During the first three months of this year alone, there were seventy reports of loose running dog incidents and five bite cases involving dogs at large. Forty percent of the dogs reported as running at large this year to date had no collar or other visible identification. We are happy to hear that your dog is not one of the problem dogs, but the city council is obligated to protect public health and safety.

Assessing Community Needs and Changes in Law

Community demographics, characteristics of the domestic pet population. and past experience can help determine what provisions are needed in law. For example, if the local jurisdiction has residents who own, breed, or keep horses or keep other livestock, do local ordinances address potential livestock problems?

Communities with numerous apartment complexes or those with many single family homes on large lots may influence the type of pets that are kept by residents and may be a factor in proposing changes in law, particularly if there are nuisance animal problems. Noisy animals in an apartment can be just as problematic as barking dogs in a large yard in a suburban community. Laws requiring dog owners to clean up their animals' waste from sidewalks, lawns, or other areas have been enacted in many communities. Where more than one language is spoken in the community, animal control officials may find it to be advantageous as well as necessary to publicize information in other languages in addition to English.

The more open space available, the more likely that dogs and cats will be allowed to run at large, especially if residences are not close together. In other words, animal owners may pay less heed to observing leash law requirements and perhaps even ignore rabies vaccination requirements for their dogs if neighbors do not complain or enforcement is lax. That is no excuse for not enacting the appropriate provisions in law. While the expense of enforcement is an important cost factor, enacting laws to address problems is a minor, one-time expense. Public health and public safety concerns may override any other objections to enacting changes in law.

Generally, animal control problems that continually recur and are brought to the attention of local elected officials will be referred to an attorney with a request to draft the necessary ordinance or amendment. Valuable input on animal issues and proposed local ordinance provisions can be obtained from police, code compliance officials, veterinarians, city council members, and residents. Local animal welfare groups can also be quite helpful.

Training Animal Control Officers to Enforce the Laws

Training officers in how to enforce animal laws is critical to job performance and may be required by statute. Training requirements for animal control officers vary from state to state. Among the training programs offered to animal control officers are those that cover enforcement of animal laws and related topics that are important in pursuing criminal cases. Pennsylvania, for example, has a state mandated training program for persons who desire to be appointed as Certified Humane Police Officers. The training is offered by the National Animal Control Association and consists of twelve training topics:[9]

Role of the Cruelty Investigator

Stages of the Investigation

The Job of the Pennsylvania Humane Police Officer

Pennsylvania Humane Laws

Laws and the Legal System

Rules of Evidence

Search and Seizure

Report Writing

Evidence Collection

Courtroom Testimony

Interview and Interrogation

Photography, Sketching, and Videotaping

The Texas state health agency offers training in animal law in its basic and advanced courses. The department also makes available an *Animal Control Officer Training Manual*[10] that contains information about several Texas animal statutes. New Jersey offers several animal control training courses including cruelty investigation. California offers an eighty hour, ten day Animal Law Enforcement Training Academy that is sponsored by Marin Humane Society, The State Humane Association of California, and Santa Rosa Junior College. Michigan requires that animal control officers have a minimum of one hundred hours of training before they can be hired by a local government, and this training must include laws and regulations. Dr. Steven L. Halstead, a veterinarian who is Companion Animal Program Manager in the Michigan Department of Agriculture, explained in a memorandum the need for one hundred hours of mandatory training required in state law: "The reason for this law is to assure that the animal control officer has had at least a minimal amount of training so that public health, safety, and animal welfare law are appropriately protected."[11]

Partnering With the Local Government Attorney

It may be taken for granted that the local government attorney(s) drafts ordinances, but that does little to explain the attorney's role or explain how animal control officials and the attorney can work productively together. The attorney is the legal advisor for local government departments and programs and is a legally trained professional whose expertise carries weight in the courts, just as an animal control professional is a specialist in animal matters. The following description of the services provided by the city attorney in a city in California illustrates the scope of responsibilities of that office:

> The Office of the City Attorney represents and advises the City Council and all city officers in matters of law pertaining to their offices; represents and appears for the City in any action or proceedings in which the City is concerned or is a party; and represents and appears for any City officer or employees, or former City officer or employee, in actions and proceedings in which such officer or employee is concerned or is a party for acts arising out of his/her employment or by reason of his/her official capacity.

> The Office of the City Attorney approves the form of all contracts made by and all bonds and certificates of insurance given to the City, and prepares any and all proposed ordinances or resolutions for the City and amendments thereto.[12]

Law enforcement is an integral part of an animal control program, and for that reason alone, animal control officials need to understand how they can work with an attorney who can advise them on enforcement and related legal issues affecting the program. The relationship may be ongoing or occasional, but it is mutually beneficial when each party understands the role of the other.

An attorney who drafts animal control ordinances and offers legal counsel in specific instances can be more helpful when the attorney understands the duties and responsibilities of animal control personnel and how those duties are linked to local ordinances and state laws. Animal control officials must be prepared to assist the attorney and provide additional information if requested.

Animal control management needs to review animal control ordinances at least annually and to recommend changes based on the past year's experiences, changes in state law, and any issues that have arisen in the enforcement of local ordinances. It should prove helpful to talk informally with appropriate senior level local government officials as well as the attorney who handles animal control matters prior to submitting recommended changes in order to get a sense of how and when to proceed further. The animal control director to the extent possible should keep the attorney informed of recent judicial decisions and statutory changes that may affect the program.

What are the animal control manager's responsibilities in this relationship? First, any issues that may have legal implications should be brought to the attorney's attention as soon as possible. Second, it is important that animal control management be kept in the loop on any matter where the attorney is involved, because management is ultimately accountable for program operations, and there needs to be a clear understanding of the advice provided by the attorney to all concerned. Likewise, the attorney also needs to be kept informed of any actions taken by animal control based on legal advice provided.

Development of a Law Enforcement Strategy

Animal control officers attending training programs learn the fundamentals of law enforcement, but that is only part of the bigger picture. There needs to be certain provisions enacted into ordinance that are priorities for enforcement and that establish a level playing field in which all the players, animal owners, the general public, and local officials, understand the ground rules. The following are some basic provisions that will help the community protect its animals, allow the community to be animal friendly, and to protect public safety all for the common good:

- Define responsible ownership requirements in law.

- Consider establishing dog and cat limits as one means of controlling the local animal population and irresponsible animal owners. It can address the problem of hoarding, but implementing animal limits per household can be controversial.

- Require dogs and preferably cats, too, be licensed. There are many health and safety benefits.

- Establish nuisance laws that define unacceptable behavior by dogs and other pets, and hold their owners accountable.

- Enact local provisions to regulate dangerous dogs, unless there are comparable provisions in state law that can be enforced.

Case Study of an Ordinance Problem

Not every ordinance creates a solution to a problem. Sometimes the ordinance is a problem as demonstrated by the following case study based on an actual experience in one United States city.

The city planning department with some input from animal control drafted a proposed ordinance regulating the keeping of potbellied pigs in residential dwellings. The proposed ordinance required the purchase of a license for the animal and limited its weight to 150 pounds. Interestingly enough, the proposed ordinance authorized code compliance officers as well as animal control officers to enforce the provisions of this ordinance, although its provisions were in the animal control chapter of the municipal code.

Once the proposed ordinance was submitted to city council for review and approval, problems arose. A city council member thought that allowing only one pig in a residential dwelling would make the animal lonely without a companion and asked to have the proposed ordinance amended to allow two potbellied pigs per household. This change was made. The second problem was one of staff oversight. The ordinance required that the city council establish a license fee for this animal by resolution. In the rush to enact the ordinance, the resolution was not prepared. When the problem was discovered four months later, a resolution was drafted, and a license fee of $50 was proposed based on the city's costs to process and issue a license. When the resolution was introduced, one potbellied pig owner appeared at city council to object to the fee being too high. Another council member asked staff to review the proposed fee and to report back to a designated council committee in ninety days. Following the council meeting, the council member who requested the ordinance be drafted and who subsequently asked to have it referred to a committee privately asked the animal control director to take no action on this matter for an indefinite period. Over the next eighteen months, three applicants for potbellied pig licenses applied and were told that the license fee had not been set by council, but they could continue to keep their respective animals and would be notified when the license fee had been approved.

Animal Lawyers

A development in recent years in the legal profession has been the emergence of a new legal specialty known as "animal law." Throughout the country there are now attorneys who specialize in animal issues. Among recent developments in animal law are courses offered in this subject at some American law schools, the publication of an animal law journal at a west coast law school, the publication of the first casebook on animal law, and the establishment of state bar committee sections on animal law. This also coincides with the enactment of new and stronger city and state animal welfare legislation and an increase in the number of animal law cases. Animal control officials should not be surprised to be contacted by one of these attorney specialists representing a client who may have an animal control grievance.

What is animal law? Animal law is very broad based and may include a wide range of legal issues that apply to animals. Animal control agencies will be more familiar with issues relating to companion animals and livestock.

What does this mean for animal control officials? Local animal control officials recognize that as times change, there are also new challenges from pet owners. Animal owners are increasingly suing local governments for damages in a whole host of animal control-related issues. Local animal control officials may find themselves challenged for their actions, even when they had acted properly, because some pet owners and others did not agree with their actions.

Animal control programs are increasingly being viewed under a microscope by animal lawyers, particularly when their clients' pets come into contact with an animal shelter and when the animal owner has had an unpleasant experience with shelter or field staff.

Local animal control advisory committees already exist in many cities and towns as a component of the local animal control program. When animal activists, who are also lawyers and may have an interest in animal law, serve on such committees, the opportunities exist for animal control officials and lawyers to engage in discussion of ideas and to work in collaboration on issues of mutual concern to improve the lives of animals.

State animal control associations may wish to consider inviting as a speaker a representative of the animal law section of the state bar association to hear his or her views on animal law as it pertains to their animal control programs.

SUMMARY

Animal control laws provide the legal basis for many services and responsibilities assigned to animal control programs and agencies. Animal laws vary by state, and local ordinances also differ from one community to another. State statutes determine what local governments must do to comply with state animal laws and what they may do if they so choose. State laws have public policy objectives to promote the humane care of dogs and cats in particular and to impose penalties upon those found to have violated those standards of care or other provisions in the statutes.

Providing humane care of domestic pets through voluntary compliance, the preferred choice of some animal interest groups, has not been effective. Continuing attacks by dangerous dogs upon animals and people and ongoing cases of animal cruelty have led to the passage of tougher local animal laws and ordinances. When owners violate these new laws, they face stiffer fines, greater restrictions imposed on dangerous animals, and the possibility of jail time for the owner in the more egregious situations. Enacting tougher local laws and ordinances requires a carefully developed strategy to ensure that there is ample local support for the proposed new laws or changes to existing laws that will not be derailed by opponents.

Another important but often underestimated aspect of developing animal laws/ordinances is the need to pay heed to the advice of the attorney charged with preparing the ordinance or changes in law. Although local officials may be clear on what they want the law to say, it is the attorney's responsibility to draft provisions that are compatible with requirements in state law and that will be upheld should the provisions be challenged in court. A collaborative and productive relationship between the animal control director and the attorney is needed and can be mutually beneficial.

The relatively new legal specialty of animal law has seen the appearance of more lawyers practicing or adding animal law to their practices. These attorneys have represented pet owners on animal control issues, and in the future, animal control directors may expect to receive more calls from attorneys practicing animal law.

Notes

1. *South Dakota Codified Laws*, Title 40, ch. 40-34, sec.9.

2. *General Statutes of Connecticut*, Title 22, ch. 435, secs. 22-327 to 22-367(a).

3. *General Statutes of Connecticut*, Title 22, ch. 435, sec. 22-336.

4. This is demonstrated in ordinance changes relating to dangerous dogs.

5. City of Sherwood, Oregon, Municipal Code, Title 6, secs. 6.04.040 and 6.04.100.

6. *Minnesota Statutes*, ch. 346.155, Subd. 1 and 2, effective January 1, 2005.

7. *Minnesota*, Ibid. Subd. 3, effective January 1, 2005.

8. Darlene Wohler Larson, ed., *National Animal Control Association Training Guide*, Chapter 4, "City and County Animal Regulations," by Mike Burgwin, 4-3. (Kansas City, MO: National Animal Control Association, 2000), by permission of the publisher.

9. National Animal Control Association, "Pennsylvania Humane Officer Training Program," by permission. http://www.nacanet.org/pahumane.html.

10. Pamela J. Wilson, ed., *Animal Control Officer Training Manual*, Texas Department of Health, Zoonosis Control Division, (Austin, Texas: Texas Department of Health, 1997), revised September 2003.

11. Michigan Department of Agriculture, Memorandum From Steven L. Halstead, D.V.M., Subject: "Animal Control Officer Pursuant to the Dog Law," May 18, 2000. http://www.michigan.gov/mda (accessed July 24, 2007).

12. City of Riverside, California, *Annual Budget 2003/04 Preliminary*, 105.

Chapter 13

Provisions in Animal Law

INTRODUCTION

There are two important questions at the outset. The first question is what provisions should be enacted into law? The second question is should it be state or local law? The response to the first question is it depends on the issue, what the state requires, and the extent of regulation sought. Statutory requirements may mandate local governments assume certain animal-related duties that will lead to the enactment of local laws to implement the mandate. Local officials may conclude that they need greater regulation than authorized in state statute and will enact provisions that go beyond what is in the statute. Having an animal issue addressed in a state statute makes it applicable and uniform throughout the state, unless the statute says otherwise. Since state law supersedes local law, local ordinances may be more restrictive than state law, but not less restrictive. The response to the second question depends on whether an animal issue has statewide implications, there is broad, statewide local support from animal control officials and animal welfare advocates, and if there is the political will and enough support in the state legislature to pass the bill. Some bills fail the first time but may be introduced again with modifications in the future to assure passage. Since some animal issues are viewed as a problem in one community but not in another, the local ordinance route may be preferred as it is quicker to implement and can be tailored to local needs if officials have the power and will to act.

This chapter lists and discusses some of the more common clauses in local laws/ordinances that are needed by local animal control officials to implement an animal services program, and there are references to state statute requirements as needed. Since municipalities and counties derive their powers from the state, local laws or ordinances cannot contravene state statutes. This can limit what local governments can regulate.

It is not uncommon to find provisions in state statutes while also seeing similar animal topics/issues addressed in municipal and county animal ordinances, because many localities share similar problems. Ordinances vary in the requirements imposed, how terms are defined, and penalties levied. State statutory provisions, the number of square miles of the community, the size of the human as well as dog and cat populations, community demographics, and what local elected officials and others consider as priorities to be enacted into law all impact what becomes local law.

A review of local animal ordinances indicates a range of issues addressed in municipal and county codes. Reviewing the scope of the topics covered in the ordinances reveals four broad topic categories and provisions that overlap from one category to another:

- Legal requirements to be met by animal owners/harborers.

- Prohibited acts against animals.

- Dangers and problems posed by animals.

- Requirements to be met in the operation of an animal control program.

Viewing animal laws by categories makes it easier to identify what needs to be enacted into law as each category has its own target of compliance. The first category aimed at animal owners is intended to make them responsible for the care of their animals. Unless some minimum standards of care are mandated by law, the care given to animals by their owners will vary, and some animals will receive an unacceptable level of care that can be harmful to them. The second category is intended to identify and define those acts that are deemed a crime committed against or upon animals and the penalties imposed upon those who inflict such acts, because they are considered to be inhumane. The third category of provisions in law addresses the perils of keeping dangerous, wild, and uncontrolled animals. In this category, the law makes clear to the owners of dangerous dogs that such animals have been found to be a threat to public health and safety, and if permitted to keep such animals, the owner must comply with terms and conditions mandated by law to remove those risks. Failure to comply may result in applying penalties, some of which are severe. The last category of laws is intended to assure that those who operate animal care and control programs provide an acceptable level of service that assures control when needed, appropriate care of the animals, the necessary authority to act, and that animal owners and the public at large are treated fairly and equitably. This last category may also impose other requirements on public, nonprofit, or private animal control entities and programs. Exhibits 13-1 through 13-4 show examples in all four categories.

Ordinances describe the powers and duties of animal control personnel and may address requirements imposed on others who care for or harbor animals such as veterinarians who administer rabies vaccinations, kennel operators, pet shops, and traveling animal exhibitions. Policies and procedures to be followed in animal control programs are either authorized by or prescribed in the ordinance. Local law (or ordinance) may confer upon local animal control officials power to enact rules and regulations to implement provisions in law. For example, the ordinance or law may specify in detail how euthanasia will be administered or may require that an administrative procedure be created to approve the transfer of animals to rescue groups for placement in new homes. Lastly, there are provisions that apply directly to animals and their owners including criteria on the care of animals. Some ordinances are only a few pages, but others are a dozen or more pages containing very detailed clauses. The detail found in each provision is an indication of the extent of regulation sought by local officials. Local laws may apply to many species of animals and not just dogs and cats.

This chapter does not profess to offer legal advice. Only an attorney can offer legal advice. The author's commentaries and recommendations are highlighting what has and can be done at the local government level.

Exhibit 13-1

Animal Owner Requirements in Law*

Care of Animals

- Provide fresh food and water daily

- Provide appropriate indoor and outdoor shelter

- Licensing and rabies vaccination

- Removal of animal waste

- Maintenance of sanitary conditions in the animal's living area

- Grooming of an animal when the animal is in pain or distress or is unable to move, rise, walk, or cries out in pain due to failure to groom the animal as needed (ordinance in Jackson County, Michigan)

Prohibited Acts

- Running at large (dogs, cats, livestock, and poultry)
- Failure to provide veterinary care to sick/injured animals
- Creating a public nuisance
- Allowing an animal to be a threat to public safety
- Animal damaging another's property
- Maintaining a diseased animal that is dangerous to public health
- Offering any live animal or fowl as a prize or giveaway in a contest, raffle, or promotion
  *Terms used such as shelter and public nuisance need to be defined.

Exhibit 13-2

Prohibited Acts, Nuisances, and Restrictions Imposed

Acts of Cruelty

- Abandonment or neglect of animals
- Tethering
- Animal fighting
- Torturing, mutilation, wounding, injuring, or poisoning an animal
- Keeping an animal in an enclosed vehicle under adverse conditions
- Use of spring loaded or foothold traps, except by government agencies
- Drivers who hit or run over a dog or cat should attempt to notify pet owner and/or the authorities (required by New York law)

Public Nuisances

- Habitual or continual barking, howling, crying, or other noise
- Allowing an animal to damage the property of others
- Maintaining an animal in an unsanitary environment
- Maintaining animal owner's property in a manner that is offensive, annoying, or dangerous to public health, safety, or welfare
- Keeping an animal that habitually or repeatedly chases, snaps, attacks, or barks at pedestrians, joggers, animals on a leash controlled by their owners, people riding bicycles, or other vehicles
- If the same animal is found at large three or more times, additional penalties may/will apply

- Causing unreasonable fouling of the air by odors attributed to animals
- Allowing a dead animal to lie exposed or unburied for more than twelve hours

Wild Animal Prohibitions /Restrictions

- Keeping any dangerous wild animals, except as provided by law. Exceptions: zoos, performing animal exhibitions, circuses, and registered wildlife rehabilitators
- Prohibiting the feeding of coyotes

Exhibit 13-3

Provisions Related to Dangerous Animals

Requirements in Law

- Registration of dangerous animals in addition to licensing requirement
- Secure confinement whether indoors or outdoors
- Leashed and muzzled when outside of a secure enclosure and in the physical control of the owner
- Posting signs warning of the presence of a dangerous dog
- Notify local authorities if the dog escapes custody of its owner
- Inspection of confinement facilities by animal control officers/officials
- Owner compliance with quarantine procedures where applicable
- Owner shall provide proof of insurance if dog is declared dangerous
- Authority of animal control director to issue regulations pertaining to dangerous dogs
- Animal must wear a collar of color and type provided by animal control that readily identifies the dog as dangerous/vicious
- Penalties for violation of those requirements (particularly if the dog attacks a human or another animal) could include but are not limited to impoundment and/or euthanization
- Spaying/neutering

Exhibit 13-4

Provisions in Law Relating to Operation of an Animal Control Program

Powers, Duties, and Prohibitions

- Authority to operate an animal control program and how it shall be operated (e.g., minimal impoundment periods)

- Enforcement of state and/or local animal laws

- Authority to enact rules and regulations as permitted by law

- Prohibit interference with animal control personnel in the performance of their duties including unauthorized removal of an animal from an animal control vehicle or animal shelter or to submit a false report to an animal control officer

- Authority to enter private property to check on animals for specific purposes as allowed by law

- Conduct hearings to determine if an animal is to be deemed dangerous.

- Collect monies for licenses, fees, etc., and remitting them to the proper authority

- Keep records of monies collected, animals impounded, bite cases, and other records as may be required by state/local law.

- Return animals to their owners in accordance with procedures stated in law

- Enforce requirements of animal limits per residence where the law limits the number of pets.

- Issue, suspend, or revoke licenses and permits.

- Inspection of facilities where animals are sold, boarded, on exhibition, or display such as pet shops, circuses, boarding, or breeding kennels

- Impoundment of stray, abandoned, abused, and/or dangerous animals

- Disposal of unredeemed animals (e.g., adoption, transfer to rescue groups, euthanasia)

- Authority to quarantine animals

- Requirement to submit for testing any animal suspected of being rabid, particularly one that has bitten a human or another animal

- Conduct investigations including but not limited to cruelty and animal bite cases

- Any exceptions/exclusions in law should be clearly stated

PROVISIONS FOUND IN LOCAL LAW/ORDINANCES

This section identifies and explains some of the more common legal requirements set forth in local laws/ordinances. Some provisions that appear in one city's ordinance may not appear in another's due to priorities, policies, and the political climate. Enacting a comprehensive animal ordinance gives animal control authorities the immediate power to address many issues and problems when needed, rather having to search for options to be used or to discover there is no power to act.

Definitions. Located at the beginning of the ordinance are terms used and defined in the law. For example, when the term "owner" is used in an ordinance, it often applies not only to the person owning the animal, but to anyone who is in charge of, has custody of, provides food or shelter for, or takes care of the animal. An ordinance may further expand the definition of owner to include a group of persons, a firm, a partnership, a corporation, organization, or an association. Some ordinances contain numerous terms and definitions while others list and define only a few. The Jackson County (Michigan) animal ordinance contains sixty definitions. The Cobb County (Georgia) animal ordinance (Ch. 10, sec. 10-1) defines the term "hoarder" three ways:

Hoarder—A person or entity that:

(a) Collects animals and fails to provide them with humane care/adequate care;

(b) Collects dead animals that are not properly disposed of as required by this chapter; or

(c) Collects, houses, or harbors animals in filthy, unsanitary conditions that constitute a health hazard to the animals kept and/or to the animals or residents of adjacent property.

Definitions are an indication of how broadly or narrowly the ordinance is to be construed. Broadly defined terms may be preferred so they may be applied to some new and unanticipated occurrences but may be challenged in court at a later date.

Penalties. Ordinances address penalties in several ways. Some define any violation as either an infraction or a misdemeanor and may state the dollar amount of the fine for the first and each successive offense. There are also other non-monetary penalties that may apply including imprisonment of the owner. Violations of state animal statutes may be a felony, misdemeanor or infraction as defined in the law and subject to monetary fines and/or imprisonment.

Powers, Duties, and Responsibilities of Animal Control Officials. Ordinances convey to animal control officials powers, duties, and responsibilities necessary to implement the program requirements. For example, the Grand Prairie, Texas, ordinance (Ch. 5, Article 1, sec. 5-2) contains a section that establishes the office of animal control and enumerates its many responsibilities. These include but are not limited to:

- Acting as the local rabies control authority

- Employment of animal control officers to assist the manager

- Administer and enforce all animal related laws and regulations of the state

- Supervise animal control operations

- Authority to impound, redeem, adopt out, or destroy animals

Similarly, a section of the Salt Lake City, Utah, ordinance lists the powers and duties of the animal control director and other animal services personnel. Other responsibilities found in local ordinances include minimum training/certification requirements, authority to enter private property to determine compliance with local ordinances and state statutes, and investigation of dangerous dog and animal cruelty complaints.

Licensing. Some jurisdictions require only dogs to be licensed, but others mandate cats, ferrets, and even potbellied pigs. Usually, dogs over the age of three or four months must be licensed or registered in the community where the owner resides. The age at which licensing is required varies by state. When combined with the requirement of a rabies vaccination, there must be documentation that verifies that the licensed animal is protected against this health risk. Anchorage, Alaska, is among those jurisdictions requiring that any nonresident who brings a dog into that municipality for a period of more than thirty days but less than ninety days must obtain a nonresident dog license at no charge, but must provide proof that the dog possesses a current rabies vaccination.

A substantial number of pet owners ignore the licensing requirement and take their chances of keeping an unlicensed animal, but there are available incentives to help reduce the number of unlicensed pets. For example, a temporary amnesty period allowed by ordinance could waive any penalties for the registration or licensing of dogs and cats over the age of four months for a period of thirty to forty-five days. Another incentive would be to reduce the registration or licensing fee to promote compliance. Evidence of rabies vaccination would still be required, because it is mandated by state law.

Many states and local jurisdictions have a provision in law for a two-tier license fee structure that sets lower fees for altered dogs and cats. Owners must show a spay/neuter certificate obtained from their veterinarian. States like New York offer reduced license fees for senior citizens. This encourages better identification and some control of the local dog and cat population. The process for adjusting license fees should be similar to that of changing other fees and charges.

Rabies Control. Rabies prevention and control is one of animal control's most important responsibilities, which it shares with state and local health agencies. Only Hawaii is free of rabies, and even that state has strict laws and procedures to be followed to make sure that rabies does not gain a foothold. Rabies vaccination is a requirement in all states, and provisions in local ordinances must at least adhere to requirements in state law. Dogs, cats, ferrets, wolf-hybrids, and other species may be required to be vaccinated against rabies. Local ordinances reflect state rabies prevention and control requirements and impose specific responsibilities on animal owners, veterinarians, animal control, and health officials. The American Veterinary Medical Association has proposed a model rabies control ordinance that can be found at www. avma.org.

Animals that have bitten a human and/or have had contact with another animal and are suspected of being rabid, exhibited signs of rabies, or have not been vaccinated against rabies must be quarantined by law. Provisions in the Cook County, Illinois, animal ordinance specify more detailed requirements on rabies vaccinations including procedures to be followed when the biting animal is capable of transmitting rabies and in confirmed rabies cases. Cook County also has detailed regulations covering animal bite report procedures for veterinarians, filing of rabies vaccination certificates, and the submission of specimens for rabies virus analysis. This ordinance also specifies penalties for owners who fail to obey rabies requirements in law.

Every ordinance has its exceptions. For example, the Garrett County, Maryland, ordinance exempts veterinary hospitals and clinics, authentic research facilities, seeing eye dogs, and governmental police dogs from the rabies requirements. Nonresidents of Garrett County who bring their dogs into that county for not more than thirty days are exempt from other ordinance provisions if they have proof of a valid rabies certificate from another jurisdiction.

Potentially Dangerous and Dangerous Dogs. These provisions are written to protect people from animal attacks and to restrict the movement of these animals. Some local ordinances have drawn a distinction between "dangerous" and "potentially dangerous dogs," which means that there is a difference in how the dogs and their owners are treated by law. Louisville, Kentucky, allows its animal control director to declare a potentially dangerous dog to include one when unprovoked and in an aggressive manner bites, scratches, or bruises a person or when unrestrained, bites, injures, or kills another domestic pet or properly restrained livestock. That city defines "dangerous" to include any dog that commits a severe attack, inflicts death or serious injury to any person, maims or kills domestic pets or livestock when not under restraint, is used in the commission of a crime as specified in the state penal code, is declared a dangerous dog by the animal control director, or any dog kept primarily for the purpose of fighting or harming other animals. Hunting dogs are excluded from this definition. The animal control ordinance of Westminster, Vermont, states that animals that are diseased and dangerous to the public health are classified as dangerous animals.

In December 2003, Pawtucket, Rhode Island, approved a pit bull ordinance that prohibited any additional pit bulls residing in that city except for those already there. Boston, Massachusetts, appears to be unique in requiring that the owner or keeper of a pit bull (a pit bull being defined in the judgment of an animal control officer) must provide a letter of permission from the landlord if the animal owner or keeper is not the owner of the premises where the dog resides.

Generally, when a dog is deemed to be potentially dangerous, it could mean that the animal has bitten someone one or more times without provocation or has injured or killed another animal. Another city's ordinance has defined "potentially dangerous" to include a dog or cat that when unprovoked approaches and chases a person in an "apparent attitude of attack" or has a "known propensity" to attack unprovoked, causing injury or otherwise threatening the safety of humans or domestic animals. Local ordinances have been found to give animal control officials authority to designate an animal *potentially dangerous* and to set certain conditions for keeping such animal.

Determining an animal to be *dangerous* (as opposed to potentially dangerous) is a more serious finding and requires the owner to comply with additional terms and conditions. Conditions include having the animal leashed and muzzled when outside of a building, kept in an enclosure in secure confinement, posting a sign of dangerous animal, notifying authorities should the dog escape from its enclosure or the custody of its owner, keeper, or harborer, and provide proof of liability insurance. Some states (e.g., New York) require dangerous dogs to be spayed/neutered. Dangerous dogs must be specially registered and have to be quarantined or confined pursuant to a court order. Some local jurisdictions have determined that pit bulls and some related breeds are not only dangerous, but have banned them as pets. Some of these laws have been overturned if the ban is solely based on the breed as opposed to actions of the dog. More discussion of pit bulls as dangerous animals is found in Chapter 14.

Dangerous Dog Registry. A few states have implemented dangerous dog registries that place an obligation to list dogs declared dangerous by local officials or the courts in a registry. Virginia requires the dog owner to renew registry information each January. The registry functions similarly to a sex offender registry and permits individuals to check if dangerous dogs reside in their area. Colorado law C.R.S. 18-9-204.05 requires that any dog owner convicted of unlawful ownership of a dangerous dog under state statute (but not city or county convictions) must register that dog in Colorado's dangerous dog registry along with other requirements imposed. New York state law requires that all dangerous dogs be reported to the municipality where the dog resides or is harbored. Texas also requires the registration of dangerous dogs with local authorities. A bill to create a statewide dangerous dog registry in Massachusetts was introduced on August 29, 2007. The registration of dangerous dogs makes animal control aware of their presence in the community, and this information can be made available to the public. However, in the interest of public safety and to ensure that the animals' owners comply with the law, animal control officials need to periodically check on these animals.

Animal Limits. Communities without animal limits encourage problems in several ways. Owners of multiple animals who do not adequately care for their pets may seek out other jurisdictions to move to that do not limit the number of dogs or cats. Failure to set animal limits contributes to expanding the workload and increases the costs of the animal control program. Multiple animals per household can contribute to nuisances such as noise and odor. Irresponsible pet owners contribute to the deterioration of the quality of life in a neighborhood when they allow their animals to be an ongoing nuisance and have neighbors complaining to animal control authorities. Animal limits help control pet overpopulation, act as an inhibitor to the growth of community animal problems, and promote pet owner responsibility by limiting the number of animals that require care. A jurisdiction that by law limits the number of dogs/cats per residence has a tool at its disposal to discourage animal hoarders and other irresponsible animal owners. If an animal limit is established, those above the limit at the time the ordinance becomes effective may be allowed to keep their animals under a grandfather clause.

There is another argument put forth by animal advocates that the solution lies in requiring all dogs and cats to be spayed or neutered rather than having arbitrarily set animal limits. Spay/neuter advocates contend that altered animals do not roam unlike unaltered animals.

Those who possess more animals than allowed by law would need to secure a permit that would require compliance with terms and conditions to assure that adequate care would be provided to the animals. Those required to obtain a permit would include kennels, catteries, breeders, and boarding facilities. They might also be subject to any applicable zoning requirements as well. Those conditions often include compliance with the zoning code, keeping the animal areas in sanitary condition, inspection of the premises by animal control, and licensing of all animals. Failure to meet the conditions would lead to suspension or revocation of the permit and removal of any animals over the legally allowed limit. Some local ordinances also impose limitations (or prohibition) on other animals such as poultry or swine, but this may be more a zoning rather than an animal control issue.

Special Permits. Local regulation of certain animal-related activities may be authorized for the purpose of promoting the humane care of animals. Local animal control officials may be empowered to issue permits that require compliance with terms and conditions that allow local authorities to act if animals are found to be abused or neglected.

Examples of Special Permit Requirements

- Pet shops
- Keeping of crime prevention animals
- Public animal assemblies (e.g., dog and/or cat shows)
- Kennels and/or catteries where animals are boarded, bred, sold, or trained
- Commercial major animal breeders as defined by law
- Minor animal breeders as defined by law
- Veterinary hospitals/clinics
- Animal grooming establishments
- Animal exhibitions where animals perform
- Large animal permits (only where zoned agricultural)
- Certain species of wild or exotic animals
- Animal rescuers, shelters, and sanctuaries

The permit fees may be enacted by ordinance or some other means. The ordinance should also contain clauses on how to appeal denial or revocation of a permit and any exemptions allowed. The Riverside County, California, animal control ordinance (Ordinance 630.7) requires animal rescuers obtain a permit from the county animal control agency and adhere to certain terms and conditions. See Chapter 9 for further discussion about animal rescuers and groups.

Impoundment of Animals. Taking animals into custody (impoundment) to protect them from further harm or to alleviate a danger to the community is one of the powers that must be statutorily delegated to animal control officers as part of their law enforcement tool basket. Abandoned, abused, lost, sick, injured, or dangerous animals may be impounded by animal control personnel and placed temporarily in an animal shelter. During the impoundment period, animal control may be required to obtain veterinary services, to search for the rightful owner, and before the owner can redeem his or her animal, it will be necessary for the owner to meet the redemption requirements in the ordinance. The requirements may include payment of a license fee if the animal has no license, presentation of a valid rabies certificate, and other fees as may be required by ordinance. Impoundment clauses specify a minimal holding period (usually seventy-two hours, but it may be longer) in which an animal may be detained in a shelter before it can be offered for adoption or humanely destroyed. Some local ordinances prohibit offering an impounded animal for adoption if it is temperamentally unsuitable or for health reasons. The Salt Lake City, Utah, ordinance (Section 8.04.330) requires that a record be kept of each animal impounded and that the record contain the following information:

- Complete description of the animal including tag numbers and other forms of identification

- The manner and date of impound

- Location where the animal was picked up and the name of the officer picking up the animal

- Date and manner of disposal

- Name and address of the person redeeming the animal or adopting the animal

- The name and address of any person relinquishing the animal to the impound facility

- All fees received

- All expenses incurred during impoundment

Increasingly, local governments are requiring animals released from impoundment and offered for adoption be spayed or neutered as part of the adoption process. Requirements may include payment of any license fees and production of a valid rabies certificate. Some jurisdictions also mandate that the animals must be microchipped before they can be released.

Quarantine. Another, more restrictive type of impoundment is known as quarantine. Animals that have bitten a human or are suspected of being rabid are placed in safe isolation for observation so as not to be in contact with other animals and to determine if the animal develops signs of rabies. Should the animal show signs of rabies, the animal needs to be destroyed, and the animal's head must be sent to the state laboratory for rabies testing and to determine if the victim needs to undergo rabies treatment. Some jurisdictions allow animals deemed dangerous (but not suspected of having rabies) to be quarantined at the owner's home or at an animal shelter at the discretion of the animal control authority.

Euthanasia. Euthanasia will continue to be a fact of life in most shelters operated by or for local governments. The law should require that euthanasia be administered humanely. There has been a greater effort in recent years to implement a no-kill policy in many animal shelters including public shelters. However, governmental shelters are still faced with having to kill some animals because of the growing number of animals admitted and the smaller number of animals that can be placed in new homes. It is common to have local ordinances require that euthanasia must be administered in accordance with state law or follow guidelines of the American Veterinary Medical Association. The Jackson County, Michigan, ordinance defines euthanasia as follows:

> "Euthanasia" means the humane destruction of an animal accomplished by a method not prohibited by law that produces rapid unconsciousness and subsequent death without evidence of pain or distress, or a method that utilizes anesthesia produced by an approved agent that causes subsequent death.[1]

Waste Removal Requirement. More popularly known as a "pooper scooper law," this local law or ordinance clause imposes an obligation on the animal owner to clean up any waste deposited by his or her animal on public or private property including the owner's property. Health and safety considerations are the rationale for this requirement to prevent the spread of disease, which is particularly important in heavily populated urban areas. Among many cities and counties that have pooper scooper laws are Cobb County, Georgia; Houston, Texas; New York City; Pleasanton, California; and Jefferson City, Missouri.

Great Falls, Montana, has one of the stricter animal waste provisions in its ordinance. The following is a summary of those provisions:

- It is prohibited to fail to remove animal feces from public or private property not owned or possessed by the animal owner.

- Owner must carry on his/her person materials to clean up animal waste when accompanying the animal off of the owner's property.

- Accumulation of animal feces on any private property is deemed a nuisance and the property must be kept free of an accumulation of feces.

- Accumulation is defined to mean a hazard to health, safety or convenience of persons other than the animal owner or any quantity that interferes with the enjoyment of any neighboring property as a result of odors, visual blight, or attraction of insects or pests.

- The owner, occupant, or agent that is in charge of the property when notified by animal control to remove such feces must do so within forty-eight hours. Failure to do so shall be a misdemeanor and may result in a fine of up to $500 plus the possibility of other penalties.[2]

Leash Law Requirement. This is a basic requirement in local animal ordinances. It is intended to prevent the danger of animals singly or in groups from running at large and posing both a nuisance and danger to humans and other animals and/or destroying property. Some ordinances apply the leash law requirement only to dogs, but others require cats and other creatures to be on a leash. Although ordinance enforcement is usually a responsibility of an animal control officer, some local government ordinances authorize other law enforcement personnel to enforce the ordinance if they witness a violation.

A leash law needs to require the animal owner to have *real* control over his/her animal. Unfortunately, some local ordinances define "control" to mean that the animal need only be under voice control of its owner. Some animal owners have allowed their dogs to run about on their front yards without any type of confinement (such as a leash or fence). This has led some local governments to approve changes in local ordinance to require a leash on any unconfined private property. The intent of such change considers the unconfined animal to be off-leash and having the potential to attack a person or other animal.

Electronic fencing, more popularly called invisible fencing, has been marketed as a means of controlling pets on the owner's property and may be suitable for some pets. A buried wire below the surface of the ground and connected to a transmitter in a building on the premises conveys a radio signal to a collar worn by the dog. An audio signal lets the dog know when the animal is too close to the property line. It is unclear whether local jurisdictions would consider this mechanism as adequate to secure an animal on its owner's property. Also, it will not keep aggressive animals or wildlife from entering private property and would not meet secure confinement requirements for animals deemed dangerous or potentially dangerous.

Leash law provisions vary by jurisdiction. Evansville, Indiana, requires when an animal is outdoors it must be on a leash not more than six feet long and under the control of a person eighteen years or older. The Evansville ordinance broadly defines the term "animal" to include domestic creatures, wild, or exotic. Gray, Maine, requires that any dog, licensed or unlicensed, may not run at large except for hunting. Bangor, Maine, authorizes the impoundment of any dog running at large and that the dog may be impounded for up to eight days. The Westminster, Vermont, ordinance states that any domestic pet (domestic cats excluded), domestic animal, or wolf-hybrid running at large constitutes a leash law violation.

Pelican Rapids, Minnesota, prohibits cats or dogs from running at large within the city limits, but a dog or cat on a leash that is not longer than six feet in length and "under the physical control of the person charged with its care" is permitted. Champaign County, Illinois, prohibits dogs from running at large in unincorporated areas of the county. The Champaign ordinance exempts dogs used for hunting or field trials, dog shows, or dogs on private property with the "actual, implied, customary or constructive consent of the owner of such private property."[3]

What happens when an animal control officer finds an animal off-leash and wandering about on public property? The first choice of some jurisdictions is to impound the animal, particularly if the animal is not wearing a license tag or other identification. Another option, particularly if the animal is wearing a license tag and other identification, is to return the animal directly to the owner with a warning that the next offense will mean a citation. Here is an opportunity to practice good public relations and teach a lesson at the same time. The fact that the animal displays a license tag and identification suggests that the owner could be considered a responsible pet owner and given a break for the first offense. If the animal has an identification tag but does not have a license, the owner can be issued a citation for having an unlicensed animal. The citation may be dismissed once the license has been obtained. Further violations can result in higher fines/penalties.

Animal Nuisances. A review of more than twenty local animal ordinances found that many nuisances were similarly defined. Nuisances commonly include:

- Noisy animals

- Fouling of the air by odor (Salt Lake City)

- Chasing people, vehicles, or bicycles

- Rummaging through garbage or rubbish

- Defecation

- Creating unsanitary conditions

- Failure to keep an animal in heat (female in estrus) in a secure and enclosed area

- Attacks other animals

- Damages private or public property (Cheyenne, Wyoming)

- An animal that has an untreated source of disease (Cheyenne and Rockingham County, North Carolina)

- Disturbs the peace, comfort, or health of persons in any manner

Animal hoarding, a major community problem, has often been reported as an animal nuisance by neighbors. When the facts become known, it may be addressed through an animal limit ordinance, as a cruelty case, or in combination. By that time it is so severe that local authorities have to take not only enforcement action against the owner, but some animals will have to be euthanized because of their condition. These cases involve issues of public health and safety, mental health of the person harboring the animals, and environmental sanitation.

Enforcement of noisy animal ordinances and alleviating noise problems have generally been difficult because of the legal hurdles in place that can take many months before the complainant experiences any relief. This is often due to requirements that two or more individuals need to have witnessed the offense and that animal owners have been encouraged to resolve the problem voluntarily, because some authorities view such nuisances as neighbor to neighbor disputes rather than animal problems. The process often involves several warnings to the animal owner before stronger enforcement measures are implemented.

One alternative to accelerate the process that has been successful is an animal court or a hearing board empowered to resolve nuisance issues more quickly through a formalized administrative procedure. This approach also reduces the processing time by an animal control officer and can avoid a court appearance. Depending on how the ordinance is drafted, repeat complaints filed about the same animal during a particular time frame can set other enforcement measures into play. The hearing board or animal court is an administrative panel that eliminates the need for judicial action except when the offending party refuses to obey lawful decisions of the administrative body. The board panel can be composed of non-animal control personnel, and the costs are minimal if the members of the panel are lay persons or local government officials. Riverside, California, created a three member animal control hearing board in 1995, which processed over two hundred noisy animal complaints in a five year period. Over 90% of the cases were heard and settled in less than thirty days. Riverside's hearing board was patterned after one operating successfully in nearby Corona, California. The ordinance was revised in 2005, and the board was replaced by an administrative hearing officer. Failure to comply with an administrative abatement issued by the Administrative Hearing Officer is unlawful and could result in civil and/or administrative remedies to gain compliance. Riverside's current noisy animal ordinance is found in Appendix 13-1.

Another available option is to expand the authority of an animal control advisory board or committee (if permitted by law) to undertake this function and establish a defined process for hearing and adjudicating complaints of animal nuisances and any appeals from decisions of the board.

Wild and Exotic Animals. Federal and state laws either prohibit keeping certain species or establish criteria for keeping certain species subject to terms and conditions. Special needs and dangers presented by some wild and exotic animals make it unsuitable to keep them on residential and other property by individuals who lack proper knowledge about the species. One city that experienced ongoing coyote problems amended its animal ordinance to prohibit the feeding of coyotes in that city with a few limited exceptions for trapped coyotes until those animals could be removed by authorities (Riverside, California). Many local ordinances ban keeping selected species, because of prohibitions in state law. Where some species of wild or exotic animals are allowed, strict terms and conditions must be met in order to keep them. Wild and exotic animals are discussed in greater detail in Chapter 15.

Cruelty to Animals. Animal cruelty takes many forms and is a nationwide problem. Although state and local laws make it a violation to fail to provide food, water, and shelter for animals or to allow animals to live under unsanitary conditions, there are also provisions that make it unlawful to harm animals in other ways.

Examples

1. Denying an animal freedom of movement for obtaining adequate fresh food, water, and shelter from inclement weather

2. Allowing an animal to fight other animals

3. Mutilating, wounding, injuring, or poisoning any animal

4. Torturing, molesting, or teasing an animal

5. Abandonment of any animal

6. Locking an animal in a closed motor vehicle during hot weather

7. Allowing dogs loose in the bed of a pickup truck

8. Failing to confine or make a dog in heat (in estrus) accessible to a male dog except for breeding purposes

9. Tethering or chaining a dog with a choke type collar

SUMMARY

Determining what animal provisions should be enacted into law and whether those provisions should be enacted at the state or local level depends on several factors. Among them are issues specific to the locality, whether there is a need to act quickly, and if there is the political will to do so.

Viewed on a larger scale, animal ordinances can be classified into four broad topic categories with different but sometimes overlapping target groups or audiences. Categories include animal owner responsibilities and requirements, inhumane acts committed against animals, perils of keeping dangerous or wild animals, and provisions relating to the operation of an animal control program. Establishing categories (which can be subjective) can make it easier to identify needed provisions in each category based on past experience and projecting future needs.

Provisions in local law reflect both similarities and differences from one community to the next in their definition of terms used, content, local issues, priorities, and penalties for violations. State requirements are a major influence on what is enacted into local law. Local laws may be more restrictive than state laws but cannot be less restrictive. Among the more common provisions found in local law are definition of terms used, penalties for violations of law, powers, duties, and responsibilities of animal control officials, licensing, rabies control, dangerous animals, animal limits, impoundment and quarantine, euthanasia, leash laws, nuisances, and wildlife and exotic animals.

Due to local interpretation, some provisions such as dangerous dog restrictions, numerical animal limits, and even leash laws have sparked considerable discussion and differences of opinion that have affected a community's ability to address ongoing problems and issues.

Notes

1. County of Jackson Michigan, Ordinance No, 1, Article 2.

2. City of Great Falls, Montana, Official City Code, Title 6, ch.8, sec. 6.8.1100.

3. Champaign County Animal Control Ordinance No.822, sec.4.

Chapter 14

Irresponsible Pet Owners and the Politics of Animal Control

INTRODUCTION

This chapter discusses irresponsible pet owners and dangerous dogs and includes an overview of breed specific legislation that has been used to address dangerous animals. These interrelated issues have been the subject of much debate nationwide and are among the most difficult to resolve. At the local government level, these issues play out in the political arena among the stakeholders and players.

THE IRRESPONSIBLE ANIMAL OWNER

The problem of irresponsible pet owners is the primary reason for the existence of all animal control programs. Although most pet owners act responsibly and value the companionship of their animals, it is the owners who flout the law who have the greatest negative impact on the community that requires enacting and enforcing animal laws. Irresponsible pet owners are those animal owners who fail to exercise their responsibilities or understand their pet's impact on the community as a whole. The list of unacceptable and unlawful pet behaviors, when matched with the list of unacceptable and unlawful acts committed against animals, combine to make up the content of animal laws enacted across the nation, designed to protect both citizens and animals alike. These acts create the need for animal control services and increase the costs for all taxpayers. The complexities of this long-standing and not well understood problem have been difficult to address, and there are limited resources to address them. This problem lends itself to be the purpose of a national conference convened to seek answers and solutions.

Who Are The Irresponsible Animal Owners?

They may be individuals you might know but do not suspect. There are others who openly defy the law. They may allow their animals to roam the neighborhood at all hours of the day or night, do not license their animals where required or have them vaccinated against disease. They may be secret hoarders who keep dozens or more animals in neglected condition behind closed doors in the mistaken belief that they are helping animals. There are others who simply abandon their animals by the roadside when they tire of them or when the animal becomes a problem. Some individuals leave their animals behind without food or water when they move away. Some owners tether their dogs to a rope or chain in the yard and forget about them. Consequently, anti-tethering laws are gaining in popularity as they are seen as a way to prevent anti-social behavior attributed to tethered dogs. Others allow their dogs to bark continuously, disturbing the neighbors and decreasing the quality of life in the neighborhood.

There are animal owners who acquire large dogs for security and encourage the animals to be aggressive and hostile, not realizing how dangerous that animal can become, or it may be as simple as the owner who fails to clean up and remove animal waste that causes odors. These are just a few examples of offensive and usually illegal behavior.

What Are The Issues?

Examples of irresponsible behavior are numerous, but the question of why people act this way needs more study that may help lead to a solution. The remaining two questions can be answered by evaluating animal control programs and legislation and by analyzing the workload data and statistics of animal control agencies:

- Why do some dog and cat owners fail to properly care for their animals?

- What action or inaction by an animal owners can be classified as irresponsible?

- How can animal control programs help make owners more responsible?

- Are some dogs more apt to attack without provocation?

How Irresponsible Animal Owners Impact Animal Control Programs

Animal care and control programs evolved over the past one hundred or more years, because animal owners abused and mistreated their work animals, dogs, and cats. Cruelty and abuse cases including hoarding, animal abandonment, and wanton disregard for local animal laws by some owners continue to keep animal control officers busy as local animal control programs are a direct response to these people-caused problems. One major effort to change owners' behaviors has been a national campaign to spay/neuter dogs and cats, but there is no nationwide consensus or strategy to comprehensively address those issues generated by irresponsible pet owners. There are, however, ample examples of how these problems impact the animal control program:

- Calls for service for abused, neglected, and abandoned animals and calls to respond to other violations of animal laws monopolize the time of field officers and other animal services personnel.

- Failure to license their animals creates a population of dogs and cats that may not have been vaccinated against disease and might be exposed to or are carriers of transmittable diseases.

- Owners who fail to claim their animals when they are impounded increase the shelter population and their chances of the destruction of more animals, because there are not enough adopters who will give the animals new homes. Animals deserve and are entitled under law to humane care. This drives up the costs of the service for which all taxpayers have to bear the burden for the minority of animal owners who are the cause of most of the problems.

- "Backyard" or "hobby" breeders who allow their animals to breed indiscriminately and then give them away "free to good homes" or sell "purebreds" that have health and personality problems perpetuate animal overpopulation issues.

- People who treat their animals as disposable commodities and when the animals have problems, they simply dump the animals somewhere unobserved and quietly slink away. The animal may become feral or be killed by other animals. Feral cats that are unaltered and unvaccinated are often the result of abandonment.

The Animal Control Response

Animal control officials have addressed these problems through educational outreach to schools, making written materials available, counseling potential adopters, promoting low cost spay/neuter surgeries, and enforcing current animal laws or enacting new ones. The response, in other words, has been two-fold: prevention and enforcement.

The author recalls from personal experience how one city council member's proposal to look into developing a solution to the increase in noisy animal complaints drew a crowd in a city hall hearing room. The outcome was a unique solution that substantially reduced the noisy animal problem.

True Story

The city council appointed a task force of three city council members to develop approaches to address the increasing number of noisy animal complaints received by council members. The task force held several public meetings that drew an audience that filled the hearing room. Initially and incorrectly, many in the audience believed their personal pets were being targeted for noise restriction measures. Several in the audience defended barking dogs as normal canine behavior.

A staff member assigned to the task force addressed those present to reassure them that neither they nor their animals were the reason for the task force, but there were some in the community who failed to act responsibly by allowing their pets to unreasonably make noise at all hours of the day and night. It was emphasized that any proposal to address the problem would be fair to all and that due process would be assured to any animal owner whose animal was charged with being a public nuisance. The meetings led to a proposal for an animal control hearing board to adjudicate noisy animal cases. The hearing board proposal was based on a similar panel operated successfully in a nearby city.

The proposed ordinance to create the hearing board was explained to the public. Members of the public raised questions and others offered suggestions to be incorporated into the proposal. The final draft ordinance submitted to the city council included ideas generated at these meetings.

When it came before the council, some spoke in favor of the ordinance, and little opposition was expressed. Although some would have preferred to believe that the proposal was not necessary, they indicated that they would accept it. The proposal was approved by city council, and those who had attended the task force meetings also attended the city council meeting where the proposal was approved. In the view of some local officials, the proposed remedy was approved in part because public input was accepted and carefully considered at the informal meetings held before the city council voted on the matter.

What Have Been the Results of Animal Control Efforts?

Spaying/neutering of animals adopted from shelters is becoming mandatory, but until recently, those who own unaltered dogs and cats could only be encouraged to have them altered. In a small number of communities, legislation requiring spaying and neutering of pets is often based on whether the animal is allowed to roam, whether it is a multiple leash law offender, or has been deemed dangerous, so pet overpopulation issues still remain a challenge in most localities. Overall, only a small percentage of dogs are licensed, despite efforts to increase canvassing, which is labor-intensive and can be expensive. There are communities with high rates of licensed animals that have an active and ongoing effort to license new animals and to renew expiring licenses. Some communities claim to have had success with animal limits to control the size of the domestic pet population, but there is strong opposition to enacting animal limits where historically they have not existed. Many communities are making great efforts, but most still pursue a piecemeal approach.

The Response of the Courts

In communities where animal laws have not been evaluated or updated in many years, penalties imposed by those laws may be too weak to provide a deterrent to irresponsible pet owners. Courts have not traditionally given animal control violations a high priority, because they have been classified as infractions or misdemeanors, and because these same courts are clogged with felonies and more high profile crimes. Increased media attention on heinous animal cruelty cases and high profile dangerous dog incidents appear to have driven efforts by local officials to enact laws with higher monetary penalties and possible jail time for more egregious violations. New felony classifications of animal violations are being prosecuted, and animal owners are being held more accountable.

STRATEGIES FOR ADDRESSING IRRESPONSIBLE OWNERS

Animal control issues are almost always community-driven, often controversial, and require the support of many in the local community to find an appropriate response. Animal control laws that have not been updated in many years may need to be reviewed and changes proposed to bring the laws into sync with reality. New legislation may be warranted to address issues that simply did not exist in the past. Proposals for new legislation that come from the local community itself and that have broad support have a greater chance of local enactment than proposals to amend state law where vested interests may push for compromises that may not effectively address the issue.

Most irresponsible animal owners who are at the root of local problems will not attend public meetings. A few might tell the media or animal control that they had no idea their animals were causing problems, or they will deny there is a problem. Some owners will go on the offensive and blame the victim or complainant for instigating the problem. New legislation may be one more step in a chain of events that includes warnings given to offenders, court appearance citations, and meetings with animal control officials. Removal of animals may be authorized by law in some jurisdictions.

Establishing an administrative panel by law to adjudicate certain kinds of nuisance animal problems may be one way to expedite solutions rather than pursue a case through the courts. Due process and the right to appeal needs to be included to assure fairness and provide the animal owner the opportunity to appeal the panel's decision.

It falls to local government officials to provide the necessary leadership and to work with key individuals in the community and credible local groups to forge needed alliances to make the needed changes. Alleviating if not eliminating animal control problems is a large undertaking, but if carefully planned and executed, it can be successful. There are several steps that can be taken in the process of developing this strategy.

Bring People Together: Create A Blue Ribbon Task Force

Convene an advisory group of respected local individuals who can help identify and assess the problems at hand. Give them a specific mission and a timetable to complete their work. Ask them to prepare a report assessing the problems, their causes, and to offer recommendations that might include a combination of responses, for example, amending laws, new outreach efforts, and perhaps new priorities for animal control staff. Consider as members in this group individuals who bring certain professional skills and experiences to the table. A veterinarian, animal behaviorist, animal trainer, someone involved in animal rescue work, police officers, mediators, and perhaps a psychologist or other therapist can bring needed new insights to this process. Those with experience in business and particularly in strategic planning may be able to offer new ideas and strategies.

After reaching consensus on the issues and developing a strategy as part of their mission, task force members need to reach out to everyone in the geographical area to publicize their efforts. Speaking engagements before local civic groups, writing letters to the editor of the local paper, or writing a guest column or editorial can give the matter a higher profile and make the information more readily available. Being interviewed on a local radio or television talk show is another way to reach more people. Commentaries offered on blogs are another popular way of communicating more informally with people who visit your Web site. Ask local animal welfare organizations to publish information in their newsletters, and offer them talking points or other assistance. The work of the task force may be in combination with efforts of others or a separate project.

What Can Animal Control Directors Do?

Directors of animal control agencies need to explore the issues associated with animal control problems with their colleagues in the state and through state associations of animal control officers or animal control directors. Find out what other jurisdictions are doing to address their problems and learn from their experience. It may be necessary to propose changes in state law in order to give all local authorities power to act. If so, the support and lobbying efforts of state associations that are able to present data documenting the problem can enhance chances for passage. Other statewide organizations representing municipalities and counties should be brought into this process as there is a mutual interest to do so. Nationally, animal control problems cost local governments millions of dollars in staff time, monies that are expended from local government general funds, a finite resource. Asking to have a topic on the conference agenda of the state association of municipalities or counties or an article on this topic in their newsletters or periodicals will call attention to the problem and help encourage a statewide approach if that is deemed the best way to address these concerns. Identifying rising costs, impact on public safety, and potential local liability are sure to be noticed by municipal and county officials.

Directors may want to apply for grants to develop pilot programs to cover added personnel costs or outreach efforts to address the most common issues facing animal control such as the low rate of animal licensing or how to reduce leash law violations. Providing handouts summarizing state and local animal laws and asking all dog owners to voluntarily sign a pledge promising to exercise animal care responsibilities at the time their animal is licensed can be a useful public relations and outreach tactic. Asking owners to sign a statement saying "I support pet owner responsibilities" costs nothing, but it makes owners more conscious that their animals are entitled to proper care by law and makes it harder for them to deny that they were not aware of their legal responsibilities.

THE PROCESS AND POLITICS OF PASSING ANIMAL CONTROL LAWS

Local government officials confronted with publicly acknowledged animal control issues that decrease quality of life or threaten public health and safety can expect a lot of advice from those served and even people living elsewhere. Local government and animal control officials will need to define the issues and problems and explore options to resolve them, but in their deliberations, they must realize that animal owners, breeders, animal welfare organizations, and animal care professionals have a stake in the outcome and are not shy about asserting their views that may differ from those of local government and animal control officials.

Dog and cat issues tend to attract large gatherings at local governing body meetings, especially when sweeping changes to local laws are being considered. The audience will include those with strong opinions and varying viewpoints. One group will no doubt be demanding that local officials take any and all steps to curb the problems. Others may express their resistance to change and who believe additional regulation is not needed. Those opposed to changes in law may assert that owners of problem animals should be held accountable on a case-by-case basis. Some in the audience may represent animal groups outside the community who are there to listen to the discussion and perhaps monitor the proceedings.

Formal and informal networks of animal owners and advocates quickly spread the word when animal issues are scheduled to be discussed before a governmental body. Elected officials can expect numerous calls from individuals and organizations expressing their views. Local officials may receive considerable and often contradictory advice and may need extra time to sort through information provided. The news media loves to report controversy and will report views of individuals and organizations. The media may have also staked out an editorial position on the issue at hand. Local government public meetings are often covered by both the broadcast and print media.

Why Are Some Animal Control Issues So Controversial And Political?

The question is important and the answers complex. The response to this question can be influenced by the following factors which help to frame the issues realistically:

- *Animals are considered to be property.* Animals are considered to be personal property, and people and the courts take property rights very seriously. However, animal owners may see new regulations as unnecessary governmental influence in their lives, but it must be pointed out that municipalities have always set and enforced provisions for keeping animals. A nuisance animal ordinance in Riverside, California, gives the city the option to remove any animal that has been declared a nuisance if the owner fails to comply with an order of the city's animal control hearing board, which has since been replaced by an administrative hearing officer. Over a five year period, not one animal was ordered removed from the city as compliance was obtained without having to resort to exercise this authority. Although some local governments including Denver and some Kansas cities have prohibited keeping certain breeds of dogs, banning dogs by breed remains a controversial issue. Many cities prohibit keeping some species of wildlife, regardless of whether the owner claims it is domesticated.

- *Animals are viewed by many as family members.* Dogs, cats, birds, small reptiles, and and some members of the rodent family have a valued place in many homes and are considered part of the family. Other pets have been known to accompany their owners everywhere. Americans care about their pets as evidenced by the amount of money spent on their animals. American pet owners spent an estimated $43.2 billion on their pets in 2008, according to the American Pet Products Manufacturers Association.[1]

- *Animal issues are complex and arriving at solutions takes time and effort.* Local government officials may need to become more informed about the complexity of the issues at hand. Although cognizant of the bond between human and animal, officials may be ignorant of the many local and state animal laws, trends in animal control, and legislative solutions that have worked or failed to work in other communities. Local authorities need to balance matters of quality of life, health and safety, liability concerns, and the public interest, however that may be defined.

- *Animal interests will make their positions clear.* Unlike some other local government issues that draw little community-wide interest from the public, animal issues almost always draw the attention of individuals and organizations concerned with animal interests. Positions on the issue may be quickly reached with few remaining neutral. Elected local governing body members are soon faced with this reality as they attempt to gather the facts and assess the need to act. Developing a consensus on how to respond in this environment requires considerable political skill and commitment to determining and protecting the interests of the broader community.

Animal issues tend to generate perspectives from many individuals and groups, but those expressed by pet owners, victims, or complaining parties and government have particular relevance because of how it affects them.

The pet owner perspective. An animal owner who testifies or speaks before a public body on a pet-related issue speaks from personal experience and frames the issue in personal terms. For example, why is this proposal directed at so many people, myself included, when the problem is limited to a few animals and their owners? The owner may believe that further animal restrictions are overkill, that there are already laws in place that can address the problems, and that the majority of animal owners are law abiding citizens. You may hear, "Let's not punish innocent animal owners as a group."

The victim's or complainant's perspective. The complaining party or victim is also speaking from personal experience and relates what happens from that perspective. Injuries, deterioration in the quality of life, and expenses incurred are among the victim's or complainant's grievances. The victim will remind public officials that they have a duty to act and may feel that speaking out at a public meeting is needed to bring more attention to issues when other efforts have failed. Whether the issue is loud peacocks or dangerous dogs at large, the message is clear: immediate relief is needed because the problem is not going away. Victims may also bring up the issue of restitution.

The governmental perspective. Local government officials are ever mindful that they represent their constituents, and their responsibilities are to the community as a whole. Where policies need to be approved or changed, priorities established, or resources appropriated, decisions must be for the greater good. A child being mauled to death by a dangerous animal, for instance, will characterize the problem in stark terms and give the political process a critical sense of urgency, even if there is but one incident. Public outcry over a recent horrific event may create a demand for immediate action, though a workable solution may not be readily apparent or easy. It may take time to develop an appropriate response.

DANGEROUS DOG LEGISLATION

About 4.7 million Americans are bitten annually by dogs,[2] and about 800,000 Americans suffer dog bites and seek medical attention.[3] Reducing the risks of attack, intimidation, and injuries caused by dangerous dogs requires time, effort, and community support for proposed remedies to be successful. Updating weak state or local dangerous dog legislation, creating specific regulations for "dangerous dogs" and "potentially dangerous dogs," and increasing fines, restrictions, and penalties are among the options for lawmakers. Addressing the associated crimes of illegal drug trafficking or dog fighting may also be part of a community solution.

Local Government's Internal Efforts

A first step is preparing an internal report for senior level local government officials as well as defining the problem and how it impacts the public and local government. The report should include the number of dangerous dog calls for assistance during the most recent three year to five year period, how many cases were resolved and closed, and how they were resolved. The number of open cases needs to be reported and why they are still open. Information about deaths and injuries attributed to these cases needs to be included in the report. Relevant data can be gathered from law enforcement and health agencies and other applicable sources. Other issues to consider for inclusion in the report are:

- How many dogs are licensed in the jurisdiction versus total estimated dog population?

- How many dangerous dogs (those that bit/attacked a person or another animal) were found to be unlicensed?

- How many incidents occurred where a dog bit/attacked a person or another animal when the biter or attacking animal was at large?

- How many dogs were found to have attacked without provocation, and what breeds were involved?

- How many dangerous dog citations have been issued per year and by breed?

- A summary of the circumstances of each incident by category of incident

- Has there been a recent animal census and how many dogs were counted?

- How many owners were cited more than once for dangerous dog or leash law violations?

- Are law enforcement officials finding an increase in dog fighting rings and arrests?

- Are state and local laws prohibiting these activities sufficient?

- Are local law enforcement officials finding dangerous dogs to be associated with known drug traffickers and have drug-related crimes increased?

It would be useful to note how other municipalities and counties acted when confronted with similar problems. Other issues to be addressed in the report should include limitations and loopholes in state and local laws, costs of answering and investigating these matters, and any liability issues that affect local government. Input from senior level law enforcement and local government officials will be needed before proceeding further.

External Efforts to Develop Recommendations

Another option is creation of an ad hoc committee to consider dangerous dog issues and to develop recommendations for the local governing body. The role of the committee is to develop a unified approach on what needs to be done, taking advantage of the experience and expertise of its members. The committee's support and expertise can provide the political support for elected officials who may need to make some hard decisions.

The committee chair could be one of the elected governing body members, because he or she will be knowledgeable about the role of the governing body and will be able to assess how the governing body may react to specific recommendations. The chair needs to be able to keep the committee's focus on the mission as defined by the governing body. A governing body is more likely to support recommendations by a panel it created, headed by one of its own members.

Membership on the committee might include representatives of the police and health departments, a few community representatives including a veterinarian, an animal trainer/behaviorist, and a dog owner. Animal control officials can be a useful resource to this group aided by a staff person to provide administrative and technical support. The local government attorney should be invited to attend meetings, and if unable to do so, he or she should be kept informed of the committee's work and consulted as needed.

"Marketing" the Committee's Recommendations

A necessary aspect of the political process is the need for public relations. If the committee's recommendations will create sweeping new regulations where there were previously none at all, the public may balk at the changes, so they need to be explained. Care should be taken to present an initiative that appeals to one's sense of community responsibility while protecting people and pets alike and assuring that animal owners and the pets are being treated fairly.

The development and distribution of a fact sheet with expected questions and answers will help clarify the proposed recommendations and counter any false rumors that may be circulating. Calling the report and its recommendations a "Companion Animals Protection Initiative" has a more positive connotation than saying new dangerous dog laws are needed. Another name to consider for this campaign might be "Keeping Pets and People Safe" (KaPPS).

Role of the Elected Governing Body

The committee chair needs to have the opportunity to present an oral report to highlight key points in the report to the governing body when the written report is transmitted to that body for review. The governing body will decide what action to take on the report. The elected governing body may choose to schedule a public hearing on the report before taking further action. The public hearing or public meeting is an opportunity for all parties to make their views known and hopefully support the committee's recommendations. It also serves the purpose of the governing body to get a better sense of what others in the community think about the issue(s). Some changes may be needed following the public hearing to make the proposed legislation more fair or to address concerns raised by those in attendance.

It is not uncommon at these public meetings for individuals and representatives of out-of-town organizations to want to speak on the issue. One city, DeSoto, Texas, held a two-hour public meeting on December 7, 2006, to discuss what to do about dangerous dogs but allowed only local residents to speak at first. When all local residents had finished speaking, in the time remaining, nonresidents were permitted to express their views.

At the end of the process, the governing body may decide to push for a more restrictive local dangerous dog law. The local law should define parameters of what constitutes a potentially dangerous dog (i.e., dogs that have been shown to have injured another domestic animal or have harassed or intimidated but not injured a human). The legislation may provide for a hearing after which a judge may make a declaration and place restrictions on such dogs to decrease the likelihood that a human will be injured. Muzzling in public, confinement on an owner's property, obedience training, and neutering are all possible requirements. The legislation may also include even stricter provisions for those dogs that have been shown to have injured a human. A judge may have the option to order these dogs to be even more restrictively kept or even humanely destroyed. Owners may be forced to purchase expensive liability insurance policies in addition to other restrictions.

BREED SPECIFIC LEGISLATION

In recent years the media has reported many dangerous dog incidents in which both humans and animals have been injured and/or killed. This has led to a variety of responses at the local government level to abate the dangers. The two approaches most often pursued are the amendment of existing dangerous animal laws to impose greater requirements on the owners and their animals or the enactment of breed specific legislation, the latter of which has been quite controversial. Regardless of which option is pursued, both have a management and political impact. The final decision of how to address the issue rests with local authorities and must take into account local considerations including the degree of urgency, how widespread the problem, and what the community will support. This section summarizes some of the major arguments for and against breed specific legislation in an effort to help animal control and local government officials gain a better understanding of the issue before deciding which approach to pursue. The author is not advocating one approach over the other but is simply expressing concern that dangerous dog incidents affect health and public safety, an issue that cannot be ignored and is also a management and governmental responsibility to be addressed.

This is currently one of the most hotly debated issues for local government officials, animal owners, animal interest groups, and the citizenry of the community. Keep in mind the following three questions when reviewing the arguments for and against regulation:

- How can animal attacks causing serious injury or even death of a person or animal be prevented?

- What steps should be taken to gain compliance from animal owners to act responsibly?

- What should local government officials do to protect people and animals from serious harm by dogs?

The Rationale for Dangerous Dog/Breed Specific Legislation

The rationale in support of breed specific legislation is centered on a group of dog breeds collectively known as pit bulls and is about the characteristics and traits of the dog together with a series of legal arguments. Proponents argue that most dangerous dog laws were enacted before pit bulls became popular and did not anticipate addressing the problems of specific breeds that are trained to fight and attack.

Proponents of prohibiting pit bulls point out that these muscular animals can attack without warning or provocation and may even attack the owner or a member of the owner's family, even if the animal has been with the family for many years and has shown no evidence of aggression . Because the animal has strong jaws and a high tolerance for pain, it can be difficult to stop a pit bull attack. Some critics of the breed(s) claim that genetic breeding over the past one hundred or more years has made them into fighting animals, and most owners are not aware of the animals' past breeding history or behavior. The media has given wide attention to attacks by these animals, emphasizing the harm they have caused and this has lead to an outcry against pit bulls, causing the public to fear these animals. Some pit bull advocates have acknowledged that these animals require special care and a secure environment. Some animals have been used as guard dogs by drug dealers, and shelters have expressed a reluctance to offer them for adoption. During the twenty year period from 1979 to 1998, pit bull-type dogs and Rottweilers were implicated in more than one-half of the deaths attributed to dog attacks.[4]

Courts have upheld the constitutionality of breed specific legislation (BSL) whether it is to impose restrictions on the breed or to prohibit keeping of specific breeds. More specifically, one-half of the states and many cities have enacted dangerous dog laws that apply to all breeds, although some have enacted breed specific legislation, the reason being to address dog bites and attacks. Dangerous dog laws typically include due process provisions that include a hearing to determine if the animal is dangerous. Some jurisdictions have authorized a less serious designation called potentially dangerous. This latter category allows conditions to be imposed on both animal and owner when the animal's actions do not quite rise to the level of danger as defined in a dangerous dog determination.

The Rationale against Breed Specific Legislation (BSL)

The rationale offered in defense of pit bulls and against BSL is centered on the characteristics of pit bulls, constitutionality issues, and the effectiveness of BSL laws.

The term "pit bull" does not describe any one breed of dog, but rather it includes three breeds of dogs and many crossbreeds as well. The physical characteristics of pit bulls are similar among the three breeds, and even experts have difficulty identifying an animal that is a mixed breed from a pure bred. Further, all dogs bite, and singling out certain breeds will not reduce the number of dog bites or serous attacks. The problem with BSL is that any dog can bite, and it puts all dogs in danger of being banned or subject to restrictions, because BSL states that pit bulls are whatever local authorities say they are. The burden is on the owner to prove that the animal is not a pit bull or that is it is an allowed breed.

BSL is being challenged in the courts because owners of specific dog breeds contend that it singles out one breed and the owners of that one breed and is a violation of the equal protection of the laws and violates due process as guaranteed by the Fourteenth Amendment. BSL has nothing to do with an animals' behavior. It is about possession of an animal. It violates owners' constitutional rights to equal protection of the laws, because it unfairly singles out one breed among many. Other breeds of dogs have caused serious injury or death, but they are exempt. Does this mean any dog over one hundred pounds will be subject to regulation? Dogs are not bad, it is the owner who is at fault, because the owner failed to socialize or control his or her animal or failed to properly train it, so the owner needs to be held responsible.

BSL laws are not effective, and some cities have repealed BSL due to the costs of enforcement and the need to hire additional staff. There is the increased cost of kenneling these animals that are awaiting a determination of breed and for those dogs whose owners are appealing such determination. There is also no guarantee that pit bull owners will obey the law, and they have been known to hide their dogs, or bad owners will simply focus their aggression on finding a replacement breed.

According to studies published in the Journal of the American Veterinary Medical Association, there are no reliable data associated on biting dogs by breed. A report from San Francisco states that 21% fewer pit bulls were impounded after that city /county enacted a law requiring pit bulls to be sterilized.

SUMMARY

"Irresponsible animal owners" create the need for animal control services and increase the costs for all taxpayers. This broad and complex issue has been addressed in many ways at the local government level depending on the extent of the problem and local priorities. Local government officials must provide ongoing leadership and work with influential individuals and groups to forge alliances to make needed changes. A blue ribbon task force to help identify the many components of the problem and to offer recommendations is vital if the scope of the problem is to be reduced. State and local efforts in partnership with each other can accelerate the process.

Animal issues bring out peoples' passions like no other and quickly become controversial and political, because there are many on both sides of the issue. There are three perspectives that will be heard: complaining parties or victims, animal owners and their supporters, and government. It is government at the local level that is charged with responsibility for public health and safety, enacting and enforcing laws, and the powers of governing. These three viewpoints contribute passion and tension to the debate.

The case for greater regulation of dangerous or potentially dangerous animals is about putting into place safeguards to protect the public and prevent dangerous dog attacks. This requires investigation and a carefully conceived strategy that assesses and addresses the problem and determines how it impacts the public. Animal control programs need to have hard data available to verify the problem. Due to the politics of the situation, support of a majority of the community is needed to find a workable solution. Whatever the choices, they are important public policy decisions.

Notes

1. American Pet Products Association, Industry Statistics & Trends, "Spending," www.americanpetproducts.org/.

2. Centers for Disease Control and Prevention, "Dog Bite Prevention," www.cdc.gov/, (accessed November 14, 2007).

3. Centers for Disease Control and Prevention, "Dog Bite Fact Sheet," Ibid.

4. Jeffrey J. Sacks, MD, MPH; Leslie Sinclair, DVM; Julie Gilchrist, MD; Gail C. Golub, Ph.D, DVM; Randall Lockwood, Ph.D. "Breeds of dogs involved in human attacks in the United States between 1979 and 1998." *Journal of the American Veterinary Medical Association*, 217 (September 15, 2000): 836-40.

Chapter 15

Wildlife and Exotic Animals as a Management Concern

INTRODUCTION AND OVERVIEW

Public health and safety of people and domestic animals the priority of animal control officials, has over the years been broadened to include wildlife and exotic animals. Reasons include the potential for transmission of disease, the possibility of a wild animal's escape from captivity, and the consequences of being attacked by a wild animal. Regulation of wildlife and exotic animals can be attributed to a number of factors:

- Recognition of an increased need to protect the environment, natural resources, and wildlife due to global warming and the increased depletion of forests and other wildlife habitats necessary for the survival of animals in the wild.

- Unlawful hunting of some wildlife species that has endangered their survival.

- Increased interest and fascination of animal hobbyists and collectors to possess wild and exotic animals, both legally and illegally, and ignorance of the special needs of these animals.

- Reported abuses of some wild/exotic animals by their owners.

- Protection of public health and safety to prevent the dangers presented by some species that are not and cannot be domesticated.

Calls seeking help with wildlife problems are increasing, and despite the public's fascination with wildlife in general, when wild animals enter their properties and become a perceived nuisance, people's attitudes change. Locally, animal control personnel are usually expected to respond to calls for assistance with wildlife. The response may require special training as some animals are dangerous and others can be harmed through careless handling.

Wildlife advocates believe that man and beast must live together in harmony and that many wildlife problems are caused by man. The destruction of natural wildlife habitats has changed how wildlife forage for food. This brings wildlife in closer proximity to man and new problems follow. Preserving and protecting wildlife is a matter of public policy and is an ongoing effort involving public and private organizations.

Animal control plays a small but important role at the state and local levels to preserve and protect wildlife (e.g., providing initial assistance in cases of dangerous, injured, or abandoned wildlife). Management needs to anticipate the challenges of these animals and to be prepared to assist with any problems at a moment's notice. The following example is based on an actual incident.

Example

> An unexpected call from a printing plant manager and calls from several nearby homeowners reported a band of feral pigs had invaded the company's property and several nearby residential properties and had dug up and destroyed their respective irrigation systems. The animals were dangerous, because they charged anyone who attempted to get close to them. Police officers who were first dispatched to the scene had to use their weapons to defend themselves against these invaders, and one of the animals had to be destroyed before the others could be captured and removed.

Geographical location and climate influence which species of wildlife will be encountered, but not always. It is not unheard of that non-native species of wildlife may be encountered anywhere, just as exotic animals often mysteriously appear locally. Discovery of illegally kept exotic animals may come to the attention of animal control officials because a complaint was received or because the animal many have escaped its confinement. The enactment of a new ordinance prohibiting or restricting the keeping of exotic animals could force owners to comply with the new laws.

This chapter emphasizes management's need to concern itself with both wildlife and exotic animals, which are addressed here as two separate but sometimes overlapping issues. An argument can be made that issues about wildlife merit a separate discussion, because wildlife issues by common usage mean those animal species that are either native to a particular state or region or are found in every state in the nation and are not kept as household pets, because they cannot be domesticated, or keeping them is prohibited by law.

Exotic animals have by common usage come to mean members of the animal kingdom that are not native species, are kept in confinement, and/or under the control of humans, and may be kept for purposes of exhibition, education, or personal pleasure as permitted by law. Sometimes they are kept in violation of federal state or local laws by those willing to take the risk. These animals are not to be confused with native wildlife species that inhabit local woods and forests or that frequently enter private properties at will. There are exceptions to these general differences, and definitions of wildlife and exotic animals are subjective. The definition of each is whatever the law says it is, and the laws vary considerably between levels of government and among the fifty states.

Animals Exempt from Wildlife/Exotic Animal Regulation

Through common understanding, some small cage animals such as gerbils, guinea pigs, small, non-venomous reptiles and amphibians, canaries, parakeets, other caged birds, some rats and mice, rabbits, and most aquarium fish are excluded from state and local regulation and may be kept as household pets.

WILDLIFE/EXOTIC ANIMAL ROLE

Wild or exotic animal issues will not get much attention unless animal control seizes those animals, because they have been abused, neglected, abandoned, escaped captivity, injured, or killed someone. What goes unnoticed is the routine work of inspecting pet shops where exotic animals are sold and circuses where animals perform and are on display. Other duties include enforcing local wildlife ordinances, loaning traps, and disposing of wildlife caught in traps. Animal control is usually the first responder when calls for assistance are received by police officers, sheriff's deputies, or other local authorities. Other local law enforcement agencies and the state wildlife agency will often dispatch officers to the animal incident scene to assist animal control personnel because of the danger in capturing and containing certain wildlife species.

Animal control's role and responsibilities are defined in local ordinance and/or in state law and are discussed later in this chapter. State statute may delegate to local authorities certain powers in addressing wildlife issues including enforcing provisions in state law. Even if state and local laws are silent regarding wildlife, the problems exist nonetheless, and major wildlife problems cannot be ignored.

Defining Wildlife

Since animal care and control programs differ from one community to another, it should come as no surprise that there is no universally accepted definition of what is meant by the term "wildlife" when used by municipalities and counties. Similarities as well as differences can be seen when comparing one ordinance to another, and it may be a matter of semantics. There is general agreement that dogs, cats, horses, and aquarium fish (with the exception of piranhas) are excluded from the definition of these terms, and rabbits, hamsters, and guinea pigs are regarded as domestic pets. How is the term "wildlife" defined? The answer is whatever the local or state authorities determine. In is broadest sense, Nevada's definition of wildlife in a state statute is useful in the context of this chapter. The statute reads, "'Wildlife' means any mammal, wild bird, fish, reptile, amphibian, mollusk or crustacean found naturally in a wild state, whether indigenous to Nevada or not and whether raised in captivity or not."[1]

This definition of wildlife would seem broad enough to include wild animals found in any state and particularly those most apt to be reported to animal control as a problem or a danger. Conceivably, deer, bears, mountain lions, venomous snakes, alligators, feral pigs, coyotes, and fisher cats easily fit into the wildlife category. Some species are considered endangered under state laws and are protected. Other species are not protected and may be hunted. Some state laws contain detailed listings of undomesticated animals that may not be kept in captivity and those that can. Some states follow federal law in declaring which animal species are endangered and thus affording them protective status.

Management's Concerns about Wildlife

Over the years, animal control management has paid more attention to wildlife matters because of the increasing presence of wildlife and wildlife problems in urban areas that require not only a response, but in some cases the application of local laws. Wildlife concerns and priorities for animal control directors and managers include:

- Training staff on how to respond to calls for assistance

- Whom to call for advice and assistance when confronted with dangers and special problems posed by these animals

- Preparation of a wildlife response plan to calls for assistance when dangerous wildlife pose a real or potential threat to the human population and to domestic pets

- Temporary impoundment of some wildlife species or transfer to another facility

Management has a responsibility to make sure that staff is trained to handle the more common wildlife problems and that staff knows when and who to call upon for assistance. Planning ahead by asking in advance the right questions and having some answers before the need arises will help expedite an appropriate response.

The Call List. For example, does the animal control agency have a list of organizations, agencies, and individuals who can be contacted for advice or assistance as the need occurs? Each potential resource should be contacted before being placed on the list to determine if it is willing to be included as a resource. If so, information about that resource needs to be included on the call list. The list can be organized by subject so that any resource can be readily accessed. A standardized format should be used to record needed information that can be obtained quickly from the list. A master copy of the call list should be maintained in the shelter office and a hard copy given to every officer on field duty. It also needs to be updated as often as necessary. The list should typically contain the following basic information and the answers to the following questions:

- Name, address, telephone number, and e-mail address of the wildlife resource
- Does the organization or individual have a valid permit or license to qualify as a wildlife resource?
- Does the organization or individual have a facility to care for wildlife on a short-term basis?
- Does the organization or agency have exclusive or primary jurisdiction over selected wildlife/exotic animal species?
- Does the agency have law enforcement powers?
- Description of the services it can provide or its area of specialized expertise.
- Charges for services rendered, if applicable.
- Name of contact person in the organization and that person's direct telephone number.
- Days and hours of operation.
- After hours telephone numbers and contact person(s).
- Will the organization send representatives to the incident scene if needed?
- Does the organization offer training, and if so, what type of training?
- Does the organization maintain data on species of animals?

- Does the organization have publications available for free distribution or for sale?

- Date when each entity or individual's information was last updated.

Mutual Aid Agreements (MAA). Mutual aid agreements that most often come to mind are the ones that fire departments implement with other firefighting agencies. MAAs go hand-in-hand with the call list. But it need not be an emergency to activate an arrangement when various animal control entities assist their colleagues in a nearby community with an animal problem. Questions about liability and responsibilities could arise, so an attorney should be consulted. Similar mutual aid agreements can be beneficial for animal control, too. A city or town with a single animal control officer may find that on occasion it may take two or more trained personnel to resolve a wild animal problem, because the response plan cannot be implemented by only one person.

Contingency Funding. Communities that periodically experience problems with dangerous wildlife should consider funding a line item in the budget to remove dangerous wild animals when animal control personnel are unable to handle this task and where professional wildlife removal specialists are needed. When local officials need to act quickly to eliminate the danger to humans and companion animals, prior authorization to act and having funds available can mean a more rapid response. Any unused funds can be re-appropriated for the next fiscal year's budget. One west coast city that experienced recurring coyote and feral pig problems appropriated funds to hire an experienced wildlife removal specialist who was able to act quickly when called upon to eliminate the danger and to limit property damage caused by wild animals.

Wildlife organizations and wildlife advocates. As the number of calls received by animal control agencies for assistance with wildlife problems continues to increase, animal control management needs to rethink how it will respond to these calls. Wildlife issues are not the agency's primary mission, and there are many wildlife rehabilitators that are licensed by the state and federal governments who have the necessary experience to treat sick and injured wildlife. Rehabilitators work cooperatively with animal control agencies to save wildlife and return them to the wild. Developing cooperative relationships with wildlife organizations, rehabilitators, and wildlife advocates can be mutually beneficial, and there is the reassurance that the animal will receive the care it needs. The role of animal control in transporting or rehabilitating injured wildlife is limited by law. For example, raptors (birds of prey) are best left alone, or in special circumstances, they can be transported by animal control personnel to licensed rehabilitators. Wildlife organizations, rehabilitators, and others with training in wildlife issues can help educate the public about wildlife and may be able to assist animal control personnel with some aspects of training.

RESOURCES TO CONTACT FOR ASSISTANCE

Local animal control officials often contact other agencies for advice or assistance when they encounter wildlife problems with which they are unfamiliar or when a wildlife issue falls under the jurisdiction of another agency. The time to develop relationships with others who are potential resources is *before* the need occurs. Recently there have been efforts to bring together those with an interest in urban wildlife issues who want to learn more about the subject. An example of this effort was "Managing Urban Wildlife: Planning for Success," a one-day regional workshop held in Dallas, Texas, in February 2007, for local government officials, animal control personnel, regional planners, park and nature center staff, and local wildlife rehabilitators.

Federal and state wildlife agencies, zoos, wildlife rehabilitators, trappers, pest control, and animal removal companies have a wealth of information about various species of wildlife, and they are sometimes invited to speak and participate at conferences, workshops, and in-service training programs attended by animal control personnel. Most are happy to share their knowledge and experience with others. Not only will it be a learning experience for animal control personnel, but the exchange of information and experiences among the participants benefits all.

Other law enforcement officials such as state game wardens, local police, sheriff's deputies, state police, or state highway patrol officers may be called upon for back-up support, particularly if there may be a need to use firearms.

Resource Entities

State wildlife agencies. Every state has at least one agency that is responsible for wildlife protection and regulation. These agencies go by various names, but their roles are similar in each state. The agencies have names like Department of Fish and Game, Department of Conservation and Natural Resources, or Division of Fish and Wildlife. Using Google's search engine and the name of the state followed by "department of fish and game" will direct the user to the state wildlife agency.

Among the wildlife agency's responsibilities is the enforcement of wildlife laws that either prohibit or restrict the killing of certain animal species or keeping some animal species designated as exotic animals for reasons of public health and safety. Game wardens or other enforcement personnel such as state conservation officers, rangers, and other wildlife personnel with enforcement powers will pursue and destroy wildlife responsible for injuring or killing people and that pose a danger to the public. These same officials are also available to advise and assist local animal control officials on wildlife problems where specialized expertise is needed, how state laws affect local options for addressing wildlife problems, or where state wildlife officials' consent is needed to pursue remedies locally.

Their Web sites also contain information for homeowners and pet owners who encounter wildlife problems on their property. Advice is also available on the agencies' Web sites for those who find sick or injured wildlife or who want to know how to protect their companion animals from nuisance or dangerous wildlife. Several agency Web sites have links to frequently asked questions (FAQ). The New Hampshire Fish and Game Department FAQ link, http://www.wildlife.state.nh.us/Wildlife/faqs_wildlife.htm, addresses such issues as:

- What to do if someone finds an orphaned fawn or other animal.

- How to respond to a family of fox living in someone's backyard.

- What happens when a bay bird falls out of its nest.

- What to do when a fisher, fox, or coyote is in someone's yard and chasing after the pet cat or dog.

The Ohio Department of Natural Resources (DNR) offers advice to urban dwellers on how to prevent nuisance wildlife from taking up residence in or under a home or rummaging through garbage. Information is presented on how to remove them if they are already there. The Ohio DNR Web site is located at http://www.dnr.state.oh.us.

Wildlife rehabilitators. The role of the wildlife rehabilitator is to care for sick, injured, or abandoned wild animals until those animals can be returned to the wild. Rehabilitators must have a state permit to assume these duties and must meet certain requirements before a permit can be issued. Animal control officers by law may be allowed only limited contact with sick or injured wildlife before transferring them to a rehabilitator possessing a state permit. Names and contact information for wildlife rehabilitators are available through state wildlife agencies.

Rehabilitation of migratory birds is federally regulated. Individuals desiring to rehabilitate migratory birds need to contact the nearest Migratory Bird Permit Office of the U.S. Fish and Wildlife Service to obtain a permit. Migratory birds apply to all birds protected by the Migratory Bird Treaty Act (MBTA).

Pest control and wildlife removal companies. Some firms work closely with animal control agencies. Pest control companies, for a fee, will remove nuisance and endangered small animals whether it is bats in an attic, gophers digging up a lawn, or a bird trapped in a chimney. Some companies also specialize in removal of large wildlife.

Zoos. Although most zoos do not normally accept sick, injured, or abandoned wildlife, they do possess considerable knowledge about many wildlife species, particularly those that are on exhibit in a zoo setting. Another resource is rescue zoos and animal sanctuaries that accept animals that were given up by their owners or had been seized by authorities because of mistreatment. Many rescue zoos and sanctuaries are open to the public. These include the Popcorn Park Zoo in Forked River, New Jersey; Safari's Sanctuary in Broken Arrow, Oklahoma; the Luray Zoo in Luray, Virginia; the Austin Zoo in Austin, Texas; and East Coast Exotic Animal Rescue in Fairfield, Pennsylvania.

Nuisance wildlife trappers. Some state wildlife agencies keep lists of licensed and experienced trappers who will remove nuisance wild animals for a fee. Florida and Virginia are just two examples. Cortland, an upstate city in New York, has appropriated limited funds to pay for removal of nuisance skunks or woodchucks by a state licensed trapper. There are also federal trappers who work in association with federal and state agencies and perform a similar service. They can be reached by contacting the United States Department of Agriculture's Animal and Plant Health Inspection Service (APHIS).

EXOTIC ANIMALS

Defining Exotic Animals

Aiming for a useful definition of "exotic animals" is more complicated, because the terms "wildlife" and "exotic animals" are often used interchangeably. A wild animal need not be native to another part of the world to be classified as exotic. A bear, coyote, wolf, or bobcat are defined as wildlife that inhabit and are native to several states, but some local jurisdictions have chosen to define them also as "exotics" that are prohibited from being kept in those jurisdictions.

There are many contexts in which the phrase "exotic animals" can be used. People who keep unusual pets as opposed to keeping the more common dogs, cats, parakeets, and small cage mammals such as gerbils or guinea pigs may be considered to have an exotic pet. Keeping certain species of permitted reptiles would be commonly characterized as keeping an exotic animal, particularly if it was a non-native species. Animals that are native to other parts of the world that are on exhibit at a zoo, wildlife park, or perform in circuses and carnivals are often described as exotic animals. Although some species are available for purchase and some people keep wildlife species designated as exotics in their homes, it should not be presumed to be legal, wise, or safe to keep such animals. Keeping an undomesticated animal in captivity is not always in the best interests of the animal. Exotic animals, besides being unusual and not domesticated like a cat or a dog, may require special care and diets. Removing these animals from their natural habitat may place them at some health risk. Many are dangerous, but some individuals choose to ignore the risks to keep a tiger, rattlesnake, or bear on their property, even when prohibited by law. If individuals are willing to ignore the dangers and violate the law, they may also be willing to challenge legal action to remove the animal(s) or interfere with other enforcement efforts. Animal control officials should be prepared when confronted with an uncooperative owner and plan accordingly.

Knowing which animals are considered to be exotic can be found in definitions of exotic animals in municipal and county ordinances. Although there are differences from one ordinance to the next, it becomes clear that animals classified as exotics are either prohibited from being kept as pets or are regulated by law, and the owners must comply with certain conditions if they wish to keep them. The common characteristic in local ordinances is that those deemed to be exotic are found in nature as wild animals and there is no general agreement that they are or can be domesticated or are safe to keep around people.

REGULATION OF WILDLIFE AND EXOTIC ANIMALS

The regulation of wildlife and exotics in law consists of prohibitions on keeping certain species, restrictions on species that may be kept by individuals and organizations, and the exceptions to the rules. It is becoming more difficult for individuals to keep certain species of wildlife or exotic animal species because of government policies that determine some species are endangered and need greater protection. The following examples are illustrative of regulated species.

Definitions used to prohibit certain animal species. The Arlington, Texas, ordinance defines exotic animals as any animal in the following nine classes or orders that are also prohibited in that city. Within each order are families.

Class Mammalia (e.g., wallabies, kangaroos)

Order Perissodactyla (e.g., tapirs, zebra, wild horses)

Order Artiodactyla (e.g., giraffes, antelope, deer, camels)

Order Chiroptera (e.g., bats)

Family Siluridae (e.g., pandas)

Family Viverridae (e.g., civets, mongoose, binturongs)

Family Protelidae (e.g., aardwolves)

Order Proboscidea (e.g., elephants)

Order Primates (e.g., monkeys, marmoset, tamarin)

Section 6.18.010 of the Arkansas City, Kansas municipal code defines an exotic animal to mean "Any poisonous reptile or other wild animal or reptile or any vicious or dangerous animal or other animal or reptile of wild, vicious or dangerous propensities, requiring a standard of care and control greater than required for customary household pets sold by commercial Pet Shops or domestic farm animals…"

The ordinance goes on to describe nineteen prohibited animals and species. Simply put, exotic animals are whatever the laws say they are. Bloomington, Indiana's ordinances identifies exotic animals as those "…not native to the United States, or an animal that is a hybrid or cross between a domestic animal and an animal that is not native to the United States." Stokes County, North Carolina, bans the piranha an aquarium fish.

Ordinances use either broadly defined or detailed descriptions of animal species and subspecies to ban such animals and impose penalties for violations. Ordinances may also contain exceptions. Pet shops, zoos, circuses, carnivals, educational, scientific, or medical institutions are usually exempt. An exempt entity under the law may still be subject to some limited conditions. The Arkansas City ordinance requires exempt entities to comply with zoning ordinances, and all animals must be kept in clean and sanitary condition. The city requires animal quarters be free of objectionable odors and must be secure enough to prevent the animal's escape. The West Jordan, Utah, ordinance defines wild animal as "any animal of a species that in their natural life are wild." The ordinance goes on to list categories of animals designated as wild animals, whether or not they have been domesticated, and to state that these animals may not be kept in that city. The exceptions to the West Jordan ordinance are animals at a veterinary hospital, an animal shelter, humane society shelter, or scientific facilities. The ordinance also states that it is unlawful for anyone to keep a species that is prohibited or protected by Title 50 of the Code of Federal Regulations or any state law in Utah.

Restrictions on keeping certain species. Some local governments have allowed certain wildlife to be kept in their respective jurisdictions if the animals resided there prior to the effective date of the ordinance that prohibited them. Local ordinances in Spokane and Puyallup, both in Washington State, and Stokes County, in North Carolina, have these provisions.

Stokes County's local law that became effective on October 26, 2004, is one of the most restrictive. The owner of a pre-existing exotic animal in that county before the date the more restrictive law took effect has thirty days from the effective date of the new ordinance to initiate the permit/registration process for that animal. If the animal owner fails to meet the thirty day calendar requirement, the owner will be treated as the owner of a new animal and must remove the animal from the county within seven days or face a fine of $1,000, plus $250 per day for each day the exotic animal is in the county's custody. If the animal is permitted to be kept in this county, it could be subject to such terms and conditions as a non-refundable permit fee of $1,000 per exotic animal, a signage requirement, implant of a microchip in the animal, a written emergency response plan, the requirement of a veterinary health certificate, specially designed housing facilities to secure the animal to prevent any dangers the animal presents, and inspection by Stokes County animal control. The ordinance can be reviewed at www.stokes.nc.us.

New York enacted an amendment to the General Municipal Law requiring everyone who owned, possessed, or harbored a wild animal to report the animal to the city, village, or town clerk where the animal is kept. The purpose of this provision is to protect public safety and the safety of emergency services personnel (fire, police, and ambulance personnel) when performing their duties. Animals to be reported are found at http://www.westseneca.net/animals.html.

Florida allows some wildlife to be possessed by individuals as personal pets pursuant to Section 372.922 Florida Statutes. To be eligible to keep Class III wildlife, the applicant needs to obtain a no-cost permit issued by the Florida Fish and Wildlife Conservation Commission (FWC). Wildlife in this classification includes but is not limited to small monkeys, racoons, opossums, skunks, lemurs, and wallabies. Further details can be found at the FWC Web site located at http://myfwc.com/permits/.

Other requirements. There are many other wildlife provisions too numerous to mention, but there are two cited here that are not uncommon. Local laws may prohibit feeding wildlife (e.g., coyotes and deer) to discourage wildlife from entering populated areas in search of food. Another example found in the Stevens Point, Wisconsin Municipal Code requires any person bitten or scratched by any wild animal to report the incident to the local health officer or attending physician.

Local Role in Regulating Performance Animals

Many municipalities and counties require that some temporary animal exhibitions such as circuses and carnivals must have proper licenses and permits, be subject to inspection, and must adhere to some terms and conditions to operate locally. Some local laws exempt dog and cat shows from these regulations, but others do not. Casper, Wyoming, requires a permit for a dog show or exhibition. The Cobb County, Georgia, animal ordinance requires six conditions to be met and defines which exhibitions are legal and those that are illegal. The full ordinance is found at http://animalcontrol.cobbcountyga.gov. Local regulation of performing animals may be limited as the federal and state governments have regulatory powers that may supersede local laws.

Some animal advocate groups have recommended local governments enact ordinances outlawing the use of performing animal acts. These acts are most often cited by animal rights groups in their campaigns to ban exotic animals from being placed on public display.

Other Concerns

Exotic animals kept as pets pose another challenge. They may be docile with their owners, but because they are not domesticated, they could become dangerous at any moment. Some species prohibited by law from being kept as pets may be hidden by their owners and away from public view. Should a prohibited species that is dangerous, whether it be a tiger or a venomous snake, escape from its confinement and find its way to freedom, it could pose an immediate threat to humans and other animals. Regulation and registration of wildlife kept in residential dwellings, where permitted, keeps animal control officials aware of their presence and helps them prepare for an appropriate response should it be needed. Should a dangerous animal escape from its enclosure and pose a threat to humans and other animals, it could quickly escalate into a difficult to manage crisis.

FEDERAL REGULATION OF WILDLIFE

Federal Laws

Wildlife is regulated by laws at the federal, state, and local levels of government, but not all aspects of wildlife are covered by provisions in law, nor does every level of government have similar provisions in law. Some states and local governments do not have any law that regulates the keeping of wildlife as pets. Even at the federal level, wildlife laws are limited by the U.S. Constitution. The main federal law that applies to wildlife in the context of this chapter is the Animal Welfare Act, although The Endangered Species Act and the Lacey Act may have some limited application.

The Animal Welfare Act (AWA). The AWA is administered by the Animal and Plant Health Inspection Service (APHIS) of the United States Department of Agriculture (USDA). The AWA will be of the most interest to local animal control agencies, because this law can reach out to wildlife in the community. Animal shelters and pounds are regulated under the AWA if they sell dogs and cats to dealers. The AWA requires that minimum standards of care be provided to certain animals bred for commercial sale, used in research, transported commercially, or exhibited to the public. The latter two are probably of more interest to animal control officials. The AWA's authority covers the care and treatment of warm-blooded animals. Warm-blooded animals on display or that perform for the public must be licensed with APHIS. They include lions, tigers, elephants, and monkeys, to name a few. Licensed exhibitors include circuses, roadside animal exhibits, zoos, petting zoos, animal acts, wildlife parks, nature preserves, game farms, and marine mammal parks. This law also applies to pets transported on commercial airlines. The AWA prohibits staged dog fights, bear or raccoon baiting, and similar animal fighting ventures. Individuals and businesses covered under the AWA must be licensed or registered with APHIS, which also conducts searches for unlicensed exhibitors.

APHIS will review and investigate violations, impose penalties, issue official warnings, and set civil penalties for infractions including cease and desist orders, and can issue fines, license suspensions, or revocations. Violations that require further action are sent to USDA for further legal review.

There are exceptions. Farm animals, animals used in food, fiber, or agricultural purposes, are exempt under the AWA. Birds, rats, or mice bred for research are also excluded. Also excluded from coverage are cold-blooded animals such as snakes and alligators. Retail pet stores are exempt from regulation under the AWA except in a few instances. If the pet store sells exotic or zoo animals or sells animals to regulated businesses, it falls under the AWA. Pets that are owned by private citizens are not covered under the AWA.

The following federal laws have limited application to the work of animal control officers, but an animal control officer may discover the illegal possession of an animal that is covered by the provisions of either act.

The Endangered Species Act of 1973. This federal statute is a component of the program to protect animal and plant species threatened with extinction. Over one thousand species are listed as endangered. Protected species are not only those native to the United States, but those of other countries that are covered by the Convention on International Trade in Endangered Species of Wild Fauna and Flora. This program is administered jointly by the U.S. Fish and Wildlife Service and the National Marine Fisheries Service. A pet store selling any species that is on the endangered or threatened species list under this Act would be in violation of this law. Among the species covered by the Act are anadromous fish and sea turtles as well as birds, sea otters, and terrestrial and freshwater species.

The Lacey Act. This federal act, which was signed into law in 1900 and which has had three major amendments over the years, prohibits both trade and possession of wildlife, fish, and plants that have been taken illegally, even those taken in violation of state laws. The law is administered by three federal departments: Interior, Commerce, and Agriculture.

Federal agencies. Birds, terrestrial and freshwater species, sea otters, and sea turtles while on land are the responsibility of the U.S. Fish and Wildlife Service (USFWS) under the Endangered Species Act of 1973. The Act also covers anadromous fish and sea turtles when they are in the water, but this is a responsibility of the National Marine Fisheries Service (NFS). Birds in the water fall under Fish and Wildlife Service, not NFS. USFWS is a bureau in the Department of the Interior, and NFS is a division of the Department of Commerce.

Jurisdictional Issues

Federal, state, and local laws provide authority to agencies at every level of government to protect wildlife/exotics animals. It would appear that there is some overlap and confusion. A state wildlife law may deem a certain wild animal as an endangered species that is protected by law from being hunted and killed. A local ordinance may additionally prohibit keeping such species from being kept captive or fed by local residents.

There may be more than one agency at the state or federal levels that have roles in wildlife damage management activities. This, too, can be confusing. California, for example, has six agencies involved in these issues, of which five are state entities and one is a federal agency. They are: University of California, Cooperative Extension; California Department of Food and Agriculture; California Department Fish and Game; USDA-APHIS-Wildlife Services; California Department of Pesticide Regulation; and the California Department of Health Services.

STATE REGULATION OF WILDLIFE

State wildlife agencies manage diverse species of wildlife and their habitats. The agencies enforce regulations on the hunting and trapping of wildlife and set regulations on which animals may be possessed, taken, or controlled. The agencies also determine which species are endangered for listing and monitor the health of their wildlife populations. States define what is meant by an exotic animal, determine if it is prohibited species or if it may be kept by private individuals, and under what terms and conditions it may be kept.

Issuance of permits. Although keeping some species of wildlife are illegal (depending on the state), there are exceptions when a permit may be issued. Two examples are Pennsylvania and Texas. The Pennsylvania Game Commission may issue a permit to a person to act as an exotic wildlife dealer. The permit allows that person to import exotic wildlife into that state and to possess, buy, sell, locate, find for a fee, barter, donate, give away, or dispose of exotic wildlife. The phrase exotic wildlife under Pennsylvania law includes but is not limited to bears, coyotes, lions, tigers, leopards, jaguars, and cheetahs. The state may also issue permits to persons who possess exotic wildlife, provided that the commission is satisfied that there is adequate housing and proper care of the animal(s). Permits to operate a menagerie and publicly exhibit the animals may be issued subject to requirements imposed by the commission.

The Wildlife Division of Texas Parks and Wildlife issues permits in several categories. The following are eight examples of the sixteen categories of permits:

- Protected Wildlife Rehabilitation permit: Issued to individuals to rehabilitate orphaned and injured wildlife.

- Scientific Research permit to collect, salvage, or band native wildlife for scientific purposes.

- Educational Display permit to hold or collect wildlife or parts of protected wildlife for educational purposes.

- Zoological Collection permit issued to accredited facilities for scientific understanding and to encourage management and conservation.

- Falconry permit subject to specific conditions (must also have federal permit).

- Raptor Propagation permit to raise birds of prey.

- Endangered Species Propagation permit to propagate legally acquired species.

- Protected Wildlife Transport Letter of Authorization allows transport of wildlife under certain circumstances.

How is this information of use to animal control directors? State wildlife agencies are a source of information on state wildlife policy and about wildlife policy in general. State authorities can advise on how and when to apply state wildlife laws, and as noted earlier, will assist local animal control personnel in dangerous wildlife situations. State officials generally possess greater legal authority, experience, and expertise in wildlife matters than local officials. These agencies generate and maintain data about wildlife that can of help to local animal control officials. For example, the Maine Department of Inland Fisheries and Wildlife on its Web site, http://www.maine.gov/ifw/wildlife, maintains a list of fish and wildlife species that may be kept as pets in that state, do not require an importation permit, and may be traded by commercial pet shops.

The Rhode Island Department of Environmental Management reports that it collects useful data on coyotes including the animal's dietary habits, diseases, reproductive history, and population age structure. Additional information is available on the department's Web site at http://www.dem.ri.gov. Other useful information about coyotes is available on the Web site of the New Jersey Department of Environmental Protection, Division of Fish and Wildlife, at www.state.nj.us/dep/. Since state agencies issue permits that allow individuals to be in possession of certain species of wildlife, it is in the interest of animal control directors who maintain liaison with wildlife agencies to be familiar with these permits, particularly if animal control officials come in contact with those species where permits may be required.

SUMMARY

Wildlife and exotic animal regulation has become a matter of increasing concern to animal control management, because animal control is most often the first responder when calls are received for assistance in the capture of dangerous wildlife or to address other wildlife issues. The lawful and unlawful possession of wild animals and non-domesticated exotic species, however they may be defined in each state, present both challenges and dangers for animal control personnel. Responders from local animal control agencies need to be trained in how to respond to calls for service that involve wildlife and whom to call if they need help or if the matter falls under the jurisdiction of another agency. There are a number of resources at all levels of government that can be called upon for advice and assistance.

Defining the terms wildlife and exotic animals varies by state, and what is interpreted to be wildlife in one state may be an exotic in another. What the terms have in common is that they refer to animals that are not allowed to be possessed by individuals, or if they are permitted to be kept by individuals, their possession is based on compliance with state requirements to protect both animals and humans. Many local governments either impose restrictions on keeping certain non-domesticated animals or prohibit them altogether. Federal laws also apply to some species of wildlife and exotic animals, and there is both overlap and cooperation between and among wildlife regulatory agencies. Federal regulations are primarily found in three federal statutes, but the responsibilities are spread among several federal agencies. At the state level, there may be one or more agencies having wildlife responsibilities.

Notes

1. Nevada Revised Statutes, Title 45, Ch. 501, sec. 501.097 (2007)

Chapter 16

Reviewing /Auditing Animal Control Programs

INTRODUCTION

Audits are a routine but necessary element in the process of governmental oversight. The audit process is an effort is to verify that public monies are spent for their intended purposes and that the desired results were obtained.

Problems and unanswered questions about animal control programs may lead to a review of the program to gather facts and to obtain answers to questions. There are many reasons why programs are reviewed. They include but are not limited to a series of complaints lodged with local officials alleging inhumane treatment of animals, the high number of animals euthanized, and the low rate of animal adoptions. Personnel and management issues, questions raised by elected officials, the media, or a few major animal incidents can also be contributing factors.

Numerous complaints over a period of time may strike a chord with elected officials and local government administrators when combined with outstanding and long-term issues that need to be addressed. An outside review of the program has often been the way to get to the heart of the issues, because an outside review may be viewed as more credible with greater independence. Local governments that initiate the review process may be surprised by the number and scope of the findings and cost to cure the problems. A recommendation to build a new animal shelter may not be on the municipality's radar screen and can be an unexpected expense that will require special financing. Some recommendations can be implemented in the short term, but others may take longer, because costs need to be determined. The reports evaluating animal control programs often leave it to elected officials and others to prioritize the needs and to find the resources to make changes. Consultants or auditors retained to evaluate or audit these programs are both observers and critics with experience in this field paid by their clients to find out what went wrong and how to remedy the problems.

The audit/review process brings a big dose of reality to administrators and elected officials alike, so the process should be entered into only after careful thought and preparation by the client. A program review or audit should be viewed as an opportunity to address new needs and bring the program into line with best practices in this field. This chapter discusses the various aspects of the audit/review process and how the client can maximize the benefits of an audit or review of the animal control program. Once the audit/review has been completed, the client local government needs to prioritize the recommendations and prepare a plan to stimulate and produce improvements to regain public confidence.

The term "audit" at one time meant a type of financial inquiry (e.g., verifying accounts and records). In the past when one heard the term "auditor," what immediately came to mind was an accountant pouring over financial ledgers. Today, the term "audit" has a broader meaning beyond reviewing and giving an opinion of financial accounts and records. It now includes assessing how well the program is performing overall, not simply whether the records are accurate or properly kept. Interviews, reviewing records and documents, sampling transactions, and assessing policies and work procedures are all part of the process. The audit makes findings about how well the program is operating and how successful it has been in meeting its goals and objectives.

An audit of an animal control program would be considered a *performance audit* of which there are two types, *management and efficiency audits* and *program audits*. The former focuses on how effectively the agency or program manages its resources and how to remedy inefficiencies. The second kind of performance-type audit is known as a program audit. The focus is on determining whether program objectives are being met and if the program is in compliance with law. An evaluation of an animal control program is likely to be either type of audit or some hybrid of both. Malan, Fountain, Arrowsmith, and Lockridge in defining "performance auditing" asserted that it was a "systemic process," and that it was objective.[1] Both approaches are about discovering program shortcomings and presenting recommendations to correct them. When questions are raised about program performance and program management decisions and a program review is undertaken, it will usually cover all or the most program activities. For the purposes of this chapter, an audit has the following definition:

An organized inquiry that reports on the current state of an animal control program and objectively identifies issues and problems, and offers recommendations to encourage the correction of perceived deficiencies, and to promote best practices recognized by animal control professionals.

The audit may be conducted by a professional auditor, an animal control or management consultant, a committee, or a staff analyst experienced in preparing reports assessing government services.

There is a defined process by which a program and/or an agency is reviewed to determine how successful it has been in achieving its desired results. An evaluation of an animal control program, while it includes review of documentation, also takes into consideration the observations of an experienced and knowledgeable evaluator. It is not uncommon that auditors or evaluators are challenged on their objectivity and understanding of the program when they report negative findings. Once the decision is made to conduct an audit, it sends a message to the public and others that an objective process will begin to determine the efficiency and effectiveness of a program or organization. The terms "audit" and "review" are used interchangeably in this chapter, because auditors, consultants, and others who review and assess animal control programs have the same ends in mind (e.g., to improve the program or the effectiveness of the agency).

Auditing the Animal Control Contractor Versus Auditing an In-house Program

Since many local jurisdictions outsource their animal control programs through contract to a nonprofit, private, or another governmental entity, it is recommended that the contract document state that the client has the right to review, inspect, and audit records upon reasonable notice to the contractor. Since humane societies and local SPCAs are independent private organizations governed by boards of directors, there is some question whether they can be compelled to produce documents requested by auditors reviewing their animal control activities. If the contractor fails to produce requested documents that it has in its possession, it should be noted in the audit report. The contractor then has to defend why it did not comply with this request.

The following provision found in an animal control contract between the city of Riverside, California, and Riverside County illustrates how the parties agreed to authorize a review of the animal control program by the client city:

County shall maintain and keep records of all expenditures and obligations incurred pursuant to this contract and all income and fees received thereby according to generally accepted accounting principles. Such records shall be maintained by the County for a minimum of three (3) years. The records and/or animal control operations of County shall be open to inspection and audit by City or its authorized representative as is deemed necessary by the City Manager of City or the authorized representative of the City Manager upon reasonable notice to County.[2]

These clauses provide a basis for a client jurisdiction to review and determine whether the animal control program, which it funds, is meeting its goals and objectives and operating in a manner consistent with the terms of the contract. If the contract does not specifically state that the client jurisdiction has the right to inspect and audit the contractor's operation, an attorney's advice should be sought.

If animal control services are performed by a nonprofit or for-profit contractor, the contractor should be given the opportunity to respond to the audit report and the auditor should correct any *factual* errors that may be brought to its attention by the contractor. It is up to the client to decide if the contractor's response should be included in an audit report or reported separately.

One nonprofit contractor, after noting the auditor's comments about priorities in responding to calls about stray dogs, stated: "We look forward to discussing with county officials the manner in which this can be accomplished, and *associated additional costs*" [emphasis added]. The contractor's reply made it clear that *any* change will result in higher cost is disturbing, because it appears that the contractor has declared any change will result in higher cost without determining if the change merits an additional expense to the contractor.

Auditing an in-house animal control program is a different matter. If animal control is a stand-alone city, town, or county department or a division in another department, authority to conduct an audit or internal review and to compel the production of documents and data should not be a problem, as it is within the powers of local government officials to do so. The review may be assigned to local government staff or to an outside entity or individual. Some program reviews may be conducted by a committee that has community representation and input.

REASONS FOR AUDITING ANIMAL CONTROL PROGRAMS

Aside from any regularly scheduled financial review of accounts required by law, most animal control programs are reviewed for effectiveness for many reasons. Mostly, the reasons are about alleged inhumane care of animals, the number of animals euthanized, or the low animal adoption rate. Other reasons are issues having political implications, internal personnel, or management problems, including a change in management, external complaints, escalating program costs, and/or reduction in revenues. Personality conflicts between the animal control director and his/her critics or a breakdown in communication can quickly escalate and at some point may lead to a decision to audit the program. Programs are reviewed because of problems or issues that have not been resolved and because local officials want more information. Local government officials may feel compelled to act because of the substance of allegations levied by critics, and because if the allegations prove to be true, they may be too serious to ignore and need to be corrected. Local elected and appointed officials do not want to be accused of condoning the inhumane care of animals or anything that smacks of neglect or cruelty to animals on their watch. An audit gives the decision-making officials some political cover by assigning to others the responsibility for examining the issues, temporarily defusing what could be a sensitive political problem, and removing it for the time being from the public spotlight.

As a word of caution, animal control management should first be given an opportunity to look into and respond to complaints received by elected and appointed officials and those communicated by the public directly to program management. If management can correct the problems or the complaining party is satisfied with the response, than the matter need not escalate. If the matter cannot be resolved, if complaints continue to be received, or if local officials are not satisfied with animal control's response, then other options can be contemplated. A decision to audit the program should not be taken lightly as it can be costly, takes time to conduct a review process, and once the process has begun, it will be difficult to stop. More importantly, the process must produce a report that yields useful data and addresses the concerns of those who commissioned the study. Why spend time and money to conduct an audit if no changes will be made, particularly, if the audit findings show serious program deficiencies?

Financial Audit Findings

Local government internal auditors schedule a financial audit of departments and programs on a predetermined calendar schedule so that each department or program will be reviewed at least once in an established time frame, every fiscal year or two. The findings of a financial audit may be a reason to conduct a program performance audit that would examine in greater detail the various components of the program. When subject to a financial audit, animal control will be examined to determine if its cash controls are adequate and to determine if any funds are missing or misspent for unauthorized purposes. Among the tests applied during a financial audit is whether spay/neuter fees, license fees, and impound fees are properly accounted for. Deficiencies in those areas may be a clue to other problems. The auditor may sample license fee renewal transactions to determine if renewal notices were mailed on time, the rate of response by mail, and whether there are any processing problems. A comparison may be made of revenues generated from one fiscal year to another. Nonprofits that contract to provide animal control services are also subject to financial audits. A jurisdiction that contracts with a nonprofit for animal services should request a copy of the organization's annual financial audit, because it received public funds.

Personnel or Management Issues

Grievances filed by shelter or field personnel against animal control management or other local government officials, if not resolved, over a specified time period and seen as negatively impacting the program, may lead to a decision to review the program, particularly if the grievances were aired publicly. Grievances levied by animal service staff may include allegations of unfair workload, favoritism by management in promotions, cruelty to animals by some employees, personality clashes with a supervisor, and unpaid overtime

Questions raised by city council members or the city manager about recent decisions made by an animal control manager or the perceived failure of an animal control manager to institute changes requested by the city manager and city council may eventually lead to a program review. A report showing an increase in the number of animals euthanized and a drop in animal adoptions together with the filing of employee grievances may trigger requests for an audit if the answers received are deemed unsatisfactory or if local officials have lost confidence in the animal control manager.

Change in Management

When a long-time animal control manager or director retires or resigns, an opportunity arises to take a fresh look at the program, especially if the program has not been evaluated in many years. The transition period when one manager departs and before a new manager takes over can be a good time to conduct a review. Reviewing the program during this period may encourage staff to speak more freely. Some staff who might have held back their comments for fear of retaliation or loyalty to management may no longer feel restrained.

This period can also be used to implement some needed program changes before a new director is hired.

Elected Officials Concerns

Events external to the animal control program may trigger a review of the animal control program. Annual budgetary increases to fund animal control services, particularly those outsourced to the private sector, often have local officials demanding more cost containment and contemplating other operating options. After hearing complaints about service and failing to have their questions answered to their satisfaction, elected officials may be more receptive to a review of the program. This could lead to a request to audit either the current service and/or the provider itself. Elected officials may feel they need to act after hearing complaints from several constituents that are deemed too serious to ignore. For example, a senior citizen's receipt of a citation for a leash law violation that the owner believes was in error or hearing from a distraught pet owner whose cat was euthanized before he had a chance to redeem it, when combined with fifteen other complaints filed with elected officials in a three month period, may be all it takes to launch a review, particularly if the program has not been reviewed in many years. There is no test to determine how many complaints or other factors it takes to conduct an audit or review. It is a political decision.

One city created an ad hoc committee to review the animal control contract with a local nonprofit group that held the contract for more than thirty years. A city council member who initiated this effort (and subsequently chaired the ad hoc committee) justified the committee's need this way:

> A comprehensive look at the animal control program has not been undertaken in more than twenty years. In view of increasing costs, recent efforts to explore regional animal control options, concerns about program effectiveness and the long passage of time since this program has been reviewed in its entirety, it would seem appropriate to review this program at this time.

Over a four month period the committee was to "review in depth the city's current animal control program, evaluate the programs in place in other jurisdictions, and then formulate recommendations for improving the city's program." The eight member committee consisted of two city council members, one of whom served as chair, two local animal advocates, two veterinarians, a dog trainer, and an interested local resident. The committee became a change agent for implementing a new animal control program. The committee developed a new humane program philosophy and presented twenty-four program recommendations. The committee's report became the blueprint for a new city-county animal care and control program.

Complaints from Pet Owners and Animal Advocates

Unhappy and vocal pet owners and representatives of organized animal welfare groups are frequently the catalysts that spur local government officials to request a program review or audit. Occasionally, activists known to be affiliated with an organization seeking the animal control contract have criticized the current provider, perhaps with some justification. Complaints from animal activists should not be taken lightly as their allegations may have merit unless proven otherwise.

The Media

Local newspapers, radio, or television stations frequently report alleged deficiencies in animal control programs. Letters to the newspaper's editor and interviews with individuals who have grievances filed against animal control provide grist for the mill. Some critics or aggrieved parties actively seek media involvement to highlight the issue. Once the media goes public and reports the issue, local government officials will need to respond. The amount of publicity, the charges levied, and the length of time it remains in the news will influence whether the program will be reviewed. Occasional letter writers to the local newspaper who write to express their opinions about animal control services or to report their own personal experiences with animal control are to be expected. The animal control manager should read each piece to determine if the letters are factual. Depending on the situation, the animal control manager may want to contact the letter writer. Other letters of similar content or that share a common theme deserve attention from animal control management. Failure to do so may lead complainants to believe that animal control management is ignoring or denying problems exist.

Citizen Appearances before Local Legislative Bodies

Typically, pet owners and others seeking more program resources also appear before the local city or town council or county legislative body at budget time to request more funding. They may appear before these bodies at other times when they believe animal control officials are not responsive to their concerns. Whether the issue is about barking dogs creating a neighborhood nuisance or loose dogs running in packs that are frightening schoolchildren or older residents, animal control problems are at or near the top of the list of community problems. The complaint may be that they were denied the opportunity to adopt an animal from the shelter without explanation. When local residents speak at a public meeting, sometimes their comments appear disorganized and lengthy. Yet their message is clear that they are unhappy, and they will not hesitate to say why. Elected officials will then need to decide whether there is a real or perceived problem. The matter may be referred to animal control, to a legislative committee, or to another official for a response by a specified date. If elected officials see these comments reflecting a continuing pattern over time, they may consider requesting a formal or informal review of the issues. The inquiry may be assigned to staff, or a large-scale review may be referred to an audit firm or a consultant.

Grand Jury Inquiry

County civil grand juries may choose to investigate an animal control program based on complaints received in writing from private citizens and other sources. Interestingly, one critic of an animal control program who was not satisfied with the agency's response to his complaints about the program contacted the civil grand jury and asked that it review animal control services. The grand jury's report is usually a public document, and the inquiry is conducted by lay persons. It is intended to hold county officials responsible and encourage them to take corrective action. One county grand jury conducted an inquiry and issued a critical report of the county's animal control program. The report cited twenty-eight findings, which also included a review of internal financial controls by the county controller at the behest of the grand jury. The grand jury report in one state led to a detailed response by animal control officials, the creation of a committee to recommend program changes, and the eventual resignation of the director and other senior animal control officials.

Lawsuits

A verdict in favor of the plaintiff may prove expensive for the local government defendant. If the local government's attorney determines that the lawsuit has merit, it can be viewed as a need to make some internal organization or program changes as there could be continuing liability if certain practices continue. At a later date, after the decision on the litigation has been rendered, an audit may be conducted.

HOW CRITICS INFLUENCE THE AUDIT PROCESS

Once the decision has been made to examine the program, critics may attempt to influence the choice of consultant and the direction and scope of the audit either publicly or behind the scenes. The choice rests with local government officials who have the decision-making authority and who control the purse strings. This is all the more reason why local officials need to have a better understanding of the issues and be able to decide whether a consultant or auditor best meets their needs. The RFQ and RFP processes can be helpful in this respect, along with input from local government officials in other jurisdictions who have been through a similar process.

Some who disagree with the current program philosophy or practices, view current animal control ordinances as too strict, or would like to see a change in management or even a new provider, may encourage the need for an audit. When a local animal welfare organization perceives animal control as a competitor for animal adoptions or other reasons, it may levy criticism of the animal control provider at every opportunity.

PROGRAM REVIEW OPTIONS

When local officials recognize the need for a program review, the question becomes: what are the options? An ad hoc committee, internal review by staff, or an external review are options to review an animal control program or agency.

Ad Hoc Committee. Ad hoc committees have been used with success in some communities to evaluate the program. Their efforts have generated new ideas and recommendations to promote pet adoptions, amend animal ordinances, promote pet owner responsibility, create a corps of volunteers, find ways to raise funds, and develop consensus on issues in need of examination. Finally, the committee often consists of lay persons, some of whom have a strong interest in animal welfare, plus others who are animal professionals such as veterinarians or animal trainers as well as individuals with organizational management experience who can offer other perspectives. Members need to be fair-minded and respected, and the membership need to be balanced so that various interests are represented. The committee needs to capable of developing a consensus on issues.

The committee has the benefit of community representation at little or no cost. If funds are available, and it is within the mission of the committee, the members should visit other animal shelters in the state to see their operations firsthand or invite animal control professionals outside their geographical area to address the committee. The committee may have neither the authority or expertise to document all program shortcomings, but it may nonetheless recognize some of the more obvious problems. At minimum, it should be viewed as an advisory group to the local elected governing body, the mayor, or to some other official charged with making animal control decisions. The value of the committee is in providing support and advice that local officials can use to make program improvements.

Internal Review

A review of the program by a staff analyst, internal auditor, accountant, budget analyst, or any individual who possesses analytic skills and is capable of preparing a report of findings and recommendations is another low cost option. Many municipal internal audit offices have produced useful audit reports on animal control programs. Someone on the city manager's staff in a smaller community might be assigned this task. It is not necessary that one have experience in animal control work (but knowledge of the subject would be beneficial). It is more important to know how to gather and analyze data, understand how organizations function, and how to measure goals and objectives. The person given this assignment, who can get up to speed quickly on how animal control programs operate, could review several program activities.

There are many resources available to help someone reviewing this program. A primary resource is the Internet, where the reviewer can quickly gather information. State agencies, particularly state health or agriculture departments with responsibilities for oversight of animal control, may have publications available and specialists who are able to offer advice. For example, the Texas Department of Health publishes a voluminous but useful publication titled *Animal Control Officer Training Manual* that can be downloaded from the Web or purchased from that Department. Similarly, local animal control ordinances are also posted on the Web.

National animal welfare groups publish materials on this subject, and their Web sites contain much useful information. These groups include the American Humane Association, the Humane Society of the United States (HSUS), and the National Animal Control Association (NACA). State associations of municipal and county governments maintain libraries of reports and other documents that may be available on loan to member governments. State or regional associations of animal control directors and state associations of animal control officers are also helpful sources. Animal control audit or evaluative reports prepared for other jurisdictions are often available once the reports become public.

An in-house review means the task can be assigned quickly, a completion date set, and access to in-house records is much easier. An internal review can be broadened in scope, if necessary. An external review that extends beyond the original proposal will normally incur additional cost for extra work. Having the audit conducted by in-house governmental staff comes with official authority to assure cooperation of all parties. The cost of an in-house review is mainly staff time, and additional funding is not generally needed unless there is some travel involved or some special expense unique to the audit. An in-house work product of high quality may nonetheless be questioned by those who say the reviewer is biased and is not really independent. Those who disagree with the findings of an outside auditor or consultant may question their qualifications. Solid documentation can help refute such allegations.

External Review

Local government decision makers may decide to select an outside entity to review the program. Lack of in-house expertise, amount of staff time required, and the desire to have a neutral outside party present a report may appear more credible if major changes are expected.

Animal welfare/control organizations. Some national and state animal welfare/control organizations advertise their availability and expertise to review local animal control programs and can point to studies they have completed in various parts of the country. The evaluations are conducted by teams consisting of individuals with a broad range of experiences in animal control services. The teams use an established format to conduct the review process. Their approach includes interviews, observations, and reviewing various types of documentation, and they usually label their work as an "evaluation," not an audit, which could emphasize records review. Their reports present numerous findings and recommendations. How well animal control tasks are performed are their bread and butter, because they offer their services as *animal control* consultants.

Animal control directors associations. Another approach to evaluating an animal control program is to request help from a state animal control directors association. The membership includes experienced directors who may be willing to undertake a review as a short term assignment. This approach has the benefit of tapping the knowledge of those who understand the state's animal control requirements and are familiar with and know what needs to be included in local animal ordinances. A variation of this approach is to engage the services of an experienced animal control director from another jurisdiction whose program is well regarded by other professionals in the field, to review specific issues or to advise local officials on how to address program concerns. Written permission from the director's employer may be required before the assignment can be accepted.

Management consultants. Another option is to utilize the services of a management consultant with local government experience. The consultant may consider partnering with an experienced active or retired animal control director or perhaps a veterinarian to assess the animal control program. The advantage is that the consultant can concentrate on management issues, which can be integrated with the findings and recommendations of the animal control director or veterinarian. This approach benefits from having two different specialists complement each other.

AUDIT/REVIEW PREPARATION

Before selecting an outside auditor or consultant, local officials need to have a clear idea of what issues they would like to have reviewed and to convey them to the auditor or consultant orally and in writing before the work has begun. The client must make its priorities clear so that the resulting work product will meet its needs. The following examples illustrate this point.

Example No. 1

Local critics complained to the county administrative officer and to the county legislature that staff at the county-run animal shelter unnecessarily euthanized dogs and cats that could have been placed for adoption. Five pet owners also filed complaints that their pets were killed before they had a chance to reclaim them.

The complaints of the critics and owners should have been referred at first to the animal control director for a response. If the director's response was inadequate, then this information should be forwarded to the auditor or consultant for follow-up.

A discussion with the auditor should be followed by written provisions in the contract, if an outside auditor is retained, or in a memorandum to an internal auditor, if one is given this assignment. Priorities given to the consultant or auditor may be expressed in the following questions that policymakers want to have answered and/or addressed in a Request for Proposal (RFP). Note that these questions also address allegations levied in the above example:

- What is the policy for euthanizing animals, and how are animals selected?

- Are euthanasia procedures being followed, and are they humane?

- Do euthanasia and/or adoption policies/procedures need to be changed, and if so, why?

- How long are animals held before being euthanized?

- What efforts are made to locate the owners of impounded animals, and have those efforts been documented? Are current efforts sufficient?

- Were any animals euthanized that could have been offered for adoption? If so, please explain and document to the extent possible.

- What do the statistics show about animals returned to owners versus those euthanized?

- What can be done to reduce the number of animals euthanized?

Example No. 2

Three local breed rescue groups complained to the city's mayor that they were denied the opportunity to transfer animals from the city shelter to their organizations for placement in new homes. All allege that shelter staff refuses to allow animals to be adopted if the animals are undergoing minor treatment with medications. They further allege that the shelter's pet adoption efforts lag behind other shelters where they obtain animals.

Again, animal control should first be given an opportunity to respond. Following are some suggested questions for the auditor to address based on the complaints from the rescue groups:

- What are the current policies and procedures for adopting animals, and are they being followed?

- How many animals were denied transfer to rescue groups because of needed medical treatment, what was the medical condition(s) treated, and did a veterinarian concur with staff's decisions?

- Compare adoption statistics for the most recent four year period if possible, and how do they compare to other similar shelters?

- What priority is placed on adoptions as a program objective? Please document to the extent possible.

- What recommendations would you offer to increase the number of adoptions?

- Do the allegations levied by these groups have merit? Please explain.

- Are breed rescue and foster animal care groups pre-qualified before animals are transferred to their custody?

- Have there been any problems working with these groups? If so, please explain.

It is common when seeking an outside auditor or evaluator to prepare a Request for Qualifications (RFQ) and to send them out to various firms and individuals to determine both their interest in this project and their qualifications. Once it is determined that they are qualified and interested, then the Request for Proposal (RFP) documents will be sent to them. The RFQ should be brief, but it should ask questions needed to help determine whether the firm or individual has the experience and knowledge to conduct an audit or evaluation. It is appropriate to ask in the RFQ for the responder to cite work experience with other similar projects. The RFP will allow the interested firm or individual to submit a proposal on how the audit or review will be conducted and the proposed scope of services. The RFP package sent to interested parties should include areas of concern to the client to be addressed in the process.

The client may wish to add a question in the RFP packet whether the respondent would be willing to help implement its recommendations and the cost of this service.

The attorney representing the jurisdiction that intends to hire an auditor or consultant may be asked to draft an agreement with terms and conditions for the work to be performed. The following issues should be considered in preparing the agreement:

- The scope of the evaluation or audit shall be spelled out in the terms and conditions of the contract. This reinforces that concerns of the client will be addressed.

- The auditor or consultant, in addition to submitting a written report, shall be required to make one or more oral presentations to officials designated by the hiring jurisdiction. This will enable local officials to ask questions in person and to get clarification on any aspect of the report.

- The report shall contain an executive summary that reflects major findings and recommendations. It is advisable to request that recommendations be prioritized and that cost estimates accompany them to the extent possible.

- As part of the auditor/consultant's assignment, animal control management should be given the opportunity to respond to the report in writing, and the auditor/consultant should be required to correct any factual errors based on that response.

PERCEPTIONS OF CRITICS, DEFENDERS AND OTHERS

An evaluation of the program in part is the perception of the reviewer. Findings can be confirmed through documentation. Otherwise, perceived deficiencies will be reported as the reviewer's observations. Whether recommendations will be implemented depends on whether funds are available, commitment to change, and politics.

An animal control audit always creates intense interest among animal advocates. For example, if breed rescue and animal fostering groups for whatever reasons were denied permission to adopt or transfer animals from the shelter, based on past experience, they will criticize shelter management for failing to partner with them and how it ends up harming the animals. Other animal welfare advocates will air their criticism of the program in the public spotlight as a way of maintaining political pressure on elected officials to give the audit a high priority and to allocate more resources for animal control or to make substantive changes.

The audit also pits critics against defenders of the program. Critics may feel that their complaints will be at least partially validated if the agency or program is audited. Defenders of the program, including animal control management staff, outside supporters, and allies are hopeful that the audit will vindicate animal control management of charges levied against them or will argue that if any shortcomings are found, it is because of inadequate funding, insufficient staff, or lack of other resources.

Officials who authorized the audit may be both surprised by the number of findings and recommendations. It is not uncommon for local elected officials to review the audit report and to make some immediate but limited changes for reasons of cost. After reviewing the consultant's report, one county legislator was reported to complain about how much it would cost to fix the problems.

FOUR MISTAKES AUDIT CLIENTS NEED TO AVOID

Those who have oversight and funding authority for animal control programs need to avoid four major mistakes before undertaking an audit or evaluation of the program.

First mistake. Do not ignore what the critics are saying about the program. Their complaints may have some ring of truth. Their complaints, together with negative animal control reports in the media, should be passed on to the consultant for follow-up. Training records should be reviewed and staff and management should be interviewed.

Second mistake. Do not leave it to the consultant to set the parameters of the study and do not assume the consultant's report will address all of the client's major concerns. The response to the RFP should explain the process of conducting the review and the topics or activities that it will be included. It is the client's responsibility to set the parameters for the audit/review process, so that the process will address the *client's* questions, concerns, and needs. The governmental client should insist that the consultant address any issues that the client deems important, if the consultant has not included them in the review.

Because animal control is a community-based program, local policymakers ought to have a better understanding of the community than the consultant. The desired end result needs to be a product that the client can use and is community-specific. One consultant who veered from an assigned task submitted a report that the client refused to implement.

The town hired a consultant to review its animal control program and specifically requested that the local police department not be included in any recommendations to be developed, because the police chief was opposed to assuming any role in the animal control program. The consultant chose to ignore that request and recommended that the police department take over the program, then being operated by a local nonprofit agency. The report was promptly filed away and ignored.

Third mistake. Do not concentrate only on the management aspects of the program or solely on the animal control tasks. Both are important, and the report needs to be balanced between a management focus and a focus on assessing activities. It takes good management combined with knowledge of good animal control practices to get desired results.

Management consultants are experienced in assessing how well organizations and programs are run, but not all of them have had experience in evaluating an animal control program. Consultants from animal welfare-based organizations are selling their services based on their experience in the animal services field. When hiring either a consultant with a management focus or one specializing on evaluating animal control programs, there needs to be a balance between management and subject matter (e.g., animal control) skills and experience. Ask to see the credentials of those who will be performing the work, and also ask if a senior level person will be in charge of the work process.

Has the consultant had experience working with both governmental agencies and nonprofits? Keep in mind that governmental agencies operate differently and under different constraints than nonprofit and for-profit entities.

Fourth mistake. Do not ignore the report, do not accept the report unquestionably, and do not file it away without taking any action. Ask questions of the consultant, and become educated about the subject matter. Remember, you are the client and are paying the consultant for services. There is a presumption that commissioning the audit or review process means that there is an intent to uncover the facts and make needed improvements. Spending public funds for an outside consultant and failing to take any significant corrective action will be a waste of tax dollars, will lead of a loss of confidence in those who made the decision, and a belief in some quarters that poor practices will continue. The decision makers need to be aware at the outset that some findings or recommendations will cost money, but others can be implemented at little or no cost.

If as a client you disagree with a finding or believe that a certain recommendation is not needed, say so and explain your reasoning. Do not simply continue to study the findings and recommendations indefinitely; the critics will not remain silent or patient. Some time is needed to study the report, determine which recommendations need to be implemented on a priority basis, and identify those that will take more time and/or money. If a committee is created to review the report's findings, their mission needs to be defined and a time frame established.

Findings and Recommendations

The end result of the audit or evaluation is what everyone looks forward to with bated breath. Senior local government administrators, animal control program management, and elected officials are all awaiting the receipt of findings and recommendations for different reasons. The chief county administrator or city manager is assessing whether a major shakeup of the program will be needed, the costs to fix the problems, and if and when to replace program management. The animal control director and senior program staff are concerned about the security of their respective jobs and how to respond to the findings and recommendations. Local government elected officials who authorize the funding of the program and set policy have their own concerns (e.g., damage control, need for additional funding, and any political fallout). Outside critics are looking forward to confirmation of their complaints. If the animal control program is county funded, the county's chief administrative officer or the county's elected governing officials may be thinking ahead about the audit findings. Would a regional animal control program where several cities and towns and the county share the operating costs save money and be more effective? If so, the consultant can advise how to navigate through this concept.

Sometimes consultants may be willing to help implement their recommendations. If the consultant is retained to implement some recommendations, it may temper what is recommended. Before engaging the consultant, the agreement could stipulate that the consultant will prioritize recommendations, prepare cost estimates, and offer ideas on how to implement the recommendations if not self explanatory. Internal governmental auditors will not see that as part of their audit responsibility.

Once local officials have reviewed the entire report, they may want to appoint a task force or an ad hoc committee to review the findings and recommendations, develop a plan of action, and a time frame for implementing changes. Local government officials, residents, and animal care professionals are logical choices for this committee, which should report to the elected local governing body. Decision makers will need to determine whether they want to schedule a public hearing when the audit report becomes public or after a task force has presented its own report.

The public has a stake in the program and will welcome (if not expect) an opportunity to be heard. The release of the report presents the opportunity to hold a public hearing to allow public input from all. The hearing can be used to clarify issues in the report and to build support for needed change. Care should be taken in preparing for the public hearing. Who will chair the hearing? When will it be scheduled? Will the consultant have a role in the hearing? Will animal control make a presentation at the hearing? How much time will be allotted to each speaker? Will there be visual presentations? Will there be handouts of printed materials?

SUMMARY

Governmental business should be both transparent and subject to oversight in a system of checks and balances. Performance audits are part of that process of providing after-the-fact oversight and accountability of how public funds are spent and the results of those expenditures.

Problems and unanswered questions about animal control programs may lead to a review of the program to gather facts and to obtain answers to questions. There are many reasons why programs are reviewed. It may not only be about complaints or allegations levied against animal control officials. Personnel and management issues, overall program performance, or failure to meet goals and objectives can be counted among the reasons. Over time, population growth in the community, county, and the region can result in more animals, new animal issues, and new needs. The audit or review process can be considered a positive opportunity to take a fresh look at services in light of changes that have occurred over time.

Auditing a nonprofit or private animal control contractor may be challenging if the contractor does not accept the need to audit the delivery of services. If the contract does not specifically authorize the client to review and inspect records and have access to the shelter facility, it may be problematic. Auditing an in-house program or a governmental contractor is far less problematic.

Animal control critics will try to influence the process in a number of ways. They may complain to local officials, contact animal rights groups, offer names of consultants, and suggest what should be covered during the process. However, it is the client's decision and responsibility to look at the bigger picture and determine the needs of that jurisdiction.

Several options are available for reviewing the program including creating an ad hoc committee, internal review by governmental staff, or a review by outside consultants such as an animal welfare or animal control organization, a management consultant, or representatives from an animal control directors association.

Preparing for the review process and what to do after the report has been completed are important aspects in the process. Both deserve careful thought and planning. How the client undertakes these tasks will help determine whether the work product meets the client's needs and how and what changes will be implemented. Taking preparatory steps is like laying the foundation for what is to come next. This includes going through the process of selecting a consultant or auditor, planning ahead on how to review the report, and prioritizing and funding recommendations to be implemented.

There are four mistakes that the client needs to avoid in the review process:

- Do not ignore those who are critical of the program unless proven otherwise.

- Set the parameters of the review and determine the scope of the audit to the consultant orally and in writing. Consultants and auditors are not all alike. You as the paying client have the right to determine the scope and priorities in this process as it must meet your needs.

- Do not concentrate on either the management issues or animal control tasks, but review both as they are interdependent.

- Do not accept the report unquestionably and file it away without taking any action.

Notes

1. Roland M. Malan, James R. Fountain, Jr., Donald S. Arrowsmith, and Robert L. Lockridge, II., Performance Auditing in local government (Chicago: Government Finance Officers Association, 1984), 9

2. City of Riverside, California, Contract for Animal Control Field Services Between the City of Riverside and the County of Riverside, (Riverside, California: City Clerk's Office) 1995, 16.

.

City of _____   Date _____

Sample Cover Letter
Request for Qualifications

TO: Individuals, Firms, Companies, and Public and Private Organizations, including For-Profit and Nonprofit

RE: Request for Qualifications (R.Q.) to Provide Animal Control Field Services for the City of _____

PLEASE RESPOND BY 5:00 P.M., (date) _____

The City and County of _____ will be joining together in late fall _____ to operate a city/county animal shelter where animals from the city and the county will be brought. The shelter will be operated and managed by the county on behalf of the city and the county.

The field service for the city may be contracted out to either a public or private entity. All animals retrieved and/or impounded through the field service operation will be brought to the new city/county facility at (address) ____ _____.

The city invites the interest and response from individuals, companies, firms, for-profit and nonprofit organizations, and other entities that have had animal control field service experience and may be interested in providing animal control service in this city.

{Persons responding to this RFQ should provide the information asked in the section of the RFQ entitled "Submission Requirements," and should respond in writing by 5:00 p.m., on (date) _____ to me at City Hall, (address) _____

If you have any questions, please feel free to call me at (area code) _____ or the city's principal management analyst, Mr./Ms. _____ at (area code) _____ between the hours of 8:00 a.m. and 5:00 p.m. Monday through Friday.

Time is of the essence in order that the city proceed on schedule as directed by the city council to implement the animal care and control program. Your interest and response are encouraged.

Sincerely yours,
Director of Management Services

Attachment

Attachment 1

City of Riverside, California
Office of the City Manager

REQUEST FOR QUALIFICATIONS
ANIMAL CONTROL FIELD SERVICES

The City of Riverside is soliciting qualifications from qualified individuals and organizations to perform animal control field services in the City of Riverside. Hereinafter, the term "contractor" shall refer to: individuals, firms, companies and/or organizations including but not limited to for profit and/or not-for-profit entities.

The City's animal control program consists of numerous services divided into shelter and field services. The shelter services will be performed by the County of Riverside at the City/County Animal Shelter, 5950 Wilderness Avenue in Riverside.

BACKGROUND

The animal control field services component is intended to provide an array of activities designed to protect the health and safety of the general public and to provide humane animal care and control to domestic and wild animals.

ABOUT THE CITY

Riverside is situated about 60 miles easterly of Los Angeles and is the County seat as well as the largest City in the region. The City covers approximately 76.9 square miles and its population is approaching 250,863. There are approximately 80,000 residential dwellings units plus 8,800 commercial and industrial facilities.

ANIMAL CONTROL STATISTICS

The City has approximately 25,000 licensed dogs. Based on available data for the most recent fiscal year 1993-94, the following field service data are available for the 11 month period:

The total number of dogs and cats brought into the shelter from the field operation (dead, alive, put to sleep, returned to owner) totaled 9,674 for the 11 month period from July 1, 1993 though May 30, 1994.

14,891 dogs and cats were processed through the shelter for the same period by the current contractor. This includes 4946 animals received dead on arrival, 7361 animals put to sleep, 1559 adopted and 1025 returned to owner.

Total animals processed through the shelter, including

2

dogs, cats and miscellaneous totaled 17,025.

QUALIFICATIONS OF CONTRACTOR:

The City desires to identify contractors with appropriate experience and training to provide the field services component of the City's Animal Control Program.

Philosophy of Field Service Operations

The City desires to identify contractors who share the City's concerns on animal control practices and services. The following is a summary of the City's field service philosophy.

The services sought by the City should encompass not only protection of persons from wild and dangerous animals but also the humane care and treatment of animals by personnel providing services through this program. The City desires that good public relations practices should be a priority and that all persons in this City should expect courteous service and that animals will be treated in a humane way. The City is concerned that priority be given to the following as it applies to the field service component of the animal control program.

1. Humane care and treatment of animals while they are in custody or in contact with field personnel to assure that they remain healthy where possible.

2. Priority to field service emergencies and same day response to other field service needs with minimal next-day carryover.

2. Reuniting lost animals with their owners.

3. Development and implementation of a process for local residents to report lost and found animals.

Required Experience/Training

The contractor should possess experience and training (where appropriate) in the following field service activities:

1. Enforcement of state and local laws and/or regulations pertaining to animal control.

2. Response to animal control emergencies and use of mobile field patrols in large urban areas comparable to the City of Riverside.

3. Impoundment of domestic and wild animals.

3

3. Field investigation of reported animal bites in accordance with state and local laws/requirements.

4. Response to and resolution of noisy animal complaints.

5. Removal of dead animals from the public rights-of-way, and public and private properties.

6. Trapping and removal of animals from public and private properties.

8. Verify animal license status in the field.

9. Issuance of citations and/or warning notices for animal control violations, adequate preparation for prosecuting cases in court, testimony in court when needed and assistance to, and cooperation with the City Attorney's Office on any animal control legal matter.

10. Quarantining of sick/dangerous animals.

11. Public relations skills when interfacing with the general public, pet owners and government officials.

12. Up-to-date training of field staff to meet state and local requirements.

13. Operation of animal control vehicles (including care and maintenance of such vehicles), a record of safe driving practices and use of equipment in the field service component of animal control program.

14. Preparation of accurate, detailed and timely reports to government officials as may be required including monthly field service data.

15. Knowledge of and experience in the emergency care and treatment of sick and injured animals until professional veterinary services are available.

16. Preparation and maintenance of field service truck logs, incident reports and use and maintenance of mobile communication systems including two-way radios.

17. Responding to emergency situations any time of day or night.

18. Inspection of kennels, catteries and pet shops.

4

19. Conducting field investigations relating to cruelty, abuse of animals, animal bite cases and violations of City and state laws/regulations.

20. Supervision and management of animal control field personnel.

21. Developing and implementing staffing/work schedules for field personnel including adjusting and assigning personnel to meet fluctuating workloads.

22. Processing the returning of animals to their owners in the field.

23. Development and implementation of an animal control field services budget with appropriate support documentation.

24. Response to field service calls within one day and to minimize the number of calls carried over to the next working day.

25. Operation of a field service dispatching facility.

26. Identification of animal breeds and knowledge of animal behavior.

27. Other experience/training to assume other responsibilities as may be mutually agreed upon.

SUBMISSION REQUIREMENTS:

Any and all person(s) responding to this RFQ is (are) requested to submit in writing the following data:

1. Client Reference Information. This should include the names, addresses and telephone numbers of organizations including public agencies that the contractor offers as a reference to verify experience and qualifications. Also included should be the names, titles and addresses and telephone numbers including area codes of principals of the above named organizations.

2. Contract Experience Data. For each organization listed above, the contractor should submit to the City, names dates and locations of any and all contracts relevant to this RFQ, the status of such contracts and the dollar value and number of personnel assigned and number of animals processed annually.

3. Contractor's Principal Personnel. A listing of the

5

principals of the contractor's organization who would be in charge of and give direction and management to a field service animal control component. This listing should include in addition to names, addresses and telephone numbers, a description of the principal(s) animal control background that qualifies the contractor to perform this service for the City.

4. **Personnel Assigned.** Contractor should provide the names and titles of any and all persons who would be assigned to the City contract if said contract was awarded to the contractor.

5. **Financial Data.** Contractor should also provide appropriate documentation to the City that the contractor has the financial wherewithal to provide such service to the City including evidence of insurability.

6. **Documentation to Verify Field Service Experience.** Sufficient documentation to verify that the contractor does indeed have experience to qualify to perform animal control field services for the City.

SELECTION AND REVIEW PROCESS:

The City will review and evaluate all responses to this RFQ to prequalify candidates on the basis of their experience and credentials.

Upon an examination of the RFQ submittal, a number of the most appropriately qualified candidates may be selected and asked to participate in interviews and then may be invited to submit a Request for Proposal (RFP) to the City. The City reserves the right to accept or reject any and all submissions of the RFQ and/or to request any additional information to determine the contractor's qualifications.

Responses to this Request for Qualifications (RFQ) are due not later than 5:00 P.M. on July 22, 1994.

SUBMISSION OF QUALIFICATIONS:

Three copies of the responses to this Request for Qualifications must be submitted to:

Mr. Lawrence E. Paulsen
Assistant City Manager
City Hall
3900 Main Street
Riverside, CA 92522

6

For further information on this Request for Qualifications or the details of the RFQ process, please contact Mr. Paulsen at (909) 782-5552 or Mr. Stephen Aronson at (909) 782-5756.

CITY OF OVERLAND PARK
REQUEST FOR PROPOSAL FOR
IMPOUNDMENT AND BOARDING OF ANIMALS

SECTION I
GENERAL INFORMATION AND INSTRUCTION FOR SUBMITTING
PROPOSALS

A. PURPOSE

The City of Overland Park, Kansas (hereinafter referred to as the "City") is requesting proposals from qualified entities to provide certain services relating to the impounding and boarding of animals found to be in need of such care including, but not limited to those found running at large within the City limits.

B. PROPOSAL INQUIRIES

All inquiries concerning this RFP should be directed to Sergeant Steve Maurer at 11900 Westgate, Overland Park, Kansas 66213. His phone number is 913-895-6403 and his email address is srmaurer@opkansas.org. Inquiries that are general and informational in nature can be made at any time and responses to those inquiries will not be distributed to all respondents. Any responses to inquiries that affect all applicants will result in the answers being forwarded to all respondents.

C. ADDENDUM TO THE REQUEST FOR PROPOSAL

The City reserves the right to amend this RFP prior to the due date of proposals. If it becomes necessary to revise any part of the RFP, an addendum will be mailed to all who have received a copy of the RFP from the City. All respondents shall include acknowledgment of all addenda as part of their proposal. Failure to acknowledge addenda may be grounds for disqualification of the proposal.

D. COST OF PREPARING PROPOSAL

The cost of developing and submitting the proposal is entirely the responsibility of the respondent. This includes costs to determine the nature of this engagement, preparation of the proposal, submitting the proposal, negotiating for the contract, and other costs associated with responding to this RFP.

E. REQUEST FOR ADDITIONAL INFORMATION

The City may request additional information as needed from any respondent who submits a proposal. If additional information is requested, the City is not required to request the same information from all respondents.

F. SUBMISSION OF PROPOSALS

Three copies of the proposal must be received by the City Clerk at the below address no later than 4:00 p.m., _____, 2003. Each proposal must be submitted in a sealed envelope with the following words clearly marked on the outside of the envelope: OVERLAND PARK ANIMAL SERVICES REQUEST FOR PROPOSAL. The applicant's name and address must also be clearly indicated on the envelope. All proposals must be type written or machine printed, except that forms required as part of the submission may be hand printed in ink.

G. MAILING ADDRESS

Proposals shall be mailed or hand-delivered to the following address:

City Clerk
Overland Park City Hall
8500 Santa Fe Drive
Overland Park, Kansas 66212

H. SIGNATURE ON PROPOSALS

Each copy of the proposal must be signed by an authorized representative of the entity submitting the proposal. Each proposal must include the complete mailing address of the respondent. Proposals submitted by corporations must be signed in the name of the corporation followed by signature and title of the president, secretary, or other person authorized to bind the corporation. Proposals submitted by a corporation must include the completed Corporate Data Sheet attached hereto as Appendix B. The names of all persons signing the proposal must be typed or printed below the signature.

I. CONSIDERATION OF PROPOSALS

Any proposal that is not received by the City Clerk's office prior to the deadline date and time will not be considered. The City reserves the right to accept or reject any and all proposals and to waive technicalities or irregularities involving any proposal.

J. PROPOSAL REQUIREMENTS

A completed proposal will consist of three completed copies of the following items:

1. A cover letter stating that the vendor wishes to be considered in the selection process. The letter should also indicate the vendor is willing to schedule an interview with the City should they be asked to do so and can comply with the contract and insurance requirements listed in Section III, and the non-discrimination requirements listed in Appendix A.
2. History and description of the vendor's organization: origin, purpose, structure, and current operations including but not limited to the number of employees, volunteer base and maximum capacity for sheltering animals.
3. A description of the respondent's qualifications, experience providing the requested or similar service and summary of experience and training of personnel who will be assigned to handle this work.
4. A list of subcontractors, if any. A description of subcontractors' qualifications and experience to perform the work proposed to be subcontracted must be provided.
5. Name, address and telephone number of contact persons in agencies to whom the respondent has provided similar services within the last three years. These references shall include the name of the agency, the name of the contact person (preferably the contract oversight officer) the address, and the telephone number of the contact person. Past and current employees and subcontractors of the respondent may not be listed as references or contact persons. The City reserves the right to contact additional persons in agencies for whom the respondent has provided services.
6. A detailed statement of work outlining the respondent's proposed goals, objectives, and procedures for providing the services including but not limited to a description of the services to be provided as set forth in Section II B and the costs for these services.
7. A detailed statement of respondent's policies and record keeping methods regarding the topics set out in Section II C.
8. A copy of inspection reports for the last 12 months from the Kansas Animal Health Department.

K. ECONOMY OF PREPARATION

Responses should be prepared simply and economically, providing a straightforward, concise description of respondent's capabilities to provide the services described in the RFP. Emphasis should be on completeness and clarity of content. Repetition of the terms and conditions of the RFP, without elaboration, will not be considered sufficiently responsive.

L. ERRORS IN PREPARATION

The City has the right to rely on any price quotes provided by respondents. The respondent will be responsible for any mathematical error or incorrect extension of any calculations in the price quote. The City reserves the right to reject proposals which contain errors of any kind.

M. ACCEPTANCE OF PROPOSAL CONTENT

The content of the successful respondent's proposal, this RFP, and addenda will become part of any contract awarded to perform work described in this RFP.

N. WITHDRAWAL OF PROPOSAL

A respondent may withdraw a proposal at any time prior to 12:00 p.m., _____, 2003.

O. SELECTION PROCESS

Once the submission deadline has passed, all proposals submitted in response to this RFP will be evaluated by a selection committee to determine the most qualified respondent. The Evaluation Criteria is set forth in Appendix C. The results of the evaluation and selection process will be presented to the City Council for final approval. The City will then enter into a contract with the selected respondent.

P. APPEARANCE BEFORE THE GOVERNING BODY

Any or all respondents may be required to appear before the Public Safety Committee and/or City Council to explain the respondent's understanding and approach to providing the services requested and to respond to any questions about the proposal.

Q. REJECTION OF PROPOSALS

Issuance of this RFP in no way constitutes a commitment by the City to award a contract. The City reserves the right to reject any or all proposals or portions of proposals received in response to this RFP, or to cancel this RFP if it is in the best interest of the City to do so.

R. OPEN RECORDS ACT

All responses will become the property of the City and will be a matter of public record subsequent to signing of the contract or rejection of all proposals. To protect confidential information, respondents must clearly identify specific provision(s) of the proposal which may be exempt from disclosure and the applicable exemption in the Open Records Act (K.S.A. 45-215 et seq.). A blanket confidentiality request covering a respondent's entire proposal will not be honored and may result in rejection of the respondent's proposal.

S. CONFLICT OR AMBIGUITIES

Respondents shall notify Sergeant Steve Maurer immediately if conflicts or ambiguities are found in this RFP. Failure to do so prior to proposal submission will result in resolution in a manner deemed to be in the City's best interest.

T. INDEPENDENT PRICE DETERMINATION

A proposal will not be considered for award if the price in the proposal was not arrived at independently and without collusion, consultation, communication, or agreement as to any matter related to such prices with any other respondent, competitor, or public officer.

SECTION II
SCOPE OF WORK

A. PURPOSE OF CONTRACT

To secure services related to the impoundment and boarding of animals found to be in need of such care including but not limited to those found running at large within the City limits.

B. SERVICES TO BE PROVIDED

Services sought under this RFP include the following:

a. Vendor will provide at its own expense a suitable and adequate animal shelter for the proper handling of all lost, stray or homeless animals. The shelter shall be supervised by a competent person or persons. Vendor shall be open daily at such hours as vendor shall determine, provided it shall be open for the public to recover animals a minimum of eight (8) hours per day during normal business hours, Friday through Saturday. The vendor will have someone consistently available during business hours to answer phone and in-person inquiries regarding impounded animals.

b. The vendor will require, prior to releasing an animal, that the person reclaiming the animal show proper identification. The vendor, prior to releasing the animal, shall obtain a legible copy of this identification and a copy shall be given to the City for its records. The vendor will ensure that citizens reclaiming animals fully complete City forms. Vendor will mark each City form with the disposition of the animal (e.g. dog reclaimed - $35.00 paid by owner, euthanized, etc.), and when applicable, vendor will attach to the City form a copy of the claimant's identification described above. The vendor will maintain a log of all inquiries from citizens attempting to locate lost pets. This log will be available to animal control officers twenty-four hours a day. Vendor will provide twenty-four (24) hour access to animal control officers of the City for impoundment.

c. Vendor agrees to accept all animals picked up or delivered to vendor by the City or its employees provided; however, vendor shall not have to accept large animals such as horses, cattle, deer or other large, vicious or dangerous animals not customarily sheltered by vendor.

d. Vendor shall refer all calls concerning strays to the City's animal control officer. In the event the animal control officer does not respond within thirty (30) minutes, vendor may accept the animal on behalf of the City.

e. Vendor agrees to provide proper and adequate food, shelter, water and other humane care and treatment of the animals delivered to it by the City, (excluding medical or veterinary care, except as provided below) during all times the animals are in its possession and until redeemed or otherwise disposed. The facility must at all times keep easily accessible to impounding officers food, water, dishes and bedding material for appropriate care of after-hour impounds. If an ACO makes a reasonable request for special or additional accommodations for an animal (e.g. a sheet draped over the front of a kennel to minimize an animal's stress, etc.) the vendor will accommodate that request until otherwise directed by the ACO or until the animal becomes property of vendor.

f. All impounded animals shall at all times have clearly displayed on their cages a record of the animal's known history and origin, in addition to any other information required by the State of Kansas.

g. Vendor agrees to hold all the animals delivered to it by the City and not provided for in subsection h. below, for a period of seven (7) days or a longer period of time as requested by the City (the "Holding Period"); provided, however, that any animal so impounded may be reclaimed by its legal owner within the Holding Period. If during the Holding Period it is the opinion of vendor that an impounded animal is suffering inhumanely from illness or injury, the animal must receive veterinary treatment at the City's expense. The facility must record any and all follow-up veterinary treatment prescribed by the treating veterinarian (e.g. oral or topical antibiotics, wound care, etc.) At the end of the Holding Period, all animals that remain unclaimed shall become the property of the vendor and may be listed for adoption by vendor, or humanely destroyed at the shelter. Vendor agrees to complete the City forms related to persons recovering animals previously delivered by Overland Park Animal Control Division to vendor.

h. Vendor agrees to care for the animals delivered to it by the City that have bitten, scratched or otherwise injured a person or are suspected of having rabies, for a period of ten (10) days or a longer period of time as requested by the City. In the event such an animal delivered to vendor is determined to have an owner, the animal will be transferred to a licensed veterinarian of the owner's choice whose place of business is located within Johnson County within two (2) working days from the time of impoundment. Vendor agrees to ensure that animals that are on a "bite hold" will not be allowed off-leash and unattended during the rabies observation period.

i. Vendor has the right to worm and vaccinate all animals upon arrival at vendor's facility regardless of condition to protect the animal and others from disease. All canines shall be given Bordetella vaccine upon arrival at vendor's facility. All cats shall be given an FVRCP vaccine upon arrival at vendor's facility.

j. Vendor agrees to keep such records and make such reports as shall be reasonably required by the City concerning the animals it cares for on behalf of the City, and vendor shall render monthly statements to the City.

C. POLICIES

Vendor shall include in the response to the request for proposals a detailed description of the organization's policy and methods of record-keeping regarding the following:

a. Disposition of feral cats. This description must include the process for identification of the feline as "feral."
b. Euthanasia.
c. Spay and Neutering.
d. Breed and gender identification.
e. Vaccination of animals upon arrival at shelter.
f. Adoption of Pit-Bull or Wolf-Hybrids.
g. Location/separation of stray canines and felines.
h. Disease outbreak and containment
i. Cleaning/disinfecting
j. Exercising, feeding, watering and socialization of animals
k. Training provided to employees regarding safe handling of animals.

SECTION III
CONTRACTUAL INFORMATION

A. CONTRACT DOCUMENT

The contract resulting from this RFP shall include: 1) the executed Agreement between the parties, 2) this RFP and any amendments thereto; and 3) the successful proposal , and any amendments thereto, submitted in response to the RFP as agreed to by the City.

B. CONTRACT AMENDMENTS

Any contract for services described in this RFP shall be amended only if in writing and agreed to by both parties.

C. SEVERABILITY

The invalidity in whole or part of any provision of the contract that results from this RFP shall not void or affect the validity of any other provision.

D. TERM OF CONTRACT

The term of any contract that results from this RFP shall be in effect for one (1) year from the effective date. It shall automatically renew for successive one (1) year periods unless either party gives ninety (90) days written notice to the other party prior to the expiration of the year.

E. ASSIGNMENT, TRANSFER, CONVEYANCE, SUBCONTRACTING, AND DISPOSAL

The contract resulting from this RFP may not be assigned to any other person, company, or corporation, or entity without the previous written consent of the City.

F. INSPECTION

The City and its authorized representatives have the right at all times to inspect or otherwise evaluate the services provided under any contract resulting from this RFP.

G. PAYMENTS

Vendor shall submit a monthly report to the City. This report shall include reference to and a copy of the entire City's impound sheets for the month. The report shall reflect the disposition of every animal and any and all fees paid by those citizens reclaiming animals.

For those fees submitted for the City's payment, Vendor understands and agrees that the City will pay for the administration fee and seven (7) days boarding for animals that are not reclaimed. If the animal is held longer than the seven (7) days at the request of the City, and the animal is not reclaimed, the City will pay for the administration fee and the days boarded at the City's request. All other payment of above fees will be sought from and rendered by the owner or person reclaiming the animal. The City shall not be responsible for any unpaid charges except as specifically agreed to above. In the event a litter or a litter with the mother is impounded, no more than two administrative fees will be charged.

H. NOTICES

Notices by the parties to one another shall be given in writing to the persons identified in this RFP or to such other persons as may be subsequently identified in the contract. Such notice shall be effective on the date of receipt if sent by U.S. first-class mail, postpaid, or by overnight delivery, prepaid.

I. GOVERNING LAW

Any disputes arising with respect to the contract shall be governed by and construed in accordance with the laws of the state of Kansas.

J. TERMINATION

Either party may terminate the contract arising out of this RFP by giving the other party (90) days' written notice.

K. HOLD HARMLESS/INDEMNIFICATION

Vendor agrees to defend, indemnify and hold harmless the City, its governing body, officers, agents, employees and representatives from and against all losses, claims, liabilities, demands, recoveries, judgments or expenses including attorney fees arising out of the vendor's performance or failure to perform any terms or conditions of the Agreement, to include the non-discrimination clause and including any acts or omissions by vendor, its employees, subcontractors or agents.

L. COMPLIANCE WITH LAWS, RULES, AND REGULATIONS

The entity that is awarded a contract shall at all times observe and comply with all applicable laws, procedures, rules, and pertinent regulations of the City, the State of Kansas and the United States that are generally applicable, now existing or hereafter adopted.

M. INSURANCE

Vendor shall secure and maintain, throughout the duration of this Agreement, insurance of such types and in at least such amounts as required herein. The vendor shall provide certificates of insurance and renewals thereof on forms acceptable to the City. The City shall be notified by receipt of written notice from the applicable insurer at least thirty (30) days prior to material modifications or cancellation of any policy listed on the certificate.

Commercial General Liability – Policy shall protect the vendor, City, and the City officials, officers, and employees from any and all claims arising from operations under this Agreement whether the acts or omissions are that of the vendor, its officers, directors, employees and agents, or any subcontractor of vendor. This liability insurance shall include, but shall not be limited to, protection against claims arising from bodily and personal injury and damage to property, resulting from all vendor's operations, products or services. The limit of insurance applying to bodily and personal injury and property damage shall be at least Five Hundred Thousand and 00/100 Dollars ($500,000.00) per occurrence and annual aggregate. The City shall be named as an additional insured on the policy and vendor shall provide a certificate of liability insurance confirming coverage.

Industry Rating – The City will only accept coverage from an insurance carrier who is licensed to do business in the State of Kansas and carries a rating by Best of not less than "A."

N. AFFIRMATIVE ACTION/OTHER LAWS

Vendor shall abide by the provisions of Appendix A dealing with Affirmative Action and other laws.

APPENDIX A
AFFIRMATIVE ACTION/AND OTHER LAWS

a. **Equal Employment Opportunity.** During the performance of this Agreement, the Vendor agrees as follows:

1) It shall observe the provisions of the Kansas Act Against Discrimination and shall not discriminate against any person in the performance of work under the present contract because of race, religion, color, sex, disability, national origin or ancestry;

2) It will, in all solicitations or advertisements for employees placed by or on its behalf, include the phrase, "equal opportunity employer" or a similar phrase approved by the Kansas Commission on Civil Rights;

3) If the vendor fails to comply with the manner in which the vendor reports to the Commission in accordance with the provision of K.S.A. 44-1031 and amendments thereto, the vendor shall be deemed to have breached the present contract and it may be canceled, terminated or suspended, in whole or in part, by the City;

4) If the vendor is found guilty of a violation of the Kansas Act Against Discrimination under a decision or order of the Commission which has become final, the vendor shall be deemed to have breached the present contract and it may be canceled, terminated or suspended, in whole or in part, by the City; and

5) It will include all of subparagraphs a(1) through a(4) in every subcontract or purchase order, so that such provisions will be binding upon such subcontractor or vendor; and

6) Exemptions to the above Equal Employment Opportunity conditions are contracts and subcontracts not exceeding $10,000.00; and

7) Unless otherwise provided, the above Equal Employment Opportunity provisions are required to be inserted in all non-exempt subcontracts; and

8) The vendor may be required under Section 60-1.40 Title 41, C.F.R. to develop a written Affirmative Action Compliance Program if it has 50 or more employees. If so required, it agrees to do so no later than 120 days after the effective date of this Agreement and to maintain such program until such time as it is no longer required by law or regulations.; and

9) It shall be bound by and agrees to the provisions of the Vietnam Era Veteran's Readjustment Act of 1974 and all regulations, rules and orders promulgated thereunder; and

10) It shall be bound by and agrees to the provisions of Section 503 of the Rehabilitation Act of 1973 and all regulations, rules and orders promulgated thereunder; and

11) <u>Other Laws</u>. It agrees to abide by all other federal, state or local laws, ordinances and regulations applicable to this project and to furnish any certification required by any federal, state or local governmental agency in connection with same.

b. The vendor further agrees to abide by the Kansas Age Discrimination In Employment Act (K.S.A. 44-1111 et seq.) and the applicable provisions in the Americans With Disabilities Act (42 U.S.C. 1201 et seq.) as well as all other federal, state, and local laws, ordinances and regulations applicable to this project and to furnish any certification required by any federal, state or local laws, ordinances and regulations applicable to this project and to furnish any certification required by any federal, state or local governmental agency in connection therewith.

APPENDIX B
CORPORATE DATA SHEET

1. The official company name and address:

2. Indicate the type of entity the company is (e.g. corporation, partnership, etc.) and the state in which it is incorporated or registered:

3. The name, company title, address, telephone number and e-mail address of the person the City should contact for additional information and for scheduling of a possible interview:

4. The name, company title, address, telephone number and e-mail address of the person authorized to negotiate a contract with the City:

APPENDIX C
EVALUATION CRITERIA

The selection committee will appoint a chairperson. The selection committee will interview each of the respondents. Each member of the selection committee will independently evaluate each of the entities interviewed and rank order them. The following factors will be considered in the evaluations:

a. History and years of experience of the organization doing similar work.
b. Training and experience of staff that will be doing the work.
c. Ability to handle the capacity of animals (number of employees, volunteers and space).
d. History of interaction with the Kansas Animal Health Department.
e. Quality of service previously provided to the City.
f. Willingness and ability to comply with contractual terms and insurance requirements.
g. Reference review of the organization.

Upon completion of the interviews, the selection committee shall compile the individual ratings and select the entity achieving the highest score. At the next Public Safety Committee meeting after the selection is made, the Chairman of the Committee shall recommend to the Committee that staff be authorized to enter into negotiations with the selected entity to provide the desired services. In the event that negotiations with the selected entity are unsuccessful, staff will report back to the Committee and request authority to negotiate with the second ranked firm.

When an agreement has been successfully negotiated, the agreement will be presented to the Public Safety Committee and the City Council for approval.

Floyd County Animal Control
431 Mathis Road
Rome, GA 30161
Phone: 706.236.4545   Fax: 706.233.0032
www.floydcountyga.org

Rescue Group Application

Thank you for applying for approval to rescue animals from Floyd County Animal Control. Please fill out the following form in its entirety and attach a copy of your Georgia Department of Agriculture shelter license if you are located in Georgia. Please note that incorrect information or failure to maintain minimum city, county or state requirements will result in the removal of the organization from consideration for future rescue animals.

Name of Rescue Organization, Humane Society or Animal Shelter:	How long has organization existed?
Primary authorized contact person:	Title of primary contact:
Address for correspondence to primary contact:	

Primary Contact – Home telephone:	Work or cell phone:	Fax number:

Attach the following information:
____ License from the Georgia Department of Agriculture or other state requirements
____ List of agents authorized to pickup animals from our shelter
____ Reference letter from your local animal control agency
____ Two (2) rescue references from any agency

What type of animal does your organization accept? ____ Dogs ____ Cats ____ Both

If you are a purebred rescue group, would you consider rescuing a close mix? ____ Yes ____ No

Would you accept sick or injured animals? ____ Yes ____ No

Under what circumstances would you euthanize a pet in your program? Would you euthanize an animal that develops a treatable illness such as an upper respiratory illness or mange? _____
_____
_____
_____

What is your adoption fee and what services do you provide for that fee: _____
_____
_____

What is your return policy if an adopter wants to return a pet they have adopted from you? What about a pet they've had for several years? _____
_____
_____

Do you transport or arrange transport out-of-state? If so, where to and how often? _____
_____
_____

Page 1 of 2

Floyd County Animal Control
Rescue Group Application
Page 2

Do you screen all out-of-state rescues? If so, how? _____
_____
_____
_____

Will you place animals that are located at Floyd County Animal Control on the internet? If so, how often? _____
_____

Do you agree to abide by all Georgia Department of Agriculture rules and regulations in regards to animal
rescue? _____ Yes _____ No

Do you agree to abide by all Floyd County Animal Control rules and regulations regarding rescue?
_____ Yes _____ No **Failure to do so is grounds for denial of rescue privileges.**

Please list the name and phone number of your local animal control agency and attach a reference letter.
Name: _____
Phone number: _____

Please give as a reference the name and phone number of a veterinarian that you use:
Name: _____
Phone number: _____

Floyd County requires that all animals rescued from or transferred from the Floyd County Animal Control shelter
must be spayed or neutered before release to a new adoptive home. By signing below, you are agreeing to
spay/neuter all animals take from the Floyd County Animal Control Shelter prior to release and you are
confirming that the above and attached information is complete and accurate to the best of your knowledge.

_____   _____   ____/____/____
Primary Contact Person   Title   Date

For Floyd County Animal Control staff only.
_____ Approved
_____ Rejected (see attached)

_____   ____/____/____
Director   Date

Floyd County Animal Control
431 Mathis Road
Rome, GA 30161
Phone: 706.236.4545   Fax: 706.233.0032
www.floydcountyga.org

Authorized Agents List

Before any animals can be released by Floyd County Animal Control, your rescue group must have an accepted application on file at the Animal Control office and the person picking up the animals must appear on this list. It is the responsibility of your rescue group to keep this information up-to-date and accurate.

Please list all persons authorized to pick up animals for your organization.

Name		Title/Position	
Home Phone	Work / Cell Phone	Fax Number	
Address			

Name		Title/Position	
Home Phone	Work / Cell Phone	Fax Number	
Address			

Name		Title/Position	
Home Phone	Work / Cell Phone	Fax Number	
Address			

Name		Title/Position	
Home Phone	Work / Cell Phone	Fax Number	
Address			

Name		Title/Position	
Home Phone	Work / Cell Phone	Fax Number	
Address			

COUNTY OF LOUDOUN
DEPARTMENT OF ANIMAL CARE AND CONTROL
POLICY DIRECTIVE

SUBJECT: Rescue Group Policy

EFFECTIVE DATE: September 19, 2007   **APPROVED:** _____
                                                DATE:_____

PURPOSE:

The Loudoun County Department of Animal Care and Control in order to facilitate the transfer of animals that, in its opinion, do not pose a public safety risk, seeks to establish working relationships with breed rescue groups and other humane organizations.

POLICY:

With respect to placing animals, the Loudoun County Department of Animal Care and Control's (hereinafter referred to as "the Department's") placement priority will be as follows:

1. Reuniting animals with their owners
2. Adopting animals out to new homes
3. Placing animals with breed rescues or other reputable organizations

Therefore, placement of any animal with a rescue organization will not be automatic. The Department will alter its placement priority when, in its professional opinion, an animal has special needs that can be better addressed through placement with a rescue organization rather than through adoption. In certain instances, the Department may pursue both priorities simultaneously, making an animal available for adoption while at the same time pursuing rescue placement.

If an animal has a known history of aggression or serious illness/injury, and/or the Department has determined that the animal poses a potential public safety risk, the animal will not be released to any outside organization. The Department reserves the right to make all final determinations about which animals will be made available for transfer. Each rescue partner will have discretion to accept or reject any animal made available for transfer by the Department.

Application Requirements

The Department has a responsibility to ensure, to the best of its ability, that all animals are placed responsibly. Therefore, the Department has established criteria for establishing its rescue partners. The Department will consider applications from organizations that share the Department's ideals regarding the safe, humane placement of animals, including the adequate screening of animals for public safety risk, the establishment of appropriate adopter criteria, and the option of euthanasia as necessary. As a general rule, the Rescue Partner's adoption criteria should be at least as stringent as the Department's adoption level 1 and 2 criteria (see Attachment #1).

In order to be established as a rescue partner, each organization will be asked to meet the following requirements:
- All rescue partners must either be a 501(c)(3) organization or an affiliate of a national breed rescue organization.
- Organizations shall submit all requisite application materials as set forth in the Rescue Partner Application in order to be considered for rescue partnership. They also agree to submit to a foster home and/or facility (shelter/boarding facility) check by the Department or its designee.
- Rescue partners agree to submit a copy of their annual report (VA report or local/state equivalent, as required) no later than February 1 of each year.
- Rescue partners agree to notify the Department whenever there is a change in their leadership or change in their internal policy that would impact their ability to be named a rescue partner under the criteria set forth in this document (e.g., a private organization losing its 501(c)3 status, a switch from foster homes to boarding kennels, etc.).

Approved rescue partners must also agree to the following:
- Animals may not be released to rescue partners until their legal stray hold has expired.
- Animals should be spayed/neutered prior to leaving the Department; if an animal cannot be altered prior to transfer, the rescue partner assumes full responsibility for ensuring that the animal is altered prior to adoption.
- Once an organization has accepted transfer of an animal, that organization accepts full legal responsibility for such animal, including any associated liability.
- Disposition of any animal transferred by the Department shall be limited to adoption or euthanasia. Animals shall not be transferred by a rescue partner to any other organization, unless otherwise agreed to by the Department.
- Rescue organizations agree to pay the established rescue transfer fee, which is the current adoption fee for the animal less spay/neuter costs (see Attachment #2).

Note: the Department reserves the right to waive any of the criteria identified above, and/or impose additional criteria, as determined appropriate by the Department's Director or his/her designee as being in the best interests of the animal(s). The Department also reserves the right to terminate any rescue partnership at any time without notice, if the rescue partner's members or representatives violate any applicable law, statute or ordinance governing the housing, transportation, adoption and/or care of animals, or if they fail to abide by any of the requirements of provisions set forth in this document.

Placement Procedures

New Rescue Partner Applicants

In order to be considered a rescue partner, each organization must submit a completed Rescue Partner Application (see Attachment #3), along with all associated documents and information. The Department will review each application, perform a foster home/boarding facility check, and notify the organization of its determination.

Established Rescue Partners

Once staff has determined that rescue placement is appropriate for an animal, the process for rescue placement will generally be as follows:

- The Department will contact the appropriate approved rescue partner and schedule a time for them to meet and evaluate the animal. Rescue partners are welcome to contact the Department regarding any animal already made available for adoption; however, as noted above, the Department's placement priority remains reunification, adoption, then transfer.
- If the rescue partner decides to accept the animal, an authorized representative will sign the appropriate transfer papers and pay the applicable transfer fee.
- If the animal is altered and is beyond its stray date it can be released at that time to the organization.
- If the animal is still within its stray date, it will be held by the Department until that date has expired.
- If the animal has not yet been altered, it should be sent to the participating vet of the rescue partner's choice for surgery and picked up at that veterinary office by the rescue partner after surgery.

Attachment #3
Loudoun County Department of
Animal Care & Control
Rescue Partner Application

Name of Organization: _____

Mailing Address: _____

City, State, Zip: _____

Phone Number(s): _____

Fax: _____ Website: _____

Contact Person(s): _____

Title: _____ E-mail: _____

In processing your application, it would greatly help us to learn more abut your organization and how it functions. In addition, we are frequently asked questions by the public about our rescue partners and their policies regarding surrenders and adoptions.

Please provide us the following information (it can be provided in a written narrative form, as printed copies of your web page, as brochures, etc.):

- The history of your organization
- The type(s) and breed(s) of animal(s) your organization rescues
- Your admission criteria for accepting animals into your rescue
- What types of facilities does your organization regularly use to house animals (e.g., foster homes, boarding kennels)?*
- How do you make decisions regarding the adoptability of animals (e.g., temperament testing, etc.)?
- How do you make decisions regarding the suitability of adopters (e.g., applications, home checks, etc.)?

The names and contact information for other municipal shelters your organization has worked with within the past 12 months, if any

Please identify what types of facilities your organization regularly uses to house animals: Dedicated Shelter Building ☐ Yes ☐ No
Boarding Kennels ☐ Yes ☐ No (If yes, please attach a list of all boarding kennels that your group regularly uses).
Foster Homes ☐ Yes ☐ No (If yes, please attach the name and address of a foster provider able to undergo a home check by LCACC, preferably one within Loudoun County)

Do you perform formal or informal behavioral evaluations on the animals accepted into your organization? Please explain.

What behaviors, if any, might disqualify an animal from adoption once it has been accepted into your organization?

What tools do you use to screen potential adopters (e.g., application, home check, etc.)?

What criteria, if any, might disqualify a potential adopter from being approved to adopt one of your animals?

Is euthanasia ever an option for your organization? Please explain.

Do you ever transfer animals to other individuals or organizations to be made available for adoption?

What happens to an animal adopted through your organization if the adopter is no longer willing or able to keep it?

By signing below, I certify that:
- I have read the Loudoun County Department of Animal Care & Control's Transfer Policy, and I agree that the organization identified above will comply with its terms and conditions.
- The above identified organization is in compliance with the requirement of the Virginia Comprehensive Animal Law that every animal care organization obtain a signed statement from each of its directors, operators, staff, foster care providers or animal caregivers specifying that each individual has never been convicted of animal cruelty, neglect or abandonment.
- The above identified organization is in compliance with all applicable legal requirements, including annual and periodic reporting requirements.
- I am an authorized representative of the above named organization and have the requisite authority to sign this document on behalf of that organization, and to bind it to the all of the Department terms and conditions regarding animal transfers.

_____   _____
Signed   Date

Organizational Representatives

Please identify those individuals who form the current management and oversight of your organization: (e.g., officers, directors, board members, senior staff, etc.)

Please identify (name, phone, address) up to 3 individuals authorized to sign transfer paperwork on behalf of your organization (changes to this list should be made in writing).

Required Documentation

All rescue partners must submit the following:
_____ A completed rescue partner application
_____ A copy of the organization's current VA report or local/state equivalent (as applicable)
_____ A copy of the organization's standard adoption agreement (must conform to Code of VA)
_____ A copy of the organization's standard foster agreement (as applicable)

In addition, all proposed rescue partners must submit 2 of the following:
_____ A copy of the organization's IRS 501(c)3 letter of determination,
_____ A copy of a current (within the past 6 months) written inspection report from local animal control agency
_____ A written letter of endorsement from the organization's affiliated national breed association
_____ A letter of reference from a licensed vet that has worked with the organization within the past 3 months

Riverside Municipal Code   Riverside, California

Chapter 8.10

NOISY ANIMALS

Sections:

Section 8.10.010   Purpose.

The disturbance caused by excessive, unrelenting or habitual noise of any animal is disruptive of the public's peace and tranquility and represents an unwanted invasion of privacy of the residents of the City. It is declared to be in the public interest to promote the health and welfare of the residents of the City by providing for an administrative proceeding for the abatement of such nuisances, which abatement procedures shall be in addition to all other proceedings authorized by this Code or otherwise by law. (Ord 6797 § 1, 2005; Ord 6223 § 1 (part), 1995)

Section 8.10.015   Definitions.

For the purpose of this chapter, the following words and phrases shall have the meanings given herein:

"Director of Animal Services" means the person designated by the City Council as the Animal Control Director of the City whether employed by the City or by the animal control contractor retained by City to provide animal control enforcement or the designee of such Director of Animal Services, or his/her authorized designee.

"Complaining Party" means that person or those persons who contact the Animal Control Director to report a noisy animal or noisy animals.

"Noisy animal" means any animal or animals maintained on the same premises or location whose excessive, unrelenting or habitual barking, howling, crying or other noises or sounds annoy or become offensive to a resident or residents in the vicinity thereby disturbing the peace of the neighborhood or causing excessive discomfort to any reasonable person of normal sensitivity hearing such sounds.

"Responsible party" means that person or those persons in charge of the premises or location where any noisy animal is located and may include any of the following:

1. The person or persons who own the property where the noisy animal is located;
2. The person or persons in charge of the premises where the noisy animal is located;
3. The person or persons occupying the premises where the noisy animal is located;

4. The owner of the noisy animal.

If any of those persons are minors, the parent or parents or a guardian of such minor shall be the responsible party. (Ord. 6797 § 1, 2005; Ord. 6223 § 1 (part), 1995)

Section 8.10.020   Administrative Hearing Officer.

A determination whether an animal is violating this Chapter shall be made by the City of Riverside's Administrative Hearing Officer. The administrative hearing officer shall have the power to hear testimony from witnesses including complainants, peace officers, animal control officers or State humane officers or other parties including the owner or person having charge, custody or control of the animal allegedly causing the nuisance, to determine whether the maintenance of the animal is a public nuisance as herein declared by the City Council, and to order the abatement of such nuisance by taking such actions as set forth in this Chapter. (Ord. 6797 §1, 2005; Ord. 6635 §1, 2002; Ord. 6223 § 1 (part), 1995)

Section 8.10.030   Declaration of noisy animal as a public nuisance.

A. The City Council hereby determines and declares that it is unlawful and a public nuisance for any person owning, keeping, harboring or having in his or her care, custody or control any animal, to cause or suffer, or permit to be made or caused by such animal, barking, howling, crying or making of any noises or other sounds, so as to annoy and become offensive to a resident or residents in the vicinity in which the animal is kept thereby disturbing the peace of the neighborhood or causing excessive discomfort to any reasonable person of normal sensitivity residing in the area, unless such noise or sound is made by an official police dog while on duty.

B. If, in violation of the provisions of this declaration of nuisance, any person owns, maintains, harbors, keeps or has any animal who persistently emits any noises or sounds in such a manner as to annoy and become offensive to a resident or residents in the vicinity in which the animal is kept, the maintenance of such animal may be declared a public nuisance by written notice to the owner or person in charge, custody or control of the animal. If after the issuance of such notice, the person owning, keeping, harboring or having in such person's care or custody any animal has not abated the nuisance, such person shall be liable to enforcement of the provisions of this Code.

C. It is unlawful for the Responsible Party, after being informed in writing that such person's animal has been declared a noisy animal and that the maintenance of a noisy animal is a public nuisance, to fail, refuse or neglect to take whatever steps or use whatever means are necessary to assure that such animal does not again disturb residents in the vicinity in which the animal is kept. (Ord. 6797 § 1, 2005; Ord. 6223 § 1 (part), 1995)

Section 8.10.040   Noisy Animal Warning Notice.

A. When an animal control officer or police officer of the City is notified or alerted of a possible noisy animal which may constitute a nuisance and has personally confirmed the existence of a potential nuisance, or has received a written complaint under penalty of perjury of such noisy animal signed by the complaining party, that animal control officer or police officer shall issue a Noisy Animal Warning Notice to the Responsible Party. Such notice shall specify that the continued barking, howling or other noise or sounds of such animal is in violation of this Code and that the noisy animal nuisance must be abated forthwith to avoid further City action. Such notice shall be served upon the Responsible Party or, if such service cannot be safely made, posted at the premises upon which the animal is located. A copy of the Noisy Animal Warning Notice shall be filed with the Director of Animal Services. The Director of Animal Services shall, within five days of the issuance of said warning notice, make a reasonable attempt to speak personally or by telephone with the Responsible Party concerning the matter, including what efforts have been made to abate the nuisance.

B. If within five days of the issuance of the Noisy Animal Warning Notice the Director of Animal Services determines that the barking, howling or other sound or cry was provoked and that such barking, howling or other sound or cry was not excessive, unrelenting or habitual, the Director of Animal Services shall cause the Noisy Animal Warning Notice to be voided and the person to whom it was issued to be so notified. In the event a Noisy Animal Warning Notice has been voided, such warning notice shall not be considered as having been issued for the purposes of Sections 8.10.050 or 8.10.085 of this title. (Ord. 6797 § 1, 2005; Ord. 6223 § 1 (part), 1995)

Section 8.10.050   Declaration of Complaint of Noisy Animal and Petition for Administrative Hearing.

A. When the Director of Animal Services receives a subsequent verbal or written complaint concerning a noisy animal at the same location within twelve months after the issuance of a Noisy Animal Warning Notice, the Director of Animal Services shall determine whether the Noisy Animal Warning Notice went unheeded. If the determination is made the nuisance was not abated, a Declaration of Complaint of Noisy Animal and Petition for Administrative Hearing shall be issued by the Director of Animal Services to the Complaining Party.

B. The Declaration of Complaint and Petition for Administrative Hearing shall be completed under penalty of perjury by the Complaining Party and returned within ten (10) days to the Director of Animal Services.

C. The Director of Animal Services, upon receipt of a timely executed Declaration of Complaint and Petition for Administrative Hearing, shall set the case for hearing before the City's Administrative Hearing Officer. The hearing shall be set at least 10 days from the date the Declaration is received and no more than 30 days. The Director of Animal Services shall notify the Complaining Party and Responsible Party of the date, time, and place for the hearing. The notice of hearing shall advise that the Complaining Party and Responsible Party that they may present evidence at the hearing through witnesses and documents. The notice of hearing shall be accompanied by a copy of the Declaration of Complaint and Petition for Administrative Hearing form. The notice shall be personally served on all parties and witnesses. If the notice cannot be safely served by personal service, then it may be posted upon the premises where the animal is kept and sent by first-class mail. The complaining party shall be informed that further action may not be warranted if the animal is controlled, but in any case, no further action can be taken until the completed Declaration of Complaint and Petition for Administrative Hearing form is received by the Animal Control Director. (Ord. 6797 § 1, 2005; Ord. 6223 § 1 (part), 1995)

Section 8.10.065   Hearing.

The hearing before the Administrative Hearing Officer shall be open to the public. The Administrative Hearing Officer may admit all relevant evidence, including incident reports and affidavits of witnesses. The Administrative Hearing Officer may decide all issues even if the Responsible Party for the animal fails to appear at the hearing. The Administrative Hearing Officer may find, upon a preponderance of the evidence, that the animal is a noisy animal and the maintenance of such noisy animal is a public nuisance. Upon the conclusion of the hearing, the Hearing Officer shall orally announce the decision as to whether a public nuisance has been found to exist on the premises. (Ord. 6797 § 1, 2005; Ord. 6223 § 1 (part), 1995)

Section 8.10.070   Determination and order.

Within three business days after the conclusion of the hearing conducted pursuant to

Section 8.10.060, the Administrative Hearing Officer shall, by certified mail, return receipt requested, notify the Responsible Party of the Officer's determination and any orders issued. If the Officer determines that the animal is a noisy animal and the maintenance thereof, a public nuisance, the Responsible Party shall comply with the Officer's order within five days after the date of mailing of the determination and order. The decision of the Officer shall be final. (Ord. 6797 § 1, 2005; Ord. 6223 § 1 (part), 1995)

Section 8.10.080   Administrative abatement measures.

The Administrative Hearing Officer may, as part of his/her determination that the animal is a noisy animal and a public nuisance, direct the Responsible Party to perform one or more of the following actions [this list is illustrative rather than comprehensive]:

A.   Containment of the animal within an enclosed building on the premises of Responsible Party;

B. Require that the animal wear a noise suppression device obtained at the expense of the Responsible Party to reduce or eliminate the noise creating the nuisance;

C. Require that the animal undertake obedience training designed to abate the nuisance problem when appropriate and under the conditions imposed by the Hearing Officer and at the expense of the Responsible Party;

D. Restrict the time of day, days of the week and duration when the animal may be placed out-of-doors on the premises of the Responsible Party;

E. Require the animal to be debarked at the expense of the Responsible Party;

F. Require the Responsible Party to permanently remove the animal from said property and outside the City limits.

G. Any other reasonable means to accomplish the abatement. (Ord. 6797 § 1, 2005; Ord. 6223 § 1 (part), 1995)

Section 8.10.090   Failure to Comply with Administrative Order.

It is unlawful for any person to fail, neglect or refuse to comply with an administrative abatement order of the Administrative Hearing Officer within the time specified in said order. Should any party to the order issued by the Administrative Hearing Officer fail to comply with the order, in whole or in any part thereof, that party or those parties may be subject to administrative remedies to enforce the order as set forth in this Code, including administrative citations and administrative civil penalties, and any other lawful means necessary to gain compliance, including a civil action. (Ord. 6797 § 1, 2005; Ord. 6223 § 1 (part), 1995)

Section 8.10.095   Civil action.

In the event any person shall fail, neglect or refuse to comply with an administrative abatement order of the Administrative Hearing Officer within the time specified in said order and the public nuisance continues to exist, the City Attorney is authorized to commence civil action to obtain the abatement of such public nuisance. (Ord. 6797 § 1, 2005; Ord. 6223 § 1 (part), 1995)

Section 8.10.100   Not exclusive remedy.

The provisions of this chapter are to be construed as an added remedy of abatement of the nuisance hereby declared and not in conflict with or derogation of any other actions or proceedings or remedies otherwise provided by this title or other law. (Ord. 6797 § 1, 2005; Ord. 6223 § 1 (part), 1995)

Section 8.10.110   Severability.

If any section, subsection, sentence, clause or phrase in this chapter is for any reason held to be invalid or unconstitutional by decision of any court of competent jurisdiction, such decision shall not affect the validity of the remaining portions of this chapter. The City Council declares that it would have passed this chapter and each section, subsection, clause or phrase thereof irrespective of the fact that any one or more other sections, subsections, clauses or phrases may be declared invalid or unconstitutional. (Ord. 6797 § 1, 2005; Ord. 6223 § 1 (part), 1995)

Examples of Breed Specific Legislation

In recent years, some communities have addressed dangerous dog problems through enactment of breed-specific laws that restrict or prohibit certain breeds, particularly pit bulls. The Denver, Colorado, ordinance defines pit bulls as follows:

> (2) a "pit bull," for purposes of this chapter, is defined as any dog that is an American Pit Bull Terrier, American Staffordshire Terrier, Staffordshire Bull Terrier, or any dog displaying the majority of physical traits of any one (1) or more of the above breeds, or any dog exhibiting those characteristics which substantially conform to the standards established by the American Kennel Club or United Kennel Club for any of the above breeds.[1]

These new ordinances obligate all owners of the named breed to comply with restrictions on ownership at the front end (e.g., demonstrate that the requirements of the law have been met before the animal is allowed to remain in the locality). These laws are usually aimed at limiting or restricting public exposure to these dogs, and in some communities, entire dog breeds are banned. In breed-specific legislation, restrictive confinement measures designed to prevent aggressive and dangerous acts by these animals are imposed upon the animal owner who would need to meet specific requirements to keep these animals as pets. These measures are similar to those imposed on individuals harboring wild or exotic animals in jurisdictions where they are permitted. The owner would need to demonstrate that the prerequisites for keeping the animal in question have been met. Requirements may include secure confinement on the owner's land or buildings, licensing, a special permit because the animal is deemed potentially dangerous, having the animal spayed or neutered, mandatory liability insurance, muzzling the dog in public, and placing the animal on a secure leash under the control of a person over the age of twenty-one.

A review of three pit bull ordinances in Boston, Denver, and Ontario illustrate similar as well as different approaches to removing or controlling the breed.

Denver, Colorado. In 1989, Denver was one of the first municipalities to enact legislation prohibiting pit bulls, although other cities have followed suit. This city's law, among the strictest in the nation, survived court challenges and was ultimately upheld. It is important to note in the Denver case:

> ...the justification for bans or restrictions on pit bulls is that these are not dependent on a claim that every pit bull has a higher than average propensity for attacking humans. The justification is based on the clear

evidence that as a group, pit bulls, compared to other breeds, generally have a higher propensity to exhibit likelihood of causing more severe injuries or death.

There are some limited exceptions. The Denver ordinance requires that individuals whose pit bulls are grandfathered under the law must comply with more than ten mandates if they wish to keep their animals. These include having both a dog license and a pit bull license, a valid rabies vaccination, mandatory sterilization of the animal, a tattoo or other marking placed on the animal by animal control, a leash and muzzle on the animal (or the animal must be placed in a secure enclosure when off the owner's property), and posting a warning sign on the owner's property. The owner must be at least twenty-one years of age, and the owner must maintain at least $100,000 in liability insurance coverage on this animal.[1]

Boston, Massachusetts. Boston's pit bull ordinance, passed on June 23, 2004, contains several requirements that are similar to Denver's, but there are differences. The law allows two pit bulls per household, the animal owner must be at least eighteen years old, and there is no insurance requirement. Similar to Denver, Boston allows pit bulls to remain under a grandfather clause, provided that owner complies with provisions in law that took effect on August 1, 2004.

Province of Ontario, Canada. Ontario's Dog Owner's Liability Act (DOLA), as amended by Bill 132, was passed on March 2, 2005, as the Public Safety Related to Dogs Statute Law Amendment Act. The act did not take effect until August 29, 2005, to allow municipalities in the province time to ensure that the legislation would be applied effectively as animal control was deemed a municipal responsibility. Owners of existing pit bulls were given until October 28, 2005, to comply with the new law. Ontario's breed-specific ban also differed from those of Denver and Boston, and being a Canadian province notwithstanding, the differences are distinct. The new law applies to all dogs and not just pit bulls. Dogs that were grandfathered under the new law had to be owned by an Ontario resident on August 29, 2005, or born in Ontario within ninety days after August 29, 2005. The leash length could not be longer than 1.8 meters, and there was a limited exemption for the sterilization requirement for the pit bull based on a veterinarian's written opinion. A court must issue a mandatory destruction order if the dog is found to be in violation of the DOLA. Pounds and humane societies were permitted to adopt out restricted pit bulls provided that the transfer of the pit bull to a new owner would not lead to a violation of the restrictions on acquisition. A provision applicable to all dangerous dogs authorized fines of $10,000 (Canadian) and/or six months imprisonment for violations, and the court is able to make restitution orders requiring convicted persons to make compensation or restitution to victims.

Notes

1. City and County of Denver, Revised Municipal Code, ch. 8, art. II, sec. 8-55.

Index